DRAW YOUR OWN
MANGA

ALL THE BASICS

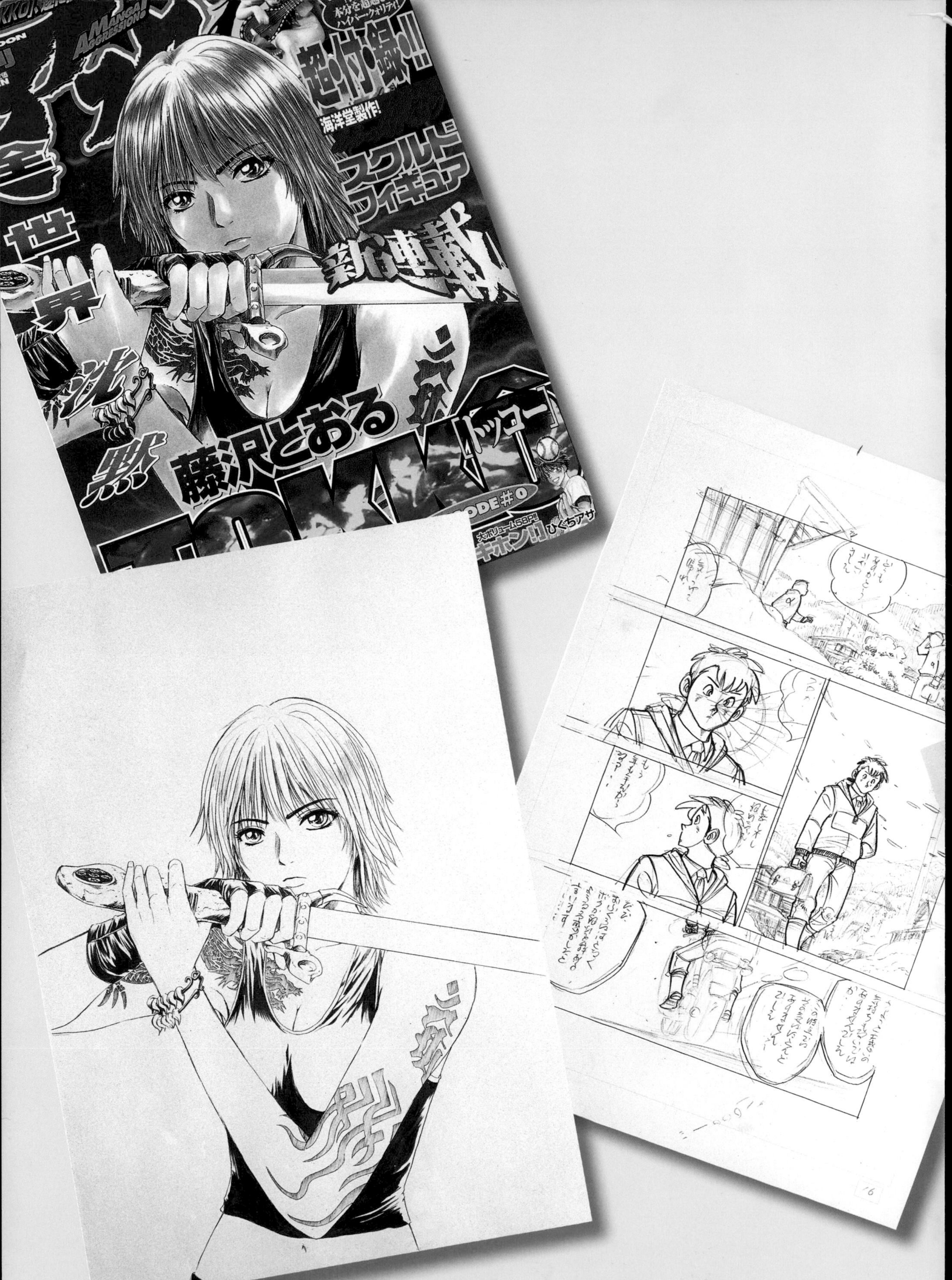

超付録!!
海洋堂製作!
スクルドフィギュア
新連載
藤沢とおる
トッコー
大ボリューム58P!
ひぐちアサ

DRAW YOUR OWN
MANGA

ALL THE BASICS

KODANSHA INTERNATIONAL
Tokyo · New York · London

Photos of Takao Yaguchi and Tōru Fujisawa by Kyūzō Akashi.
Translation by Françoise White (interviews) and Yuriko Tamaki (text).
Illustrations pp. 78–80 by Kei Katsura,
pp. 102–104 by Nanae Kusanagi,
p. 126 by Emu Yamada.

Originally published in Japanese as *Manga, irasuto no kakikata nyūmon*,
edited by I.C., and published by Coade in 2002.

Distributed in the United States by Kodansha America, Inc.,
and in the United Kingdom and continental Europe by Kodansha Europe Ltd.

Published by Kodansha International Ltd.,
17-14 Otowa 1-chome, Bunkyo-ku, Tokyo 112-8652,
and Kodansha America, Inc.
All rights reserved. Printed in Japan.

Copyright © 2003 by Coade and Kodansha International Ltd.
ISBN 4-7700-2951-9

First edition, 2003
04 05 06 07 08 09 10   10 9 8 7 6 5 4 3

www.kodansha-intl.com

CONTENTS

"Improve your technique as you learn from everyday experience!" Takao Yaguchi

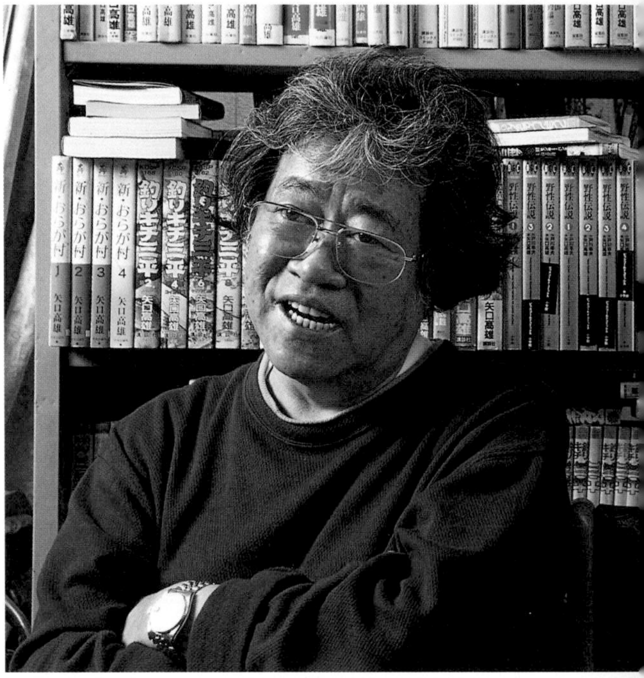

One radiant character in the Japanese manga hall of fame is Sanpei Mihira, a brilliant young fisherman (about eleven years old) in a trademark straw hat who wrestles with monstrous fish and challenges adult master fisherman. The unique "Tsuri Kichi Sanpei" ("Fishing-Mad Sanpei") has been a highly popular work for over thirty years. It's a magnificent drama, appealing even to readers who aren't at all interested in fishing.

At the age of thirty Sanpei's creator, Takao Yaguchi, gave up his secure job at a bank and launched himself into the world of professional manga. Before long he had established the new genre of "Fishing Manga."

THE PATH OF A MANGA ARTIST

In order to discover more about the charm of Yaguchi's work, I asked about his early influences. He told me that by the age of four, he had already been enchanted by the colossal scale of "Monkey: Journey to the West" (a classic of Chinese literature). A precocious child, he was engrossed in copying the pictures in his illustrated copy.

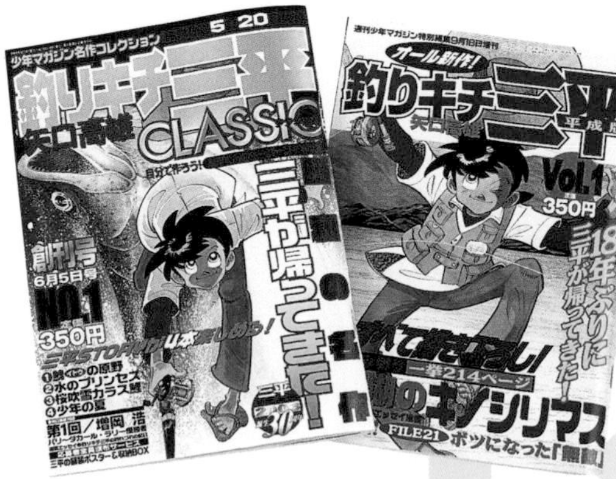
少年マガジン名作コレクション
5 20
釣りキチ三平
矢口高雄
CLASSIC
三平が帰ってきた!
創刊号
6月5日号
NO.1
350円
オール新作!
釣りキチ三平
平成版
Vol.1
350円
18年ぶりに三平が帰ってきた!

I remember during the war paper was hard to come by, so I used to draw on the blank pages in between chapters in novels. Pencils were really poor quality—you had to lick the lead to get it to draw dark lines. I also used to paint graffiti of steel-helmeted soldiers on the paper shoji screens with a brush and ink.

I've heard that when you were in the top grade of elementary school, you dreamt of becoming a manga artist like Osamu Tezuka.

In the spring break before entering the fourth grade in April, I came across Osamu Tezuka's manga "Ryūsenkei Jiken" ("The Streamlining Incident") and was stunned. It was about a car race, a competition between two automobile companies, one owned by rabbits, the other by wicked wolves. The cunning manager of the wolves' company tried to stop production at the rabbits' company by doing things like plying the workers with alcohol and food, and then encouraging them to go on strike.

In 1947, Osamu Tezuka's "Shin Takarajima" ("New Treasure Island") became a bestseller. That timeless masterpiece, the "Tetsuwan Atom" ("Astro Boy") magazine series started in 1951. "The Streamlining Incident" was published in 1948, when Tezuka was only twenty-one and a student in the medical faculty of Osaka University.

Automobiles run against the wind, so in order for them to go fast they must be streamlined to reduce the drag from the head wind. This manga was based on the principles of aerodynamics and children found it very persuasive. At that time, some cars still ran on charcoal. Gasoline cars had started to appear, although you had to crank the engine to get it going. Not even jeeps were streamlined. Tezuka's manga thus seemed new and believable, and also the quality of his pictures was excellent, really amazing.

When I was in fifth grade at elementary school, an elephant called Indra sent by the Indian Prime Minister Nehru to the young boys and girls of Japan toured the country. In 1950, when Akita prefecture commemorated the elephant's visit by holding the first prefectural children's exhibition since the war, I won the first prize. In junior high school, I usually got the first prize in the poster competitions for "Road Safety," "Prevent Dental Decay Day" and "Green Week," even though I'd drawn in the manga style.

In the second grade of junior high I wrote that I wanted to be a manga artist on a school questionnaire about my hopes for a future career. The teacher didn't even comment. At that time, neither teachers or parents considered drawing manga as a proper career. If we look at a typical self-portrait of a manga artist of that time, he has scruffy hair and patches on the knees of his trousers, and he's drawing manga under a naked light bulb on an overturned wooden fruit box. The general belief was that being a manga artist or novelist meant living in poverty. It was an age when there were lots of young aspiring manga artists working in house painting or drawing movie billboards.

You practiced drawing manga all the way through high school, but then you got a job in a bank to support your family. Your colleagues at the bank knew that you were good at manga, and sometimes asked you to draw things for them.

I drew a four-frame manga for the quarterly in-house magazine. When I was asked to introduce the branch's bank clerks on the front cover and a two page spread in an amusing way, I did manga-style portraits of everyone, which were really popular. My manga was also placed in the window display of the branch throughout the year.

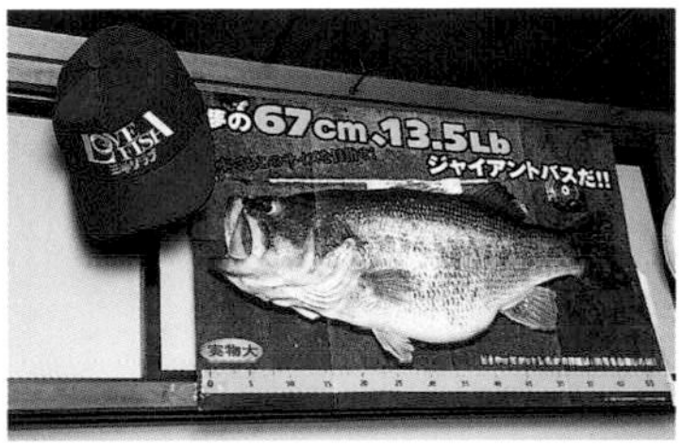
67cm 13.5Lb
ジャイアントバスだ!!

Then came a turning point for you. At the age of twenty-six, you came across Sanpei Shirato's "Kamui Den" ("The Legend of Kamui") in a bookshop. You were bowled over.

"The Legend of Kamui" was drawn from a completely fresh point of view. It was about the historical peasant uprisings, and was extremely realistic. I hadn't seen any manga for about five or six years, because I was busy at the bank. I was shocked when I saw how far Japanese manga had advanced during that time.

During that time, I liked Osamu Tezuka's style and used it as reference. I managed to draw some things, but I wasn't very good. Then I came across Sanpei Shirato's style, and it had a great effect on my work. I realized that I didn't have a flexible wrist like Osamu Tezuka and couldn't draw soft, rounded lines like he did. Sanpei Shirato's lines were rough and sharp, and I found that this style worked well for me. My hand just wasn't suited to drawing certain things, such as the strands of hair of Maitaru, the hero in Reiji Matsumoto's "Ginga Tetsudō 999" ("Milky Way Railroad 999").

Hand type determines the style! Sanpei Shirato created a style suited to his hand type with a lot of hard work. Takao Saitō apparently established his own current style because his wrist was too stiff and he started drawing long lines like in "Gorugo 13" ("Golgo 13").

Yaguchi

So then you started developing your own style, using bold, straight lines. About three years later, your debut amateur work "Nagamochi Utakō" ("The Ballad of the Wooden Chest") was published in the magazine *Garo*, an established springboard for new manga artists. Your work was not at all amateurish—the beautiful, wonderfully strong lines are impressive, and the finish is excellent.

While I was working at the bank, I made time to draw in the evenings. As I drew bit by bit, I began to realize that if I inserted an extra episode here or there, the effect would be more dramatic, and my work rapidly changed. But if I look at my first piece of work now, I want to cover my eyes. It's too flashy. When I look at work by young people who draw well but with superficial cleverness, I get the feeling that that's all it is. If it's just flashy with no substance, it's no good.

Your piece appeared in the same edition of *Garo* (April 1969) as one by Sanpei Shirato.

When you are accepted for publication, you gain confidence. With each work you think, "Ah, that's how to do it!" as you get the knack of techniques. And you get excited as the urge to draw wells up in you, and you find you really can draw. I'd never completed even one work then suddenly had five works published in one year! It felt as if a floodgate had opened.

Even so, it was around that time that you lost your determination to turn professional and you almost gave up, thinking it was impossible.

I was already 29 years old with two children. Bank employees weren't very well paid at that time, and my savings were paltry. I thought that my dream of turning professional would probably end up as just an adolescent daydream. It was the traces of my youth and would disappear, just like a tadpole loses its tail. I thought it would come to an end before long, so I drew one last piece of work as a sort of memento of my youth.

But then your branch manager told you "Your manga is good enough to be published, but that doesn't mean you'll make it as a professional. And you won't ever be successful in banking because of your drawing." These harsh words spurred you into submitting your resignation after twelve years at the bank. You left behind your family and went to Tokyo to make your way as a professional manga artist. You really dived in at the deep end. Then work began to come in, such as the series "Otoko Michi" ("The Way of the Samurai") by the popular manga writer Ikki Kajiwara.

When I was amateur, I drew my own works within my own capabilities. However, adapting someone else's work to manga opened up new worlds to me. For example, supposing there's a scene beneath the statue of the politician Saigō in Ueno, but there isn't an illustration of that statue in the encyclopedia, either the editor or myself would have to go and take a photo of the statue in order for me to be able to draw it. I realized that some manga requires extensive photographic material.

During this time, your series "Tsuri Bakatachi" ("The Crazy Fishermen") was published, and you started to build a reputation. Then from June 1973, "Fishing-Mad Sanpei" was serialized in the weekly boy's magazine *Shūkan Shōnen Magajin* and was an instant hit. You also won the Kodansha Manga Award that year. The series continued for over ten years, in which time you drew approximately fourteen thousand pages. Sales of the pocket book edition reached 25 million copies. Then there was a break of eighteen years. In 2001 you got back to work on the series and it's more popular than ever. Incidentally, young Sanpei hasn't grown at all, even though thirty years have passed since his debut.

When I decided to start drawing the new Sanpei series, some readers suggested that it would be interesting to make Sanpei a modern-day businessman. But if Sanpei had become a businessman he'd have married his childhood sweetheart, Yuri-chan, and I just didn't feel I could draw him fishing in between their domestic arguments. So I made Sanpei exactly the same as before, just changing the setting to the current Heisei period. Thus in a scene where Sanpei is out fishing and wants to phone the master fisherman Gyoshin, in the past he would have gone to the nearest house with a phone whereas now he uses a cell phone. This is the sort of change I make to create a modern setting. Essentially, though, Sanpei hasn't changed at all. The fact that this is possible is one of the strengths of manga.

You once said that "Sanpei is a facet of myself, in a certain sense he is me." I wonder if all your other characters are modeled on someone too.

I guess there's always some sort of model. Of course, my own experience counts for a lot. For example, the model for Grandpa Ippei—Sanpei's grandfather, who brought him up—is my own grandfather. Actually, my grandfather was the complete opposite of Grandpa Ippei. He was old-fashioned, unsympathetic, stubborn, never listened to anyone and was always nagging and yelling. When I thought of him, it made me think about what kind of grandfather I wish I'd had. That's how I created Sanpei's grandfather. I made him a wise character who listens to young people, a generous old man who cultivates an interest in the sciences. I think he's the sort of character that puts people at their ease whenever he appears.

DEPICTING INNER EMOTIONS IS HARD

Even though your manga is about fishing, your drawings are incredibly lively. There's no doubt that you go to extraordinary lengths to produce such dynamic pictures full of movement. I was surprised when you said "what is most difficult is depicting inner emotions, or where there isn't any dialogue."

I was once in a movie called *Itazu Kuma* ("A Bear Called Itazu," 1987) starring Takahiro Tamura. I was deeply involved with the movie from the script stage, and ended up playing the police chief in about ten scenes, with ten or so lines of dialogue. Tamura played an eccentric, violent old *matagi*, or bear hunter, who has had his gun confiscated and is in prison. When a man-eating bear terrorizes the neighborhood, however, the *matagi*'s skill is needed to kill it. The police chief therefore releases him temporarily from prison, gives him back his gun and asks him to kill the bear. At that moment, the news came that the *matagi*'s daughter, Kimi, had been attacked by the bear. Tamura's line was "What, Kimi?" Once filming finished, we went back to the hotel for a bath. I commented to him, "Tamura, filming was easy today, you only had one line!" He replied, "You must be joking! An actor has to put a lot of effort into his acting when he doesn't have any lines. If there are lines, it's not that demanding."

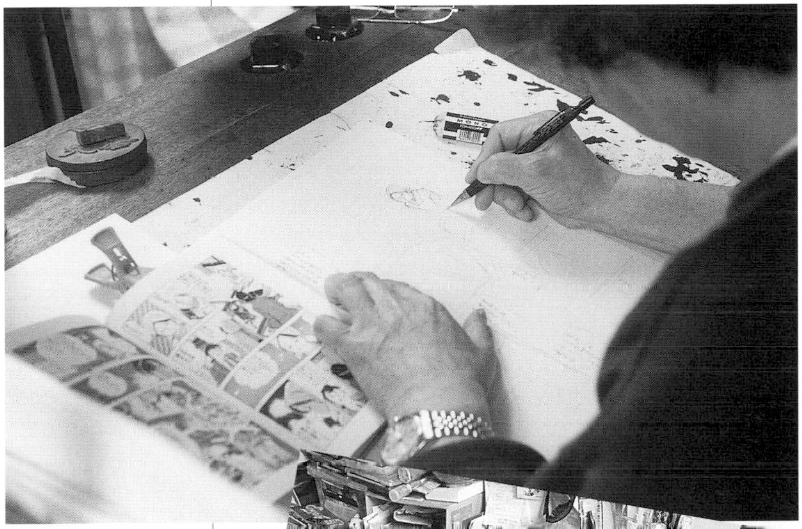

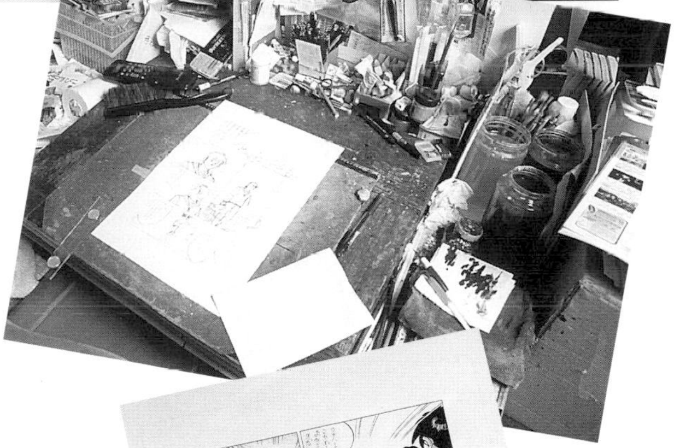

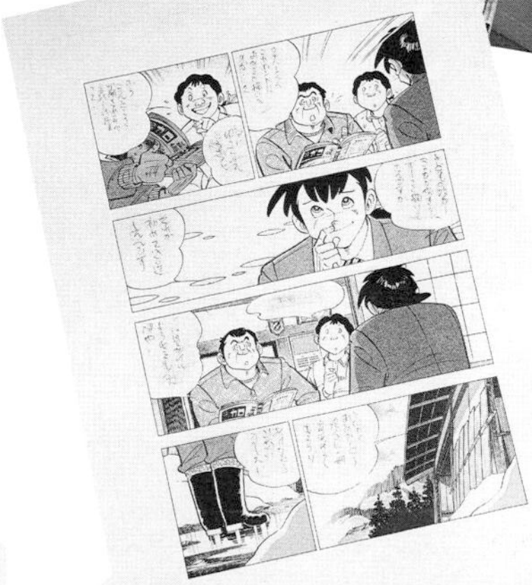

It's exactly the same with manga. I get really excited drawing scenes where there's a lot of action and jumping up and down while landing the catch, but the scenes where they're waiting for the fish to take the bait are really arduous.

So that's the really difficult part of drawing manga.

In order to create drama, you must put all your energy into building up the story, but after it reaches the climax, it's just a question of finishing it up until the last scene. That part is easy, and fun. In manga, you keep repeating this process.

I WANT TO DRAW GREAT PICTURES

Your depiction of nature in your backgrounds is really beautiful, it's one of the special charms of your work. Do you go to different places as part of your research?

Yes, of course. I like making my pictures detailed. Manga is a drawing, but it's also art, and it's important to try to achieve a beautiful picture. After I turned sixty, I felt strongly that wanted to draw quality manga. With "Heisei Sanpei" ("Sanpei in the Heisei Period"), I am putting all my energy into achieving high quality even in the tiniest details.

While talking about the special features in manga, can you comment on the latest trends in manga?

If you wrote out in words the amount of information contained in just one manga story, you would probably run to hundreds of thousands of words. First the image is embedded in the reader's mind, then they read the story.

Manga artists like Osamu Tezuka, Sanpei Shirato, Ikki Kajiwara, Kazuo Koike, Takao Saitō, Tetsuya Chiba, and Shinji Mizushima, all learnt by trial and error as they started drawing large-scale, fantastic, epic-style manga. They had a great influence on manga in the Shōwa period. It would be great if the youngsters of today would take up their legacy and develop it further, but there are those who are not doing this. Some young artists tend to neglect the background with the excuse that they haven't got enough time or that they lack the necessary skills. There have also been a lot of works with successions of close-ups, relying on exciting dialogue to carry the story. I feel there's a danger that this will result in an overall decline in the quality of manga.

MOTIVATION IS ESSENTIAL!

In the fine arts, an artist's work is said to improve as he gets older. Is this true for manga too?

You can't draw manga unless you are brimming with power. Energy and physical strength is everything. Readers love passion. Manga from the age when theories were still incomplete and immature is more likely to please today's readers in some ways, although the strong morals and philosophizing won't hold their interest.

You can't draw manga without being intensely motivated. If that motivation is lacking, you won't be able to produce good manga.

You have been a manga artist for thirty-three years now, since you left your job at the bank. If you had stayed on at the bank, you would have retired by now.

I was about twenty-eight when I took my work to the editorial department of *Garo*, but I told them I was twenty-six. They said, "The right age to start out in manga is eighteen or so, but you're twenty-six!" Even so, I made my debut after turning thirty and am still drawing manga and developing my skills. So it's not true that your age is crucial. An opportunity to fulfill your dreams will always present itself.

Have you got any advice for readers who are into drawing manga and maybe hoping to become manga artists?

However young you are, a basic requirement is to be able to accurately assess social conventions and the way the world works. If you tell a biker gang that they're causing a nuisance, their response will be "So what?" Grasping this sort of essential rule is the key to creating drama. Furthermore, you have to complete the drama with all aspects of the gang's nature, such as their lifestyle, what they're rebelling against, what sort of anti-moral they espouse. If you're not suitably acquainted with the structure of society, you won't be able to create drama.

What about the sort of character one needs to become a manga artist?

Firstly, you need a good stomach. Secondly, you shouldn't be prone to headaches. Thirdly, you must be able to bear confinement at your desk. You have to be able to endure being alone. Being alone is hard. If you can't cope without talking on the phone or going out with friends, you'll never be a writer or artist.

Does the manga artist lifestyle require you to sometimes sit at your desk drawing for three days on end?

Yes, it does. That's when the ability to concentrate is indispensable. Motivating yourself to draw until the work is finished is something you can train yourself to do, but if you don't have that sort of disposition in the first place it won't work. There is nothing cool about the lifestyle. For two or three days, as soon as I wake up I head straight for my desk and sit down without even brushing my teeth. Apart from the essentials like going to the bathroom, I concentrate completely on my work. If the finished work is good, though, then it's cool. For the last ten or fifteen years I've gotten used to only sleeping three or five hours a night on average.

Since Osamu Tezuka and Shōtaro Ishinomori, many manga artists have been energetically publishing their work even though they've been going without sleep to produce new material.

Whatever the experience, you can always get something out of it. Any experience—short of murdering someone or causing a traffic accident—is excellent for someone drawing manga. For example, you often hear things like, "I wish I'd never met that guy!" or "If only I hadn't been taken in by that sort of woman!" but it's precisely because of these experiences that you are the way you are now. Of course you should learn from your experiences. Good and bad experiences are all part of living.

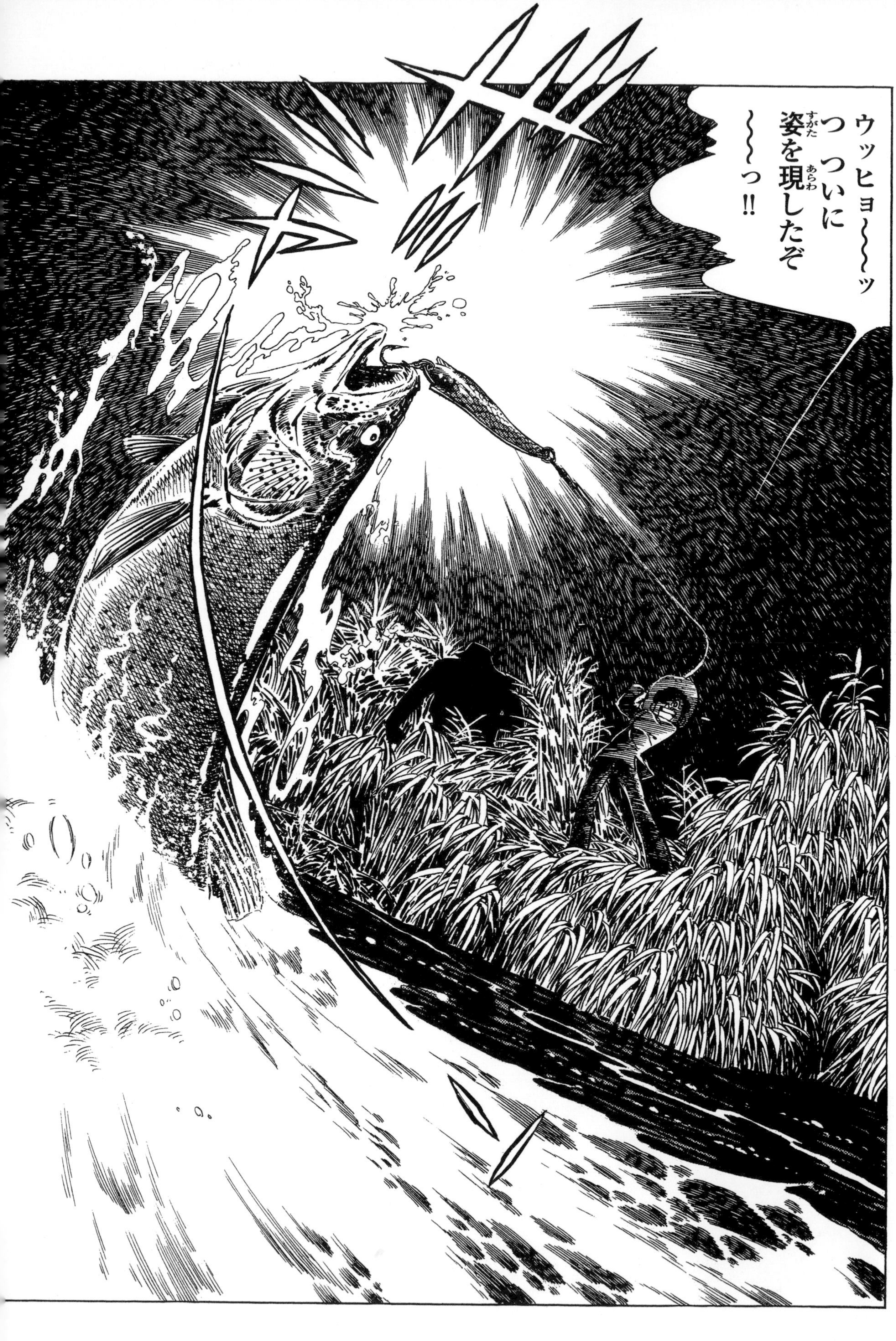
ウッヒョ〜〜〜ッ つ ついに姿を現したぞ〜〜っ!!

Left: Sanpei lands a fish.
From the original "Fishing-Mad Sanpei" series.

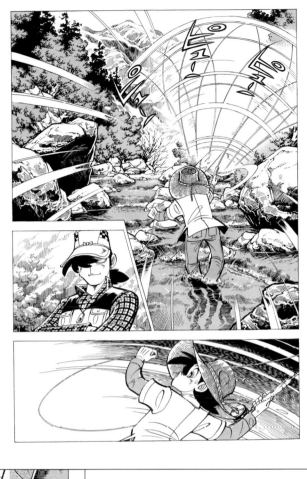

Right: Sanpei goes fishing with Gyoshin.
From the new "Sanpei in the Heisei Period" series.

三浦さん ちょっと見てください!!
なんか珍しい魚でも送られて来たのけえ

Left: the experts are astounded to see a fish they'd thought was extinct.
From the new "Sanpei in the Heisei Period" series.

"Just Draw a Lot!"
Tōru Fujisawa

Internationally famous Tōru Fujisawa is the author of "GTO: Great Teacher Onizuka," which is about a former biker gang member who becomes an enthusiastic teacher at a girl's senior high school. He resolves the succession of problems he encounters by dealing with them head on. This unconventional school story manga has garnered unprecedented popularity and has been adapted as a TV drama series, movie and cartoon series, all of which have been widely acclaimed.

Fujisawa's studio is in the Tokyo residential district of Kichijōji. The reception is on the top floor of the two-story building. Bright light filters in, and background music is being played in the work place, where six assistants sit around a table chatting and drawing intently. Four of them are women. It occurs to me that each of them vaguely resembles characters such as the teacher Fuyutsuki from "GTO," or Kasumi, the protagonist of "Rose Hip Rose," a series that is currently popular.

THE PATH OF A MANGA ARTIST

Fujisawa takes a break from his work to talk to me, and I start by asking him about his recollections of manga.

It was already the age of manga when I was a child. I used to read things like Ikki Kajiwara's "Love and Sincerity" in the weekly *Shūkan Shōnen Magajin*, and the works of Go Nagai. I also liked anime and admired the heroes. During this time, I started drawing my own heroes and robots. I started drawing in kindergarten, and those drawings became manga from the sixth grade of elementary school. It was story manga with a frame layout, so you could call it "amateur manga."

It was in the sixth grade that I started drawing manga specifically to make my friends laugh. It was almost entirely dirty material (laughs). I was

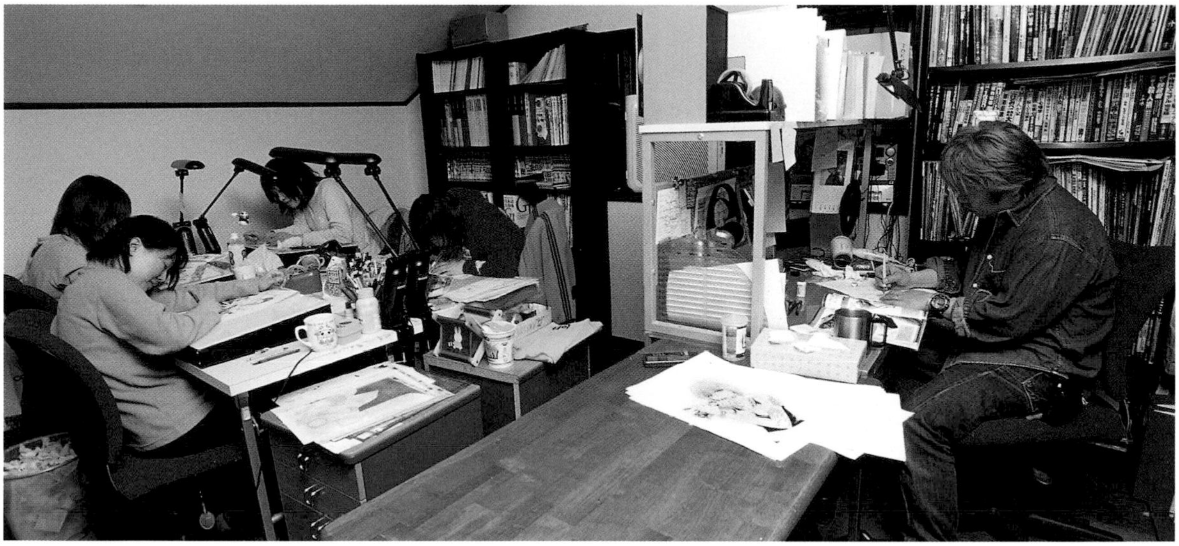

in elementary school, so I really liked drawing things like poo. I drew my own comic manga stories, and I also often drew manga parodies of TV animation series.

It seems that you didn't have any friends into manga who you could work with.

The other kids in elementary and junior high school didn't draw much. I drew pictures a lot by myself. In junior high I started drawing manga in color, and I forced my friends to buy them (laughs).

Did you get good grades for drawing at school?

No, I never got top grades, just average. I wasn't really the serious type, I fooled about a lot. Even when there was a competition for all the kids in town to paint the station building, I was bored, so I imagined a night sky setting and just drew what I felt like, which was Reiji Matsumoto's "Milky Way Railroad 999." The teacher was furious (laughs). But I won the third prize even though I drew for fun and everyone else drew seriously.

Even in your current work, if we look at the background carefully, we can see your playful side in some imaginative and unexpected details. The amount of information in one frame is incredible. Your style was already established from that time.

'Yes, I like making people laugh. The starting point is a gag.'

When exactly was it that you set your sights on becoming a manga artist?

It was after starting senior high school. A few of us formed a club to start our own magazine. There weren't many guys who drew manga, but we forced more to join in! We all created a book together to sell by mail order all over the country. After that somehow I felt that I really wanted to become a manga artist.

Was the response good?

No, it wasn't. Deep down, though, I believed that I was good at it. Even though it didn't sell at all (laughs).

After graduating from senior high, you went to Tokyo and joined an amateur magazine, so you continued to draw manga.

At first, I was told that my work was quite sloppy. But while I was there, a commercial magazine offered to publish my work, so I started working on a series for them—and that's how I entered this world.

Interestingly, after beginning that series you were offered a job as a certain manga artist's assistant, and so you worked as an assistant for some years. Although you must have been busy, you still found time to draw and publish your own work as a professional.

Fujisawa

There's something called perspective. Mr. E. taught me that you've got to get the perspective right for even the smallest object. That was a very valuable lesson for me. Furthermore, in crowd scenes where there are a lot of characters—in one frame there may be fifteen or twenty people—there'll be, for example, thin people and fat people. They should all have different hair styles, and move in their own way, otherwise it'll seem fake.

HOW DO YOU CREATE INDIVIDUAL CHARACTERS?

In your works, there are a lot of unique and individual characters, not least Onizuka from "GTO." It's not uncommon for characters to reflect an alter ego of the author. How do you come up with such charismatic characters?

Onizuka's character developed gradually as the biker protagonist of "Shōnan Jun'ai Gumi" ("Shōnan Pure Love Gang"). When I started the sequel—"GTO"—I thought it would be interesting if he were in an occupation and situation as different as possible to his biker gang days, so I decided to make him a teacher. It was easy to create this manga.

Are the characters and stories closely related to your experiences from your childhood and high school days?

I use things that are available to me—friends, the way friends speak, stories I hear from people, and stories I see on TV and in the movies. I probably get my influence from a lot of things. However, depending on the contents of manga, for example in "Rose Hip Rose" which is currently out, I can't always project myself onto the story. Just the overall theme of the work and how the story develops are close to my own thoughts.

The theme of the work becomes clear to the reader as the work progresses. Is it already clear to you before you begin drawing?

To begin with, only to the extent that it's fragmented and vague. The characters start to move, they talk, and bit by bit they start to do things, and it's only then that the theme becomes clear. So in the case of manga, I don't think the characters are complete at the beginning.

Does this mean that early on you don't know how the story will develop or how it will end?

There is a vaguely straight path, but it meanders around a bit. I think the story gradually becomes more clearly defined as it develops.

It seems that as the characters become more rounded, amazing words start appearing from their mouths, appropriate to the situation.

I WANT TO LEARN THIS TECHNIQUE!

The special features of your works are clean lines and bold, lively compositions, with dramatic double page spreads and strong pictures over three-quarter spreads. Your characters all have bright shining eyes, which fascinate readers. When you draw a character, what points do you pay attention to?

The ambience of the entire face is extremely important. I pay attention to getting the facial expression right as much as possible. In Bunraku puppet theatre, for example, a mere shift of the eyebrows can completely alter the puppet's expression. It's amazing. Even an inanimate object has that much power, so naturally in my manga I take the utmost care over the eyebrows and expression.

Some manga artists correct their rough sketches many times. What about you?

I'm forever correcting, time and time again. Even after inking in, I'm still correcting. And even when doing detail in pen, I'm extremely particular about the facial expression. I think it's terribly important to draw until you are satisfied. Being satisfied is foremost, even more important than meeting a deadline. It can be hard.

I've heard that people who see your manuscripts are always amazed. Even around the mouth there are traces of about five layers of correction fluid. Looking at the final work, it's hard to believe. The interesting thing about your work is that from one frame to the next, the protagonist's facial expression utterly changes.

'It's impact. I try to lay out the frames and speech balloons in such a way that will suddenly surprise readers.

So the flow is as important as impact?

Maybe you can call it the flow of the image. There are long perspective scenes, in which there are a lot of people. I then consider what kind of picture should follow—is it bold, has it got impact? If there is a close-up of just the face, you don't know where the character is. I'm constantly thinking along these lines while I'm drawing.

Precisely because of this, your work is very cinematic, more so than cinema even.

That's because the tempo's fast, isn't it? Tempo is difficult—if it's excessively fast the reader won't be able follow it. The important thing is to create tension. I make the slow places slow, and build up the tension, then I quickly condense it, and the sensation of speed comes across. It's a difficult process that only comes with practice.

When did you develop this skill?

I came to understand that composition is important from the latter half of the "Shōnan Pure Love Gang." My emphasis had been on the character and the story, but when I started adding tension, my work gradually became easier to read.

THE MOST IMPORTANT THING IS TO DRAW REGULARLY

The ordinarily gentle face of the manga artist often transforms into a grimace as soon as they step into the studio. What about you?

Well, if a deadline is close, I can't help looking serious (laughs). However, I can draw better if I'm relaxed can't I? If I'm too tense, the work will become stiff. Especially with funny stories, if you are enjoying it the character will look good too. Of course it's not good to be tense when you're drawing something like that. I think it depends on the theme and content of the work.'

What things are you as a manga artist mindful of every day?

Well, things like going to bars, or watching TV and movies. My method is to use whatever is available. For example, just the way we're speaking now—I'll use whatever's usable. If I find something even slightly interesting, I store it away somewhere, file it away for later use.

For example, I'll use a particular way of holding a cigarette. There are many ways to hold cigarettes. There are even lots of different ways of smoking—some people keep their cigarette dangling from their lips, and others swagger while smoking. These become the idiosyncrasies of the character, so I'm always constantly mindful of whatever I see and absorb.

Even different people's use of language—when you get on the train, you should listen to people. It is important to keep on the lookout. While you're watching, if something catches your attention, it means that you can use it. If you emphasise it, it will become a characteristic. That doesn't mean everything is usable. Don't use it all, just a bit of it.

For example, while I'm speaking you keep on nodding, don't you? And you tilt your head to the left or right when you nod—that is idiosyncratic. I memorize only the part that I latch onto.

Finally, can you give me a message for people who draw manga and especially for those who wish to become manga artists?

Generally speaking, I think the most important thing is to draw a lot. If you don't draw, you don't get any practice, do you? If you're going to run a marathon without training for it, it's just not going to work. The basic training beforehand is extremely important, so if you want to draw interesting things, if you want to draw manga, you should start drawing now. This is generally the most important point. Show it to the people around you—if they say "this is interesting" it'll be an incentive to draw more. In any case drawing a lot is the important point, so you should persist with that.

But some people say that a manga artist will never be much good unless they're already good at manga from elementary school age.

That's not true. In manga there are a lot of styles. It's just that when you're young you can really immerse yourself in drawing. When you become an adult, you don't listen to people's opinions, you tend to become less flexible, and you end up regretting that lack of flexibility. I suppose that if someone's flexible as an adult, they'll probably be able to go on drawing forever.

It's a strong message that age doesn't matter, but is it alright to start from, say, thirty-five years old?

Such late bloomers do exist. It's not enough for manga to be just a beautiful picture. The story reflects the things a person has seen in their life. They've accumulated invaluable life experience, which is interesting in itself. In that sense, I think that anyone is capable of creating manga.

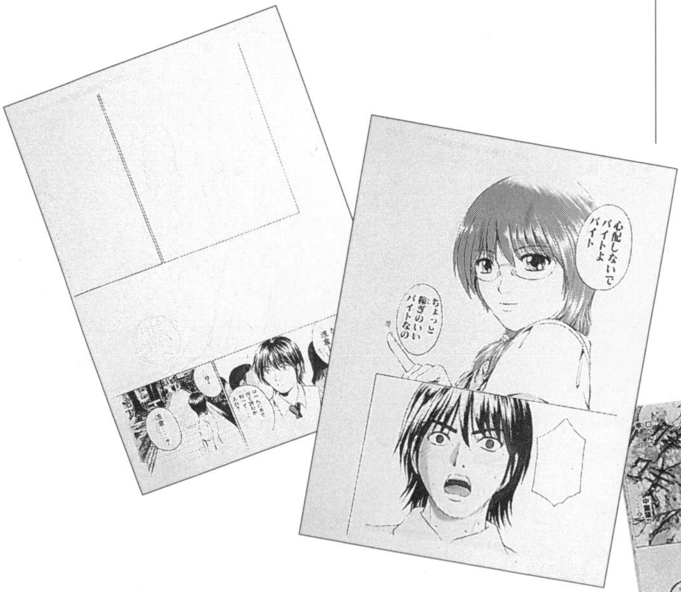
心配しないで バイトよ バイト
ちょっと稼ぎのいい バイトなの

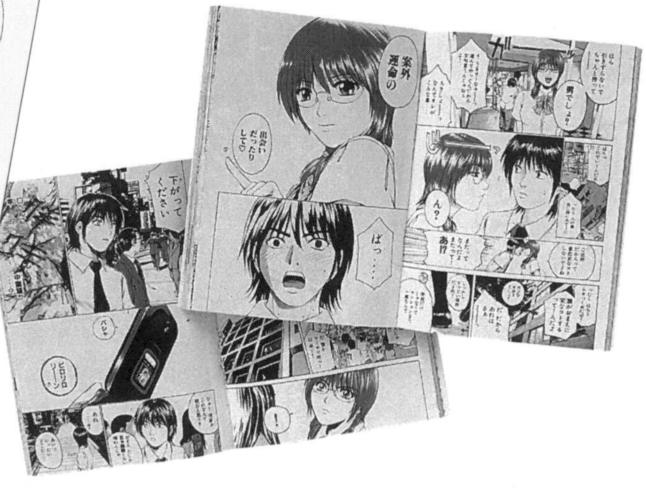
案外運命の
出会いだったりして♡
ばっ……
下がってください
ん？

DRAW YOUR OWN
MANGA
ALL THE BASICS

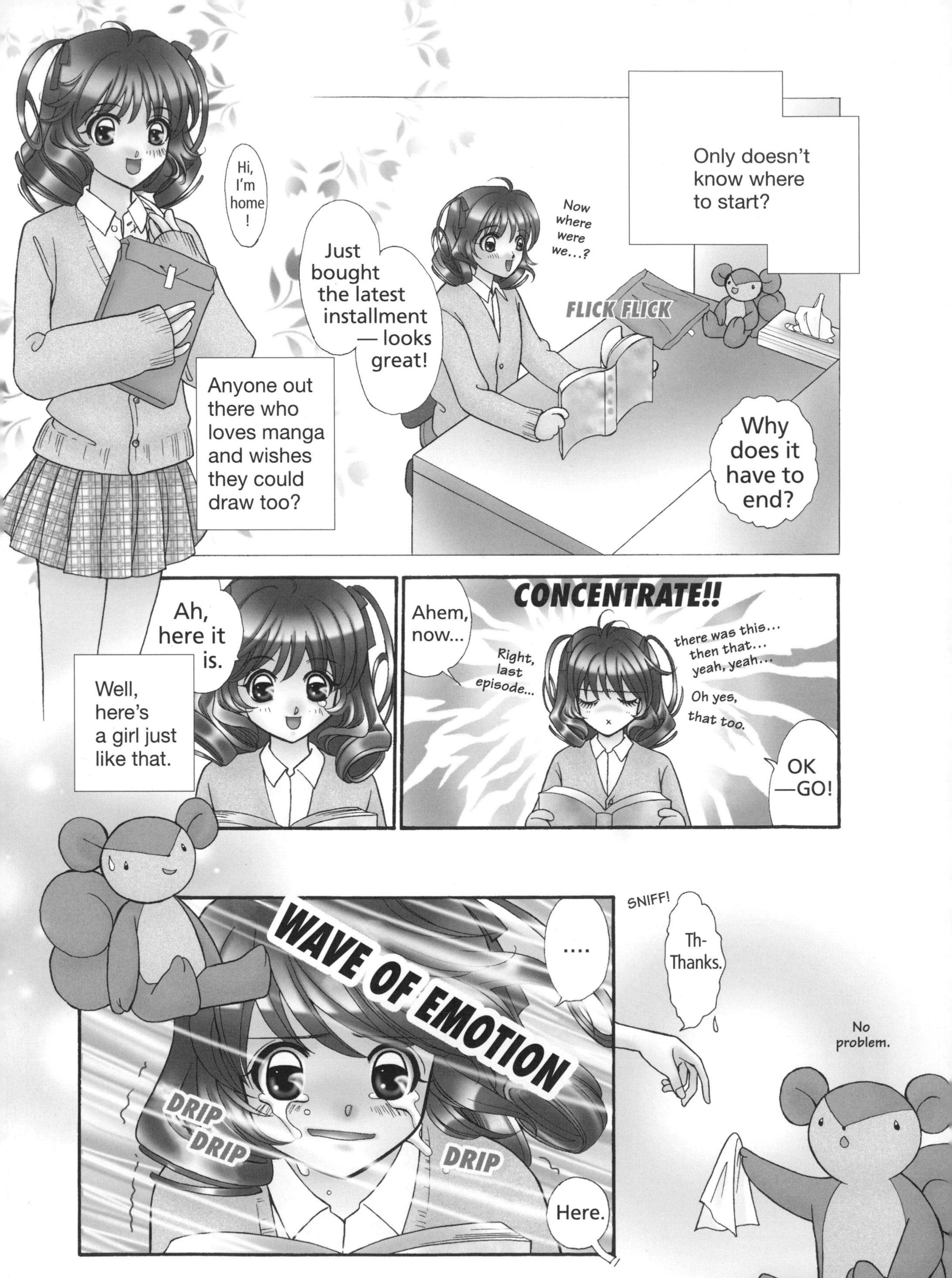
Hi, I'm home!
Anyone out there who loves manga and wishes they could draw too?
Just bought the latest installment — looks great!
Now where were we...?
FLICK FLICK
Why does it have to end?
Only doesn't know where to start?
Ah, here it is.
Well, here's a girl just like that.
Ahem, now...
CONCENTRATE!!
Right, last episode...
there was this... then that... yeah, yeah...
Oh yes, that too.
OK —GO!
WAVE OF EMOTION
DRIP DRIP
DRIP
....
Here.
SNIFF!
Th- Thanks.
No problem.

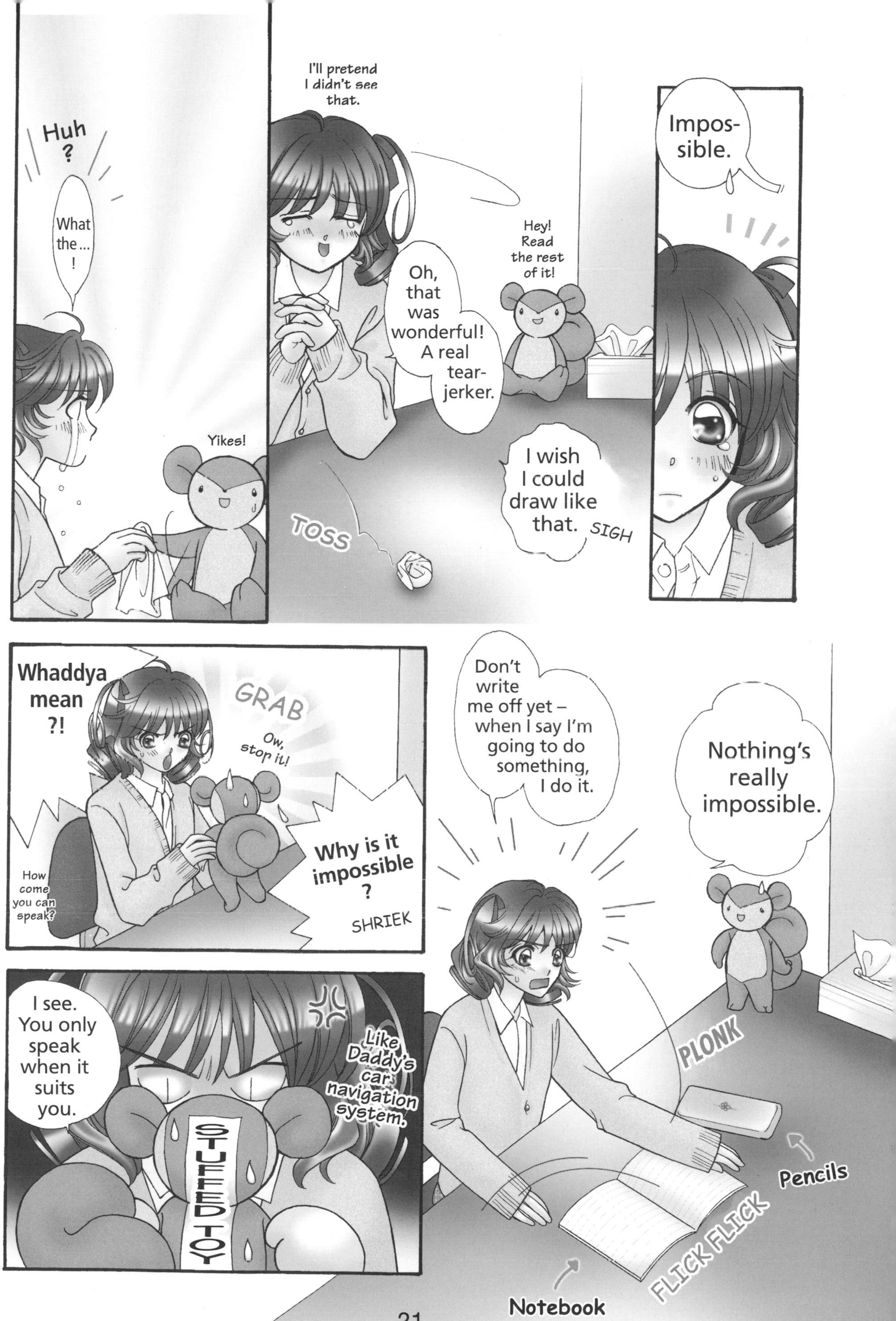
Huh ?
What the ... !
Yikes!
I'll pretend I didn't see that.
Oh, that was wonderful! A real tear-jerker.
Hey! Read the rest of it!
I wish I could draw like that.
SIGH
TOSS
Impos-sible.
Whaddya mean ?!
GRAB
Ow, stop it!
Why is it impossible ?
SHRIEK
How come you can speak?
I see. You only speak when it suits you.
Like Daddy's car navigation system.
STUFFED TOY
Don't write me off yet – when I say I'm going to do something, I do it.
Nothing's really impossible.
PLONK
Pencils
FLICK FLICK
Notebook

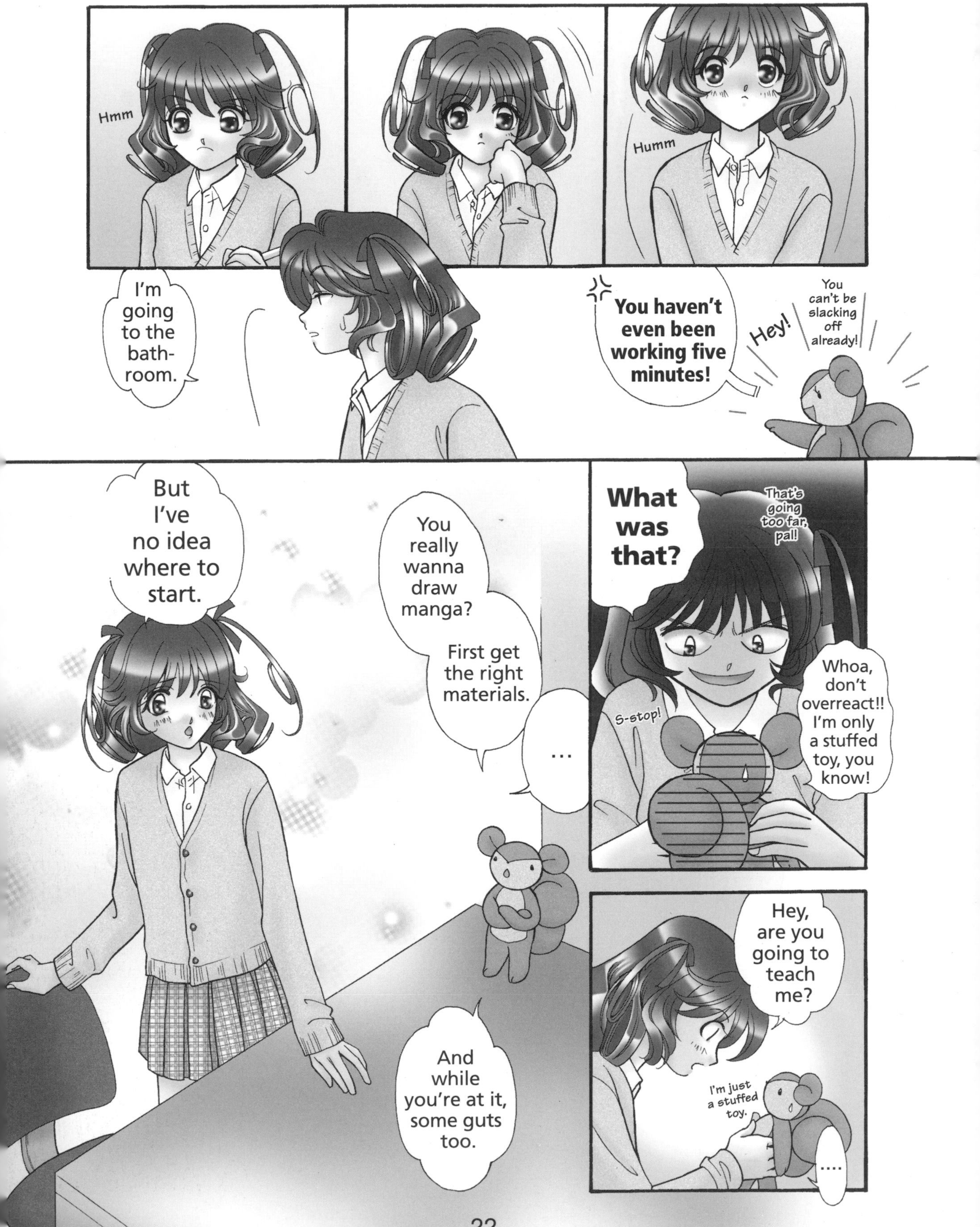
Hmm
Humm
I'm going to the bath-room.
You haven't even been working five minutes!
Hey!
You can't be slacking off already!
But I've no idea where to start.
You really wanna draw manga?
First get the right materials.
...
And while you're at it, some guts too.
What was that?
That's going too far, pal!
S-stop!
Whoa, don't overreact!! I'm only a stuffed toy, you know!
Hey, are you going to teach me?
I'm just a stuffed toy.
....

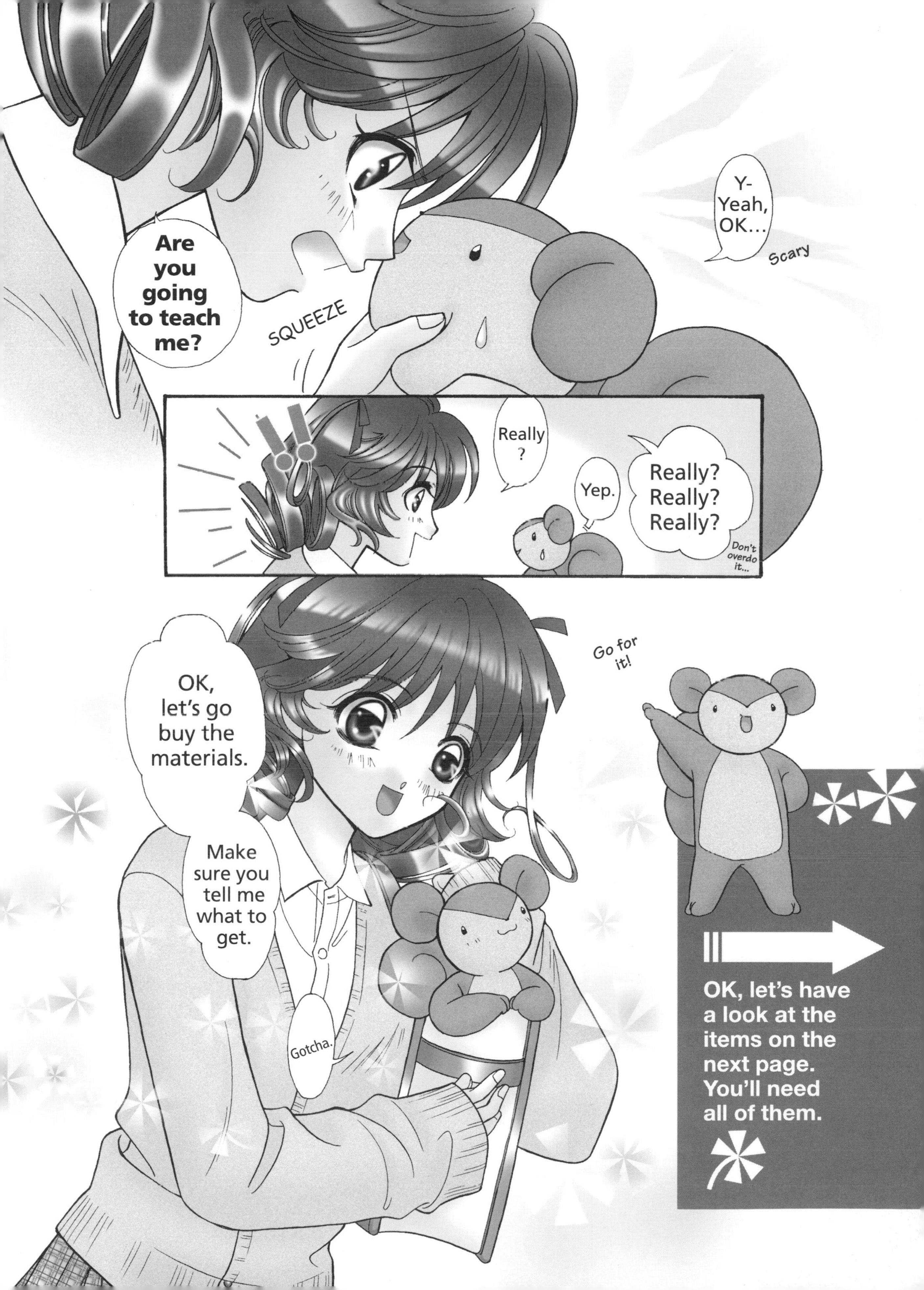
Are you going to teach me?
SQUEEZE
Y- Yeah, OK...
Scary
Really?
Yep.
Really? Really? Really?
Don't overdo it...
OK, let's go buy the materials.
Make sure you tell me what to get.
Gotcha.
Go for it!
OK, let's have a look at the items on the next page. You'll need all of them.

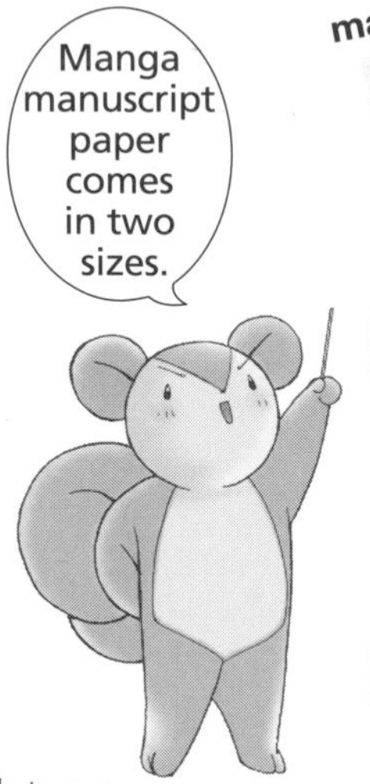

Manga manuscript paper comes in two sizes.

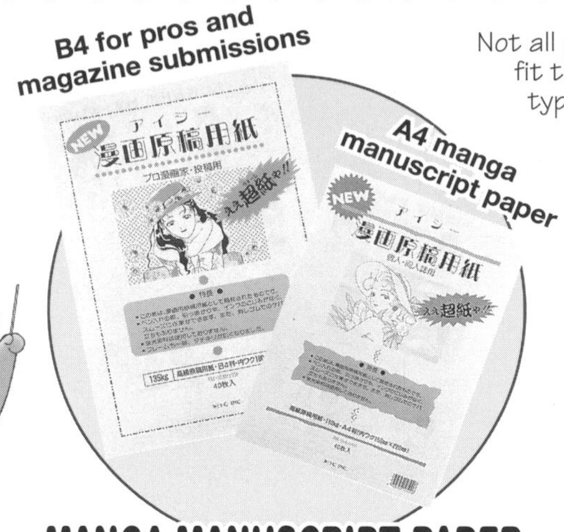

B4 for pros and magazine submissions
A4 manga manuscript paper
NEW
漫画原稿用紙

MANGA MANUSCRIPT PAPER

Not all pen holders fit the same type of nib.

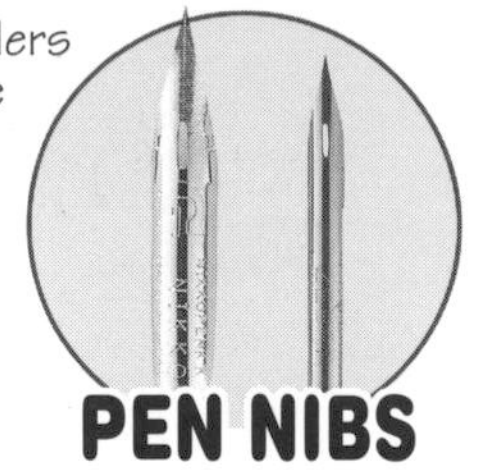

PEN NIBS

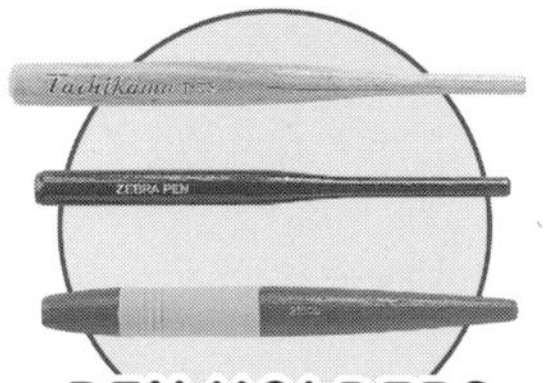

ZEBRA PEN

PEN HOLDERS

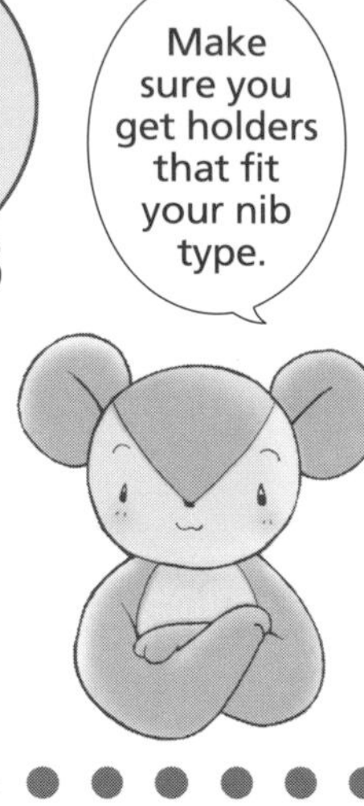

Make sure you get holders that fit your nib type.

Templates are useful for speech balloons and small objects. You can get templates for curved lines too.

Steel rulers are handy when using blade cutters.

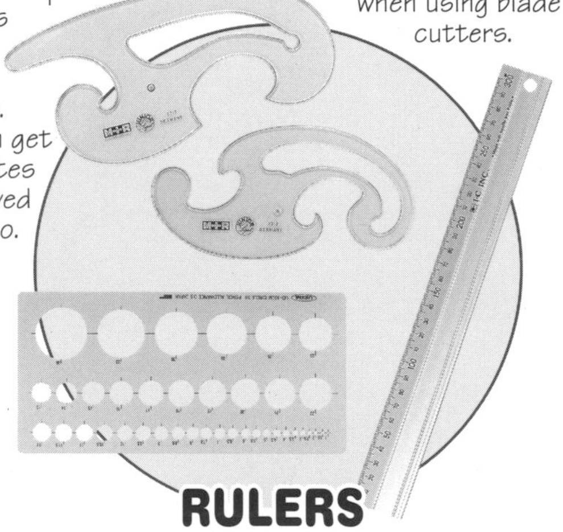

RULERS

YOUR ESSENTIAL MANGA KIT: STEP 1

Most tools mentioned here are available at stationery stores. Still, how do you choose the right pen nib, say, or cutter?
We'll give you some ideas.

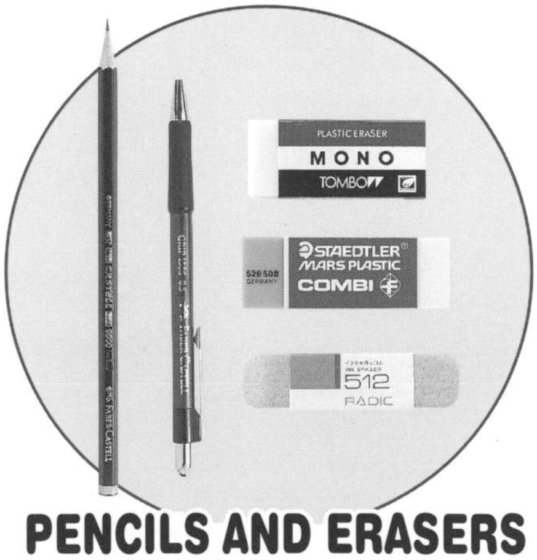

PLASTIC ERASER
MONO
TOMBOW
STAEDTLER
MARS PLASTIC
COMBI
512
RADIC

PENCILS AND ERASERS

Consider how hard you press on the paper when choosing pencils.

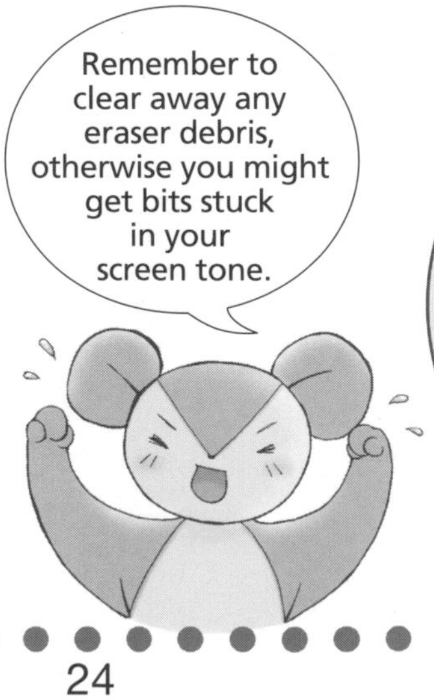

Remember to clear away any eraser debris, otherwise you might get bits stuck in your screen tone.

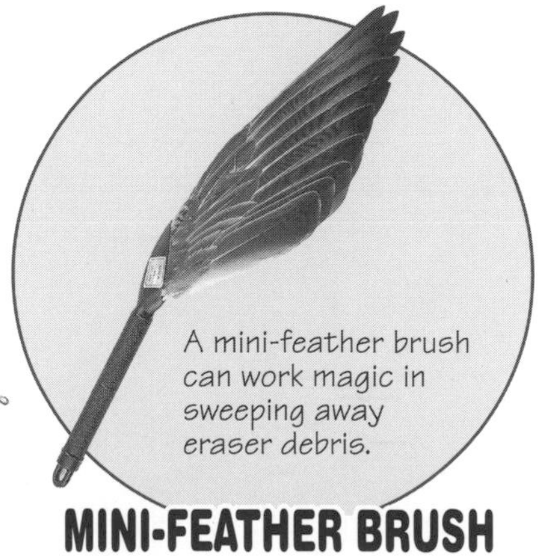

A mini-feather brush can work magic in sweeping away eraser debris.

MINI-FEATHER BRUSH

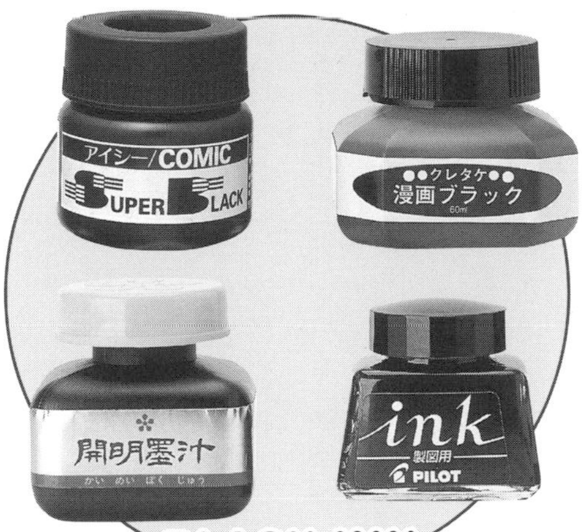
アイシー/COMIC
SUPER BLACK
●●クレタケ●●
漫画ブラック
開明墨汁
ink
PILOT

BLACK INK

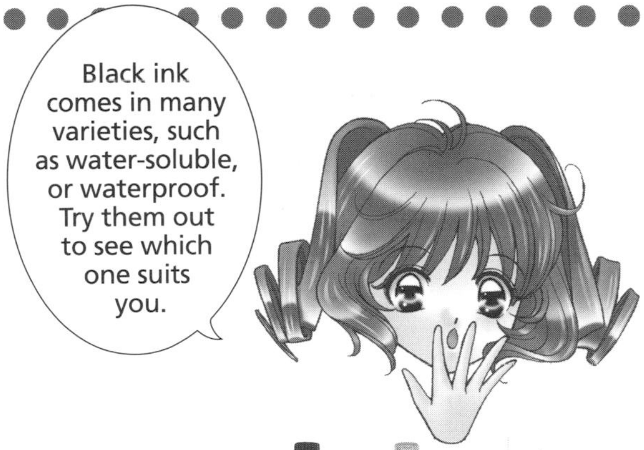
Black ink comes in many varieties, such as water-soluble, or waterproof. Try them out to see which one suits you.

Brush pens are ideal for drawing hair, and are easy to use.

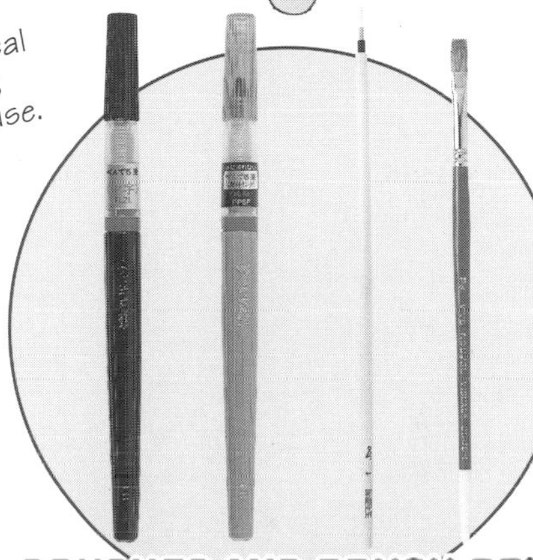

BRUSHES AND BRUSH PENS

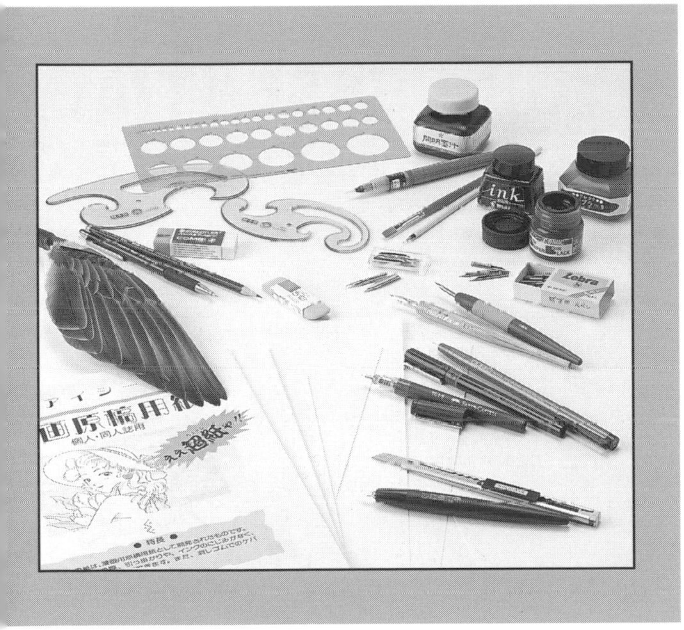

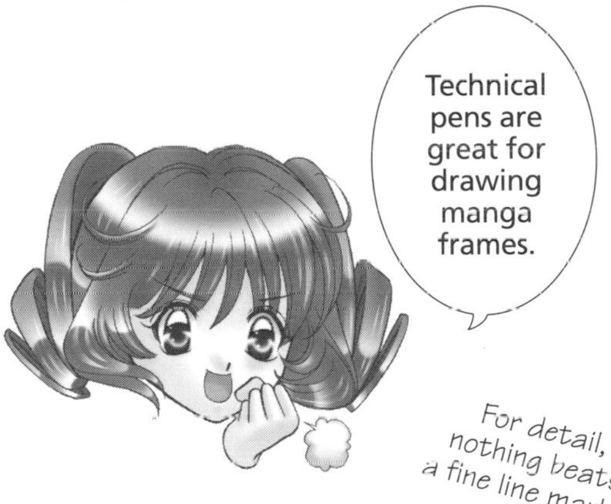
Technical pens are great for drawing manga frames.

For detail, nothing beats a fine line marker!

Cutters come in two blade angles. Choose the one you find most user-friendly.

Snap-off blade cutters work best when cutting screen tone.

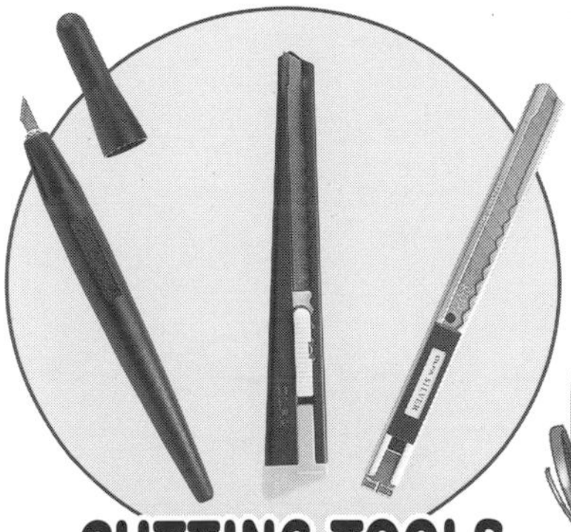

CUTTING TOOLS

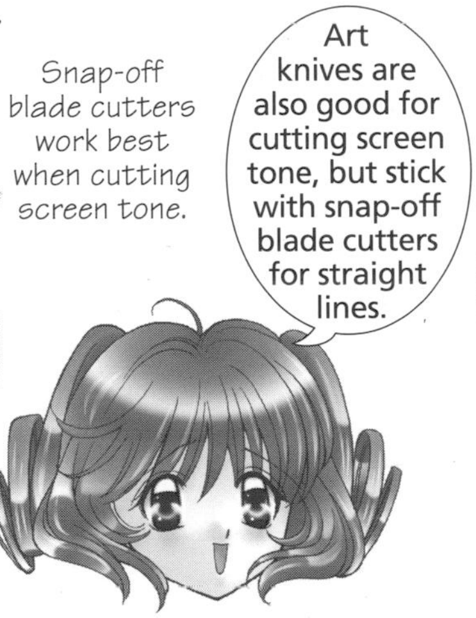
Art knives are also good for cutting screen tone, but stick with snap-off blade cutters for straight lines.

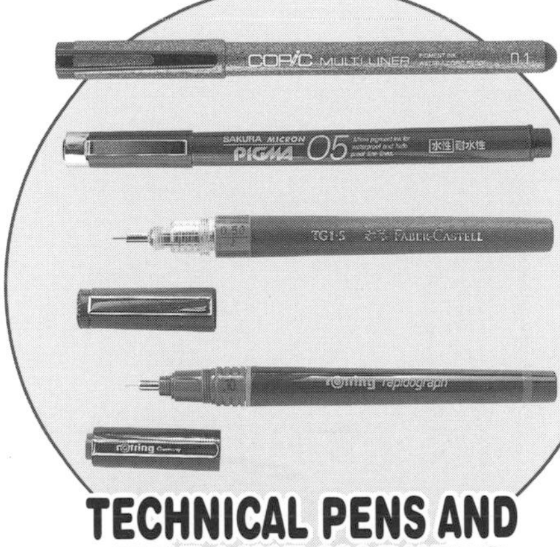
COPIC MULTILINER
SAKURA MICRON PIGMA 05
FABER-CASTELL
rotring rapidograph

TECHNICAL PENS AND FINE LINE MARKERS

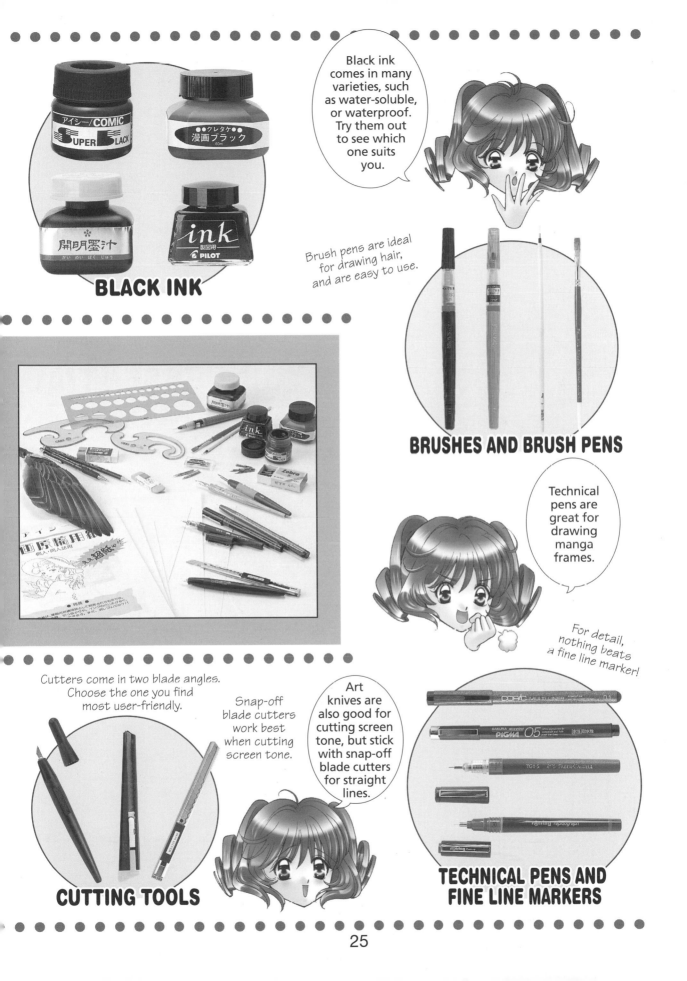

SCREEN TONE

Screen tone ↑ is film with a printed pattern on one side and adhesive on the back.

Use these tools → to stick the tone down.

TONE TOOLS

Screen tone is produced by many companies and comes in a variety of patterns.

It's easy to mistake tex for screen tone. The difference is that tone needs to be cut, whereas with tex you only have to rub over the shape you want to transfer.

T-711 ILLUST TEX   T-702 ILLUST TEX

TEX

Make sure you rub the screen tone thoroughly...

...otherwise it will peel off.

YOUR ESSENTIAL MANGA KIT: STEP 2

Once you get used to the feel of your pens, you'll be itching to get to work. You'll want to use screen tone, draw backgrounds and try various effects. Here we'll guide you to the next step.

MANIKINS

Available in small, medium and large, male and female. Good for getting poses and proportions.

There is a knack to using a ruling pen, but it's a relatively cheap option.

Masking sheets and tape are available.

Ruling pens are a good choice if you find technical pens too pricey.

RULING PEN

MASKING SHEET

When fixing screen tone on small areas, reinforce it with removable transparent tape. Use drafting tape to hold tracing paper in place on the manuscript.

Drafting tape

Removable transparent tape

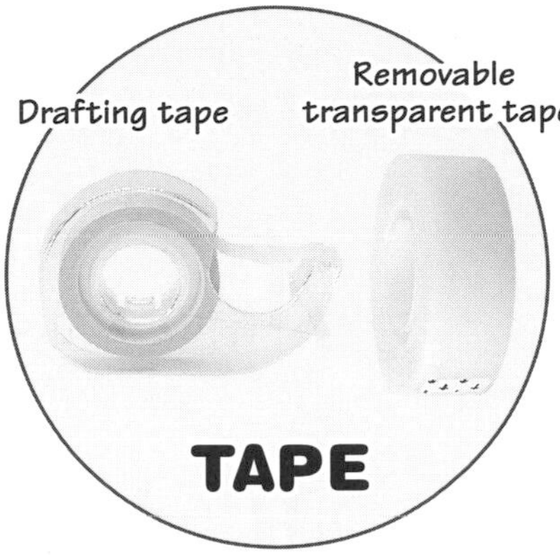

TAPE

We recommend brush-type for neat whiteouts,

pen-type for minor touch-ups.

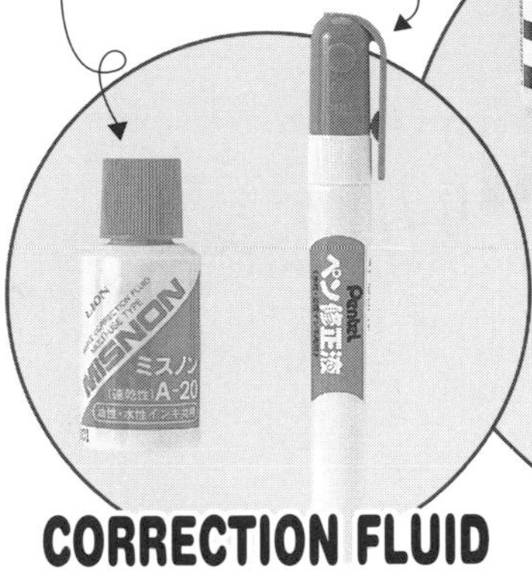

MISNON
ミスノン
Pentel
ペン修正液

CORRECTION FLUID

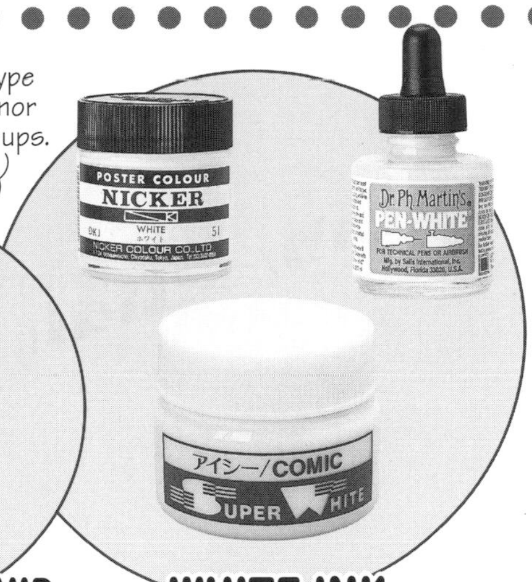

POSTER COLOUR
NICKER
WHITE
NICKER COLOUR CO.,LTD
Dr.Ph.Martin's
PEN-WHITE
アイシー/COMIC
SUPER WHITE

WHITE INK

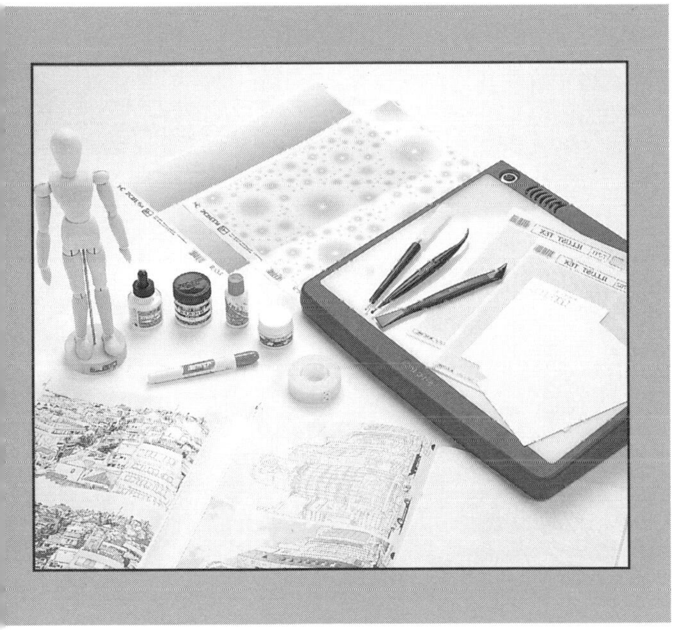

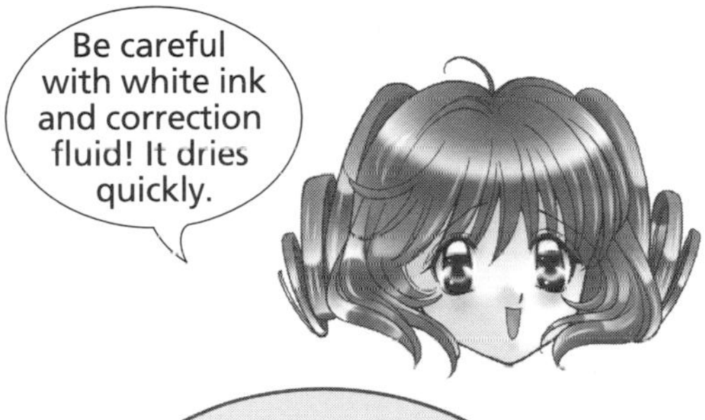

Be careful with white ink and correction fluid! It dries quickly.

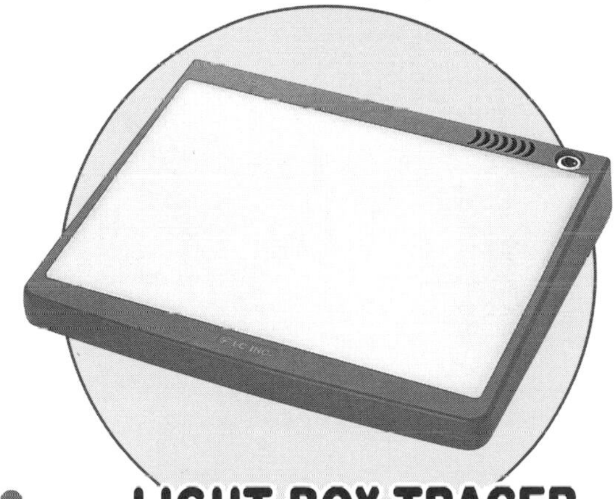

LIGHT BOX TRACER

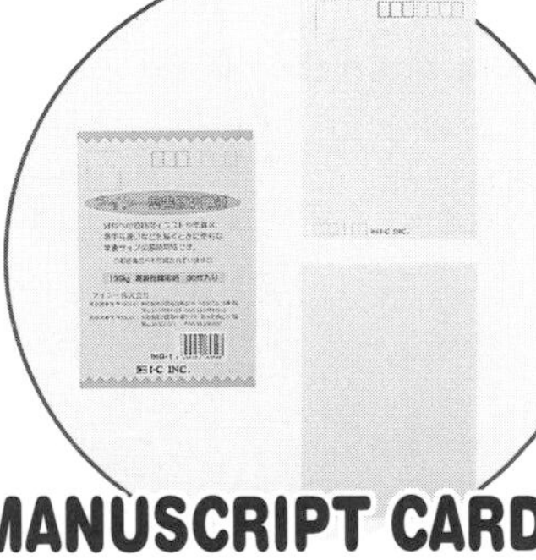

MANUSCRIPT CARDS

Manuscript-style postcards are available for submitting your manga.

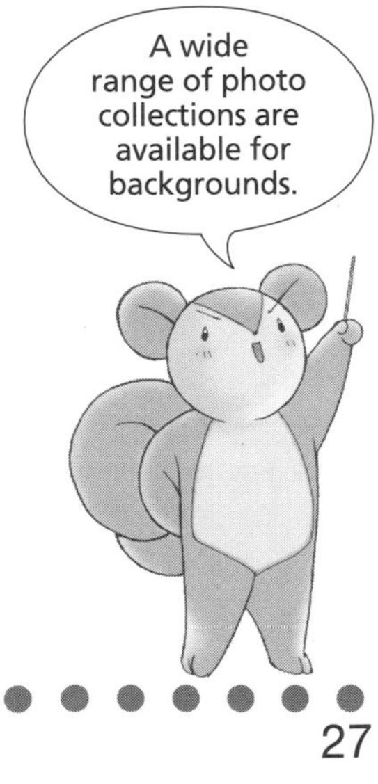

A wide range of photo collections are available for backgrounds.

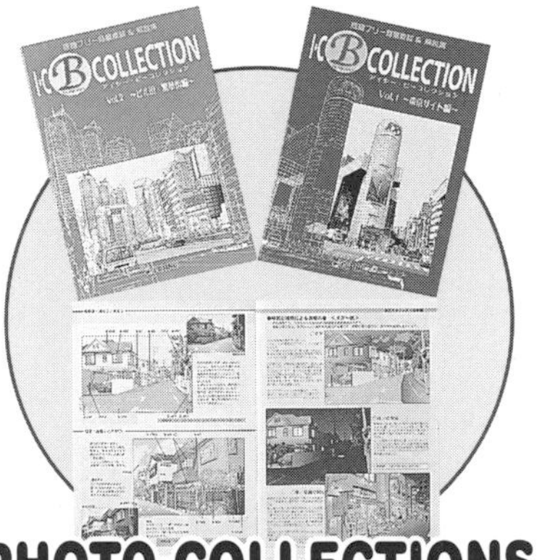

I-C B COLLECTION
I-C B COLLECTION

PHOTO COLLECTIONS

Making Manga: The Essential Steps

Now you have all the materials, you can start work.

Every step is important so learn each one thoroughly.

1. PLOTTING

Jot down your ideas for a basic storyline, the characters and what they say. Planning the story and character types is called plotting.

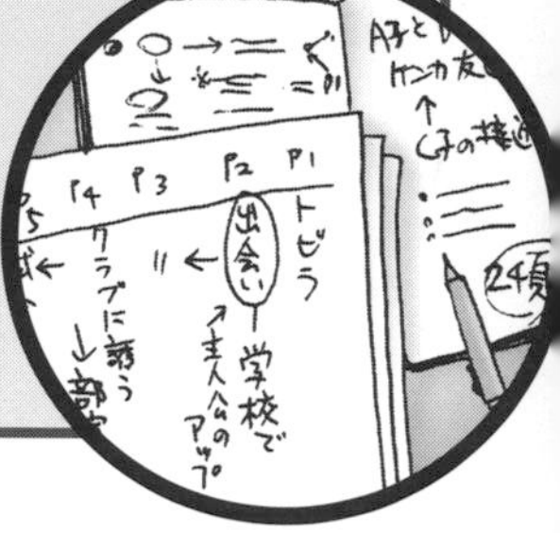

2. DRAFTING

Plan the page layout, including the frame sequences, poses and expressions of the characters, and dialogue. Then start drafting the rough outlines and sketching in special effects.

3. ADDING OUTLINE

First learn how to draw neat manga frames in ink—clean frames bring the picture into focus. Next, insert speech balloons and other words in the scene. Ink in the outlines of characters. Add special effects and background last. Be sure to clean your pen nib regularly.

Note pad

4. ERASING

Take care over erasing! Wait until the ink is dry. Use an eraser that requires minimum exertion as your arm will get tired quickly.

5. INKING IN

Fill in details such as hair, clothes etc. with ink. A fine line marker works best for tricky areas while a thick magic marker is best for larger areas. Brush pens are good for hair.

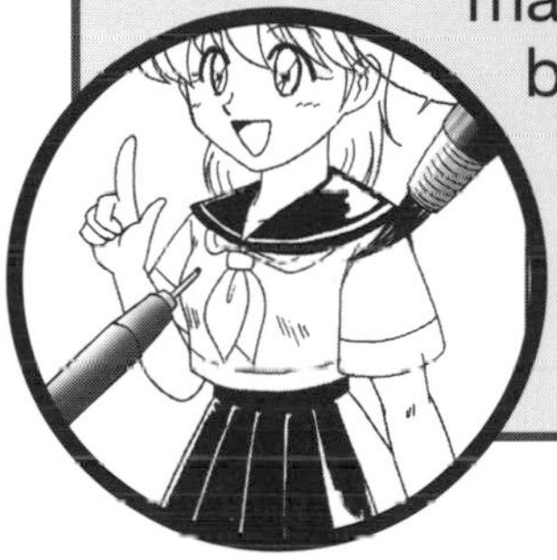

6. CORRECTING

Work carefully with either pen- or brush-type correction fluid to delete mistakes and unnecessary lines. Don't touch the manuscript until the corrections are completely dry.

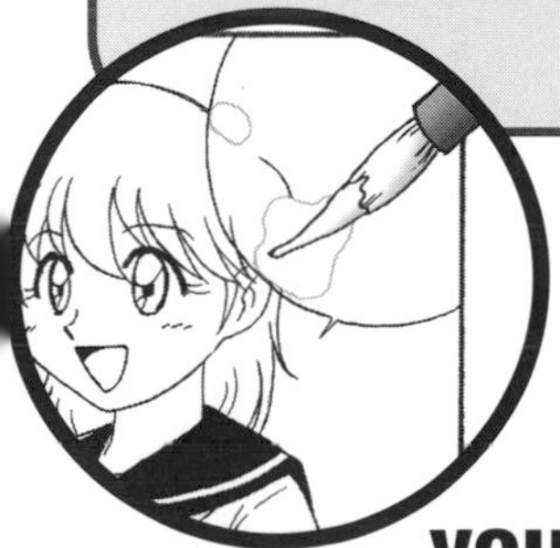

7. USING SCREEN TONE

Many types of screen tone are available, and you can cut, layer and scrape them off to achieve all sorts of effects. Be sure to remove any debris from your manuscript before using screen tone.

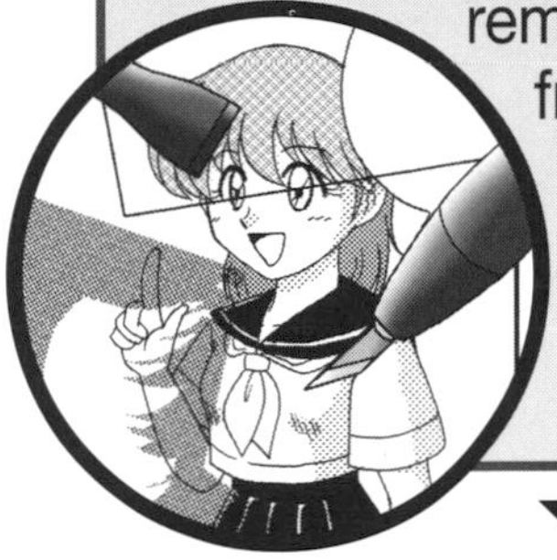

8. FINISHING TOUCHES

HIGHLIGHTING
Use white ink to add sparkle to eyes and shine to hair.

ADDING DIALOGUE
You can do this by hand, but computer printouts are easier to read. Changing fonts can make it more interesting.

Why not submit it to a magazine? Or maybe create your own magazine?

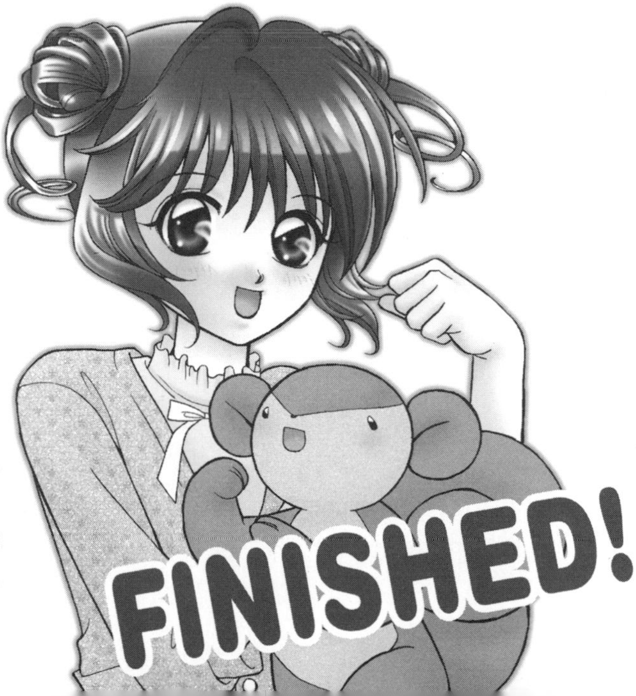
FINISHED!

AN ILLUSTRATION FROM START TO FINISH

Can you remember all the steps? Okay, let's go over the main points again.

1. First, the rough sketch

Position your characters. Sketch their expressions.

3. Then the ink outline

Go over your rough sketch in ink.

2. Next, the draft

Add details to your rough sketch, building up the characters and background.

4. Inking in and correcting

Ink in hair and other black areas. Once the ink is dry, erase the pencil sketch. Use correction fluid to delete any mistakes.

Reduced to 75% of the original.

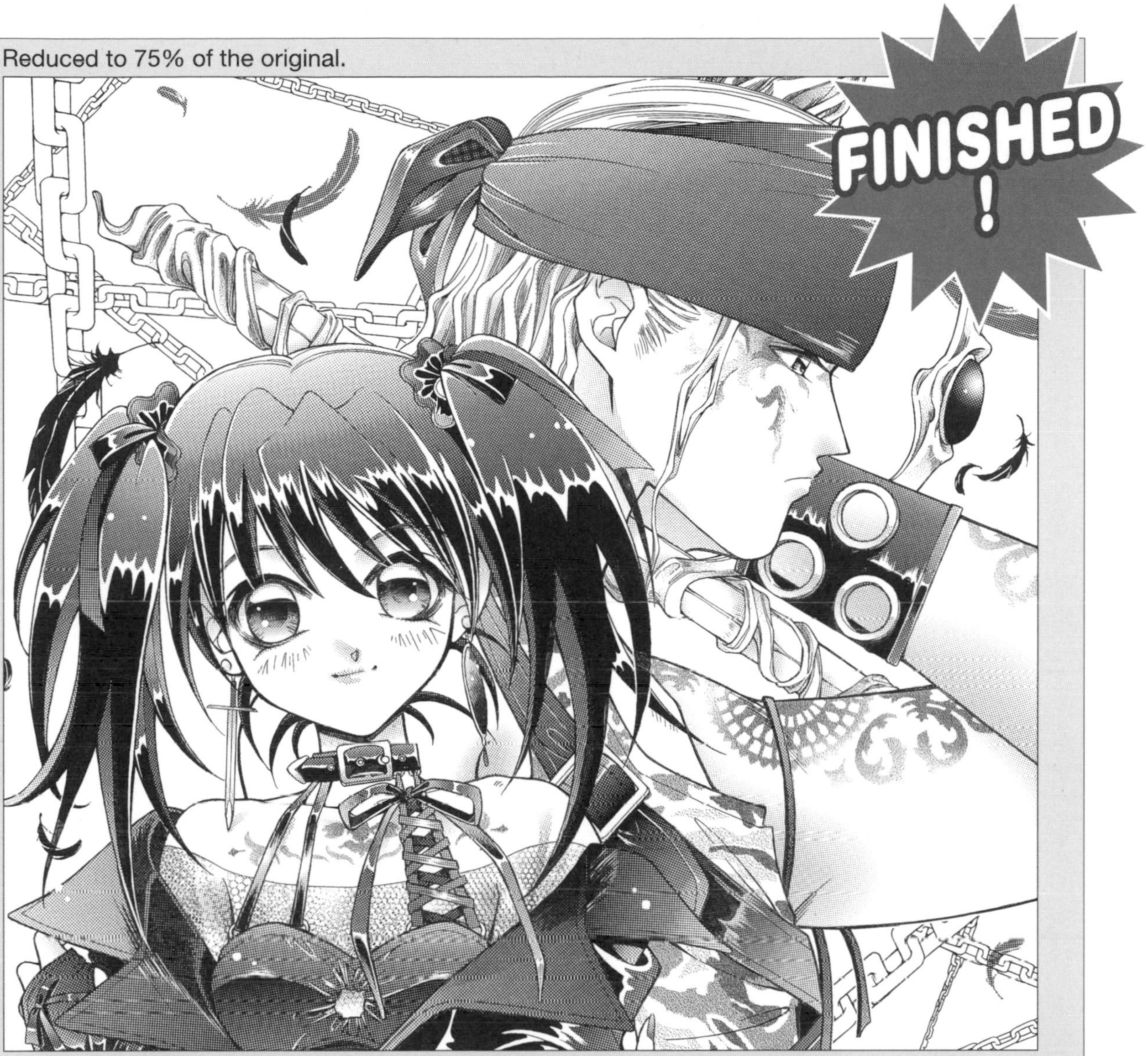
FINISHED
!

5. Lastly, apply screen tone, add highlights, and you're done!

Add the finishing touches with screen tone, and white ink for highlights in eyes, hair and clothes.

You can use gradation tone on shadows, hair, jackets, bandannas etc., keeping in mind the angle of the light.

Create a sense of volume in areas where you use dark tone, such as on bandannas, by leaving white gaps along creases.

Shadow quality will differ depending on whether you use coarse or fine dot screen tone.

We've adapted patterned screen tone to create the body paint on these two characters. You can get a lot out of one pattern if you cut it up and use the parts in your own way.

SCREEN TONE TYPES

We have used IC products here.

IC SCREEN
S-799 S-945 S-978
S-3020 S-3032
S-5012 S-5030

IC SCREEN YOUTH
Y-1242 Y-1616 Y-1648
Y-1651 Y-1652 Y-1675
Y-1676

LESSON 1
MATERIALS

What materials are essential for drawing manga?
Do I have to use manga manuscript paper?
Which pen nibs work best?
What's the difference between all
the various types of ink?
We'll answer all your questions!

MANGA MANUSCRIPT PAPER

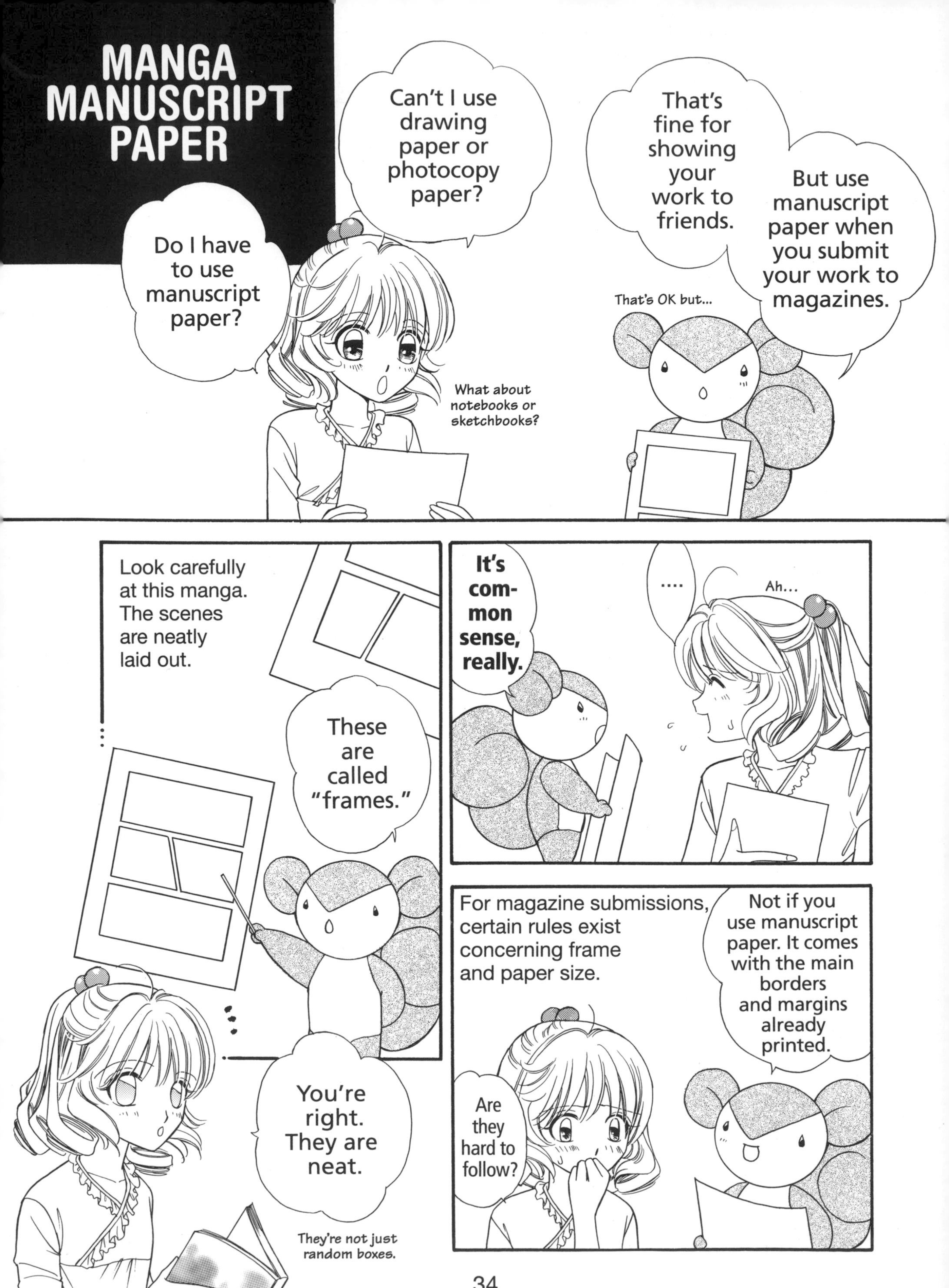

Do I have to use manuscript paper?
Can't I use drawing paper or photocopy paper?
What about notebooks or sketchbooks?
That's fine for showing your work to friends.
That's OK but...
But use manuscript paper when you submit your work to magazines.
Look carefully at this manga. The scenes are neatly laid out.
These are called "frames."
You're right. They are neat.
They're not just random boxes.
Ah...
....
It's common sense, really.
For magazine submissions, certain rules exist concerning frame and paper size.
Are they hard to follow?
Not if you use manuscript paper. It comes with the main borders and margins already printed.

OK, let's have a look at a sheet of manuscript paper.

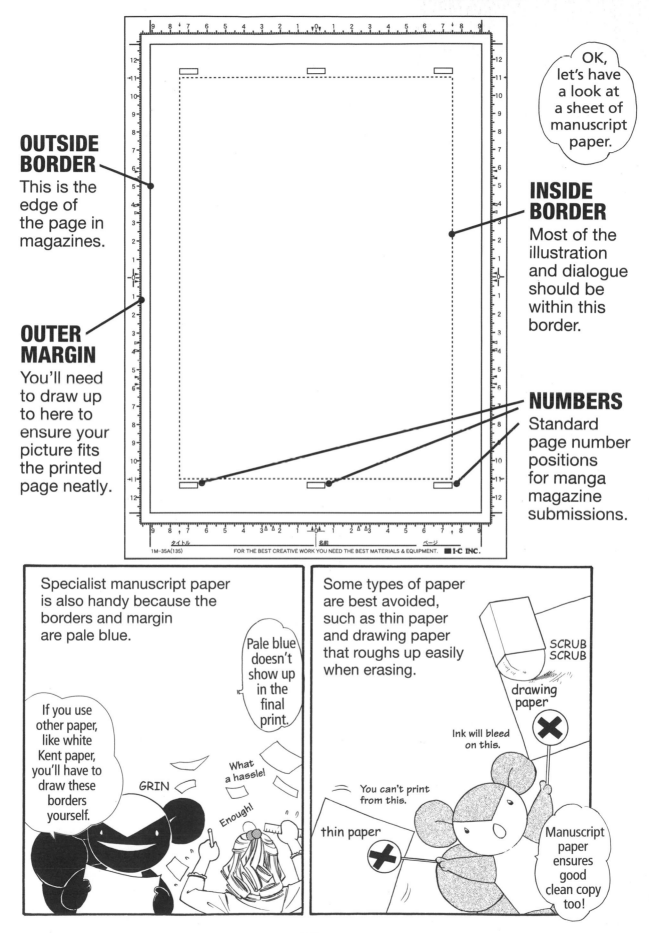

OUTSIDE BORDER
This is the edge of the page in magazines.

OUTER MARGIN
You'll need to draw up to here to ensure your picture fits the printed page neatly.

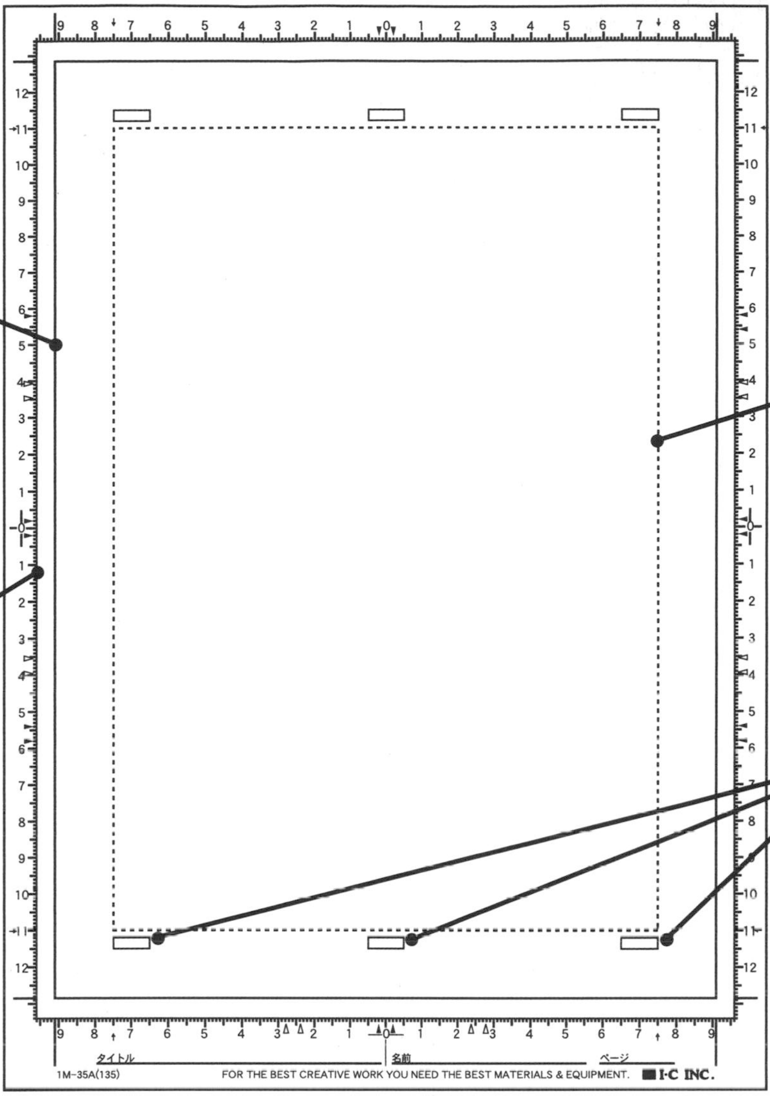
タイトル
名前
ページ
1M-35A(135)
FOR THE BEST CREATIVE WORK YOU NEED THE BEST MATERIALS & EQUIPMENT.
I·C INC.

INSIDE BORDER
Most of the illustration and dialogue should be within this border.

NUMBERS
Standard page number positions for manga magazine submissions.

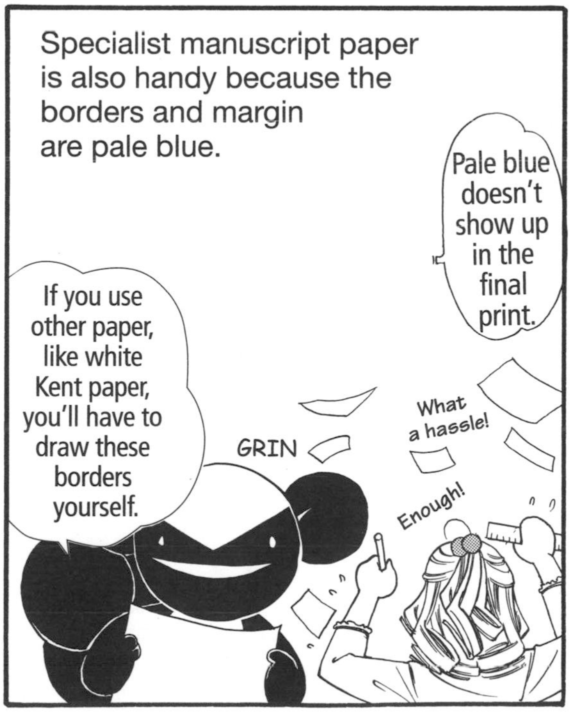
Specialist manuscript paper is also handy because the borders and margin are pale blue.
Pale blue doesn't show up in the final print.
If you use other paper, like white Kent paper, you'll have to draw these borders yourself.
GRIN
What a hassle!
Enough!

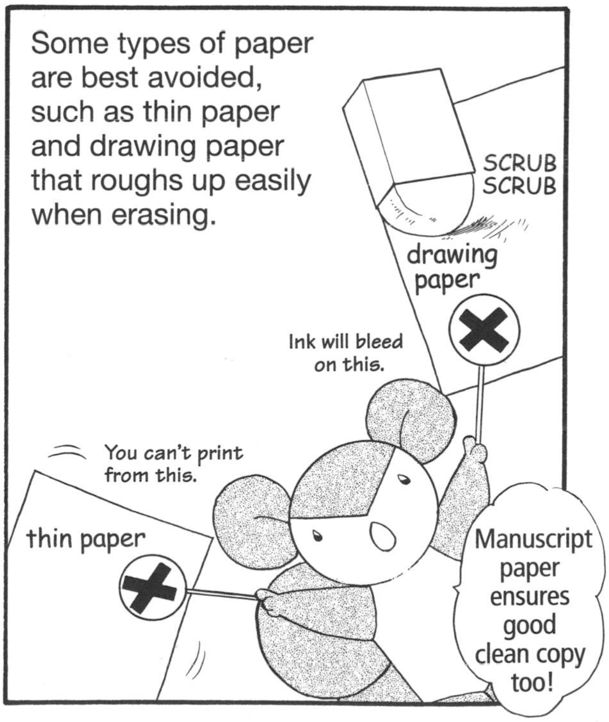
Some types of paper are best avoided, such as thin paper and drawing paper that roughs up easily when erasing.
SCRUB SCRUB
drawing paper
Ink will bleed on this.
You can't print from this.
thin paper
Manuscript paper ensures good clean copy too!

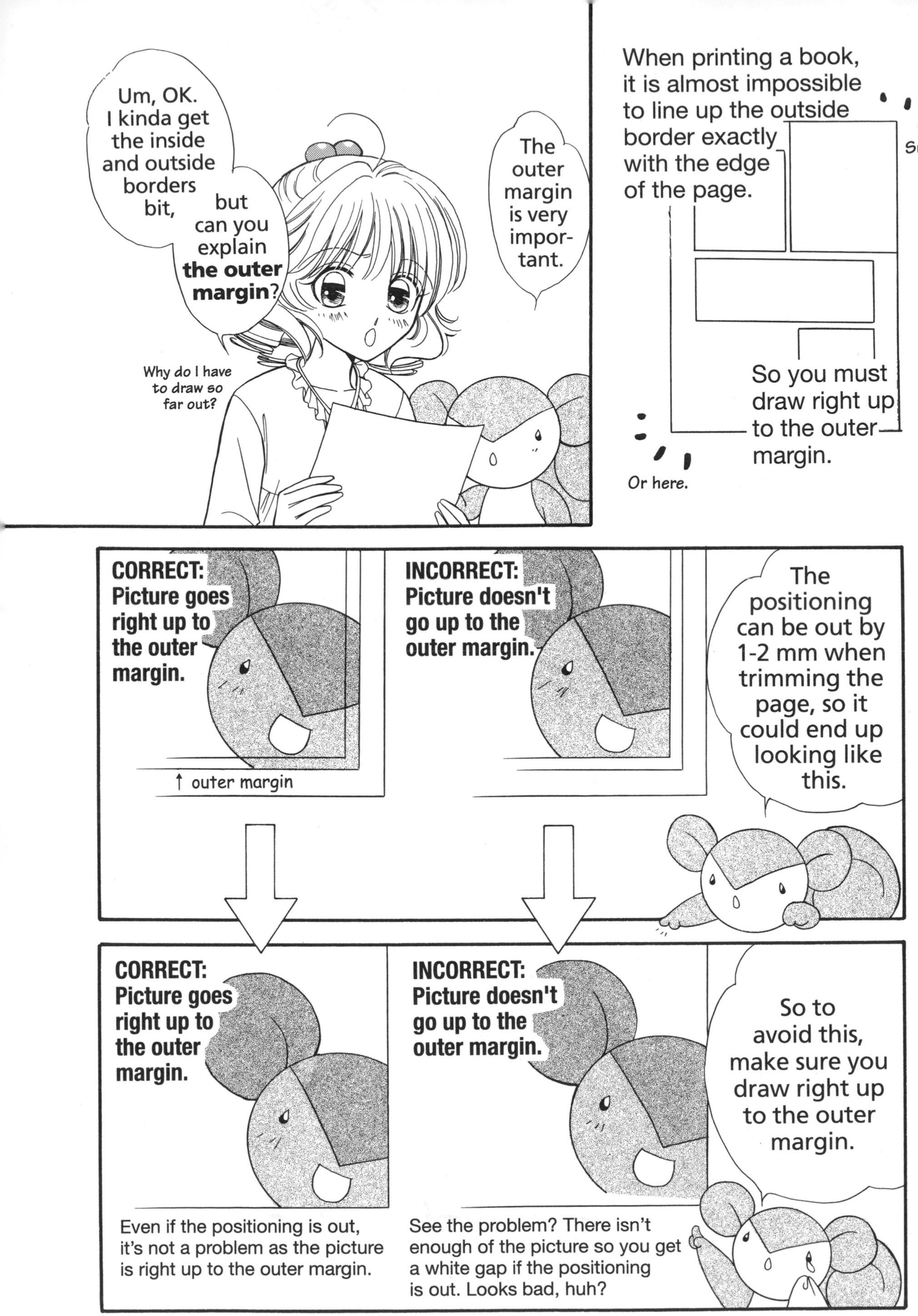

Um, OK. I kinda get the inside and outside borders bit,
but can you explain **the outer margin**?
Why do I have to draw so far out?
The outer margin is very impor-tant.
When printing a book, it is almost impossible to line up the outside border exactly with the edge of the page.
Such as here.
Or here.
So you must draw right up to the outer margin.
CORRECT: Picture goes right up to the outer margin.
↑ outer margin
INCORRECT: Picture doesn't go up to the outer margin.
The positioning can be out by 1-2 mm when trimming the page, so it could end up looking like this.
CORRECT: Picture goes right up to the outer margin.
Even if the positioning is out, it's not a problem as the picture is right up to the outer margin.
INCORRECT: Picture doesn't go up to the outer margin.
See the problem? There isn't enough of the picture so you get a white gap if the positioning is out. Looks bad, huh?
So to avoid this, make sure you draw right up to the outer margin.

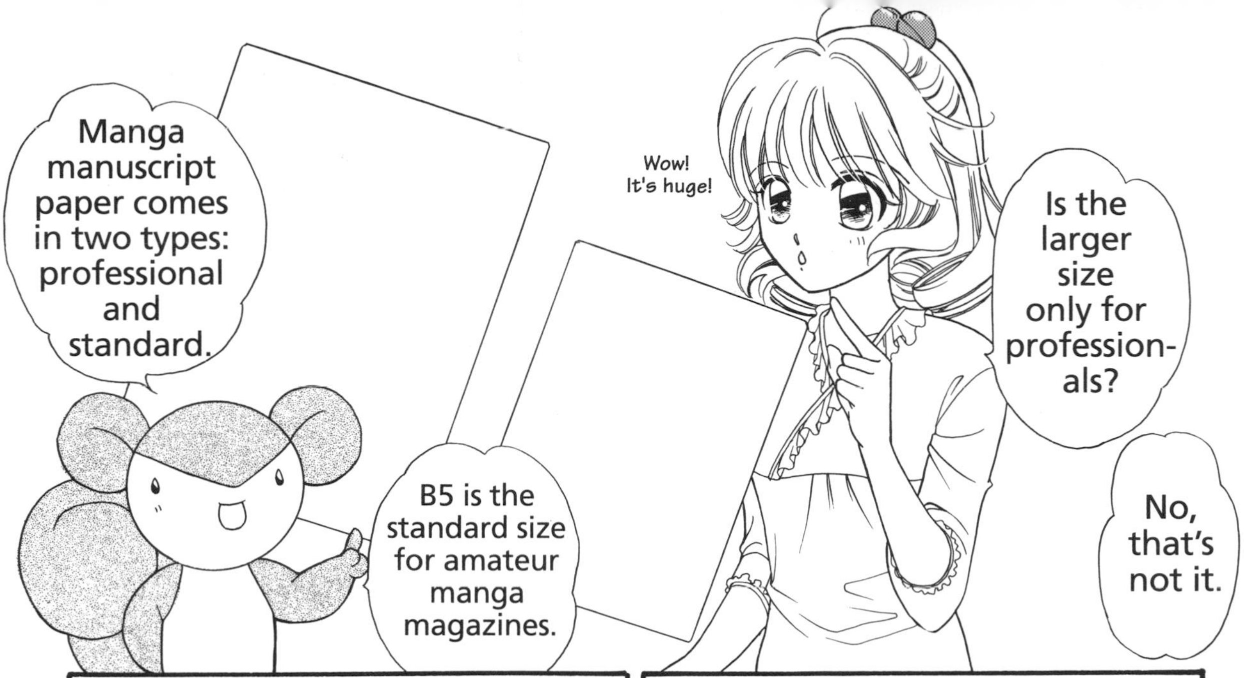

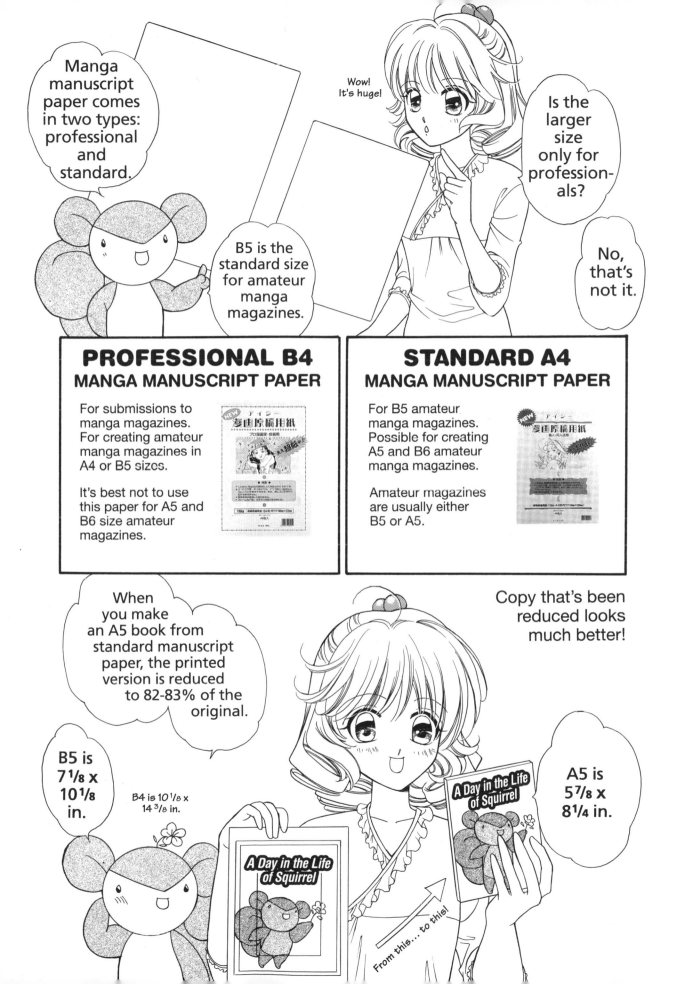

Manga manuscript paper comes in two types: professional and standard.
Wow! It's huge!
Is the larger size only for profession-als?
No, that's not it.
B5 is the standard size for amateur manga magazines.

PROFESSIONAL B4
MANGA MANUSCRIPT PAPER

For submissions to manga magazines. For creating amateur manga magazines in A4 or B5 sizes.

It's best not to use this paper for A5 and B6 size amateur magazines.

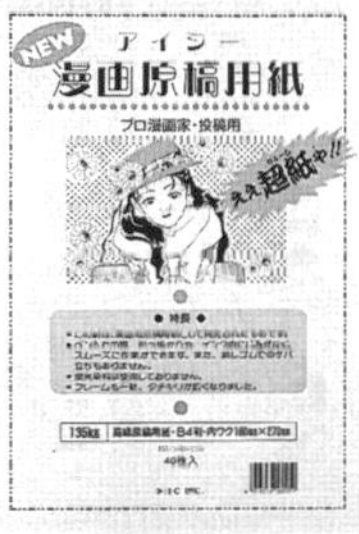

STANDARD A4
MANGA MANUSCRIPT PAPER

For B5 amateur manga magazines. Possible for creating A5 and B6 amateur manga magazines.

Amateur magazines are usually either B5 or A5.

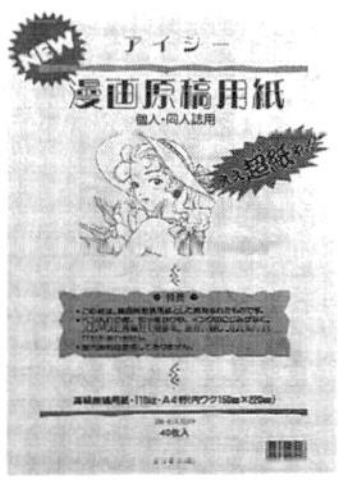

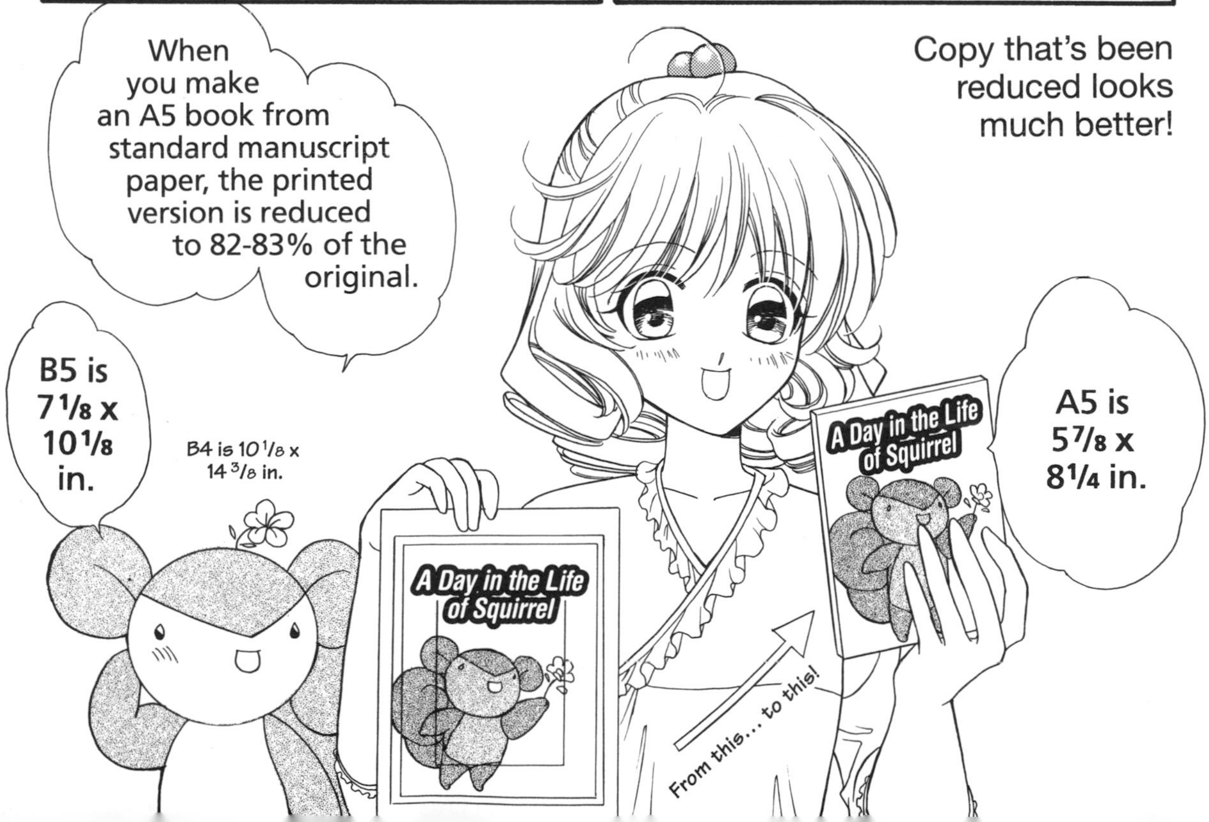

When you make an A5 book from standard manuscript paper, the printed version is reduced to 82-83% of the original.
Copy that's been reduced looks much better!
B5 is 7 1/8 x 10 1/8 in.
B4 is 10 1/8 x 14 3/8 in.
A Day in the Life of Squirrel
From this... to this!
A Day in the Life of Squirrel
A5 is 5 7/8 x 8 1/4 in.

PENCILS

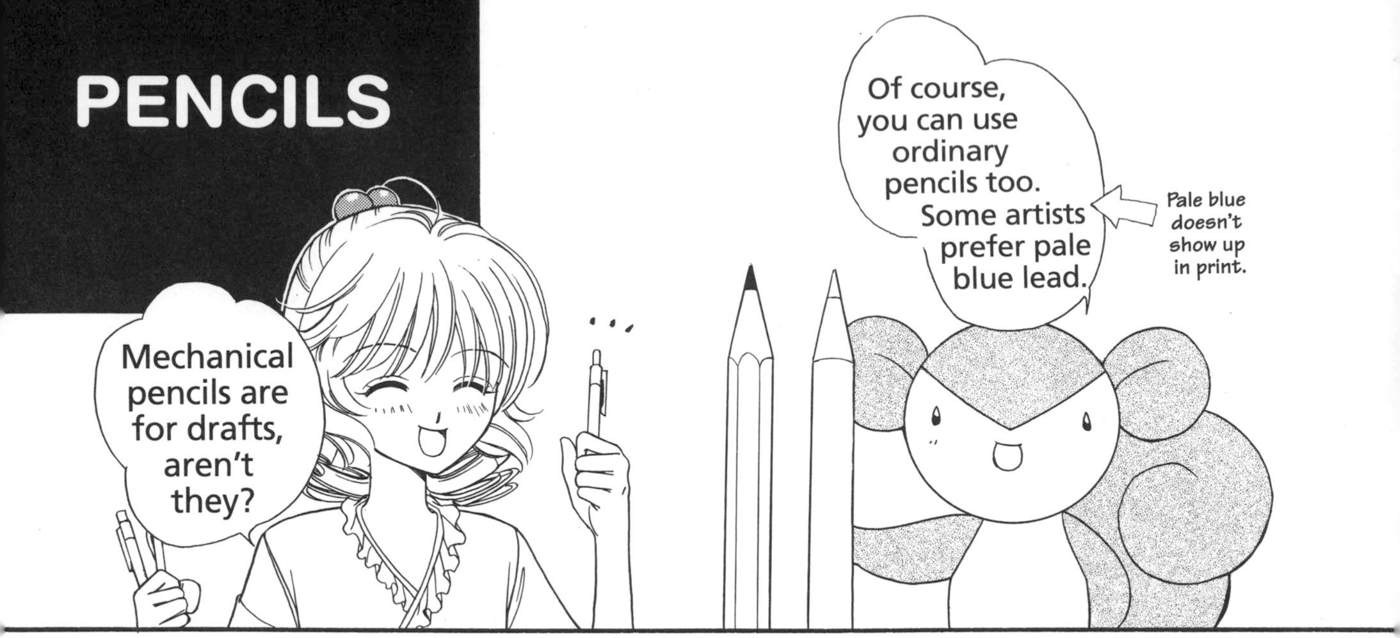
Mechanical pencils are for drafts, aren't they?
Of course, you can use ordinary pencils too. Some artists prefer pale blue lead.
Pale blue doesn't show up in print.

Mechanical pencils

These have a fine point which doesn't get blunt. They're good for delicate, detailed work.

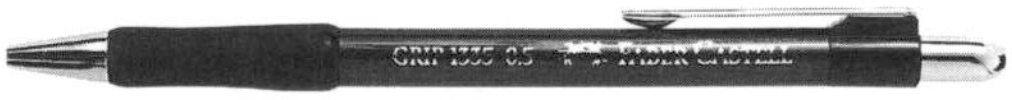

Pencils

These have a thicker lead than mechanical pencils, and are good for drawing large objects. The lead is quite soft.

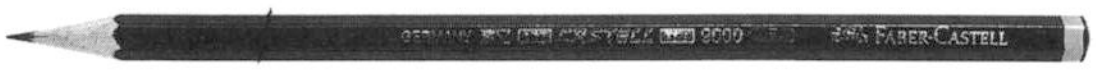

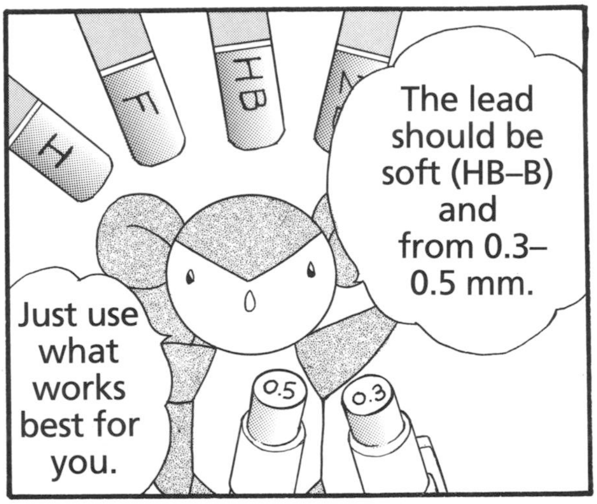
H
F
HB
The lead should be soft (HB–B) and from 0.3–0.5 mm.
Just use what works best for you.
0.5
0.3

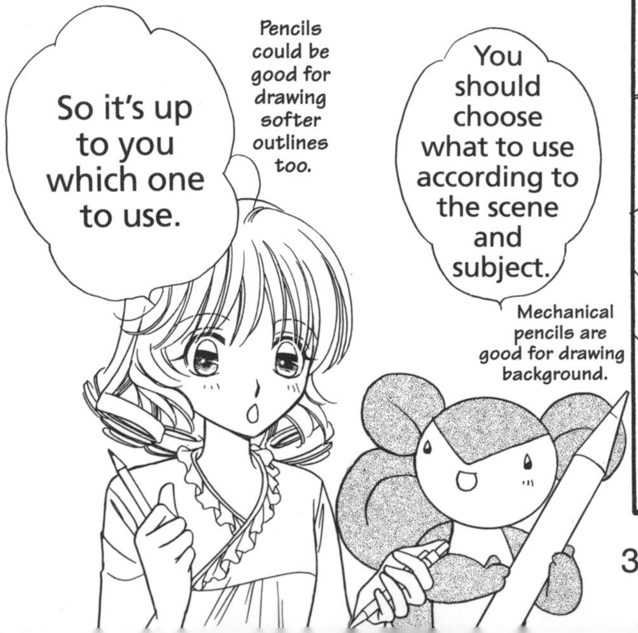
So it's up to you which one to use.
Pencils could be good for drawing softer outlines too.
You should choose what to use according to the scene and subject.
Mechanical pencils are good for drawing background.

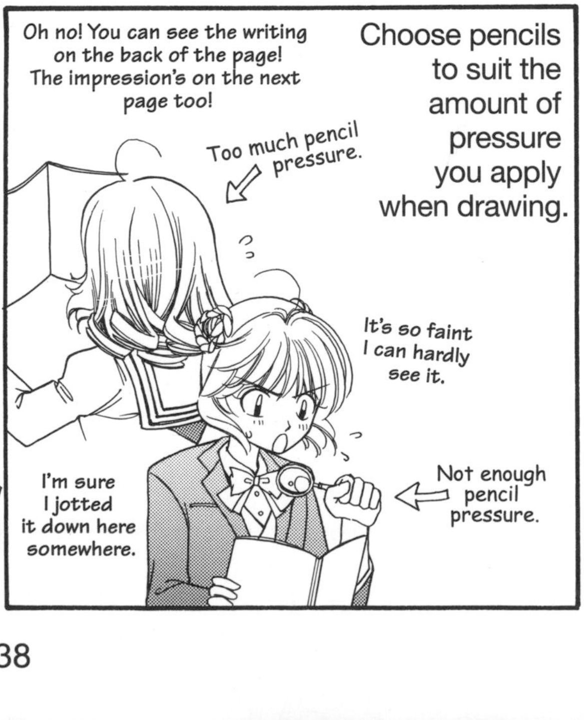
Choose pencils to suit the amount of pressure you apply when drawing.
Oh no! You can see the writing on the back of the page! The impression's on the next page too!
Too much pencil pressure.
It's so faint I can hardly see it.
I'm sure I jotted it down here somewhere.
Not enough pencil pressure.

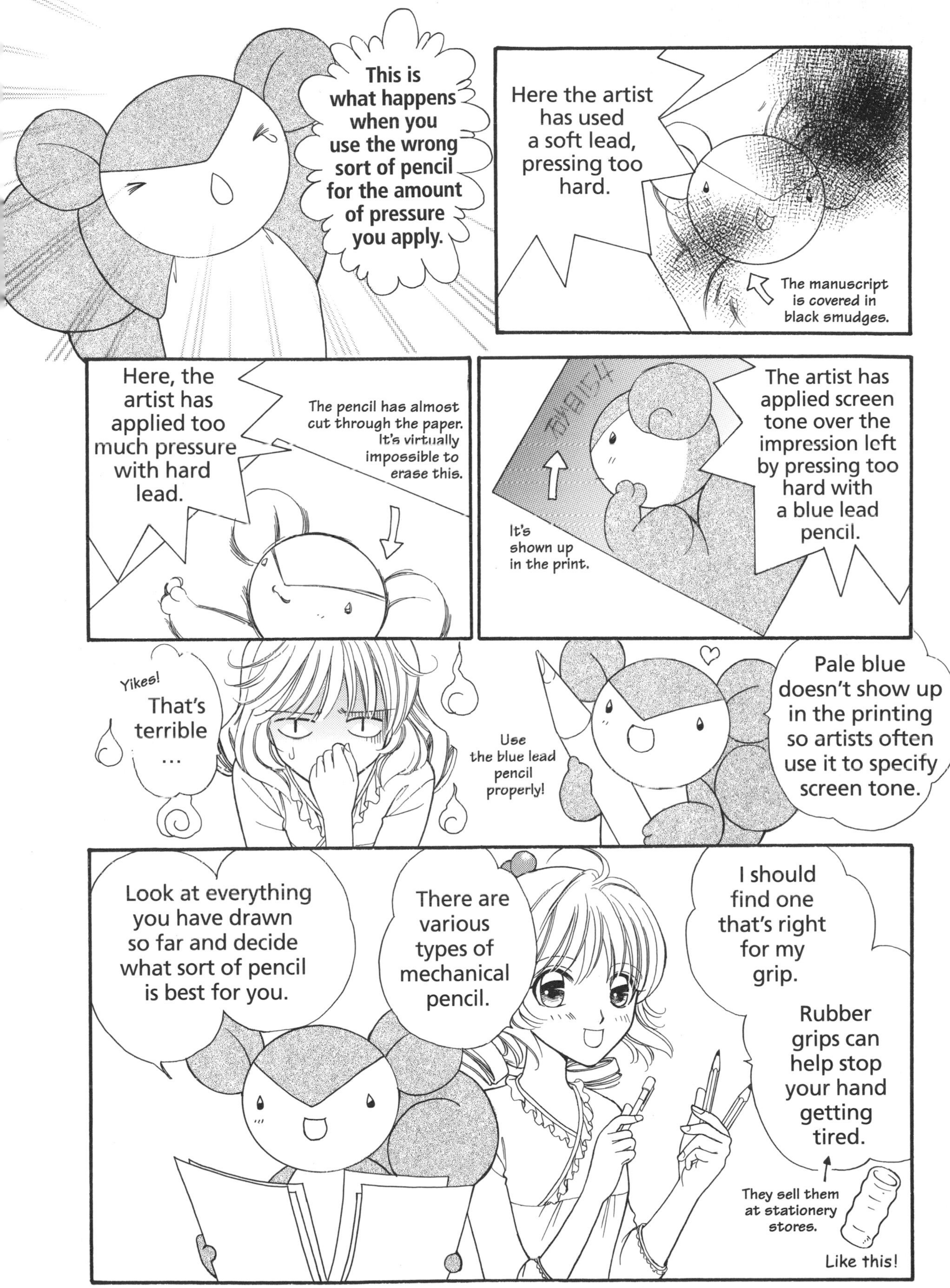
This is what happens when you use the wrong sort of pencil for the amount of pressure you apply.
Here the artist has used a soft lead, pressing too hard.
The manuscript is covered in black smudges.
Here, the artist has applied too much pressure with hard lead.
The pencil has almost cut through the paper. It's virtually impossible to erase this.
The artist has applied screen tone over the impression left by pressing too hard with a blue lead pencil.
It's shown up in the print.
Yikes! That's terrible …
Use the blue lead pencil properly!
Pale blue doesn't show up in the printing so artists often use it to specify screen tone.
Look at everything you have drawn so far and decide what sort of pencil is best for you.
There are various types of mechanical pencil.
I should find one that's right for my grip.
Rubber grips can help stop your hand getting tired.
They sell them at stationery stores.
Like this!

PEN NIBS AND HOLDERS

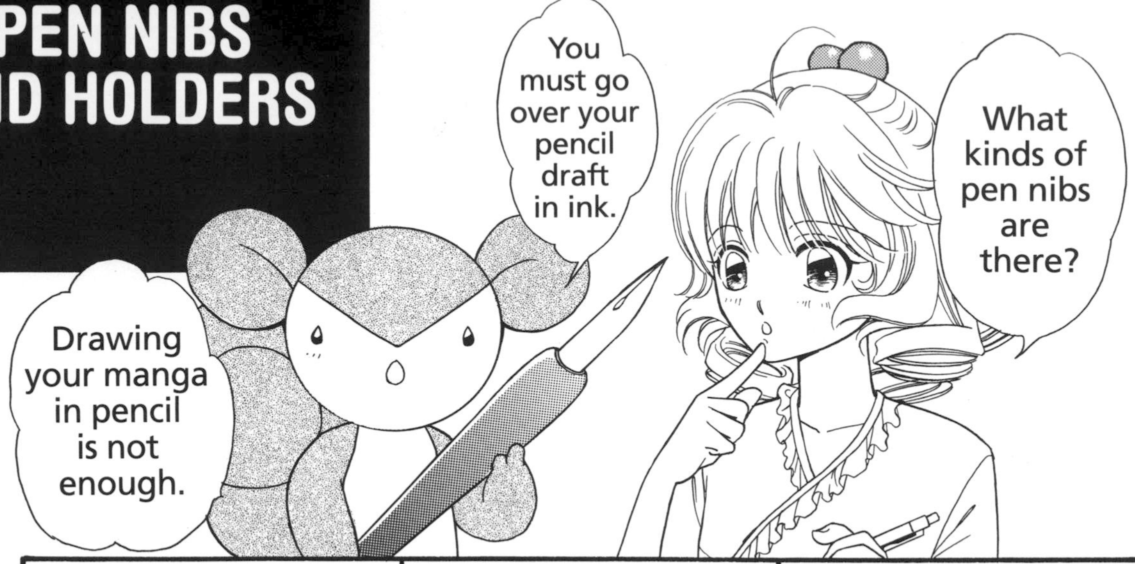

Drawing your manga in pencil is not enough.
You must go over your pencil draft in ink.
What kinds of pen nibs are there?

TURNIP NIB	G-NIB	ROUND NIB
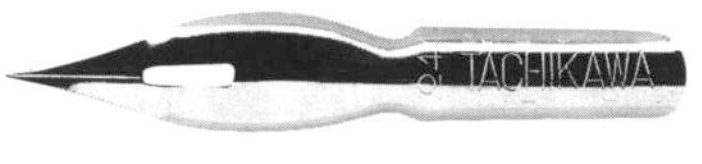	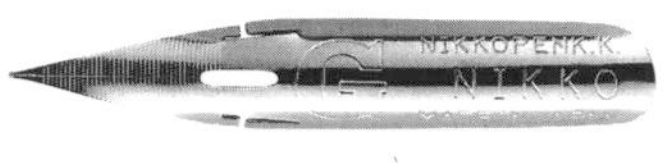	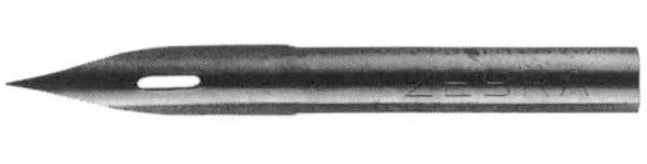
Draws fine, uniform lines. Easy to handle with a free-flowing feel even when new. Difficult to vary the thickness of lines, not very expressive.	Draws thick, uniform lines, so excellent for bold, strong outlines. Can draw fine lines too when it's new.	Indispensable for fine, delicate lines, background, and manually produced special effects. By varying pressure, it does everything from ultra-fine to thick lines.
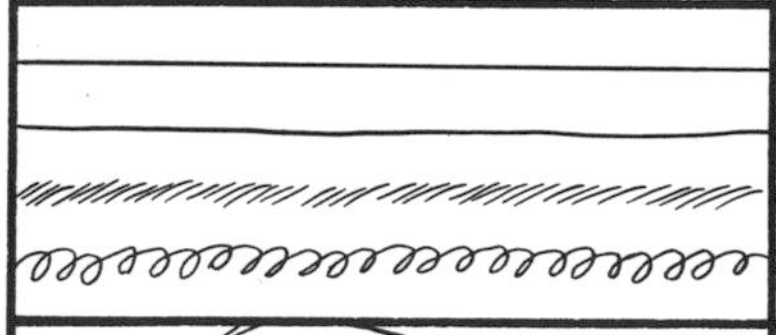	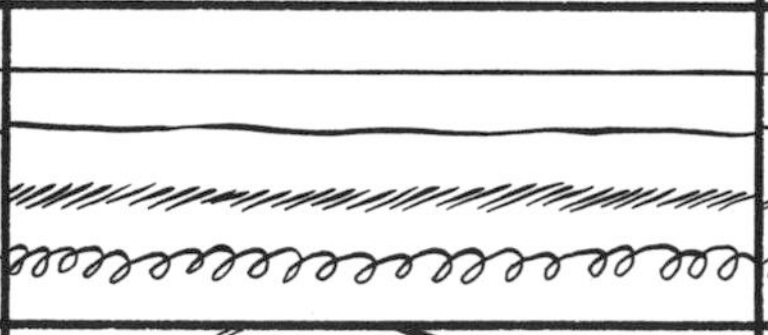	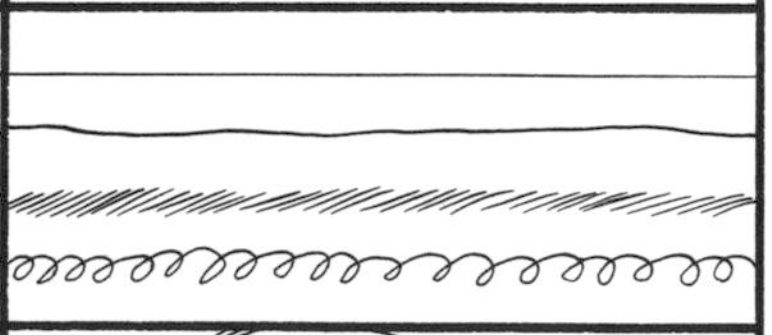
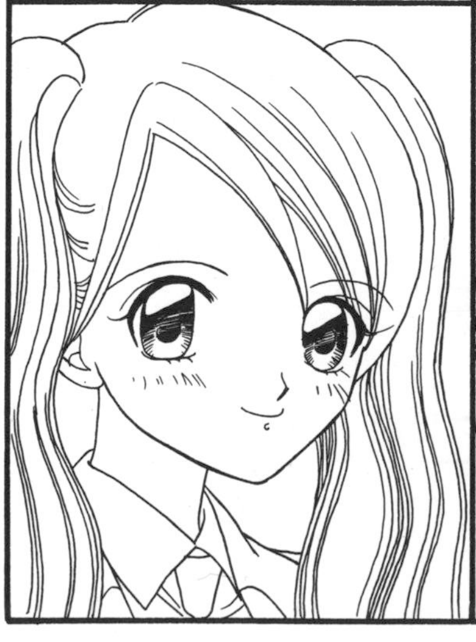	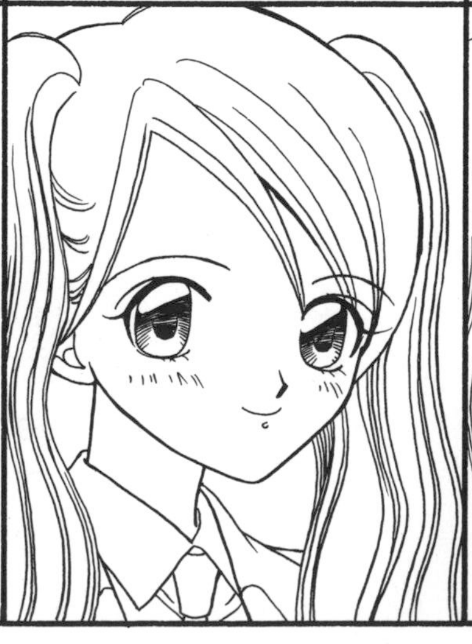	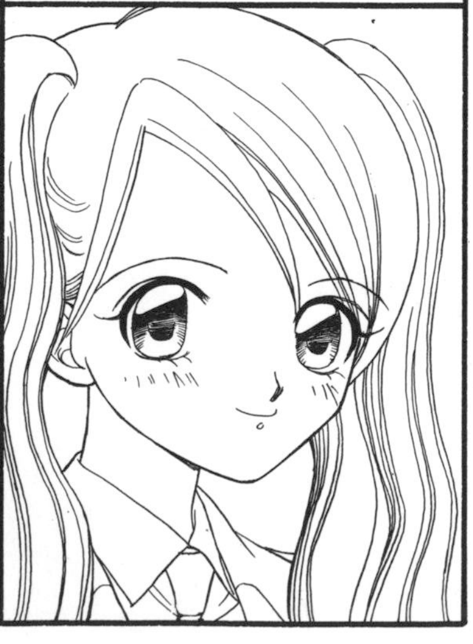

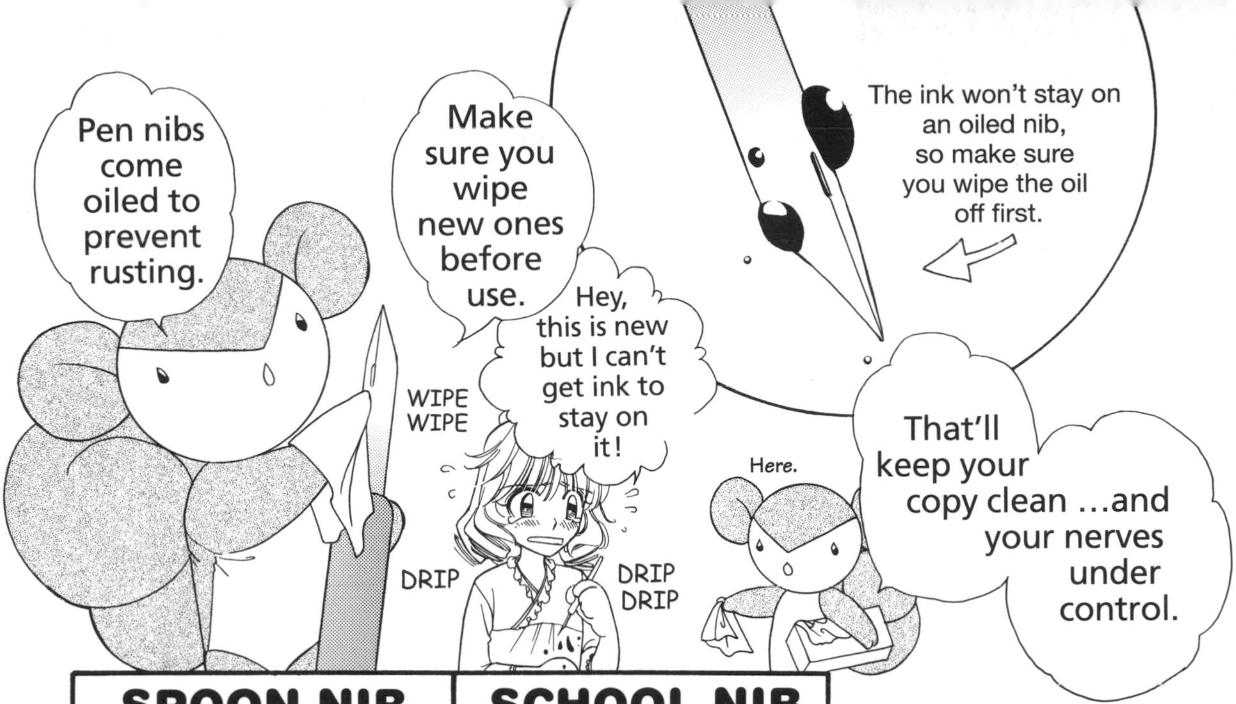
Hey, this is new but I can't get ink to stay on it!
Pen nibs come oiled to prevent rusting.
Make sure you wipe new ones before use.
The ink won't stay on an oiled nib, so make sure you wipe the oil off first.
WIPE WIPE
DRIP
DRIP DRIP
Here.
That'll keep your copy clean ...and your nerves under control.

SPOON NIB	SCHOOL NIB
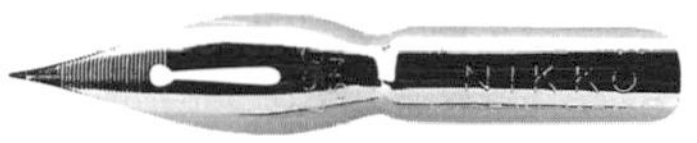	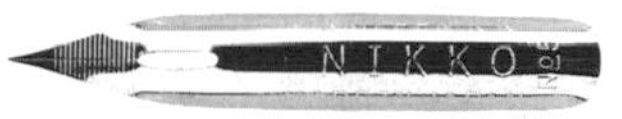
Resembles the turnip nib in feel and effect. Produces smooth, consistent lines. Hard to vary the thickness of lines.	Cross between the G-nib and turnip pen. Flows freely, produces fine lines easily. Easy to handle.
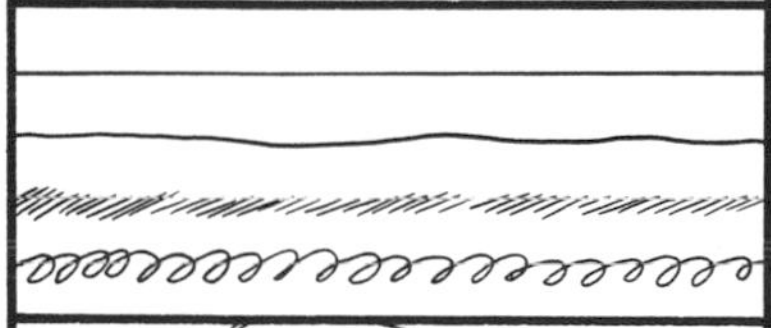	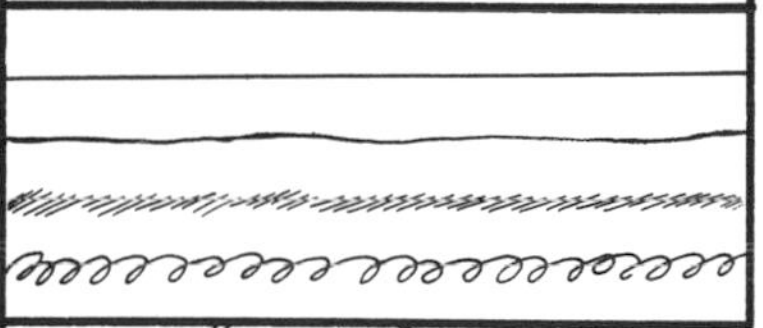
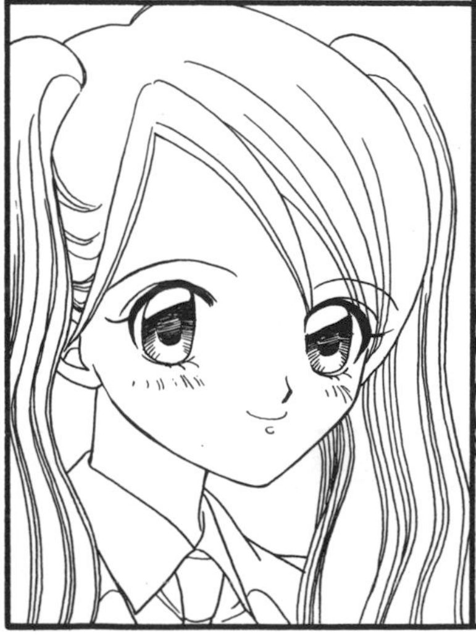	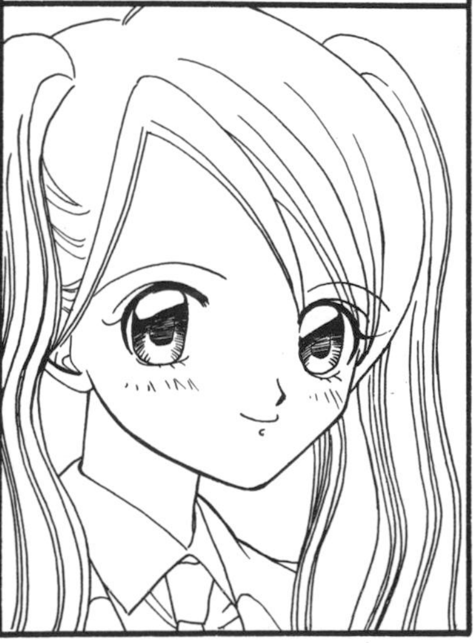

If you heat the pen nib over a flame, it will hold the ink better. Be careful!

Nibs rust easily, so keep them in a bag or case to prevent contact with moisture.

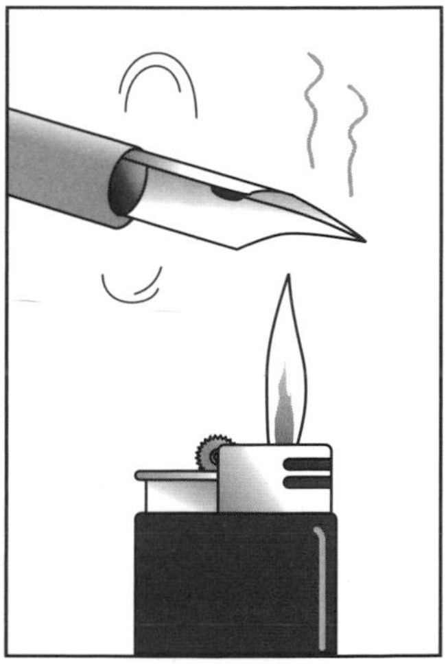

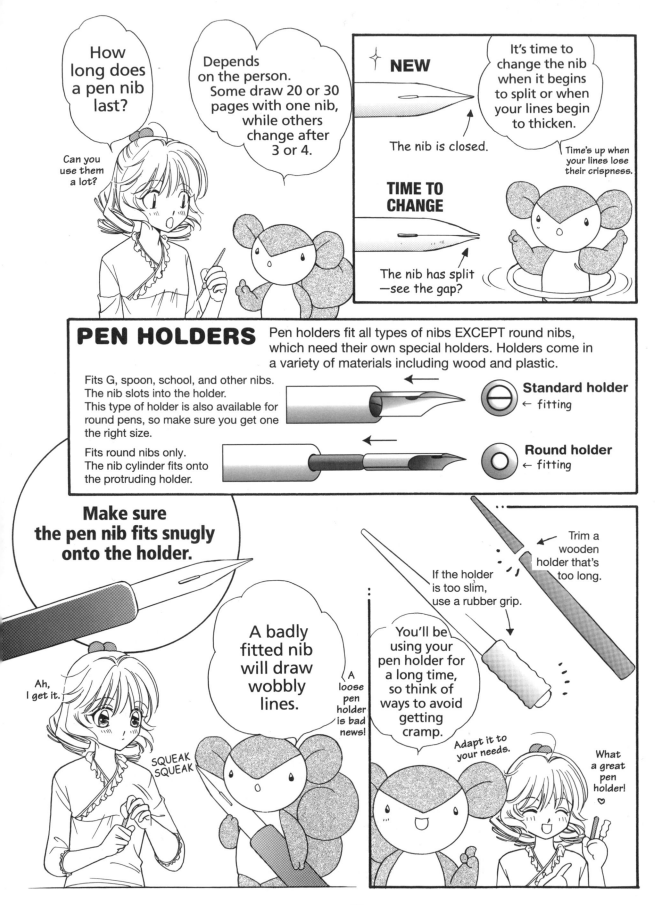

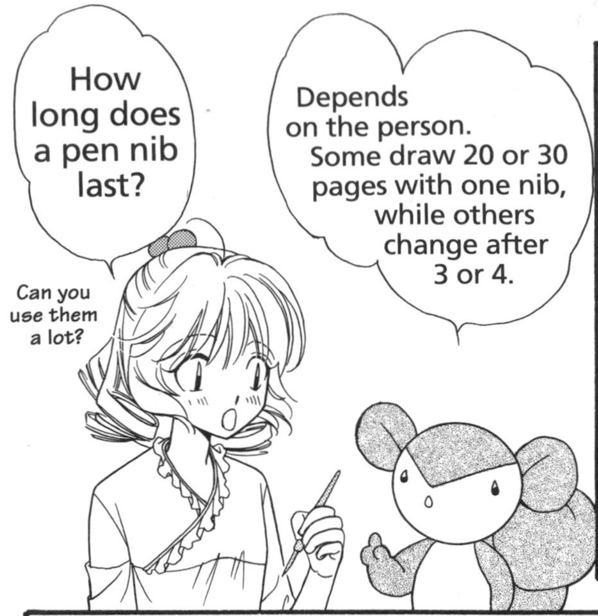
How long does a pen nib last?
Can you use them a lot?
Depends on the person. Some draw 20 or 30 pages with one nib, while others change after 3 or 4.

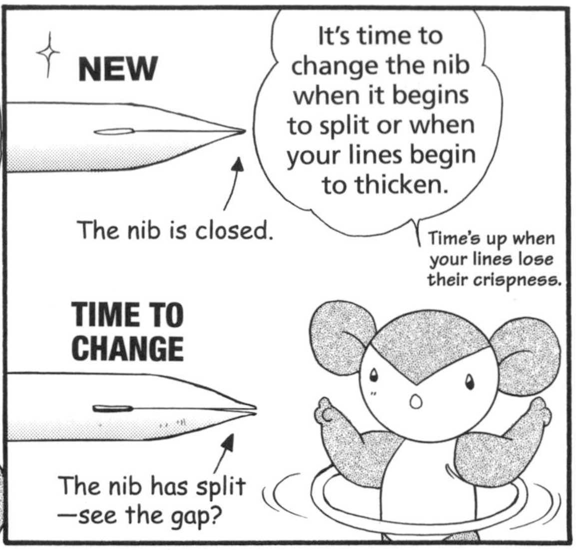
NEW
The nib is closed.
TIME TO CHANGE
The nib has split —see the gap?
It's time to change the nib when it begins to split or when your lines begin to thicken.
Time's up when your lines lose their crispness.

PEN HOLDERS

Pen holders fit all types of nibs EXCEPT round nibs, which need their own special holders. Holders come in a variety of materials including wood and plastic.

Fits G, spoon, school, and other nibs. The nib slots into the holder. This type of holder is also available for round pens, so make sure you get one the right size.

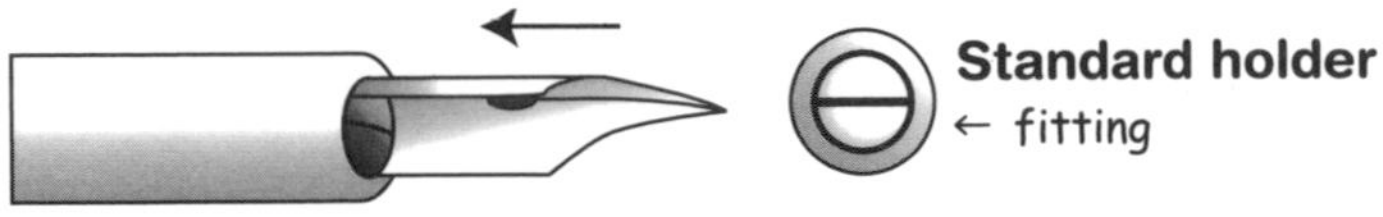
Standard holder
← fitting

Fits round nibs only. The nib cylinder fits onto the protruding holder.

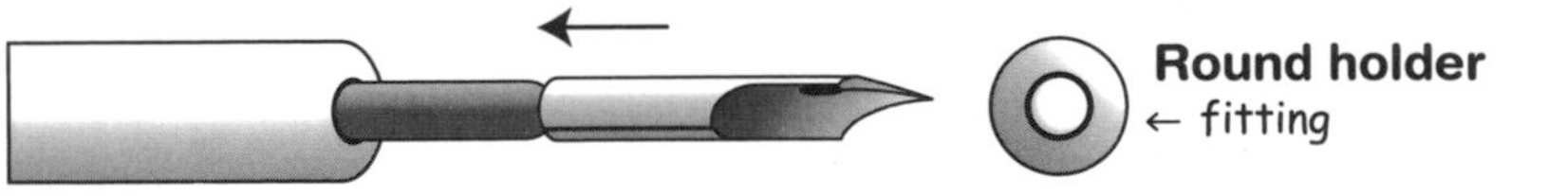
Round holder
← fitting

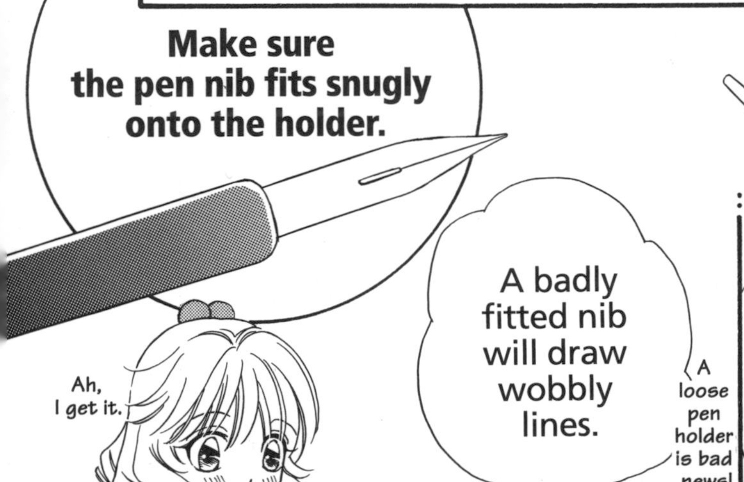
Make sure the pen nib fits snugly onto the holder.
Ah, I get it.
SQUEAK SQUEAK
A badly fitted nib will draw wobbly lines.
A loose pen holder is bad news!

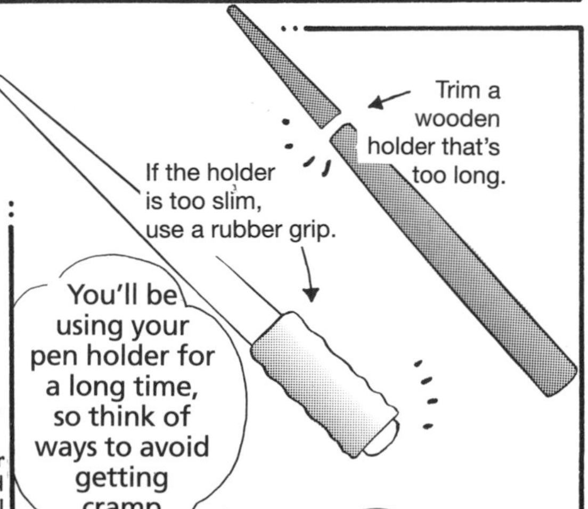
Trim a wooden holder that's too long.
If the holder is too slim, use a rubber grip.
You'll be using your pen holder for a long time, so think of ways to avoid getting cramp.
Adapt it to your needs.
What a great pen holder!

INK

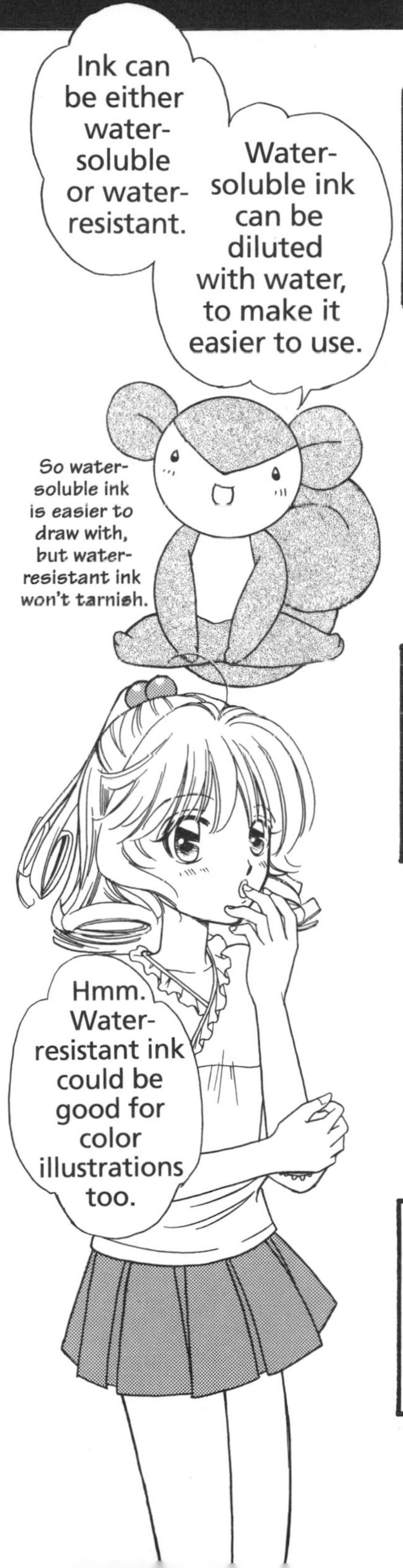

Ink can be either water-soluble or water-resistant.
Water-soluble ink can be diluted with water, to make it easier to use.
So water-soluble ink is easier to draw with, but water-resistant ink won't tarnish.
Hmm. Water-resistant ink could be good for color illustrations too.

CHINA INK

Also known as India ink, this is the blackest ink available and hardly fades when you use an eraser on it. It is water-soluble, which means that it is slow to dry, and that it is doubly important to wipe the pen nib after use to prevent rusting. It will also tarnish on contact with moisture, so try to avoid touching it with your hands even after it has dried.

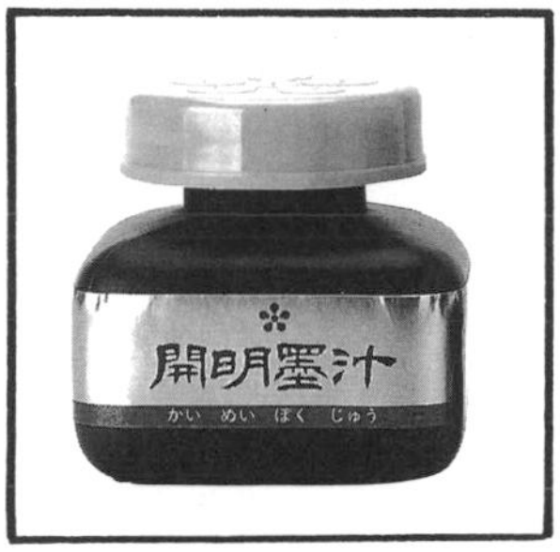

開明墨汁

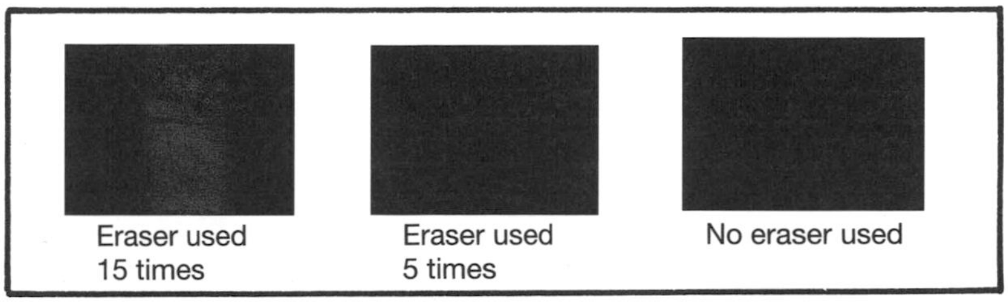

Eraser used 15 times
Eraser used 5 times
No eraser used

PILOT DRAFTING AND DOCUMENT INKS

Drafting ink is water-soluble, document ink is water-resistant. Both have a light feel and are quick to dry. Be careful when using an eraser as they fade quickly.

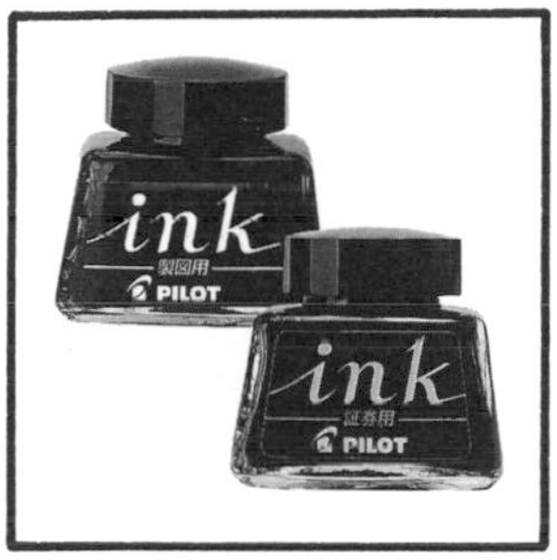

ink
PILOT
ink
PILOT

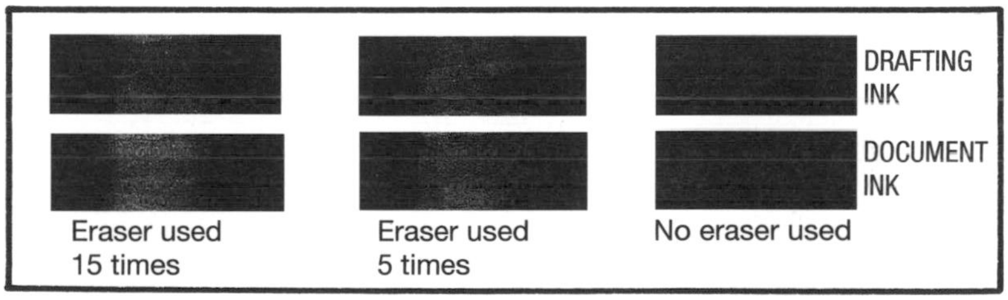

DRAFTING INK
DOCUMENT INK
Eraser used 15 times
Eraser used 5 times
No eraser used

IC COMIC SUPER BLACK

Non-gloss matte finish, and quick to dry. Goes a long way and doesn't fade when you use an eraser. It's water-resistant and dries quickly, so be sure to clean the nib regularly.

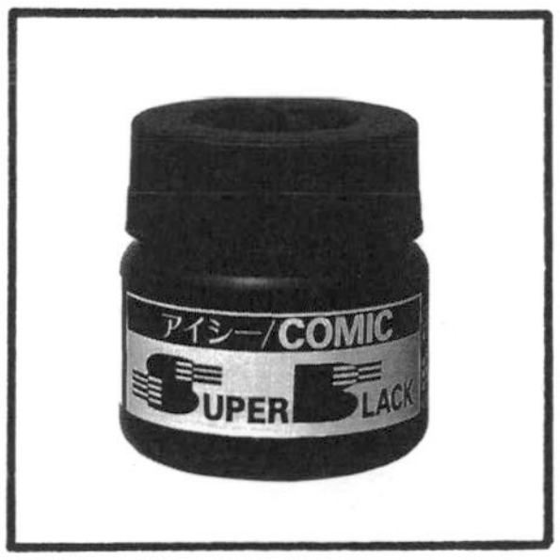

アイシー/COMIC
SUPER BLACK

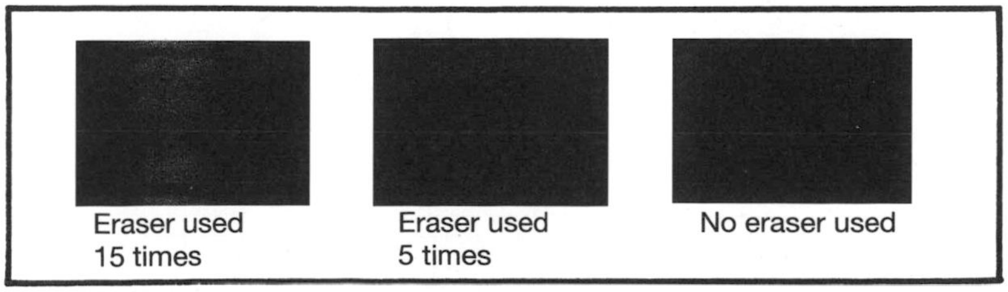

Eraser used 15 times
Eraser used 5 times
No eraser used

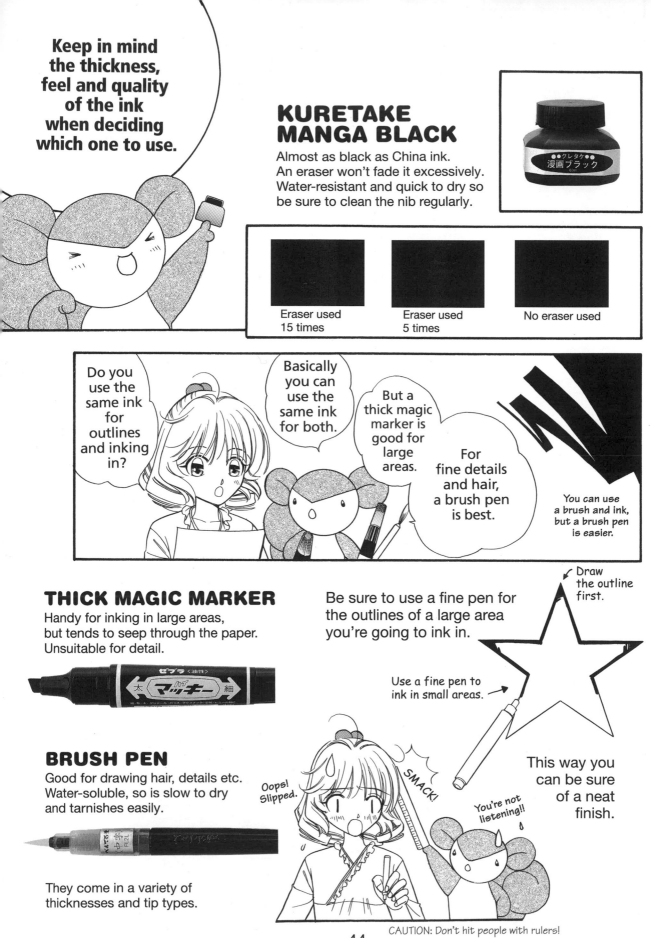

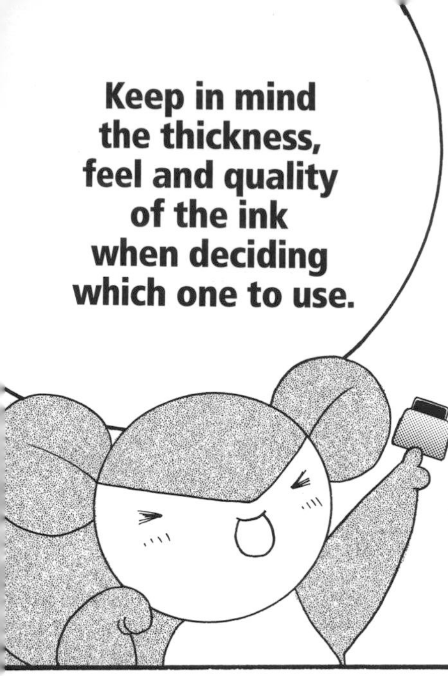
Keep in mind the thickness, feel and quality of the ink when deciding which one to use.

KURETAKE MANGA BLACK

Almost as black as China ink.
An eraser won't fade it excessively.
Water-resistant and quick to dry so be sure to clean the nib regularly.

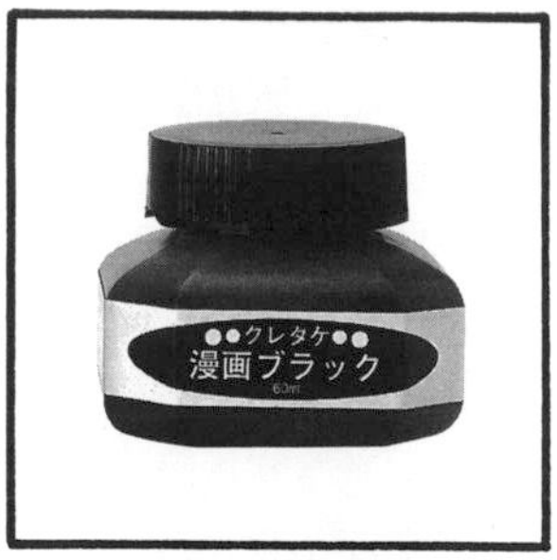
●●クレタケ●●
漫画ブラック

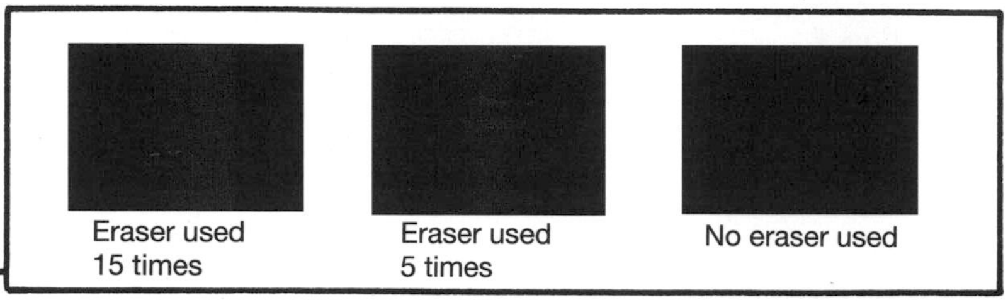
Eraser used 15 times
Eraser used 5 times
No eraser used

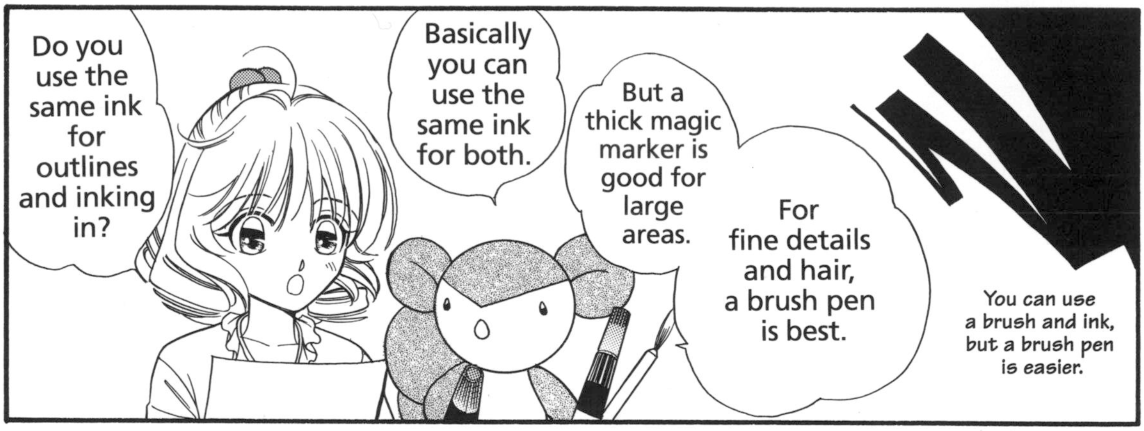
Do you use the same ink for outlines and inking in?
Basically you can use the same ink for both.
But a thick magic marker is good for large areas.
For fine details and hair, a brush pen is best.
You can use a brush and ink, but a brush pen is easier.

THICK MAGIC MARKER

Handy for inking in large areas,
but tends to seep through the paper.
Unsuitable for detail.

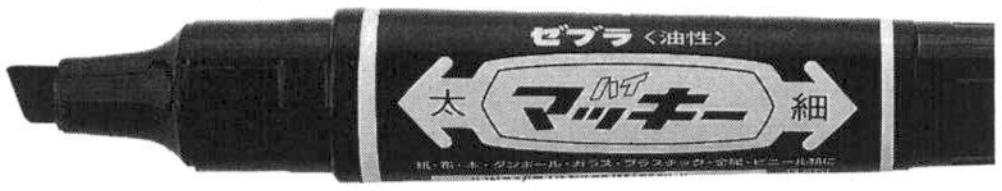

Be sure to use a fine pen for the outlines of a large area you're going to ink in.

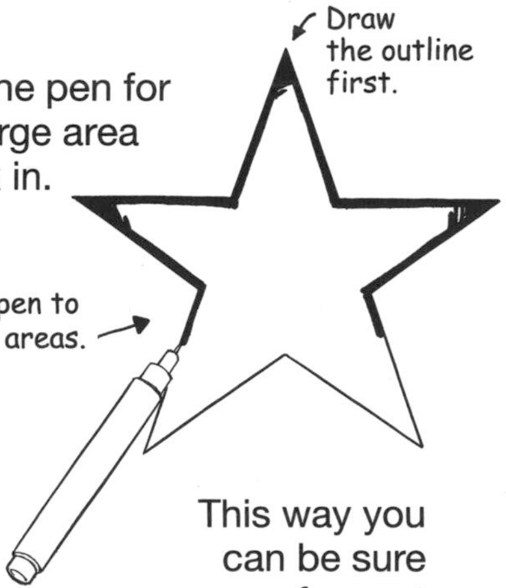
Draw the outline first.
Use a fine pen to ink in small areas.

BRUSH PEN

Good for drawing hair, details etc.
Water-soluble, so is slow to dry and tarnishes easily.

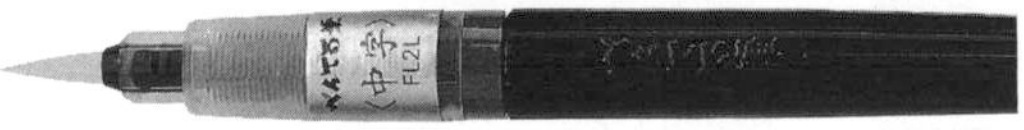

They come in a variety of thicknesses and tip types.

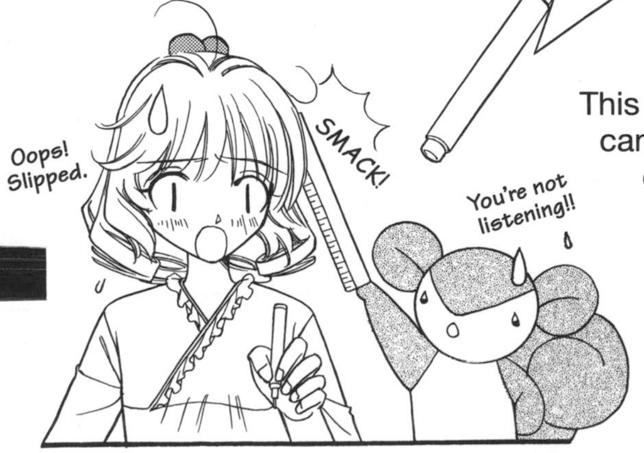
Oops! Slipped.
SMACK!
You're not listening!!

This way you can be sure of a neat finish.

CAUTION: Don't hit people with rulers!

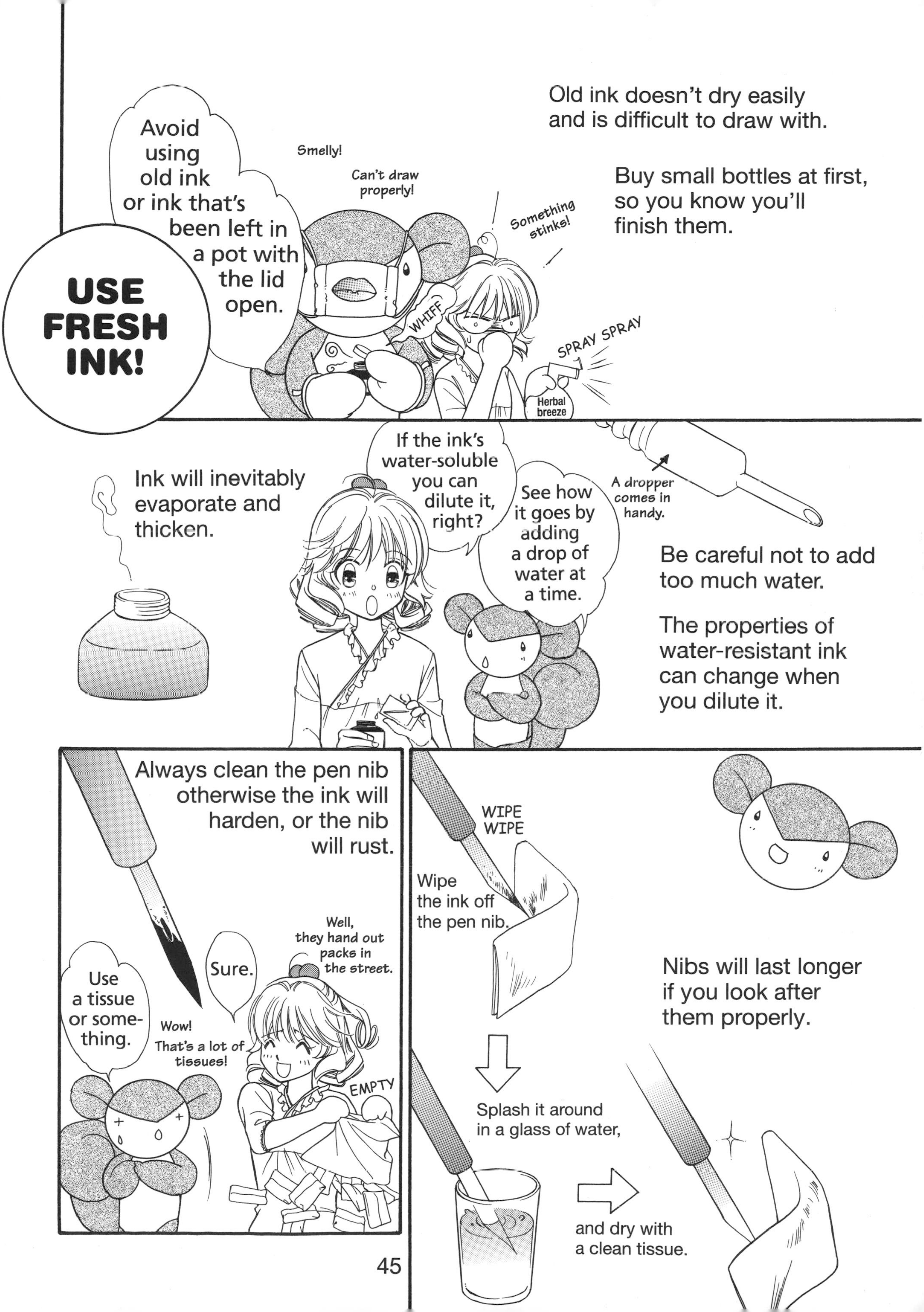
USE FRESH INK!
Avoid using old ink or ink that's been left in a pot with the lid open.
Smelly!
Can't draw properly!
WHIFF
Something stinks!
SPRAY SPRAY
Herbal breeze
Old ink doesn't dry easily and is difficult to draw with.
Buy small bottles at first, so you know you'll finish them.
Ink will inevitably evaporate and thicken.
If the ink's water-soluble you can dilute it, right?
See how it goes by adding a drop of water at a time.
A dropper comes in handy.
Be careful not to add too much water.
The properties of water-resistant ink can change when you dilute it.
Always clean the pen nib otherwise the ink will harden, or the nib will rust.
Use a tissue or some-thing.
Sure.
Well, they hand out packs in the street.
Wow! That's a lot of tissues!
EMPTY
WIPE WIPE
Wipe the ink off the pen nib.
Splash it around in a glass of water,
and dry with a clean tissue.
Nibs will last longer if you look after them properly.

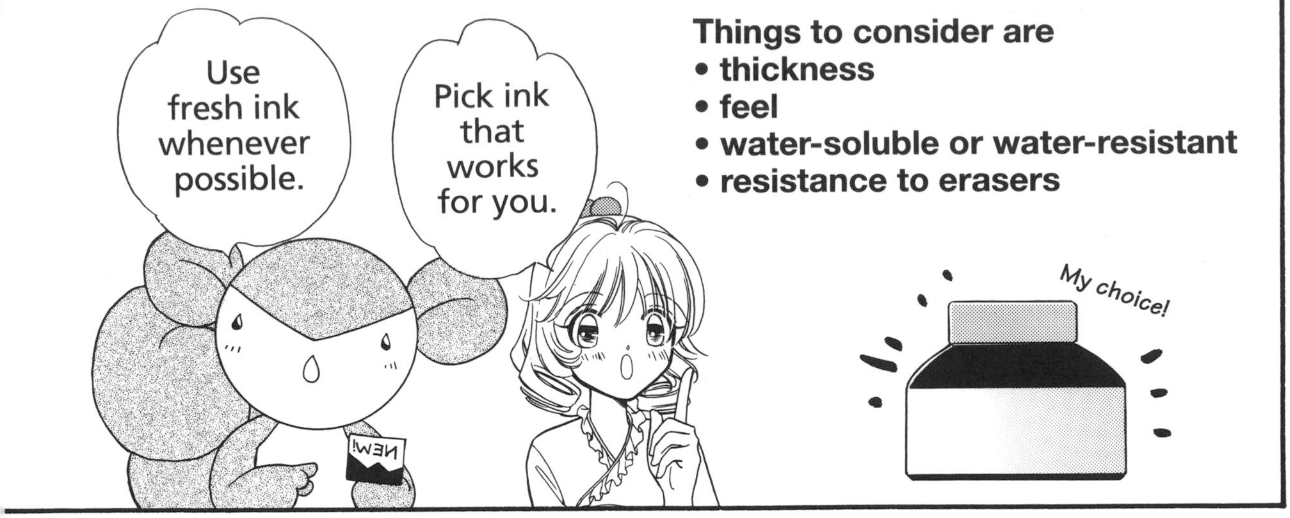
Use fresh ink whenever possible.
Pick ink that works for you.
Things to consider are
• thickness
• feel
• water-soluble or water-resistant
• resistance to erasers
My choice!
NEW!

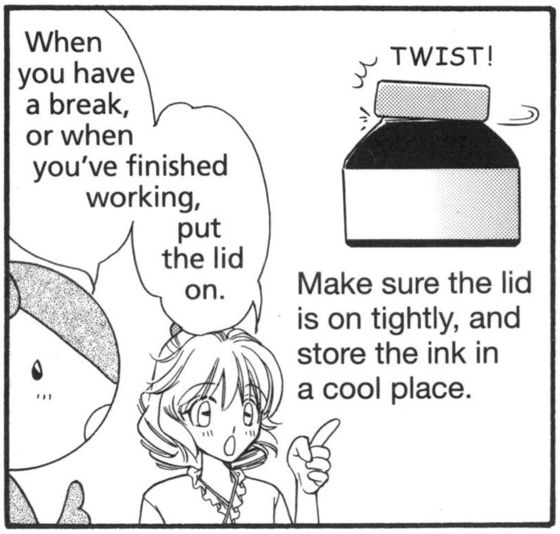
When you have a break, or when you've finished working, put the lid on.
TWIST!
Make sure the lid is on tightly, and store the ink in a cool place.

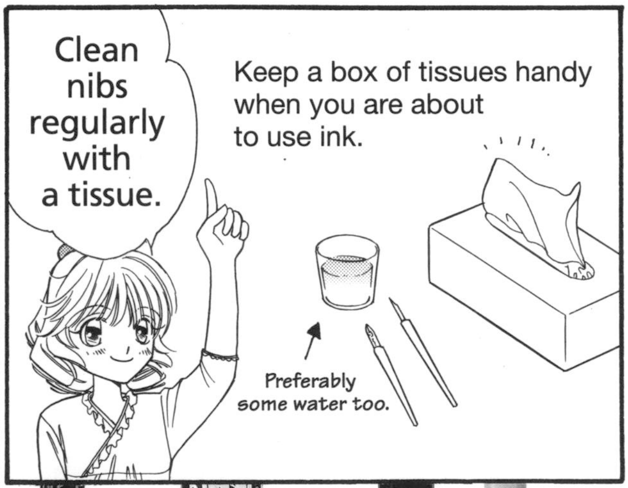
Clean nibs regularly with a tissue.
Keep a box of tissues handy when you are about to use ink.
Preferably some water too.

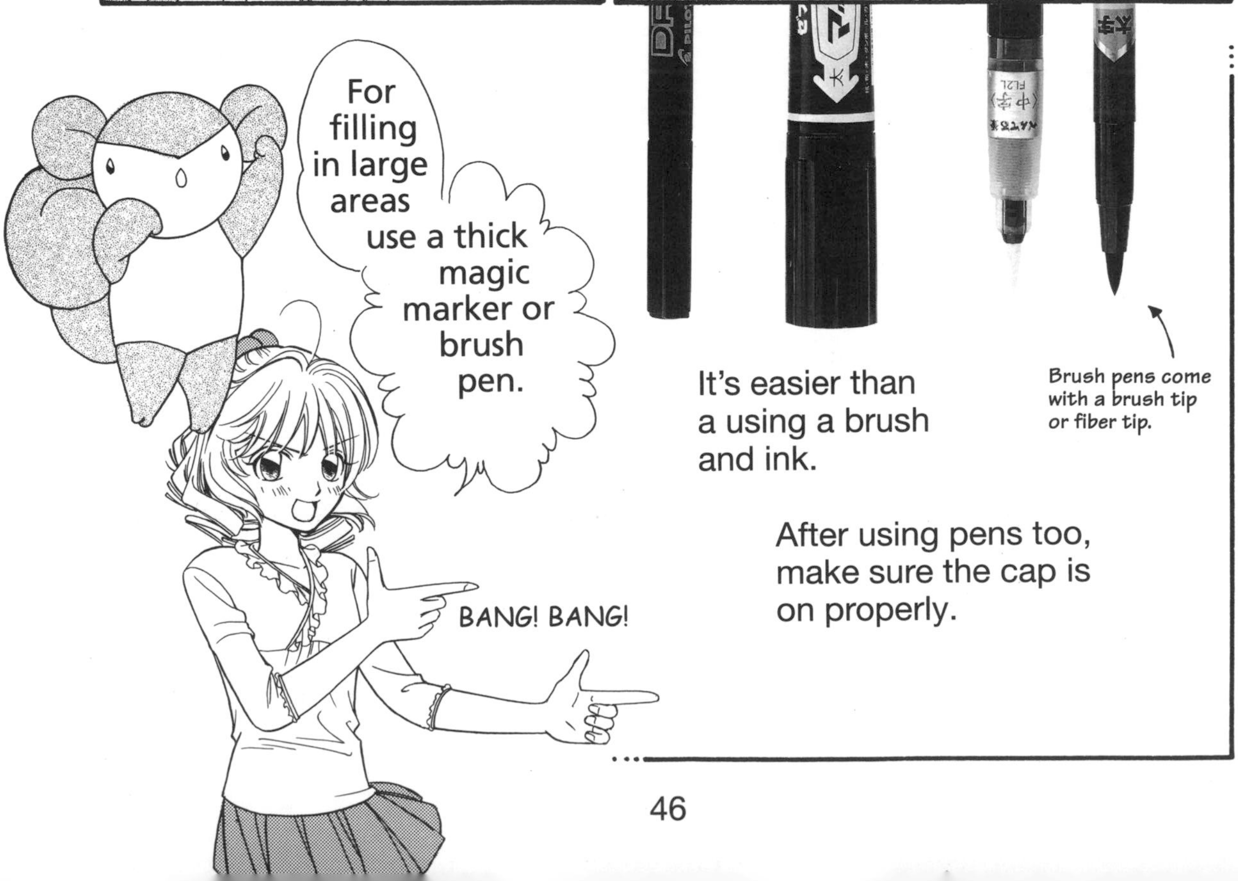
For filling in large areas use a thick magic marker or brush pen.
It's easier than a using a brush and ink.
Brush pens come with a brush tip or fiber tip.
After using pens too, make sure the cap is on properly.
BANG! BANG!

TECHNICAL PENS

Use a technical pen or a fine line marker when drawing manga frames.

You'll get a neater result than with ordinary pens.

Frame drawn with an ordinary pen.

Frame drawn with a technical pen.

frame

What's the difference between a fine line marker and a technical pen?

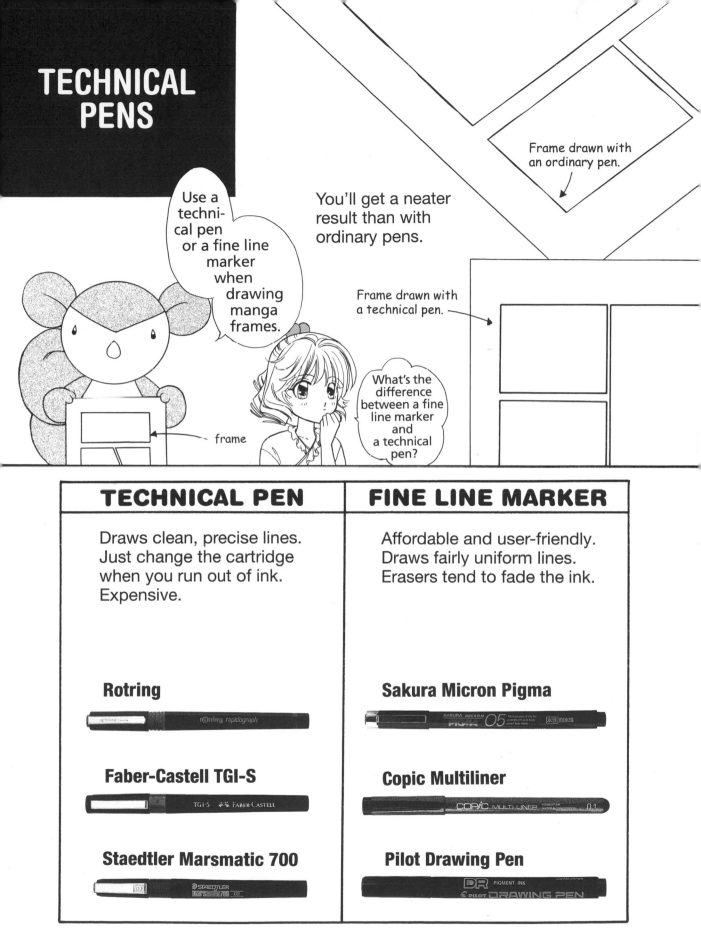

TECHNICAL PEN	FINE LINE MARKER
Draws clean, precise lines. Just change the cartridge when you run out of ink. Expensive.	Affordable and user-friendly. Draws fairly uniform lines. Erasers tend to fade the ink.
Rotring	**Sakura Micron Pigma**
Faber-Castell TGI-S	**Copic Multiliner**
Staedtler Marsmatic 700	**Pilot Drawing Pen**

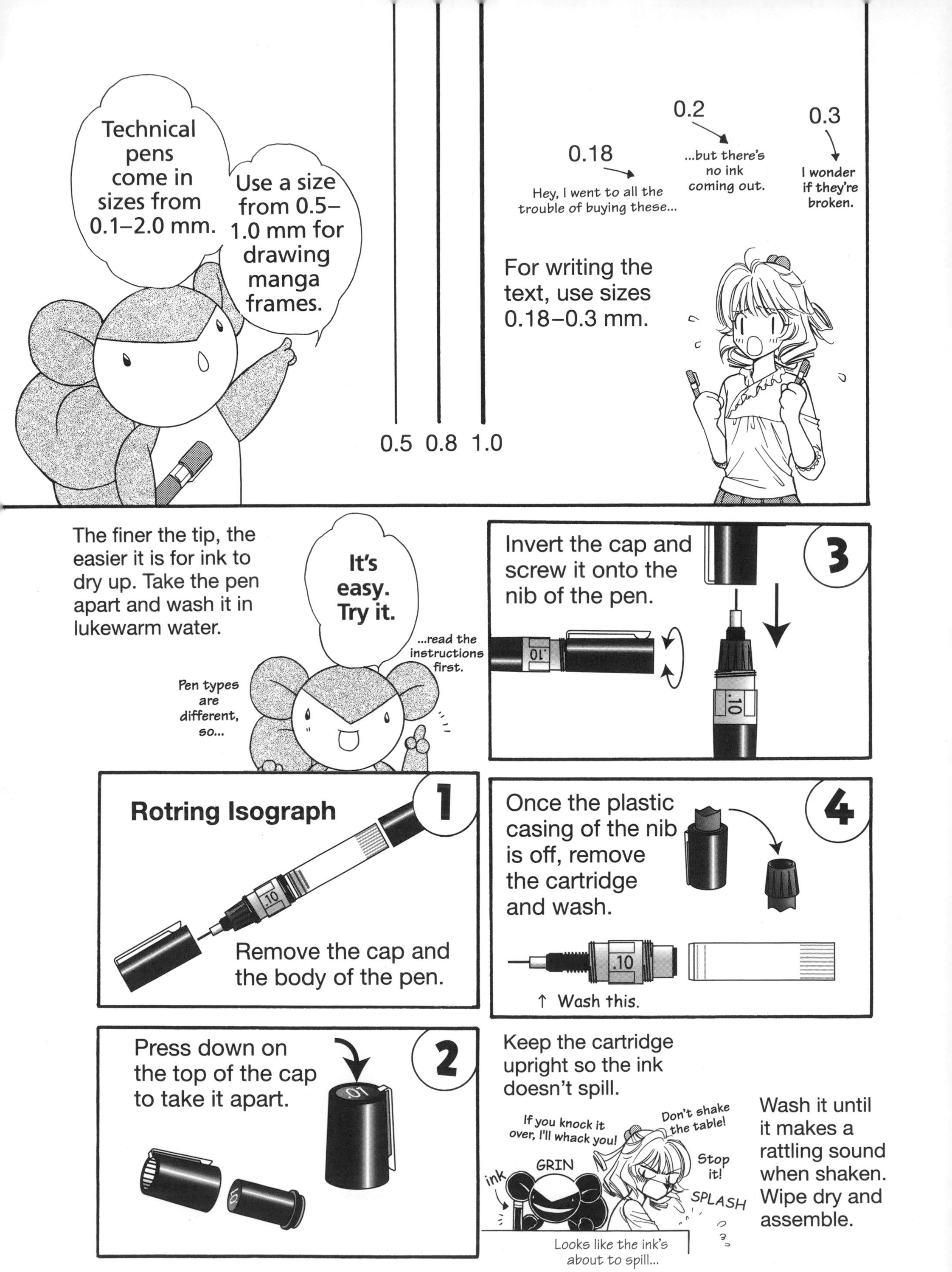

Technical pens come in sizes from 0.1–2.0 mm.
Use a size from 0.5–1.0 mm for drawing manga frames.
0.5 0.8 1.0
For writing the text, use sizes 0.18–0.3 mm.
0.18
Hey, I went to all the trouble of buying these...
0.2
...but there's no ink coming out.
0.3
I wonder if they're broken.
The finer the tip, the easier it is for ink to dry up. Take the pen apart and wash it in lukewarm water.
It's easy. Try it.
Pen types are different, so...
...read the instructions first.
1
Rotring Isograph
.10
Remove the cap and the body of the pen.
2
Press down on the top of the cap to take it apart.
3
Invert the cap and screw it onto the nib of the pen.
4
Once the plastic casing of the nib is off, remove the cartridge and wash.
↑ Wash this.
Keep the cartridge upright so the ink doesn't spill.
If you knock it over, I'll whack you!
Don't shake the table!
GRIN
ink
Stop it!
SPLASH
Looks like the ink's about to spill...
Wash it until it makes a rattling sound when shaken. Wipe dry and assemble.

ROTRING

The popular Rotring comes in refillable and cartridge types.

Be sure to use Rotring ink or cartridges. Using the wrong ink can cause blockage.

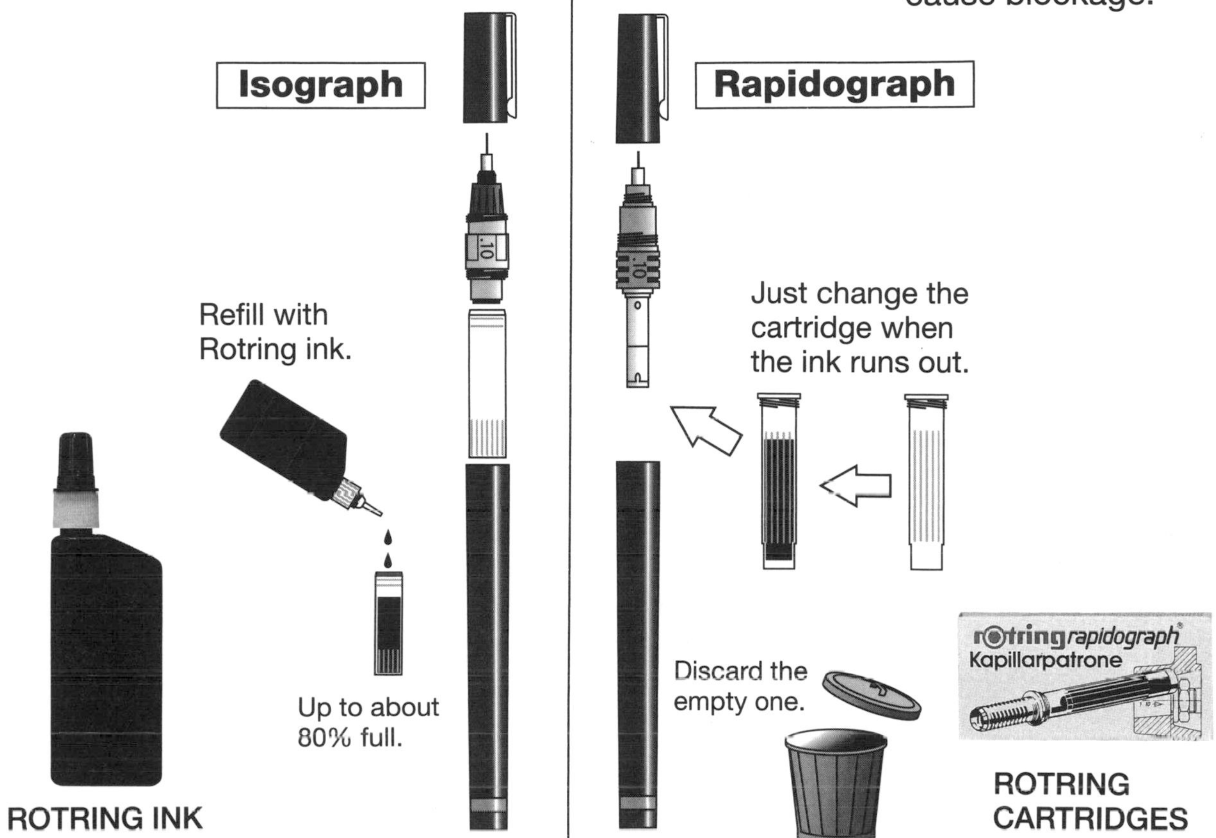

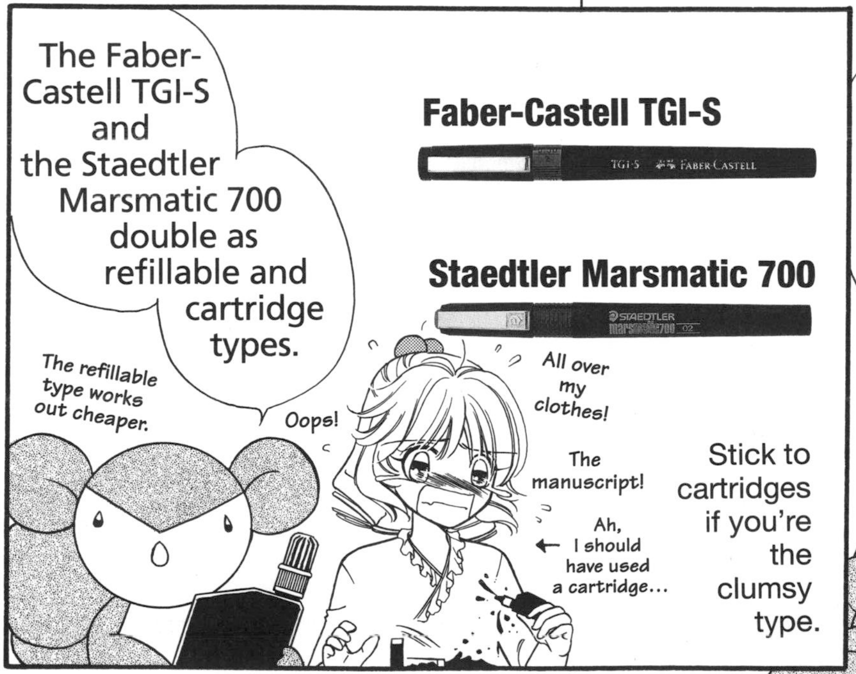

Isograph

Rapidograph

Refill with Rotring ink.

Up to about 80% full.

ROTRING INK

Just change the cartridge when the ink runs out.

Discard the empty one.

rotring rapidograph®
Kapillarpatrone

ROTRING CARTRIDGES

The Faber-Castell TGI-S and the Staedtler Marsmatic 700 double as refillable and cartridge types.

Faber-Castell TGI-S

TGI-S FABER-CASTELL

Staedtler Marsmatic 700

STAEDTLER marsmatic700 02

The refillable type works out cheaper.

Oops!

All over my clothes!

The manuscript!

Ah, I should have used a cartridge...

Stick to cartridges if you're the clumsy type.

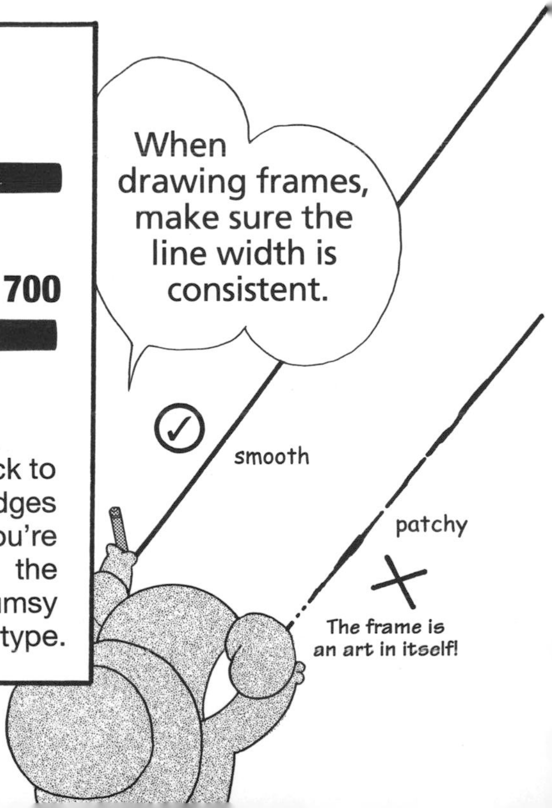

When drawing frames, make sure the line width is consistent.

✓ smooth

patchy

✗ The frame is an art in itself!

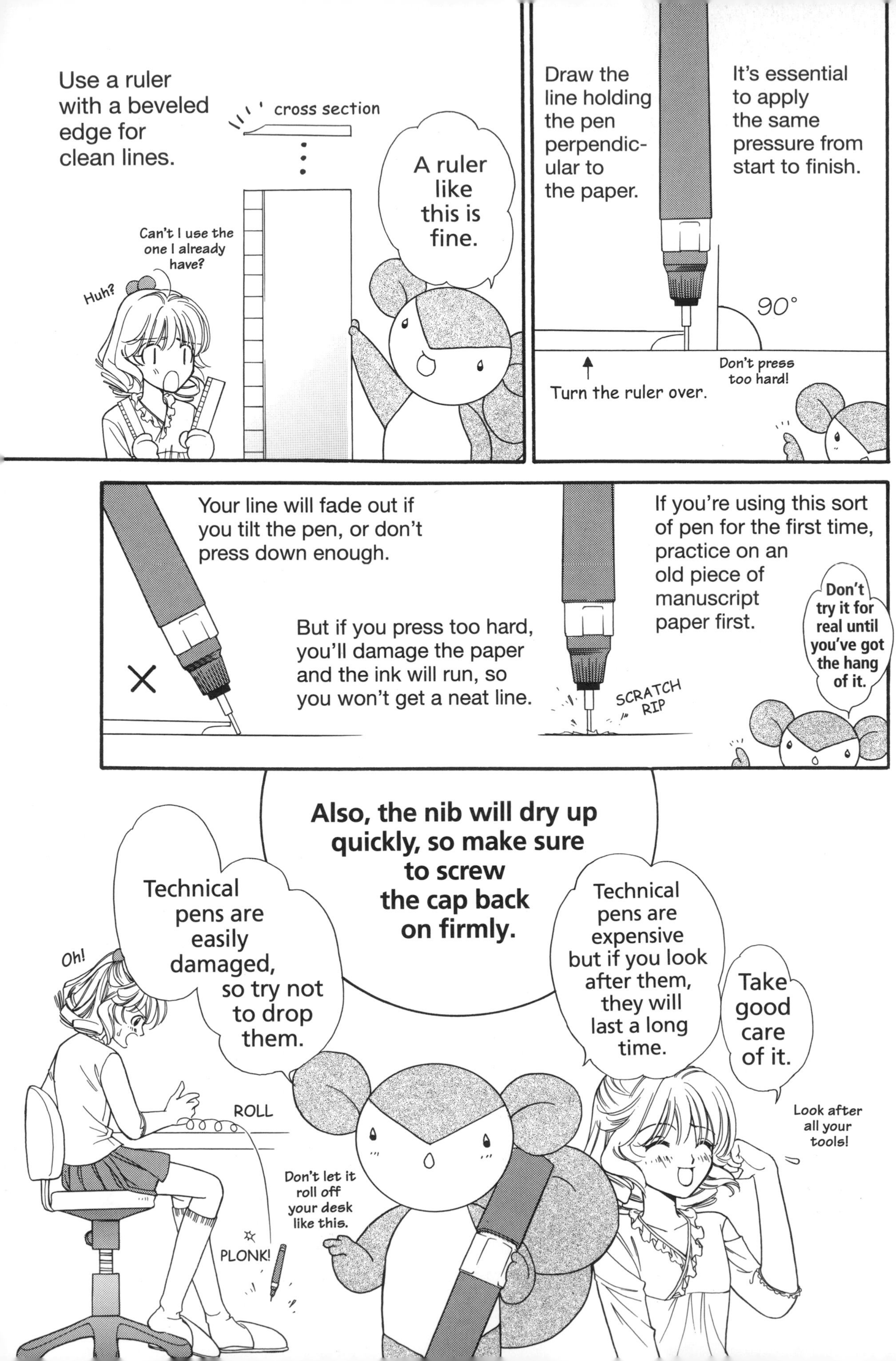
Use a ruler with a beveled edge for clean lines.
cross section
Huh?
Can't I use the one I already have?
A ruler like this is fine.
Draw the line holding the pen perpendicular to the paper.
It's essential to apply the same pressure from start to finish.
90°
Turn the ruler over.
Don't press too hard!
Your line will fade out if you tilt the pen, or don't press down enough.
But if you press too hard, you'll damage the paper and the ink will run, so you won't get a neat line.
SCRATCH RIP
If you're using this sort of pen for the first time, practice on an old piece of manuscript paper first.
Don't try it for real until you've got the hang of it.
Also, the nib will dry up quickly, so make sure to screw the cap back on firmly.
Oh!
Technical pens are easily damaged, so try not to drop them.
ROLL
PLONK!
Don't let it roll off your desk like this.
Technical pens are expensive but if you look after them, they will last a long time.
Take good care of it.
Look after all your tools!

WHITE INK AND CORRECTION FLUID

Artists use white ink or correction fluid to erase mistakes,
to add highlights,
and to add sparkle to eyes.

Use correction fluid for lines outside the frame.
Sprinkle white ink on the background for special effects.
Use white ink to create highlights in the eyes.
White ink can also be used to add white lines to clothing.

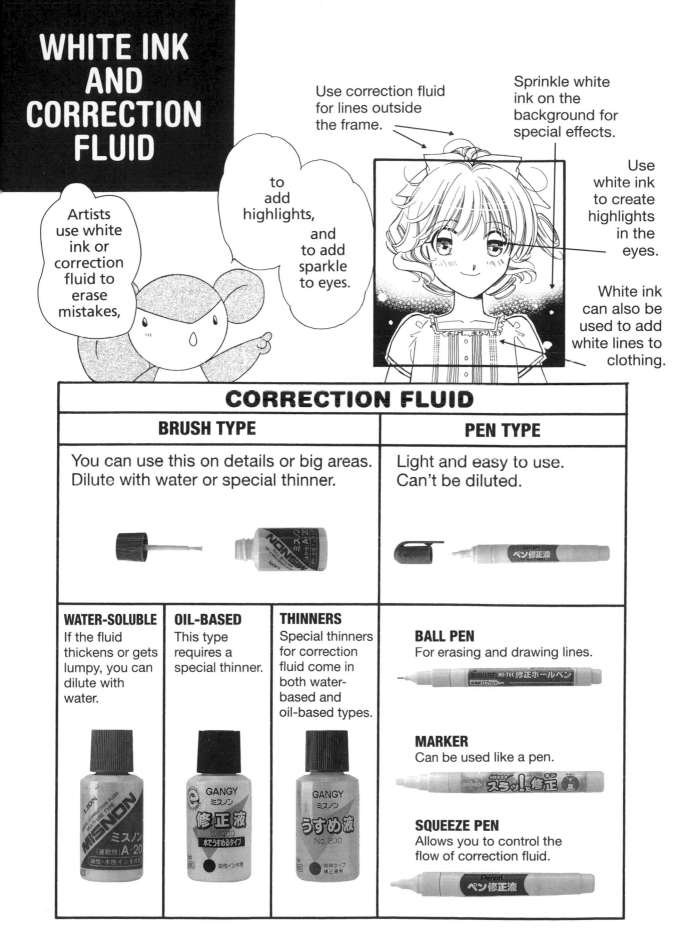

CORRECTION FLUID

BRUSH TYPE

You can use this on details or big areas. Dilute with water or special thinner.

MISNON
ミスノン

WATER-SOLUBLE
If the fluid thickens or gets lumpy, you can dilute with water.

LION
MISNON
ミスノン
(速乾性)A-20
油性・水性インキ共用

OIL-BASED
This type requires a special thinner.

GANGY
ミスノン
修正液
W-400
水でうすめるタイプ
油性インキ用

THINNERS
Special thinners for correction fluid come in both water-based and oil-based types.

GANGY
ミスノン
うすめ液
No.200
共用タイプ
修正液用

PEN TYPE

Light and easy to use. Can't be diluted.

ペン修正液

BALL PEN
For erasing and drawing lines.

PILOT HI-TEC修正ボールペン
0.7mm

MARKER
Can be used like a pen.

MISNON
スラッ!と修正

SQUEEZE PEN
Allows you to control the flow of correction fluid.

Pentel
ペン修正液

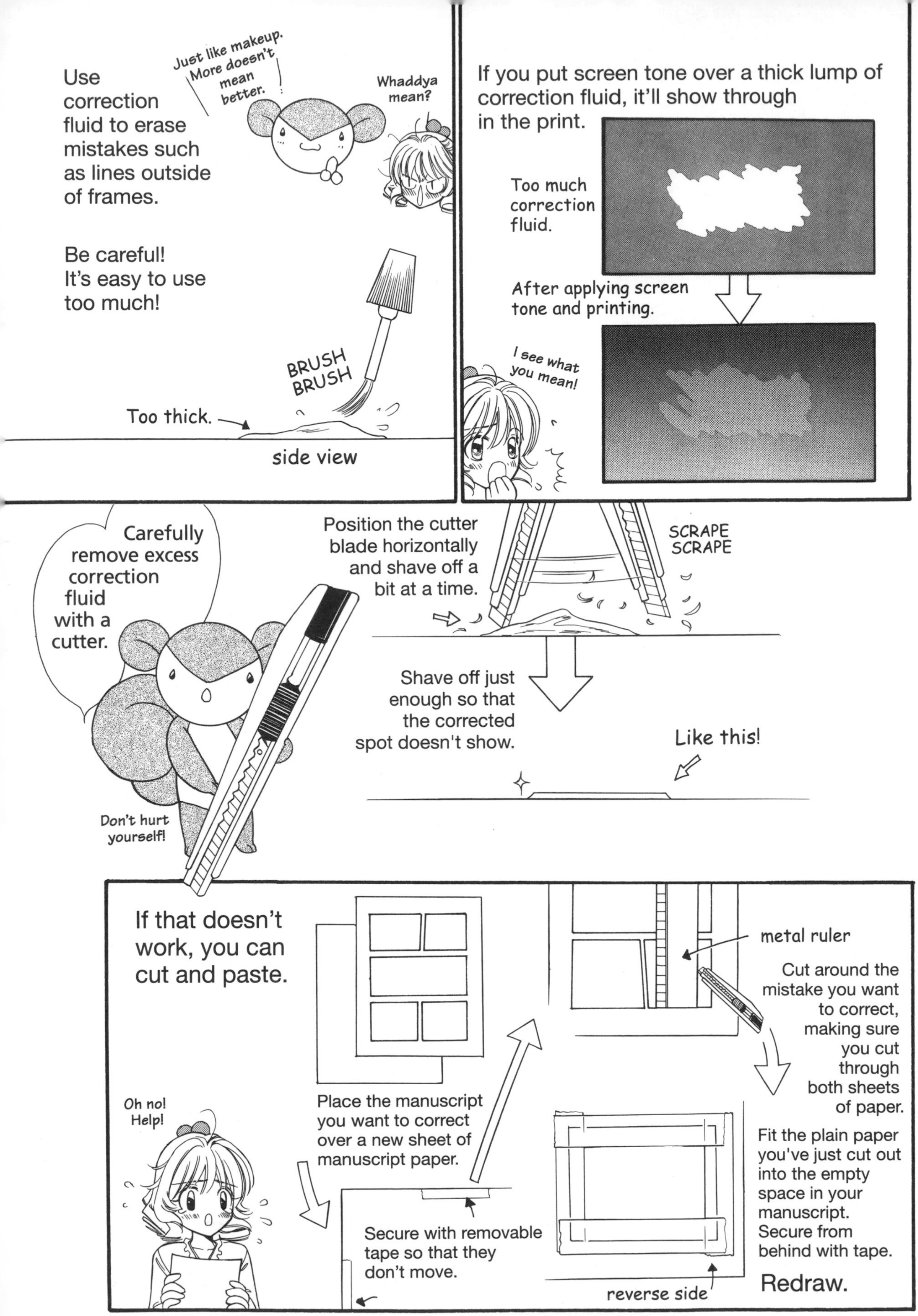
Use correction fluid to erase mistakes such as lines outside of frames.
Just like makeup. More doesn't mean better.
Whaddya mean?
Be careful! It's easy to use too much!
BRUSH BRUSH
Too thick.
side view
If you put screen tone over a thick lump of correction fluid, it'll show through in the print.
Too much correction fluid.
After applying screen tone and printing.
I see what you mean!
Carefully remove excess correction fluid with a cutter.
Position the cutter blade horizontally and shave off a bit at a time.
SCRAPE SCRAPE
Shave off just enough so that the corrected spot doesn't show.
Like this!
Don't hurt yourself!
If that doesn't work, you can cut and paste.
Oh no! Help!
Place the manuscript you want to correct over a new sheet of manuscript paper.
Secure with removable tape so that they don't move.
metal ruler
Cut around the mistake you want to correct, making sure you cut through both sheets of paper.
Fit the plain paper you've just cut out into the empty space in your manuscript. Secure from behind with tape.
reverse side
Redraw.

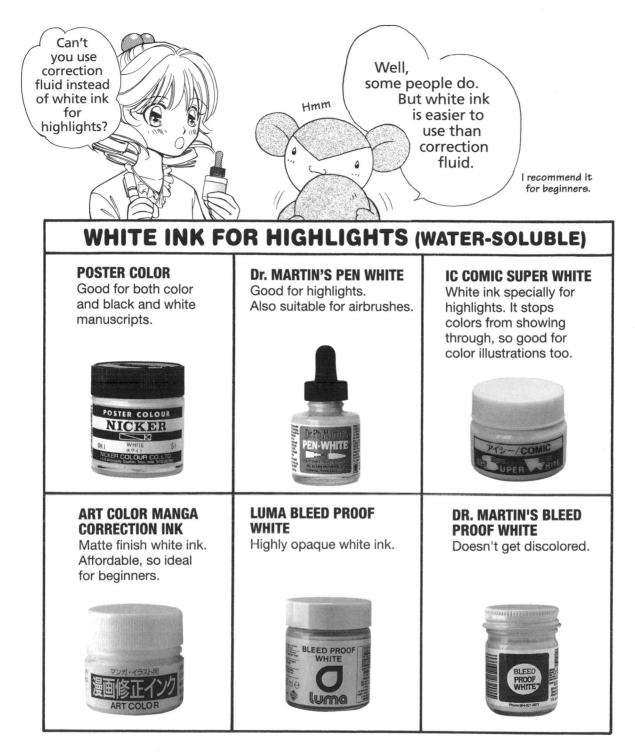

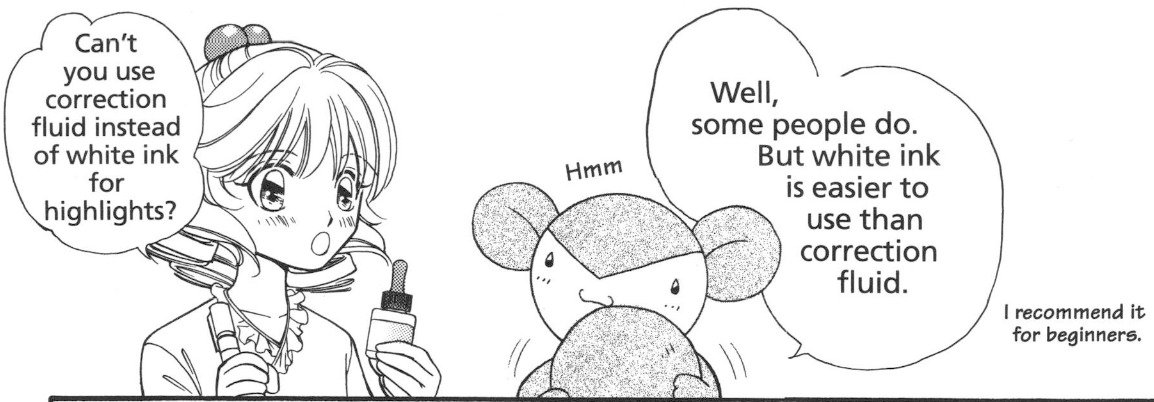
Can't you use correction fluid instead of white ink for highlights?
Hmm
Well, some people do. But white ink is easier to use than correction fluid.
I recommend it for beginners.

WHITE INK FOR HIGHLIGHTS (WATER-SOLUBLE)

POSTER COLOR
Good for both color and black and white manuscripts.

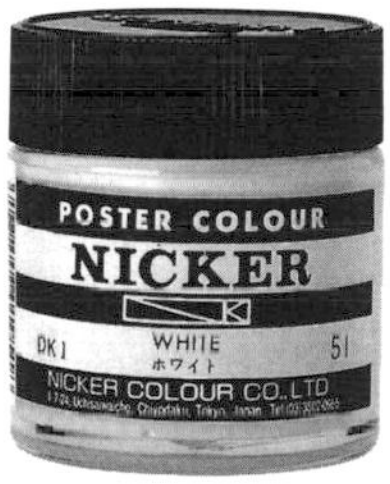
POSTER COLOUR
NICKER
WHITE
NICKER COLOUR CO.,LTD

Dr. MARTIN'S PEN WHITE
Good for highlights.
Also suitable for airbrushes.

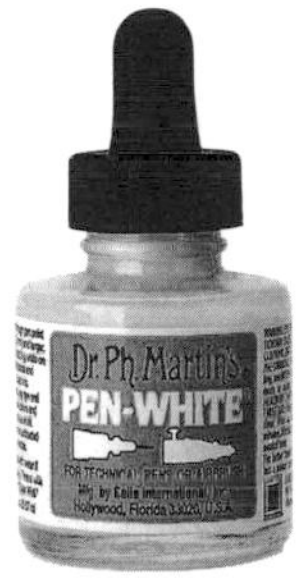
Dr.Ph.Martin's
PEN-WHITE

IC COMIC SUPER WHITE
White ink specially for highlights. It stops colors from showing through, so good for color illustrations too.

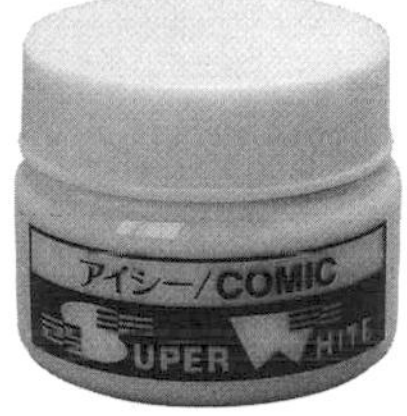
アイシー/COMIC
SUPER

ART COLOR MANGA CORRECTION INK
Matte finish white ink.
Affordable, so ideal for beginners.

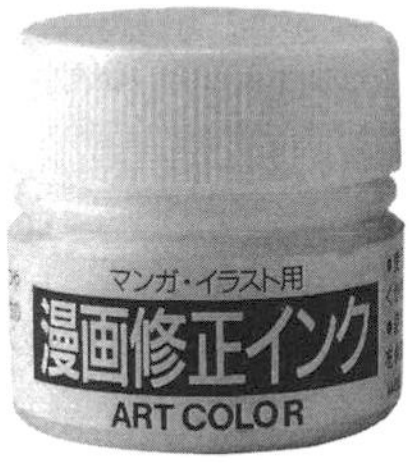
マンガ・イラスト用
漫画修正インク
ART COLOR

LUMA BLEED PROOF WHITE
Highly opaque white ink.

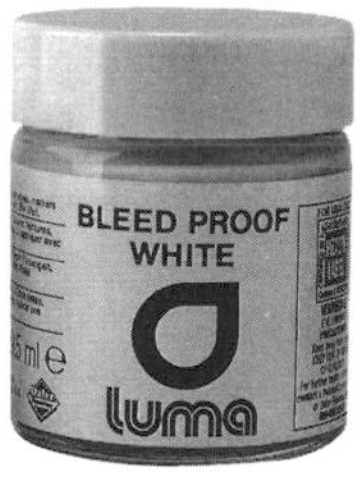
BLEED PROOF WHITE
luma

DR. MARTIN'S BLEED PROOF WHITE
Doesn't get discolored.

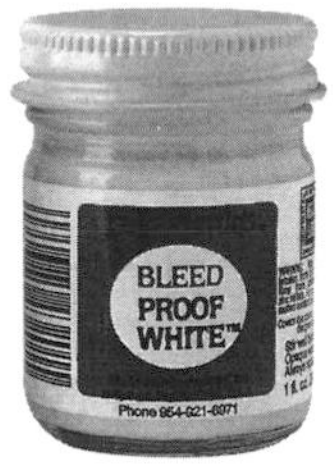
BLEED PROOF WHITE

BRUSHES FOR WHITE INK

A fine-point brush is often used for applying white ink. Its soft, narrow tip is perfect for details.

FINE-POINT BRUSHES
We recommend either the medium or fine size.
You should use a separate brush for black ink.

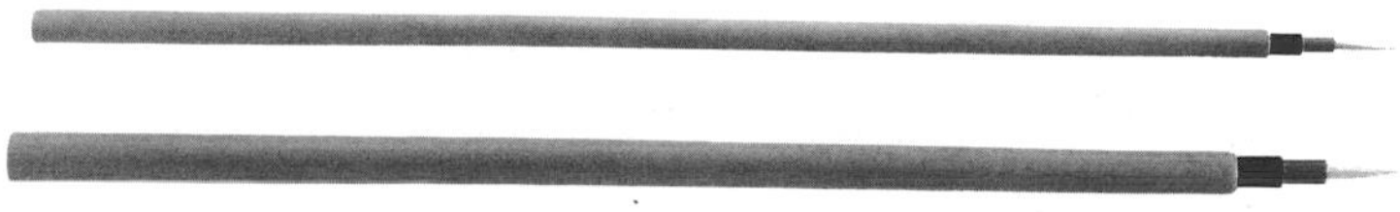

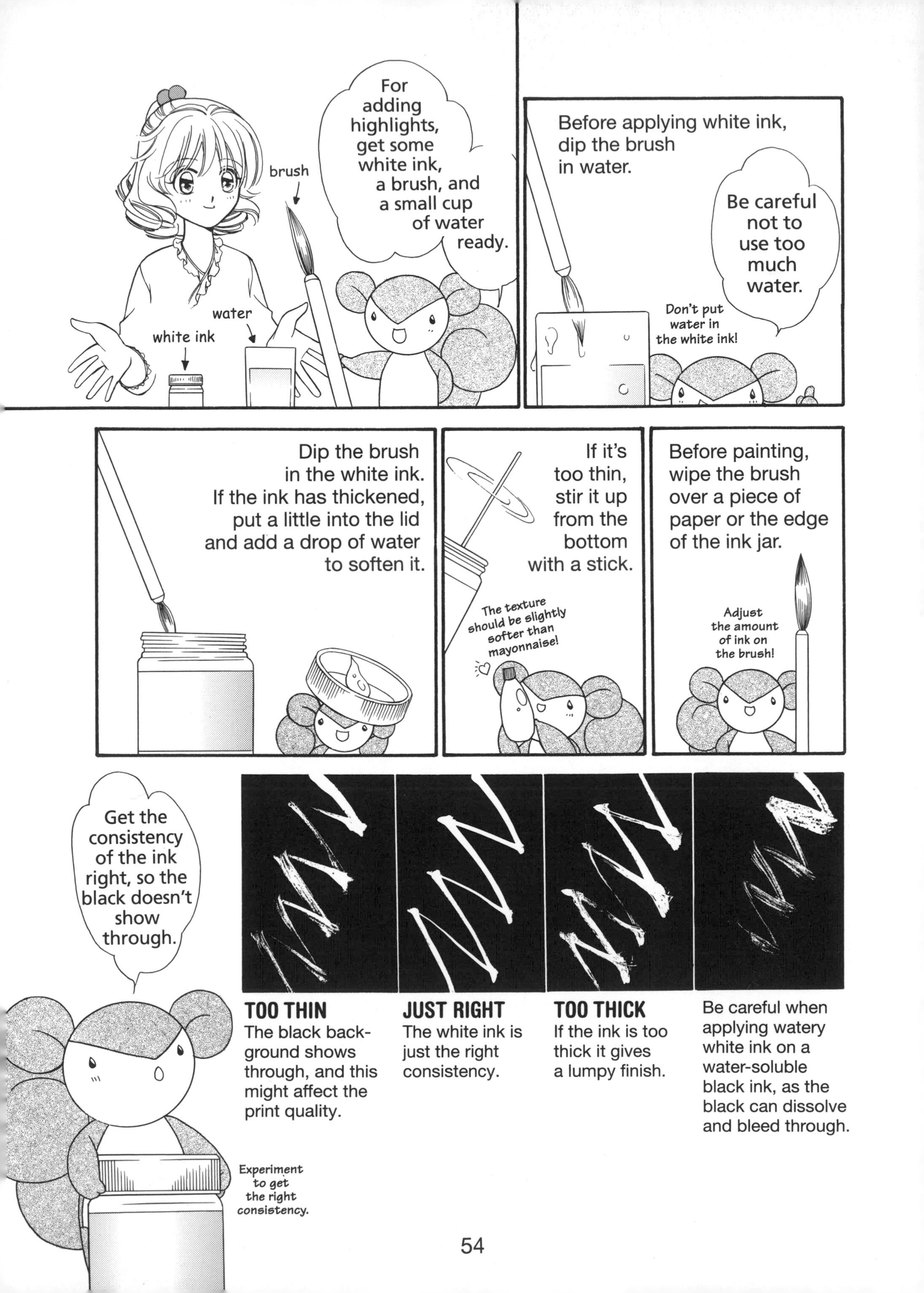
For adding highlights, get some white ink, a brush, and a small cup of water ready.
brush
water
white ink
Before applying white ink, dip the brush in water.
Be careful not to use too much water.
Don't put water in the white ink!
Dip the brush in the white ink. If the ink has thickened, put a little into the lid and add a drop of water to soften it.
If it's too thin, stir it up from the bottom with a stick.
The texture should be slightly softer than mayonnaise!
Before painting, wipe the brush over a piece of paper or the edge of the ink jar.
Adjust the amount of ink on the brush!
Get the consistency of the ink right, so the black doesn't show through.
TOO THIN
The black back-ground shows through, and this might affect the print quality.
JUST RIGHT
The white ink is just the right consistency.
TOO THICK
If the ink is too thick it gives a lumpy finish.
Be careful when applying watery white ink on a water-soluble black ink, as the black can dissolve and bleed through.
Experiment to get the right consistency.

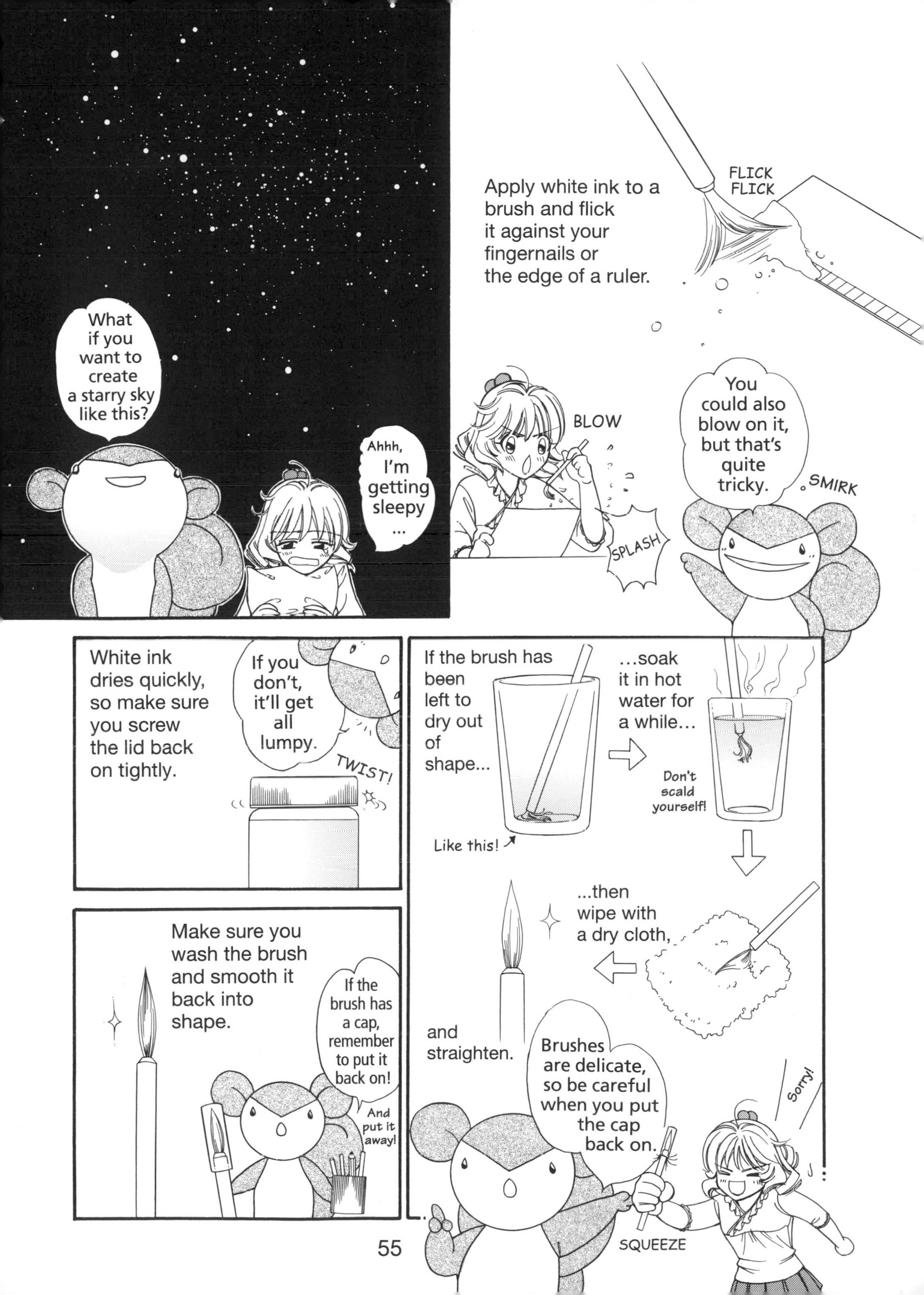
What if you want to create a starry sky like this?
Ahhh, I'm getting sleepy ...
Apply white ink to a brush and flick it against your fingernails or the edge of a ruler.
FLICK FLICK
BLOW
SPLASH
You could also blow on it, but that's quite tricky.
SMIRK
White ink dries quickly, so make sure you screw the lid back on tightly.
If you don't, it'll get all lumpy.
TWIST!
Make sure you wash the brush and smooth it back into shape.
If the brush has a cap, remember to put it back on!
And put it away!
If the brush has been left to dry out of shape...
Like this!
...soak it in hot water for a while...
Don't scald yourself!
...then wipe with a dry cloth,
and straighten.
Brushes are delicate, so be careful when you put the cap back on.
Sorry!
SQUEEZE

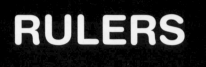

RULERS

You will need at least two rulers: One about 20 cm, the other 40 cm or over. Try to get one with a beveled edge and one with a printed grid.

For details.

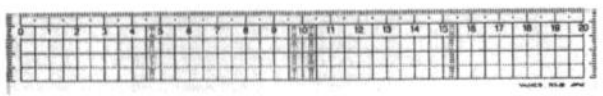

For long perspectives.

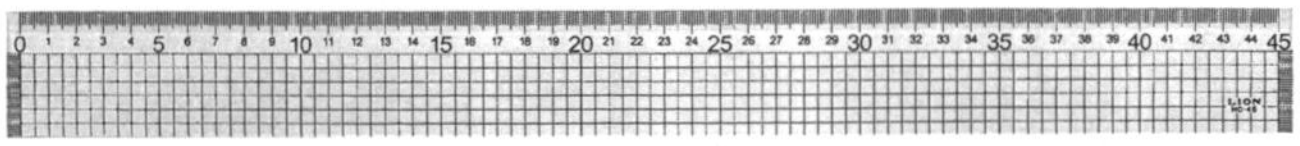

For use with a cutter.

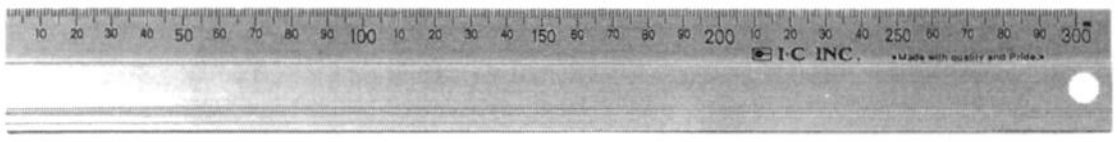

For drawing frames.

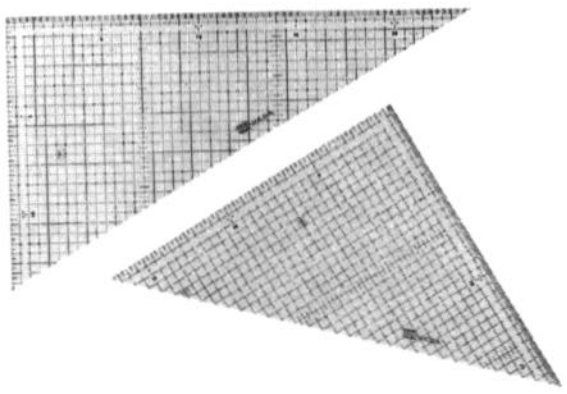

For speech balloons and effects.

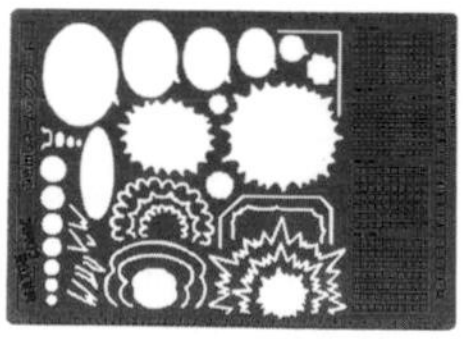

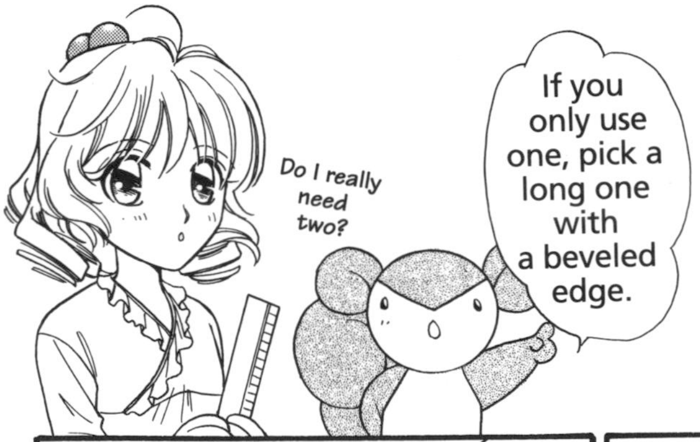

Do I really need two?
If you only use one, pick a long one with a beveled edge.

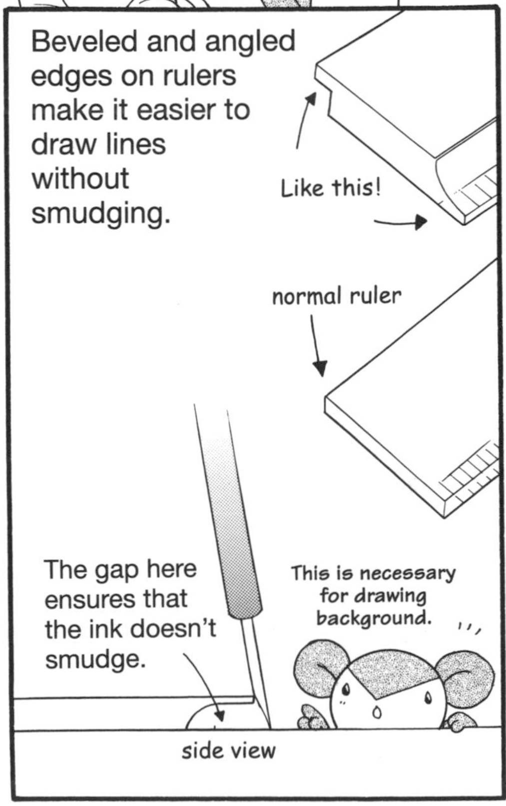

Beveled and angled edges on rulers make it easier to draw lines without smudging.
Like this!
normal ruler
The gap here ensures that the ink doesn't smudge.
side view
This is necessary for drawing background.

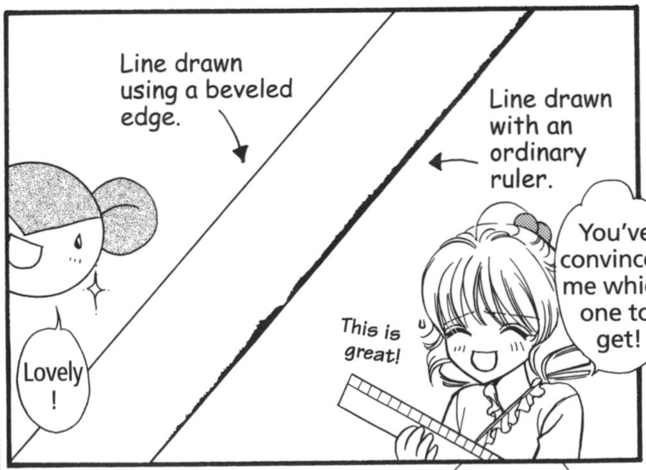

Line drawn using a beveled edge.
Line drawn with an ordinary ruler.
Lovely!
This is great!
You've convinced me which one to get!

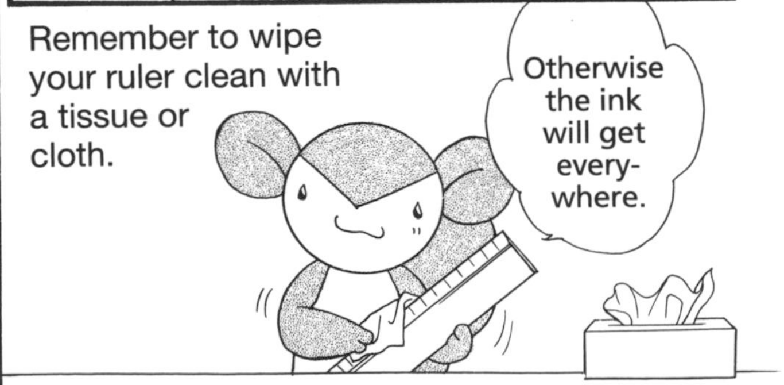

Remember to wipe your ruler clean with a tissue or cloth.
Otherwise the ink will get every-where.

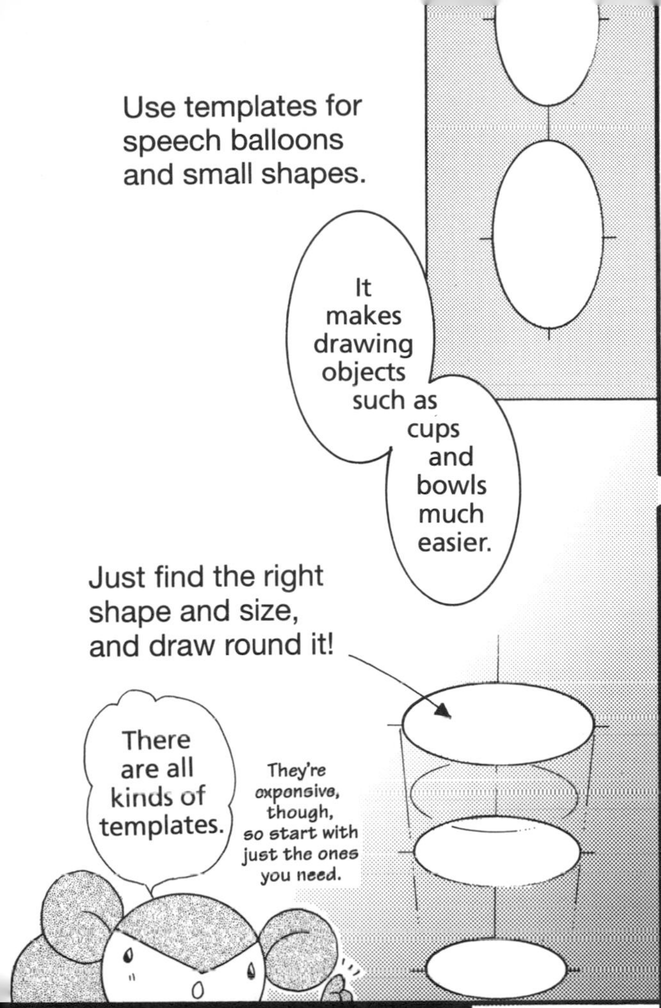
Use templates for speech balloons and small shapes.
It makes drawing objects such as cups and bowls much easier.
Just find the right shape and size, and draw round it!
There are all kinds of templates.
They're expensive, though, so start with just the ones you need.

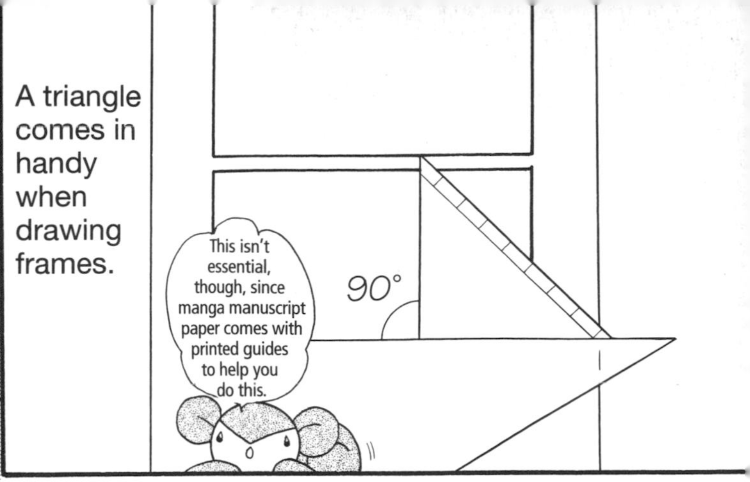
A triangle comes in handy when drawing frames.
This isn't essential, though, since manga manuscript paper comes with printed guides to help you do this.
90°

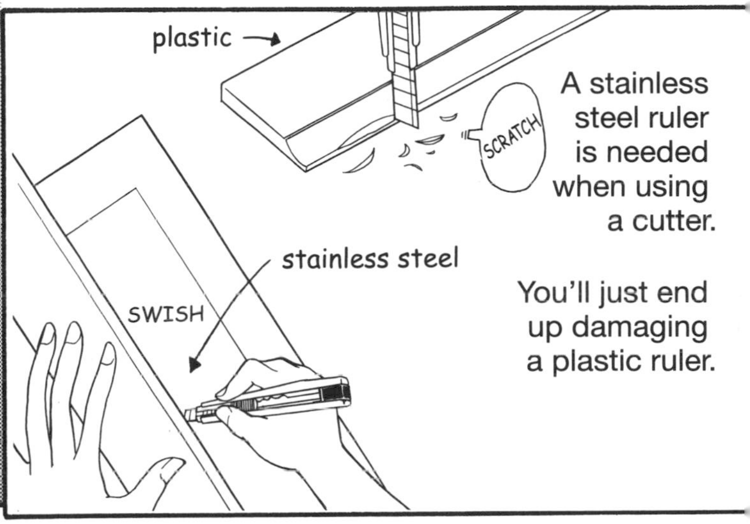
plastic
SCRATCH
A stainless steel ruler is needed when using a cutter.
stainless steel
SWISH
You'll just end up damaging a plastic ruler.

CUTTERS

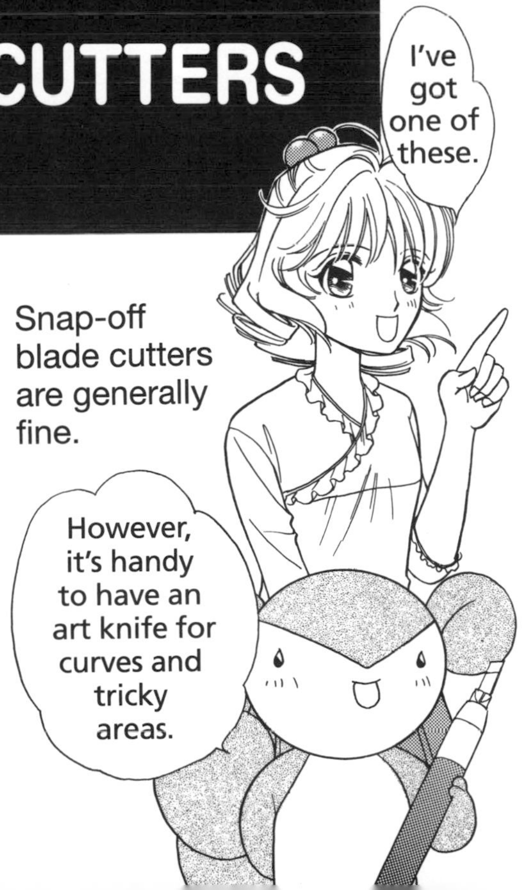
I've got one of these.
However, it's handy to have an art knife for curves and tricky areas.

Snap-off blade cutters are generally fine.

SNAP-OFF BLADE CUTTER

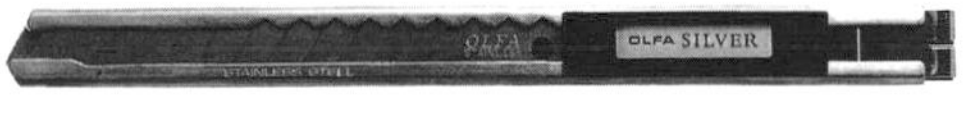
OLFA SILVER

ART KNIVES

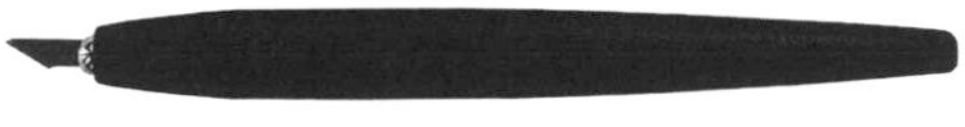

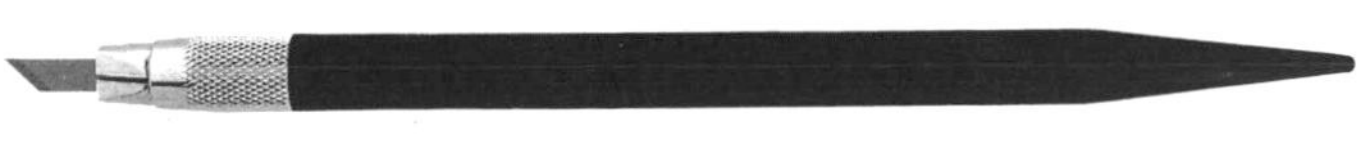

Blades come in two angles: 45° and 30°.

ERASERS

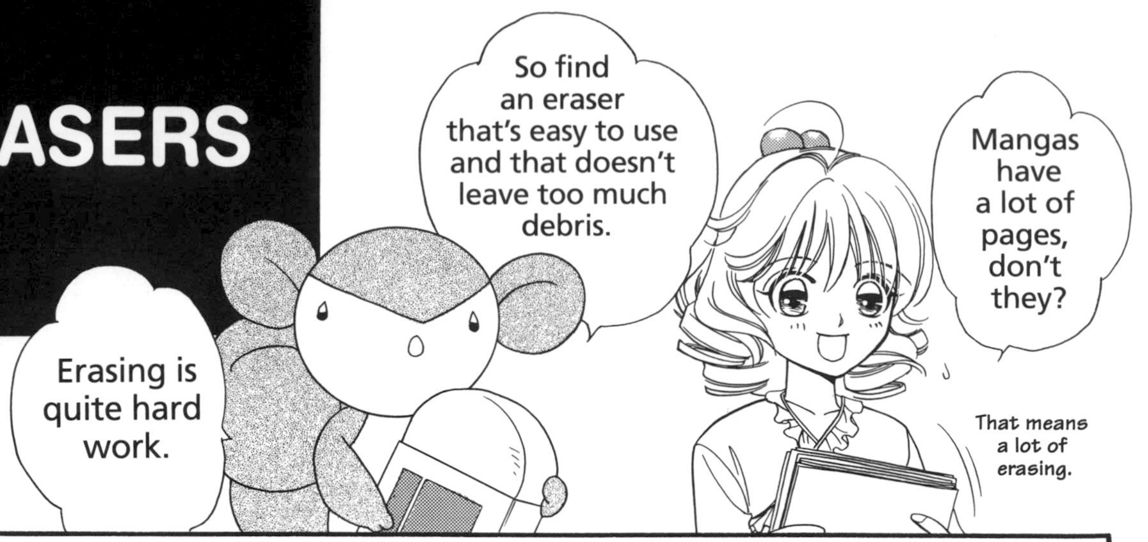
Mangas have a lot of pages, don't they?
That means a lot of erasing.
So find an eraser that's easy to use and that doesn't leave too much debris.
Erasing is quite hard work.

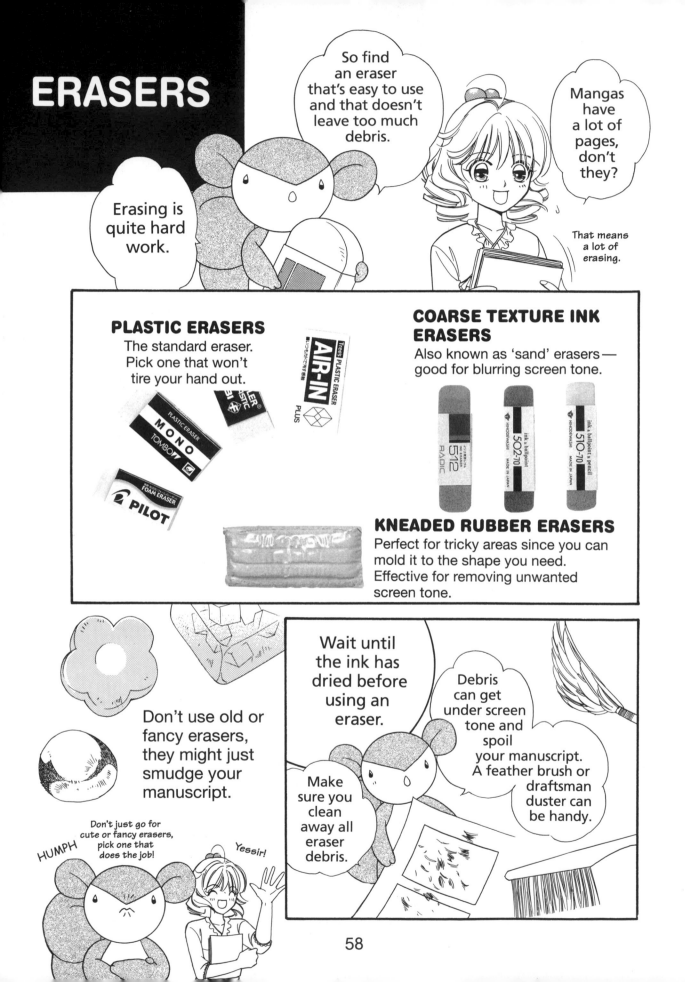

PLASTIC ERASERS

The standard eraser. Pick one that won't tire your hand out.

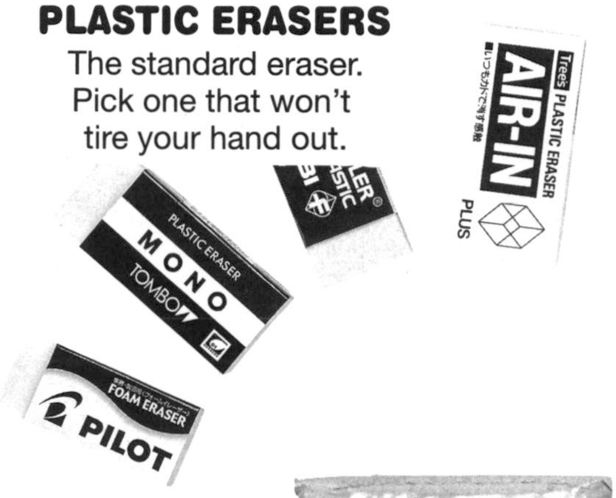
Trees PLASTIC ERASER
AIR-IN
PLUS
PLASTIC ERASER
MONO
TOMBOW
FOAM ERASER
PILOT

COARSE TEXTURE INK ERASERS

Also known as 'sand' erasers—good for blurring screen tone.

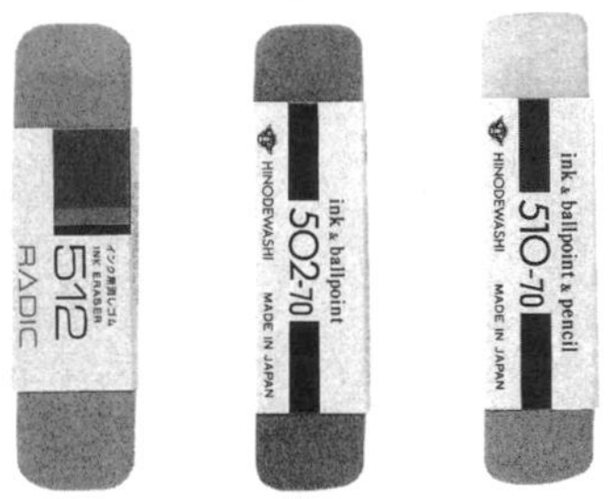
512
RADIC
ink & ballpoint
502-70
HINODEWASHI
MADE IN JAPAN
ink & ballpoint & pencil
510-70
HINODEWASHI
MADE IN JAPAN

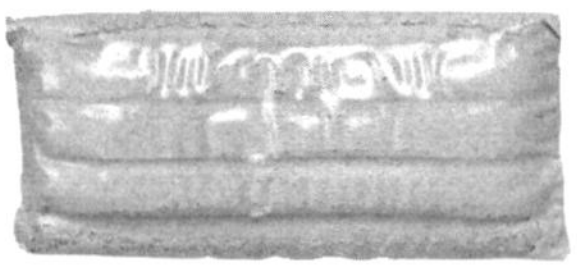

KNEADED RUBBER ERASERS

Perfect for tricky areas since you can mold it to the shape you need. Effective for removing unwanted screen tone.

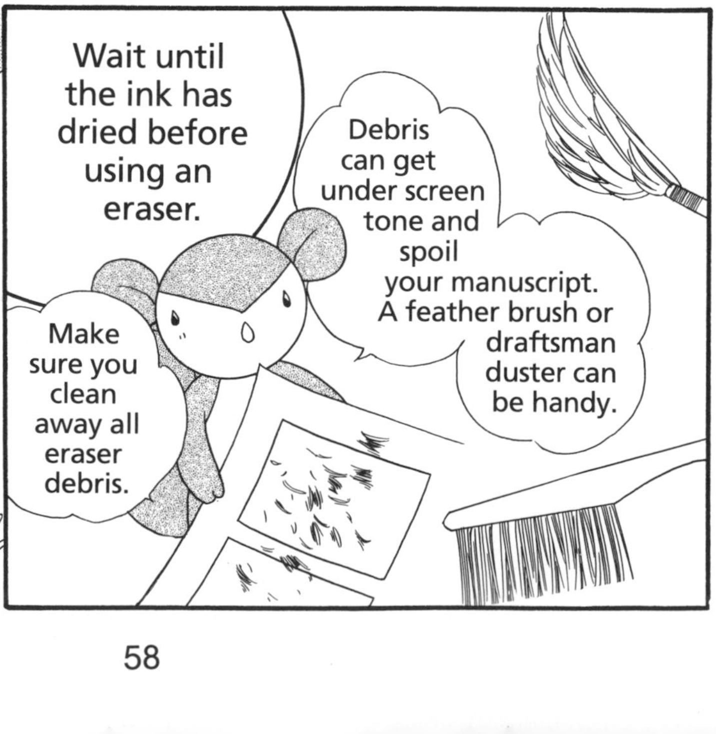
Wait until the ink has dried before using an eraser.
Debris can get under screen tone and spoil your manuscript. A feather brush or draftsman duster can be handy.
Make sure you clean away all eraser debris.

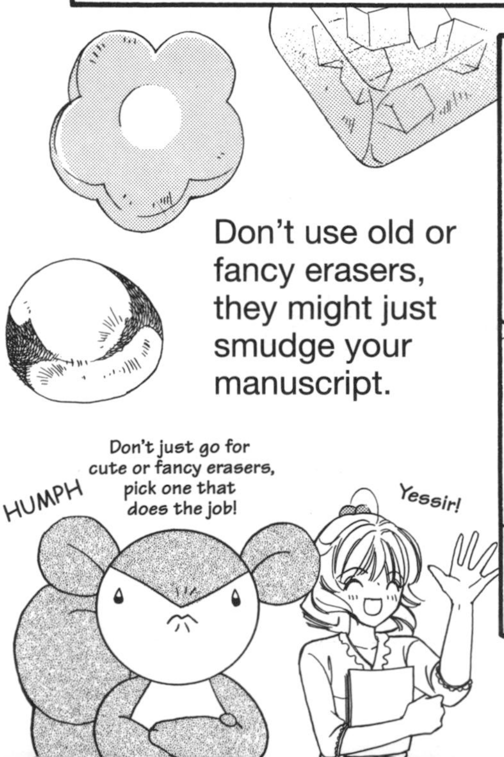
Don't use old or fancy erasers, they might just smudge your manuscript.
Don't just go for cute or fancy erasers, pick one that does the job!
HUMPH
Yessir!

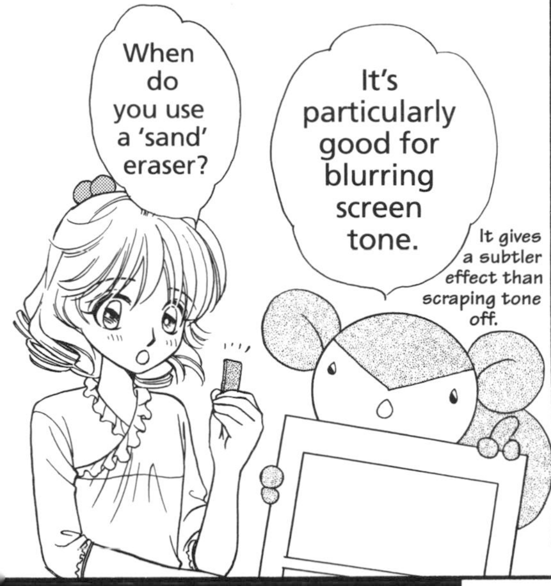
When do you use a 'sand' eraser?
It's particularly good for blurring screen tone.
It gives a subtler effect than scraping tone off.

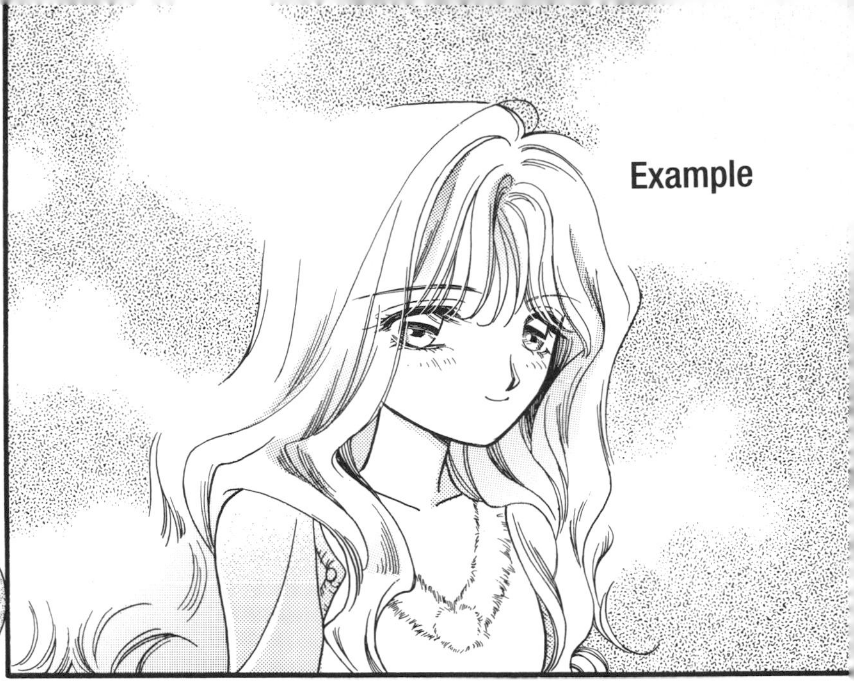
Example

SCREEN TONE TOOLS

These tools are indispensable for sticking down screen tone. Always rub the tone thoroughly.

FOR BACKGROUND

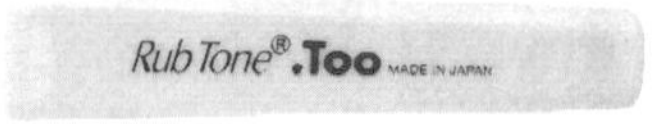
Rub Tone®.Too

Rub tone

Burnisher

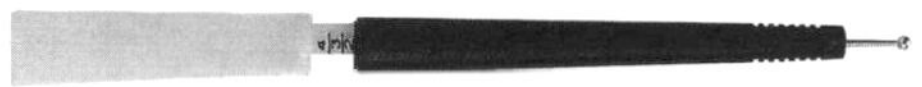

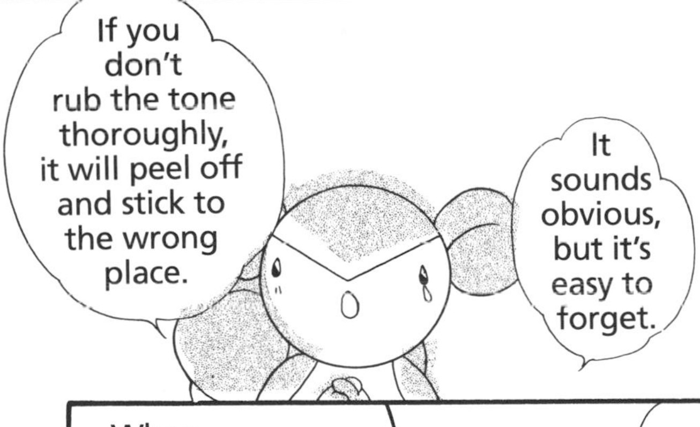
If you don't rub the tone thoroughly, it will peel off and stick to the wrong place.
It sounds obvious, but it's easy to forget.

FOR DETAILS

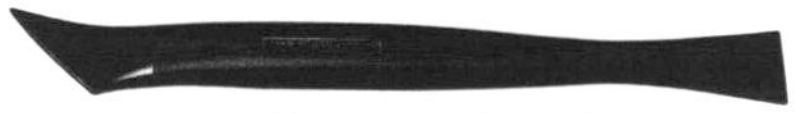

Screen tool

Burnisher 2

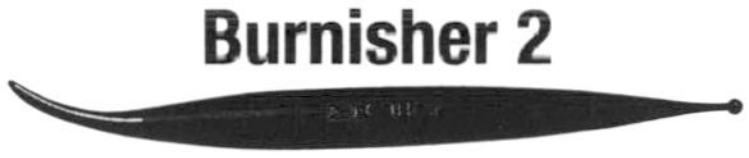

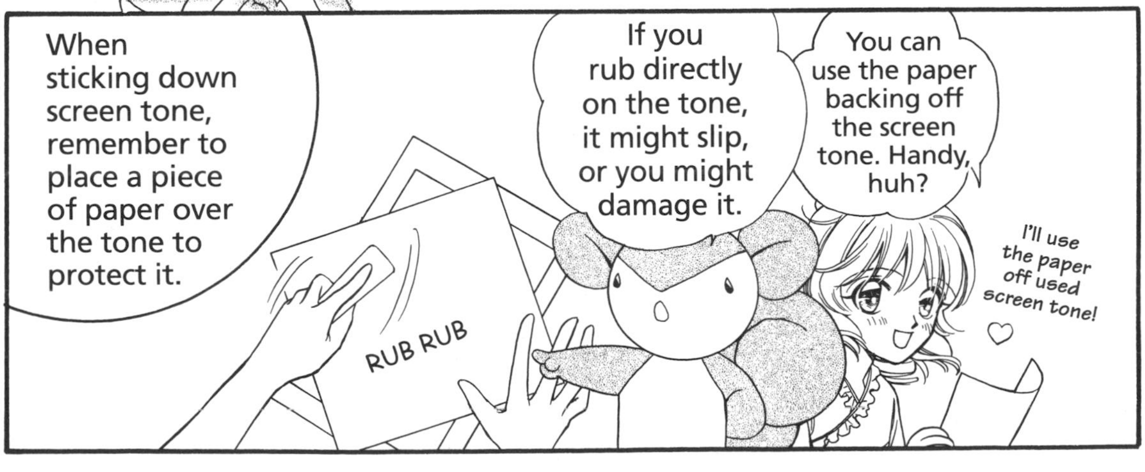
When sticking down screen tone, remember to place a piece of paper over the tone to protect it.
RUB RUB
If you rub directly on the tone, it might slip, or you might damage it.
You can use the paper backing off the screen tone. Handy, huh?
I'll use the paper off used screen tone!

TIPS FROM A PRO

RULING PENS

If you find technical pens too pricey, why not use a ruling pen? There's a knack to it, but it draws flawless lines and is much cheaper than a technical pen.

RULING PEN

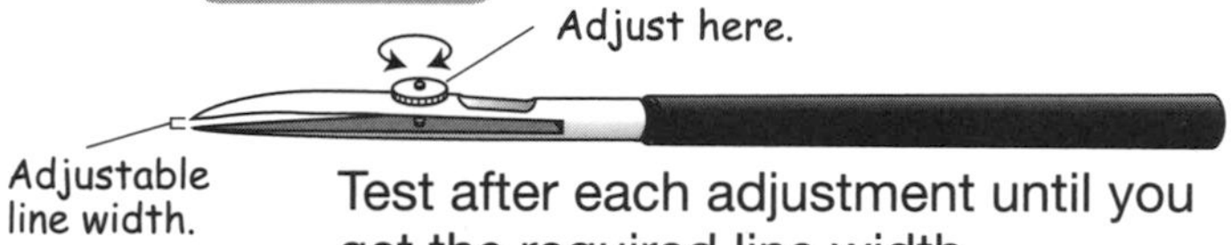
Adjust here.
Adjustable line width.

Test after each adjustment until you get the required line width.

Fill the nib with ink. Draw lines using a ruler. You can adjust the nib to draw fine or thick lines.

USING A RULING PEN

1.

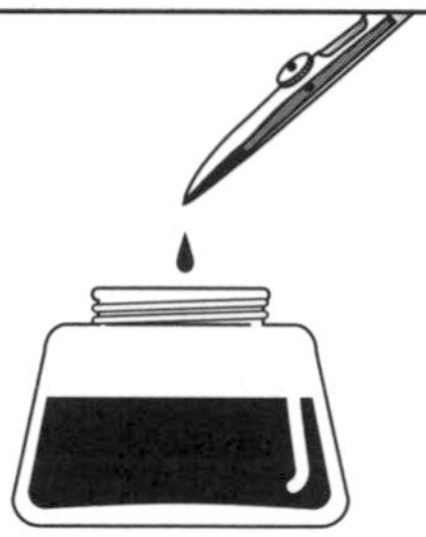

Fill about a third of the nib with ink. If you use too much, it will just cause drips.

2.

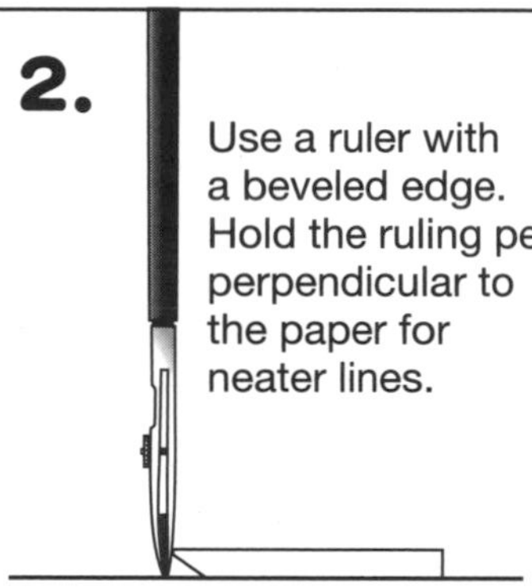

Use a ruler with a beveled edge. Hold the ruling pen perpendicular to the paper for neater lines.

After using, clean the nib thoroughly. Dried ink can clog the nib and cause messy lines.

CAUTION!

Sweaty, greasy hands!

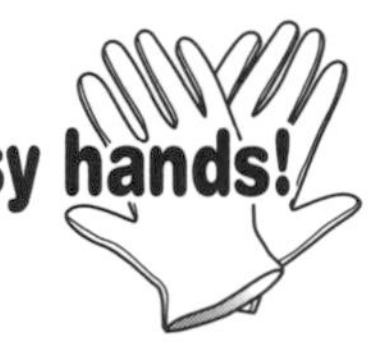

Even if your hands don't look sweaty or greasy, they might smudge the ink, and you won't be able to fix this easily. You might find it worth wearing thin gloves while you work. These are available in art supplies stores and are usually inexpensive.

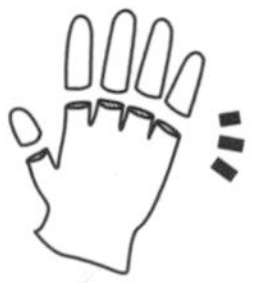
Cut off the finger tips to make it easier to work.

Another tip!

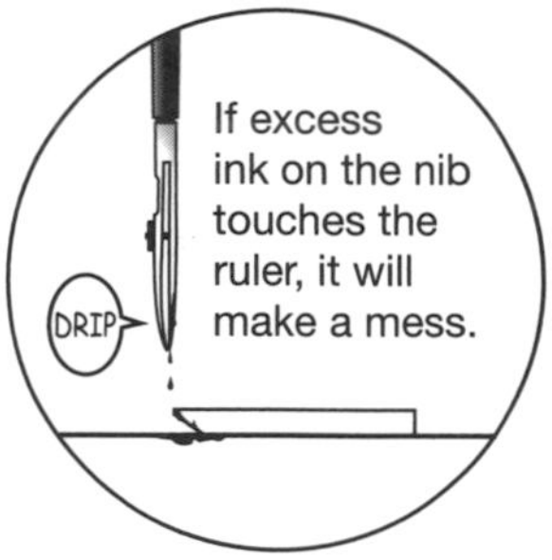
If excess ink on the nib touches the ruler, it will make a mess.
DRIP

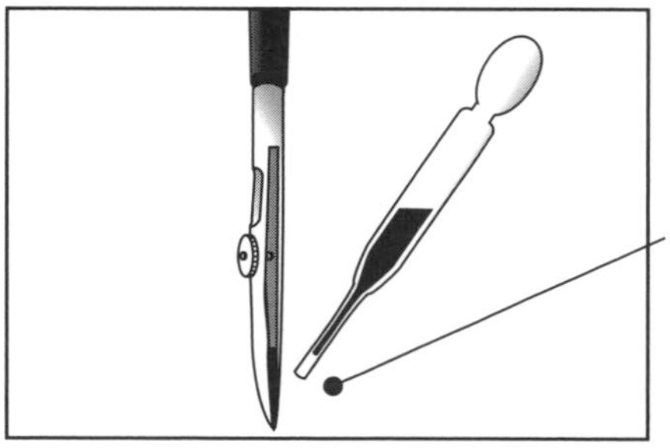

To avoid this, use a pipette to fill the nib with ink.

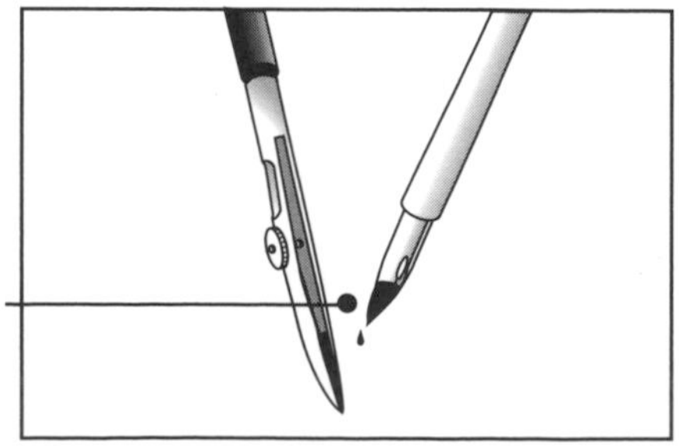

A pen nib works too!

LESSON 2
CHARACTERS

Do you have problems getting the body
proportions right when drawing people?
Do your characters end up looking too similar?
If so, then this lesson's for you.
Characters are the most important element
of manga, and their facial expressions are
what gives them their individuality.

BODIES

The head-to-body ratio uses head size as a basic unit from which the rest of the body is calculated.

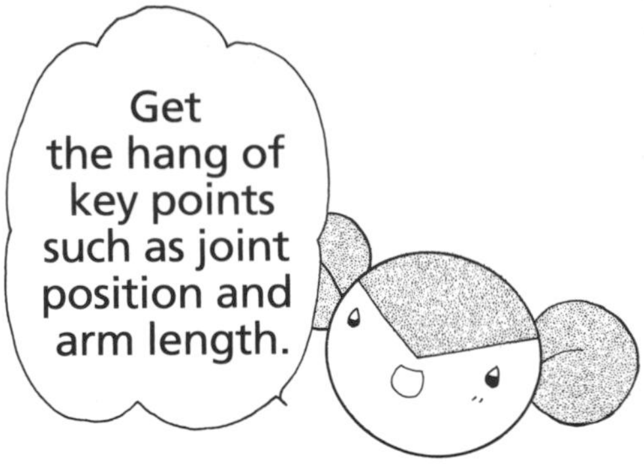
Get the hang of key points such as joint position and arm length.

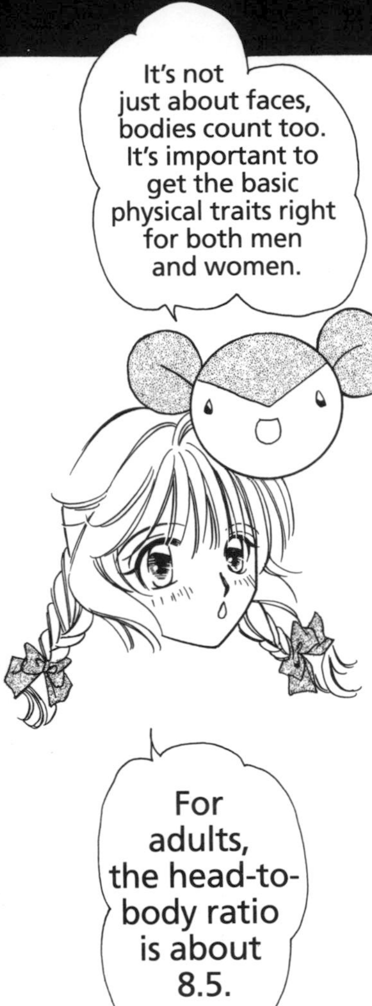
It's not just about faces, bodies count too. It's important to get the basic physical traits right for both men and women.
For adults, the head-to-body ratio is about 8.5.

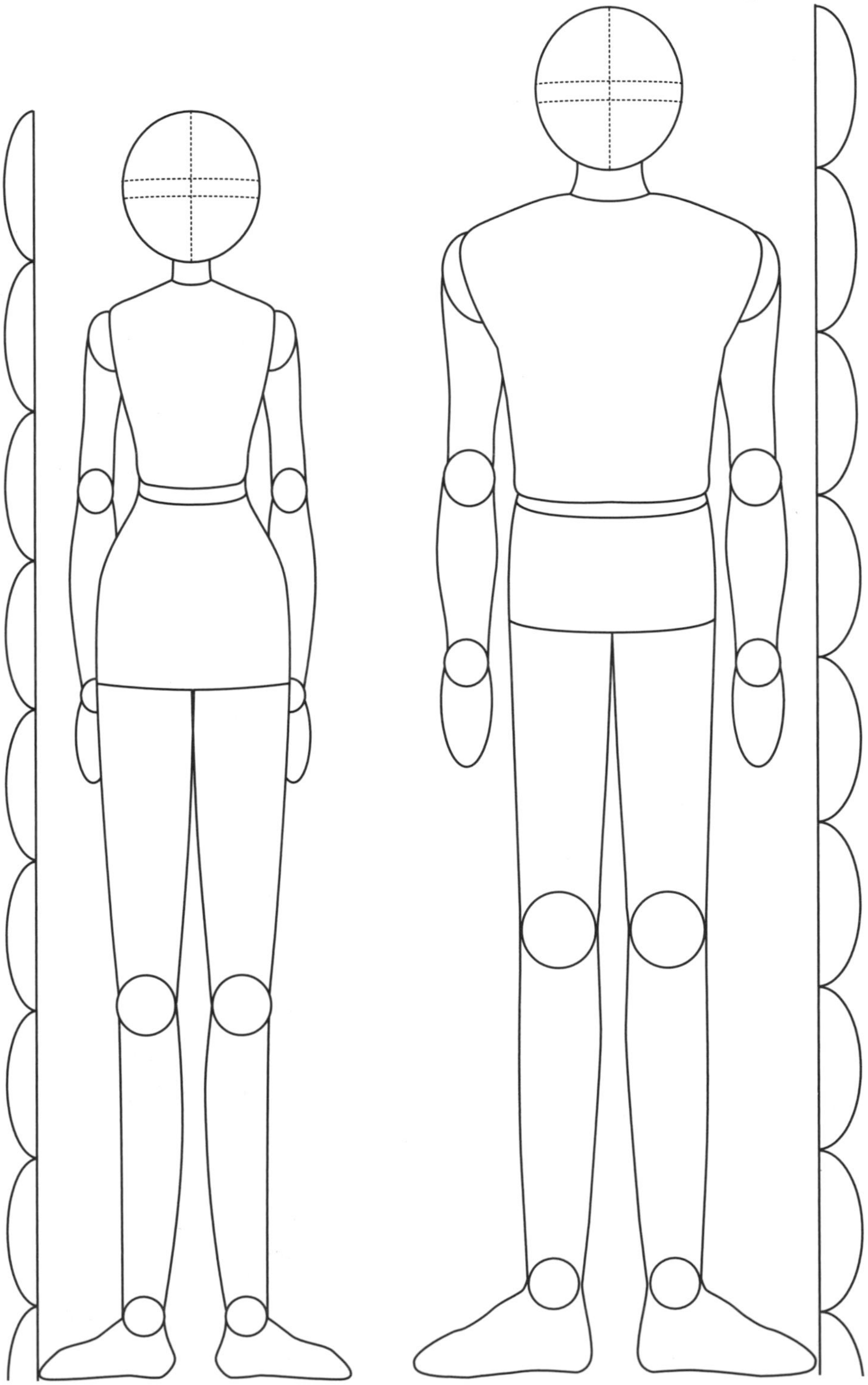

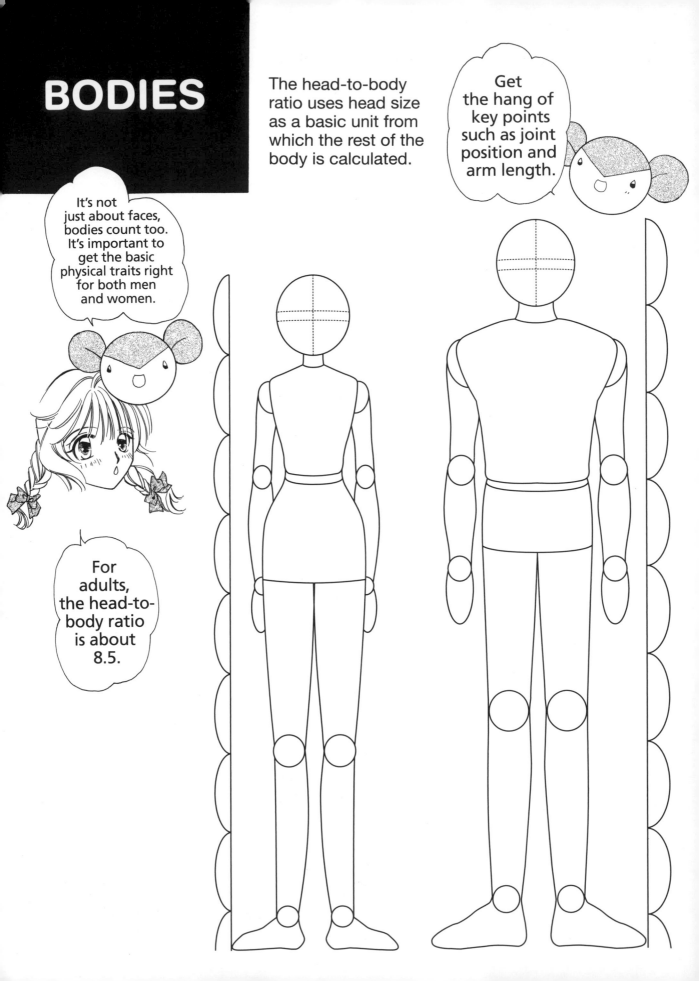

Let's look at the body's basic characteristics.

The spine serves as the body's central axis, running from the neck to the hips. Even if the character is in profile or bending over, the spine is always the central line of the body.

MEN

WOMEN

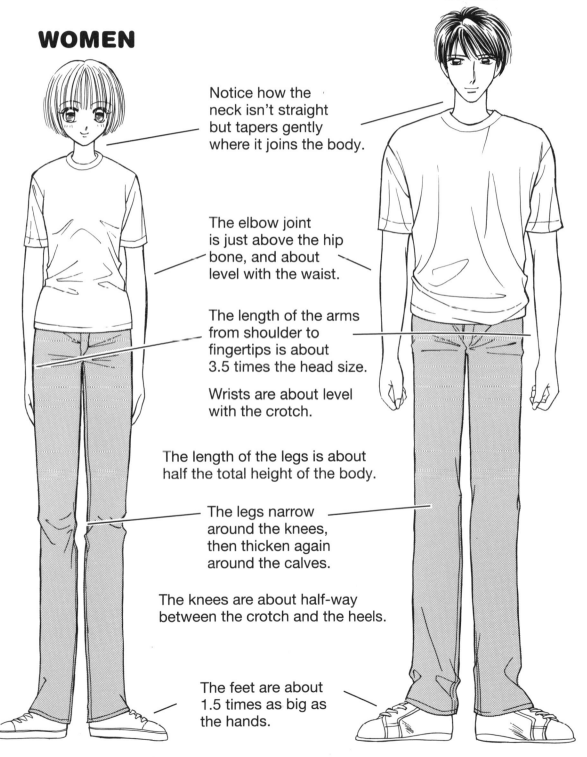

Notice how the neck isn't straight but tapers gently where it joins the body.

The elbow joint is just above the hip bone, and about level with the waist.

The length of the arms from shoulder to fingertips is about 3.5 times the head size.

Wrists are about level with the crotch.

The length of the legs is about half the total height of the body.

The legs narrow around the knees, then thicken again around the calves.

The knees are about half-way between the crotch and the heels.

The feet are about 1.5 times as big as the hands.

MALE AND FEMALE CHARACTERISTICS

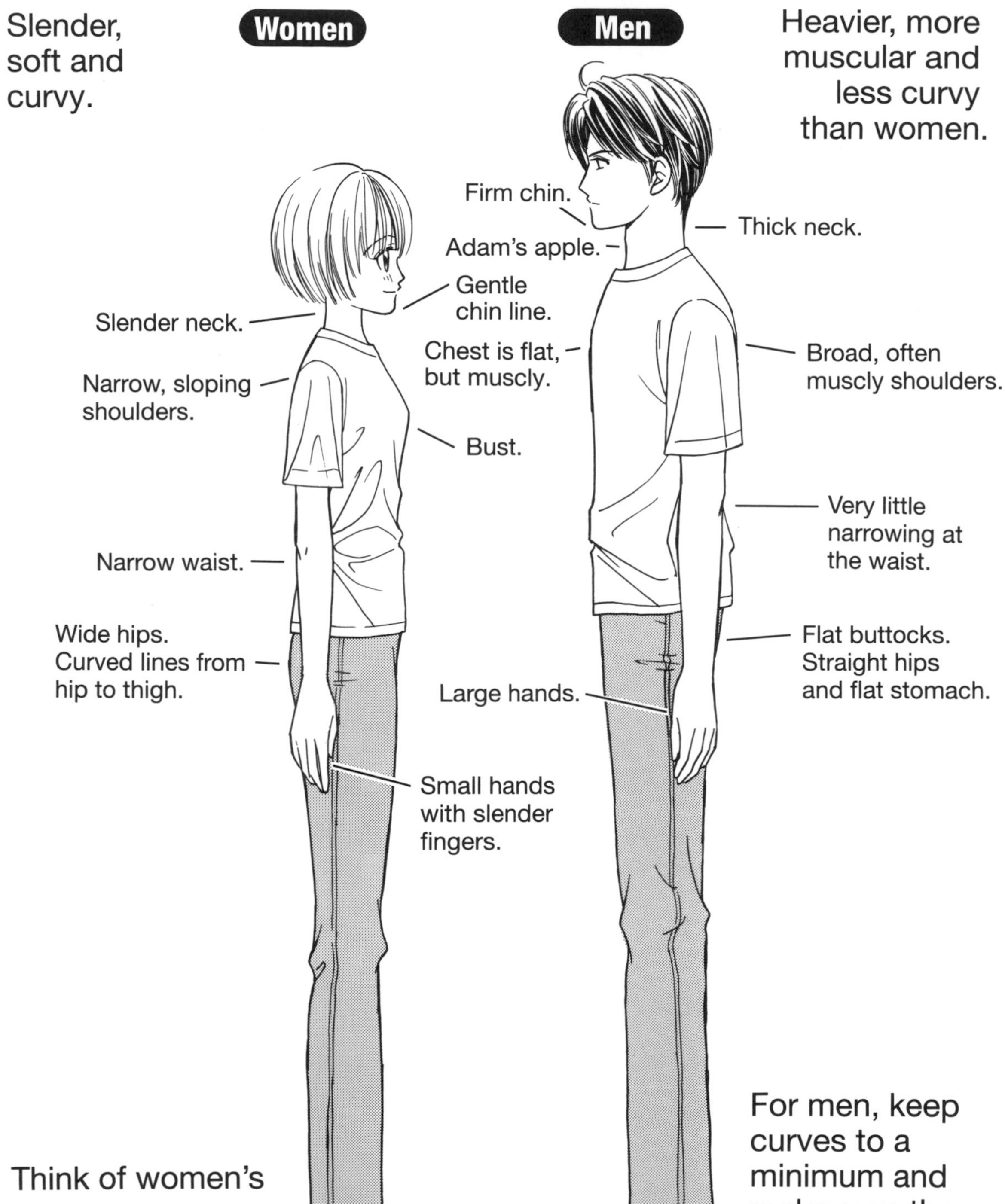

Women
Slender, soft and curvy.
Slender neck.
Narrow, sloping shoulders.
Gentle chin line.
Bust.
Narrow waist.
Wide hips. Curved lines from hip to thigh.
Small hands with slender fingers.
Men
Heavier, more muscular and less curvy than women.
Firm chin.
Adam's apple.
Thick neck.
Chest is flat, but muscly.
Broad, often muscly shoulders.
Very little narrowing at the waist.
Flat buttocks. Straight hips and flat stomach.
Large hands.

Think of women's curves as waves from the chest to the hips, thighs and feet.

For men, keep curves to a minimum and make sure the wrists and ankles aren't too thin.

Whatever the head-to-body ratio, the rules for other proportions such as arm and leg length remain the same. Just adjust hand and feet size so the proportions remain balanced.

Head-to-body ratio of 5

Common for "cute" characters. Also common in young boys and girls.

Head-to-body ratio of 4

Head-to-body ratios of 3 and 4 are mostly used for children and comical characters.

Head-to-body ratio of 3

Head-to-body ratio of 2

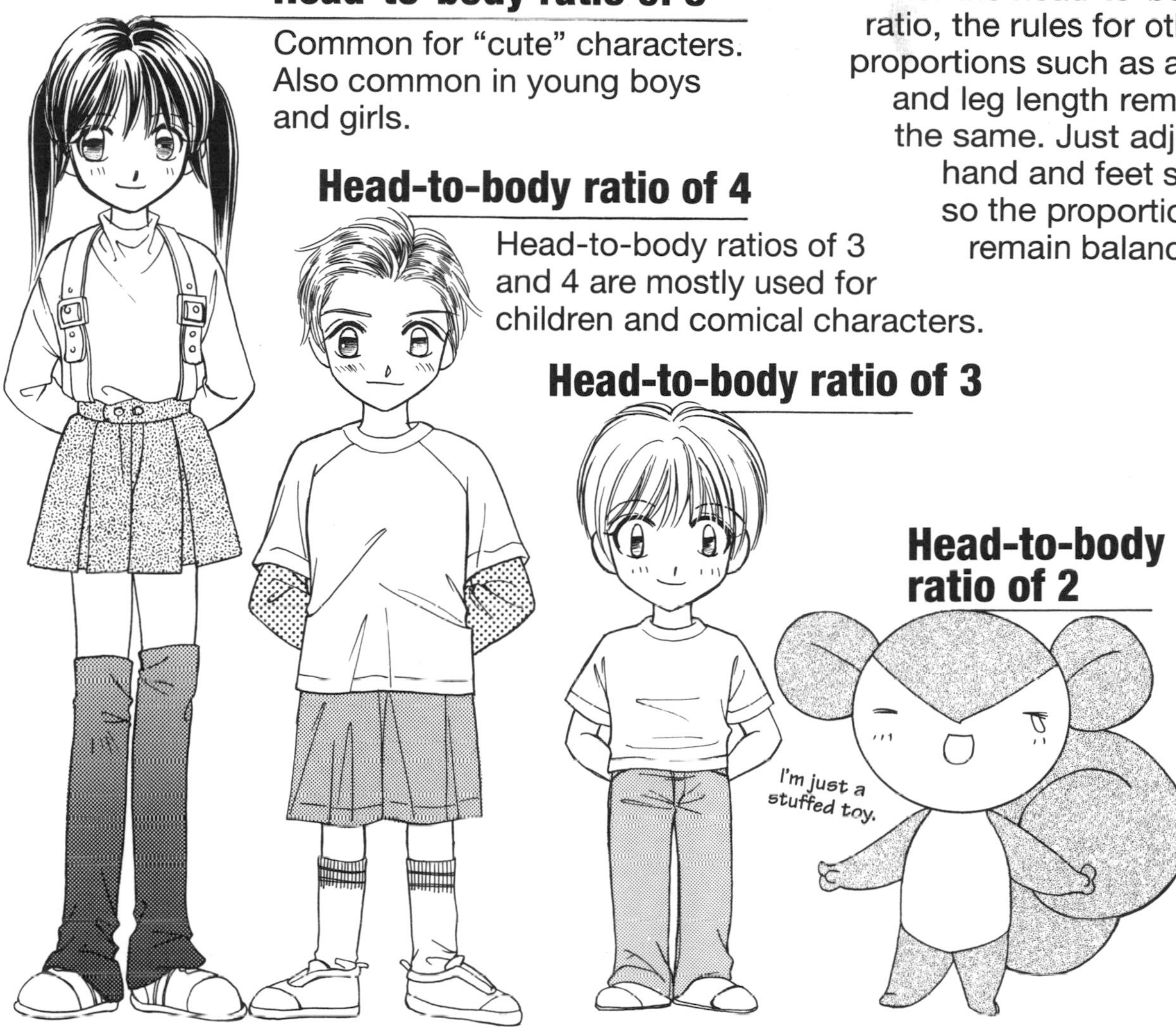
I'm just a stuffed toy.

Use your common sense when it comes to the head-to-body ratio. If you don't, figures will look awkward and the balance will be out.

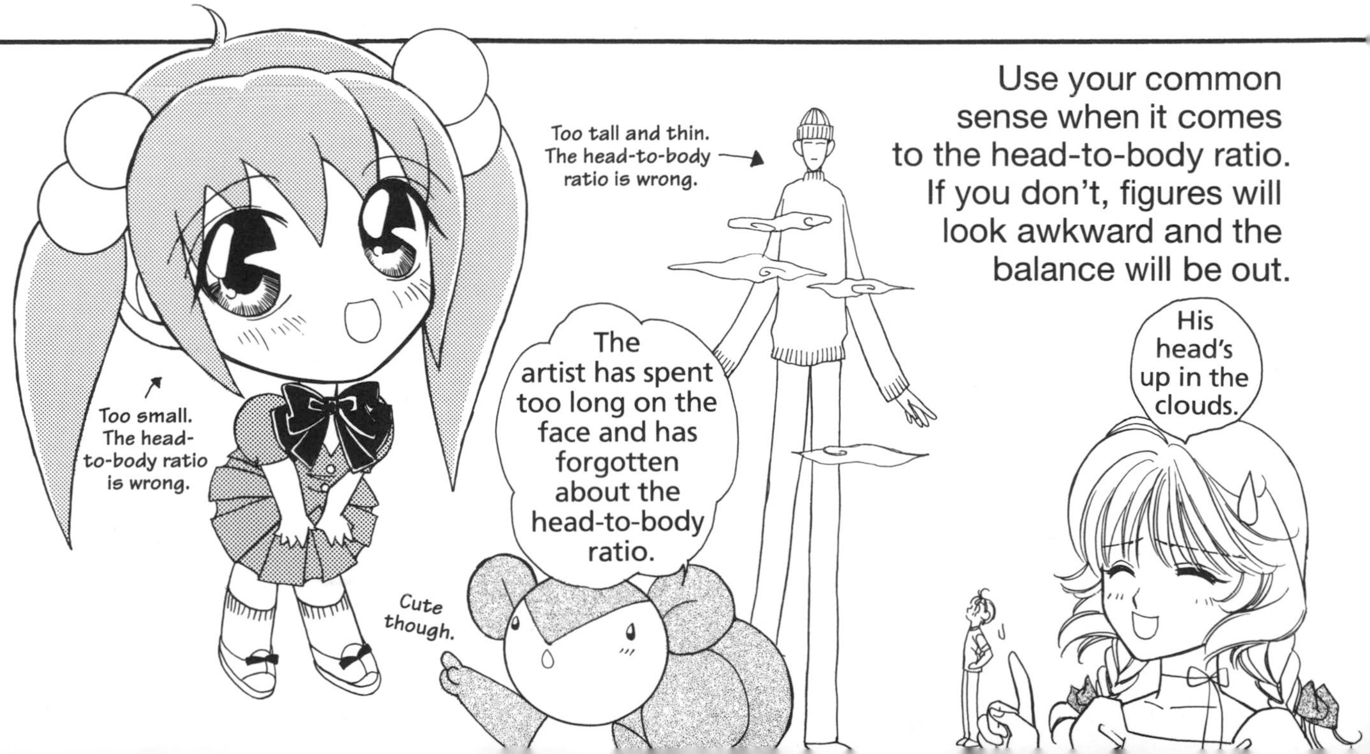
His head's up in the clouds.
Too tall and thin. The head-to-body ratio is wrong.
The artist has spent too long on the face and has forgotten about the head-to-body ratio.
Cute though.
Too small. The head-to-body ratio is wrong.

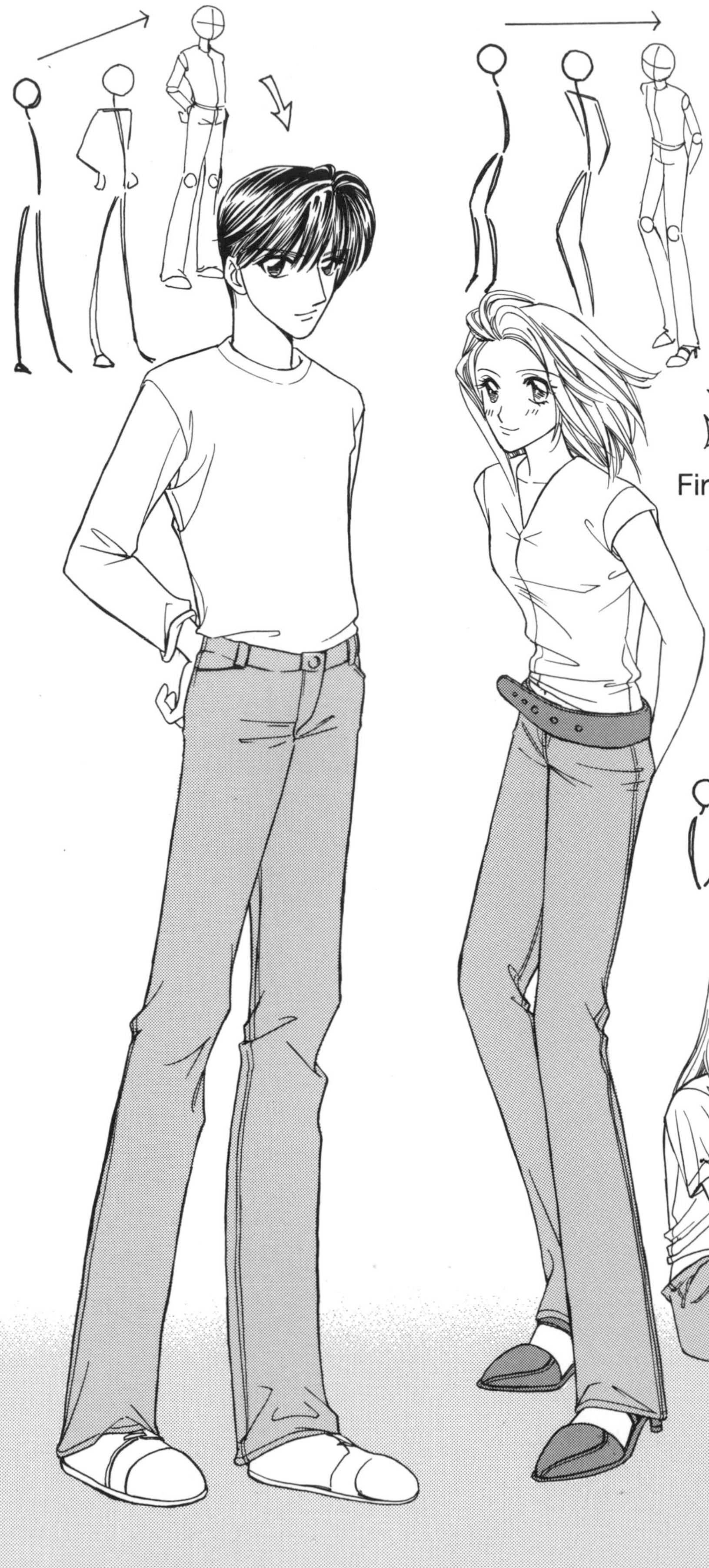

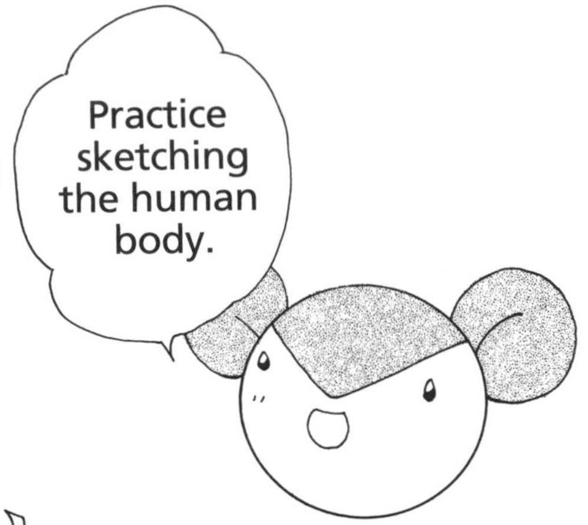
Practice sketching the human body.

First draw a rough sketch of the body bearing in mind the head-to-body ratio. Then flesh it out and add clothes.

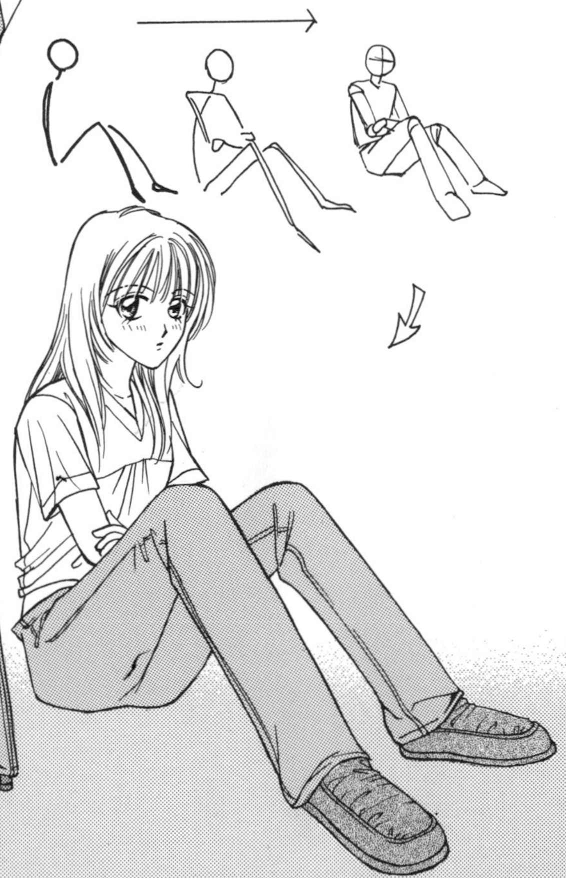

A rough sketch will help a lot when you're drawing characters in more complex positions.

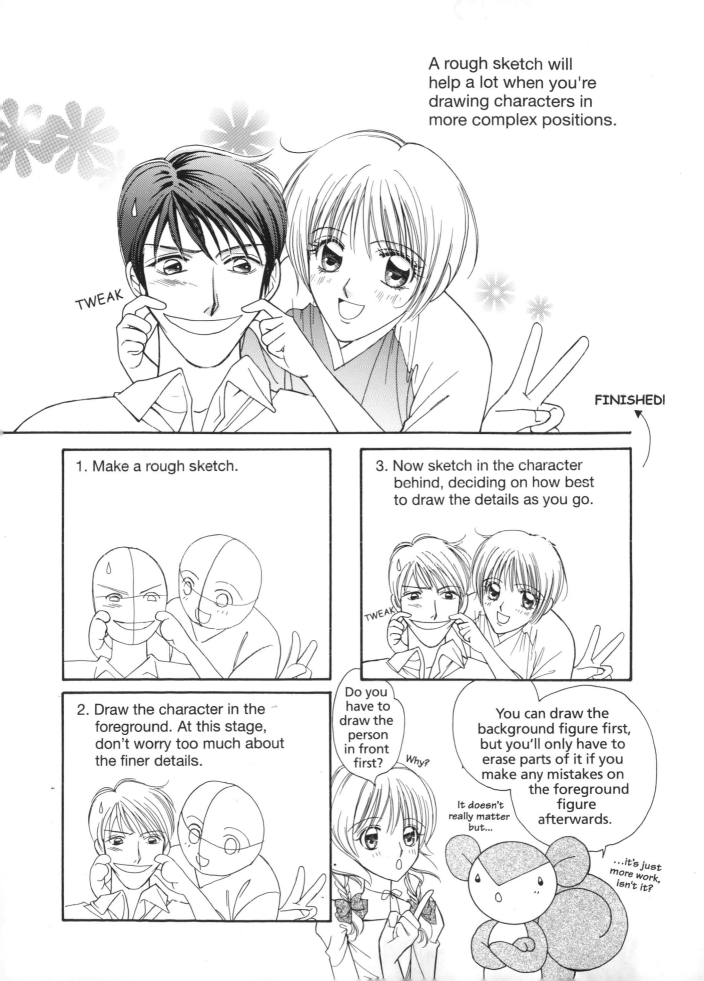

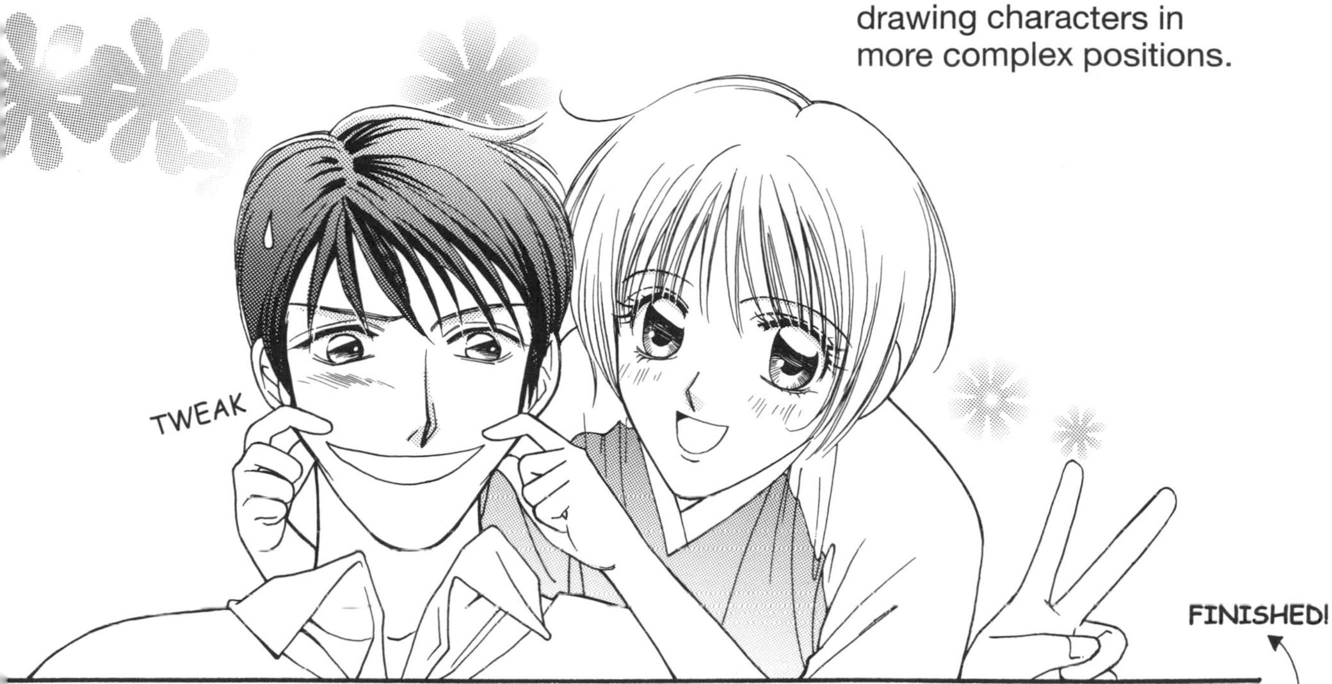
TWEAK
FINISHED!

1. Make a rough sketch.

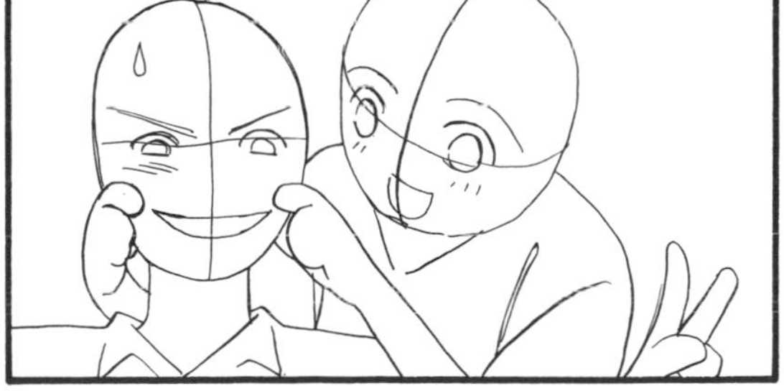

2. Draw the character in the foreground. At this stage, don't worry too much about the finer details.

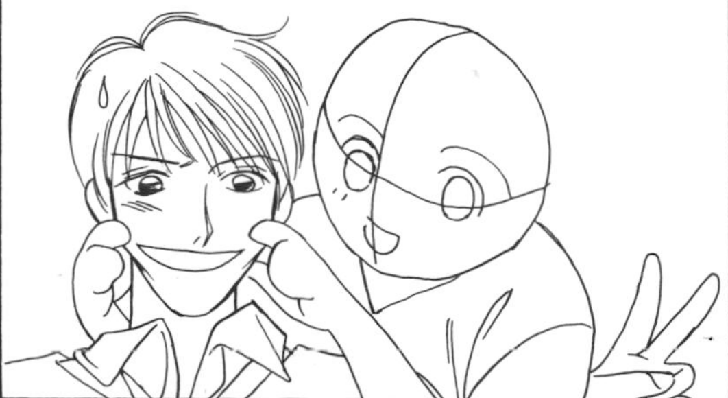

3. Now sketch in the character behind, deciding on how best to draw the details as you go.

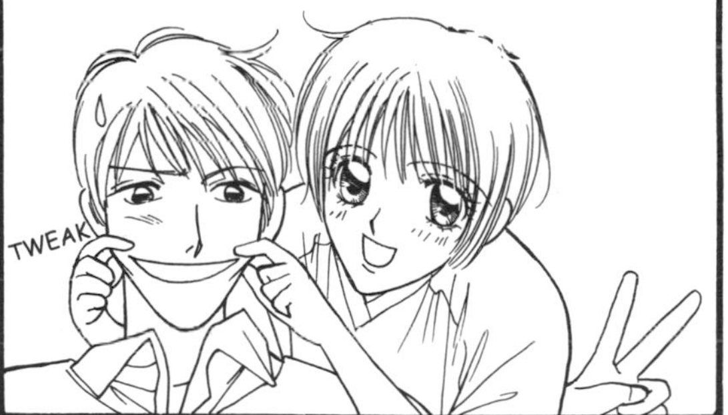
TWEAK

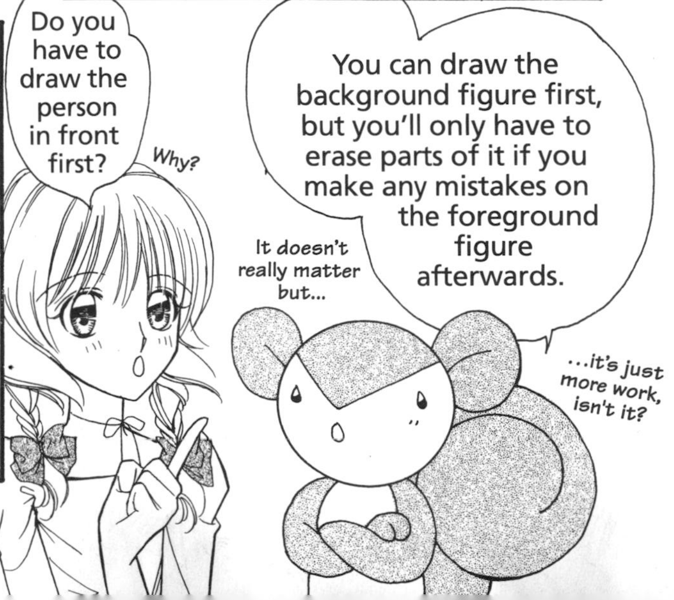
Do you have to draw the person in front first?
Why?
It doesn't really matter but...
You can draw the background figure first, but you'll only have to erase parts of it if you make any mistakes on the foreground figure afterwards.
...it's just more work, isn't it?

FACES

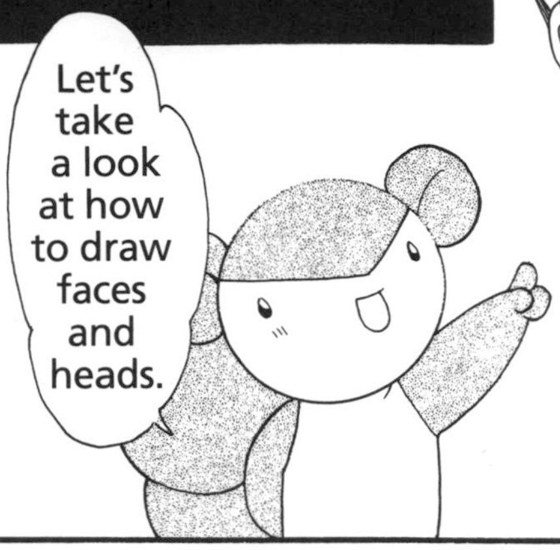

Let's take a look at how to draw faces and heads.

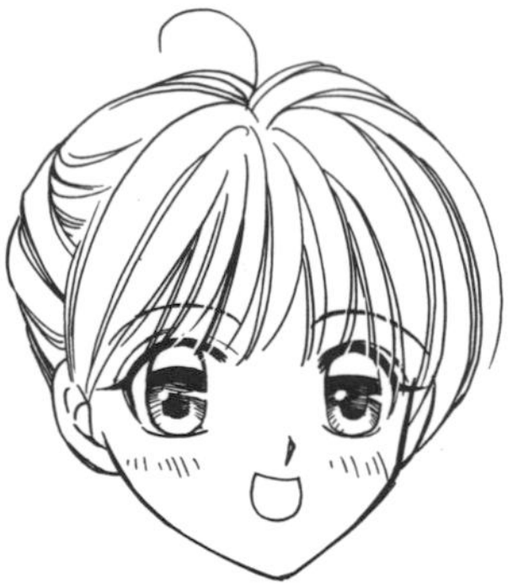

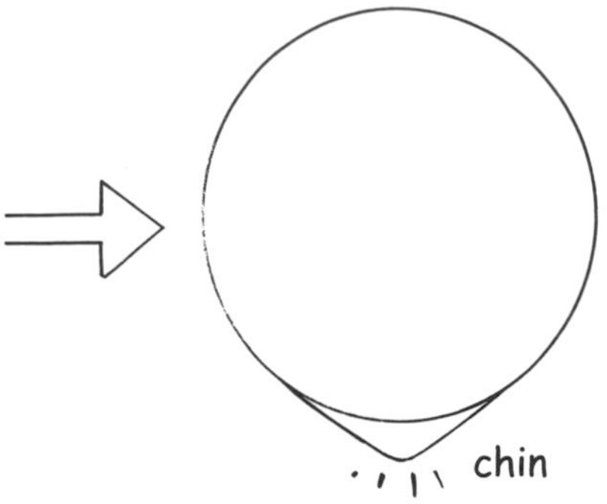

chin

Heads and faces look complex… → but basically they're just a circle with a chin, an upside-down egg with hair!

It's the same from the side.

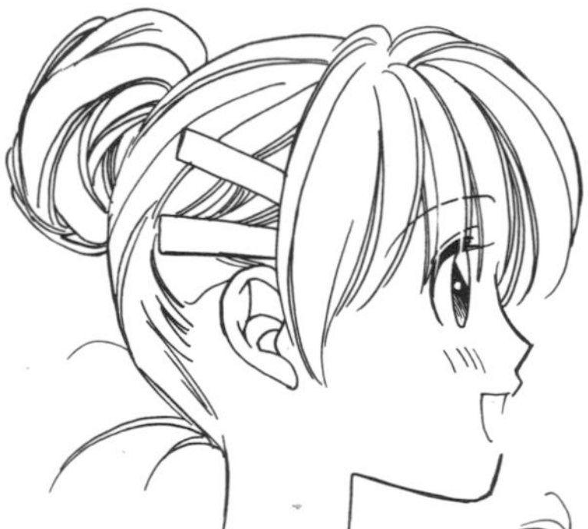

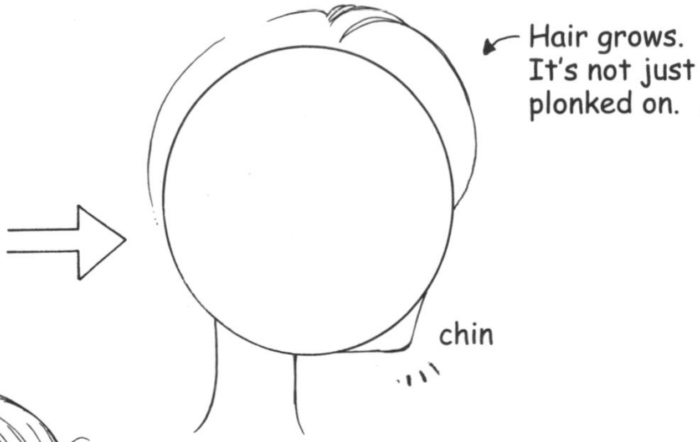

Hair grows. It's not just plonked on.
chin

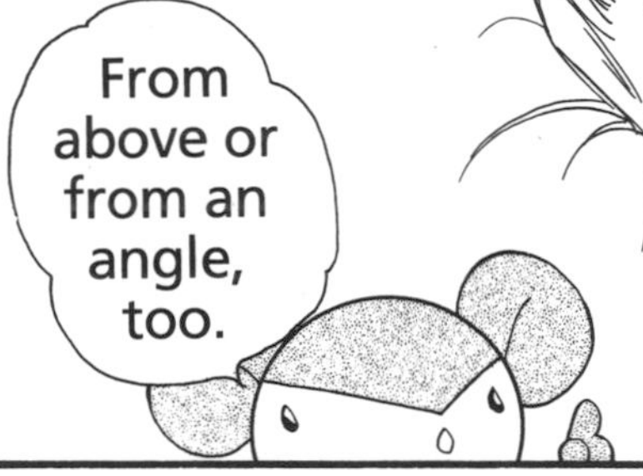

From above or from an angle, too.

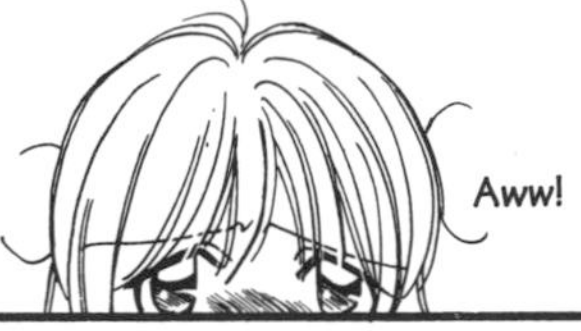

Aww!

Here are the basic proportions.

The nose should occupy the middle third of the face between the hairline and the chin, starting from the midpoint between the eyes.

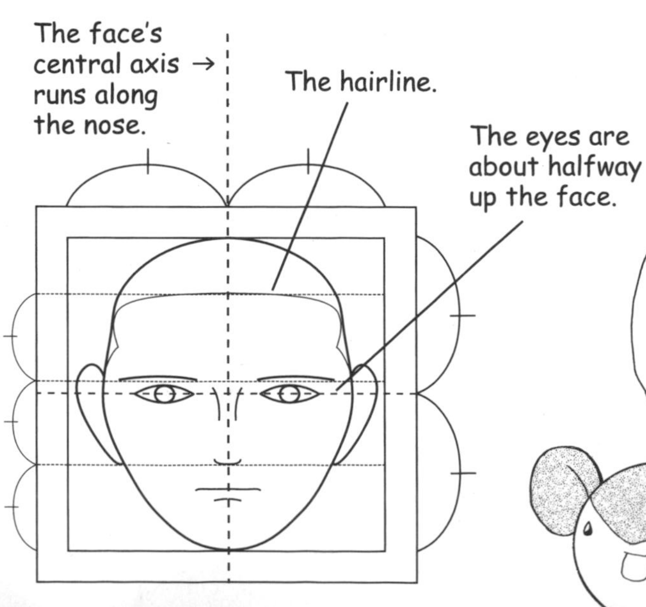

The face's central axis → runs along the nose.
The hairline.
The eyes are about halfway up the face.

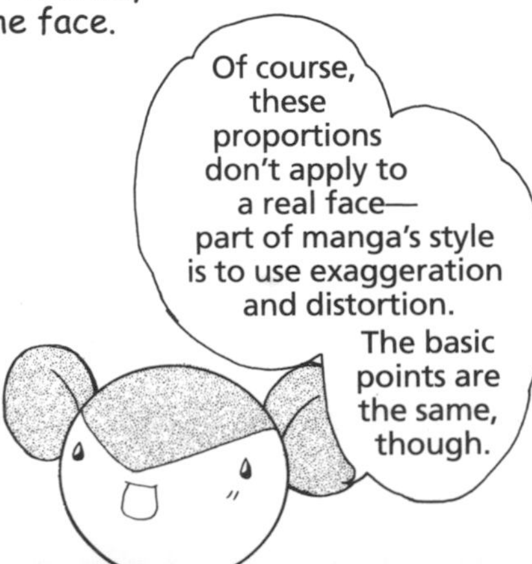

Of course, these proportions don't apply to a real face—part of manga's style is to use exaggeration and distortion. The basic points are the same, though.

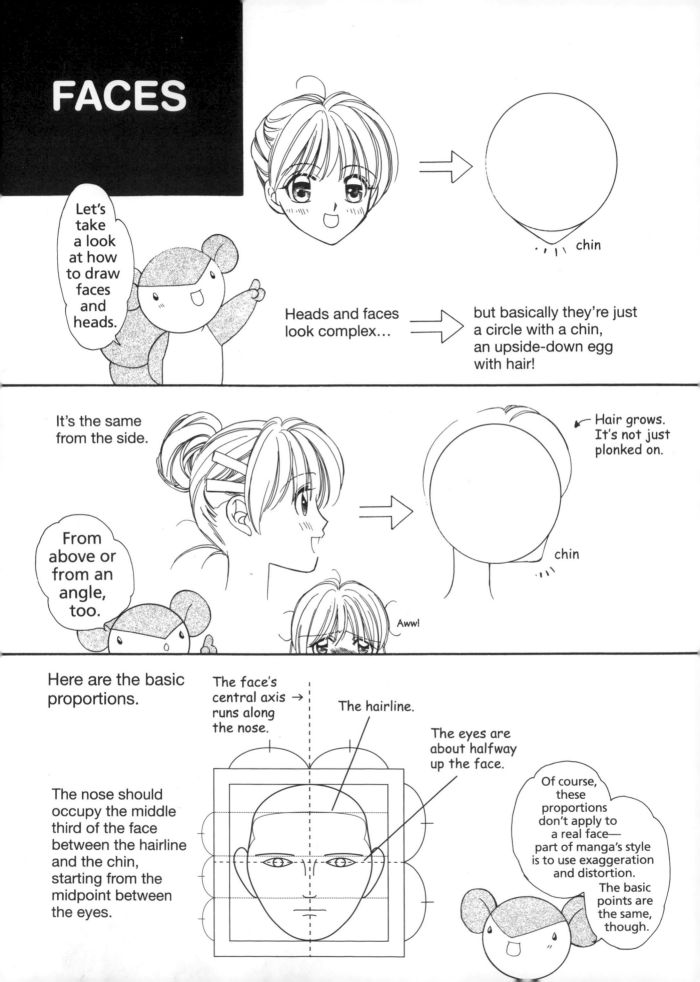

Key points for profiles.

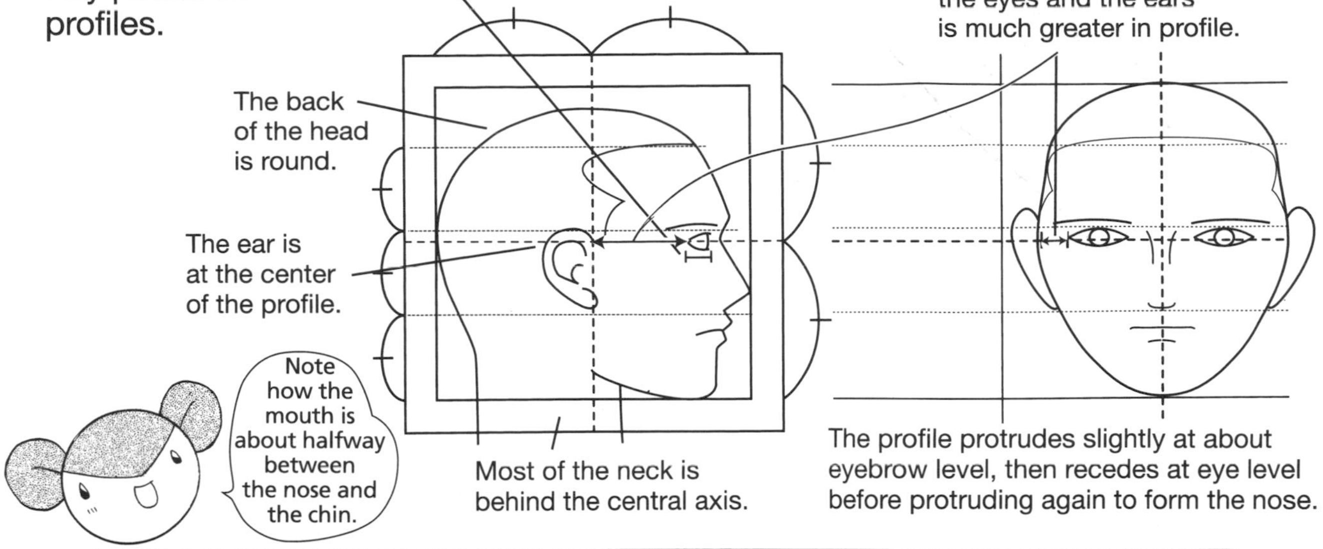
Eyes are narrower than in a front view.
The distance between the eyes and the ears is much greater in profile.
The back of the head is round.
The ear is at the center of the profile.
Most of the neck is behind the central axis.
The profile protrudes slightly at about eyebrow level, then recedes at eye level before protruding again to form the nose.
Note how the mouth is about halfway between the nose and the chin.

Get into the habit of drawing the upside-down egg model. It makes drawing faces so much easier.

This is how to start sketching your characters.

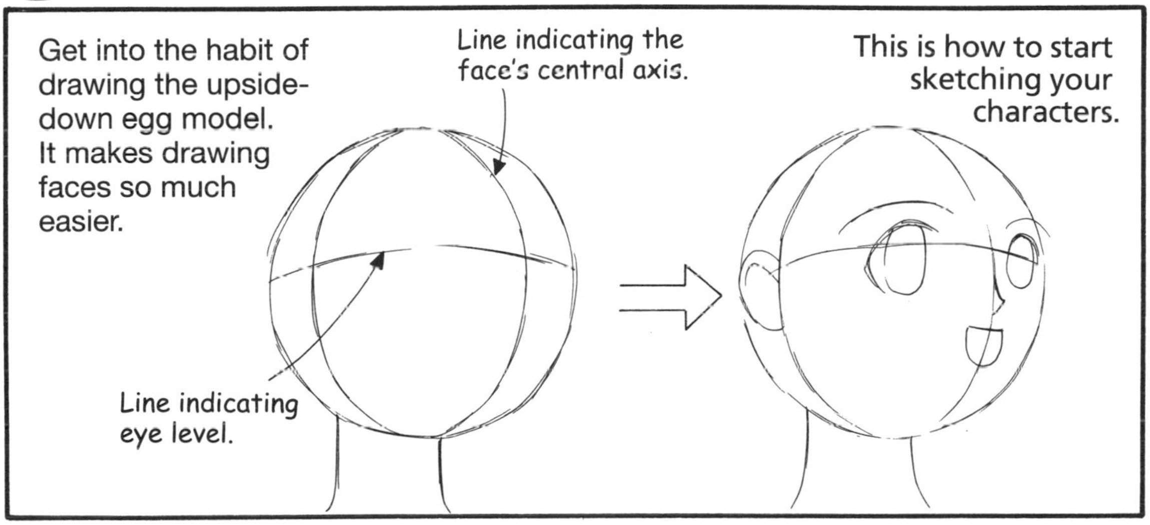
Line indicating the face's central axis.
Line indicating eye level.

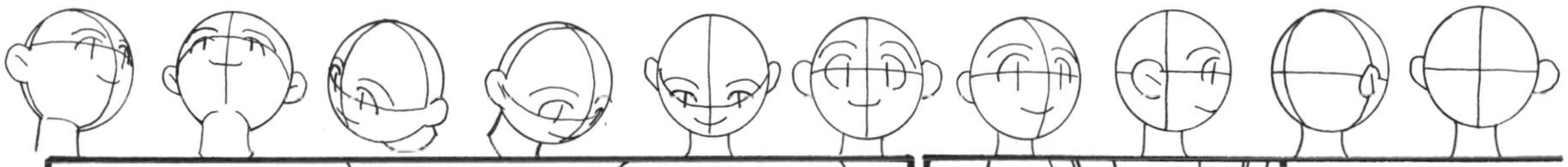

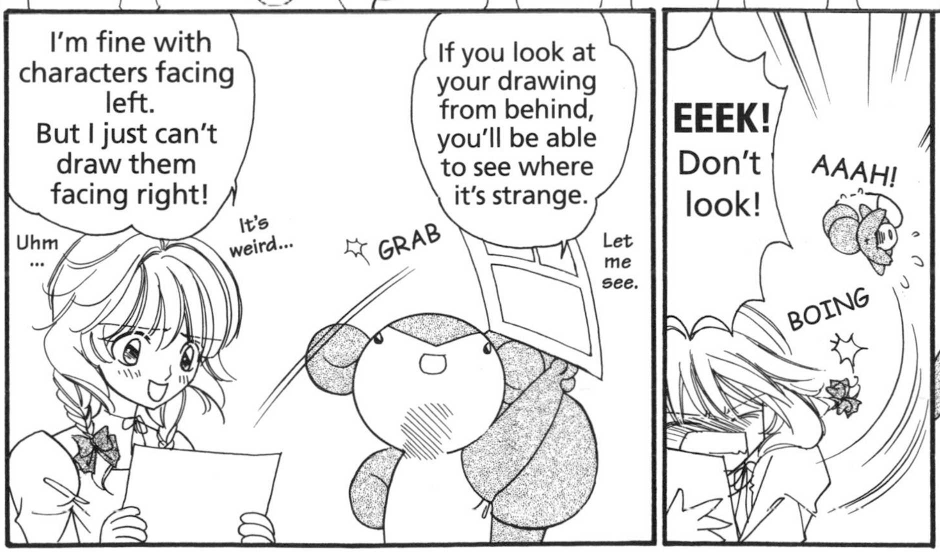
I'm fine with characters facing left. But I just can't draw them facing right!
Uhm ...
It's weird...
If you look at your drawing from behind, you'll be able to see where it's strange.
GRAB
Let me see.
EEEK! Don't look!
AAAH!
BOING

If you find it tricky drawing someone facing right, then draw an upside-down egg and add in the rest of the features.

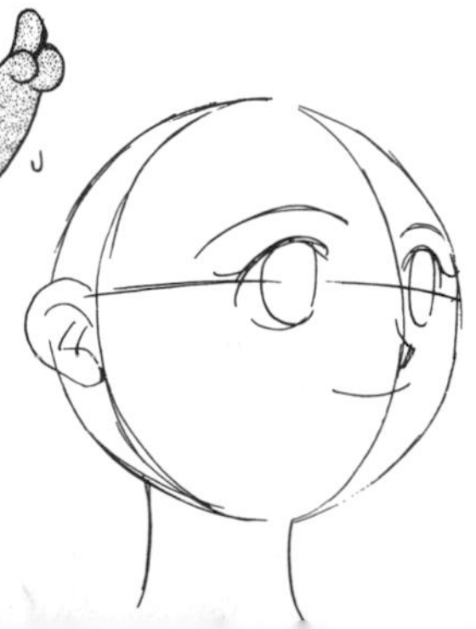

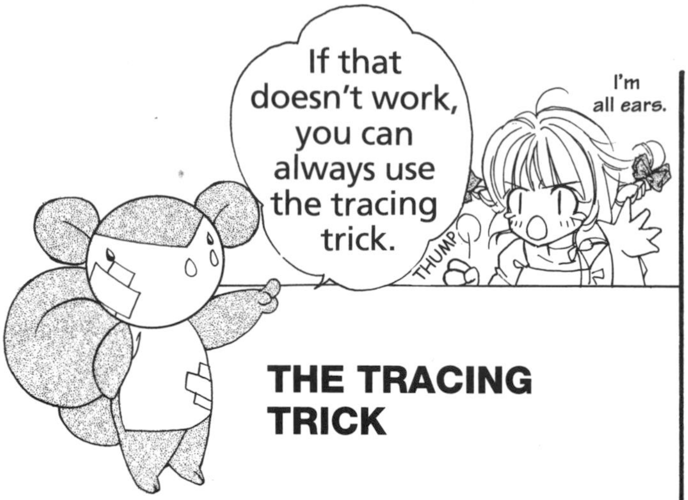
If that doesn't work, you can always use the tracing trick.
I'm all ears.
THUMP

THE TRACING TRICK

1. Get a piece of blank paper and either make another sketch in pencil or make a dark photocopy of your existing sketch.

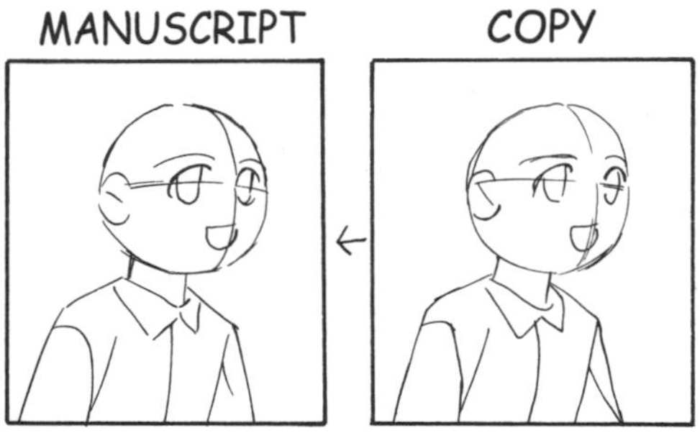
MANUSCRIPT
COPY

2. Reverse the new copy so that the right-facing head is now facing left.

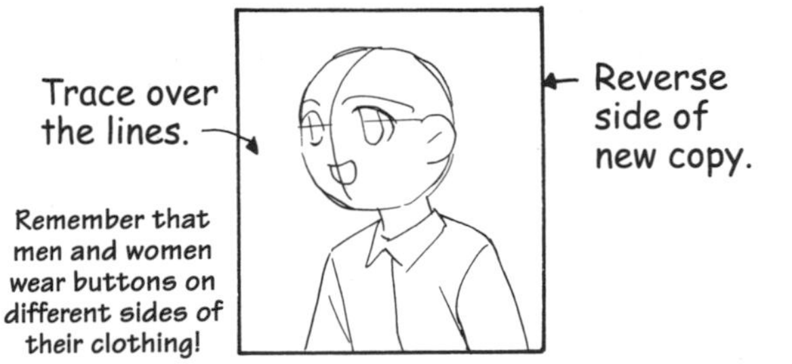
Trace over the lines.
Remember that men and women wear buttons on different sides of their clothing!
Reverse side of new copy.

3. Use this tracing to fill in the details of your character.

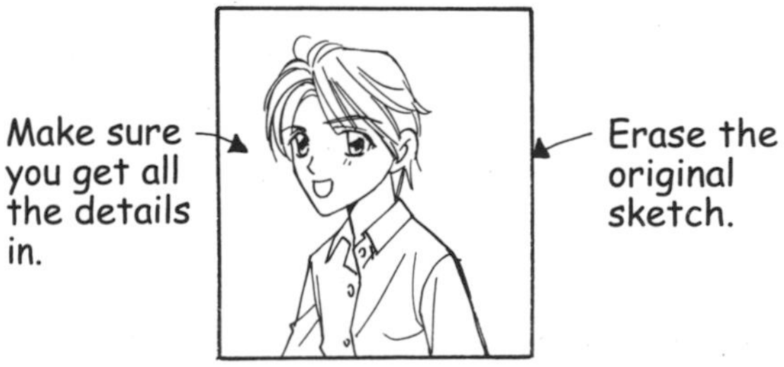
Make sure you get all the details in.
Erase the original sketch.

4. Place your completed drawing face-down on a light box.

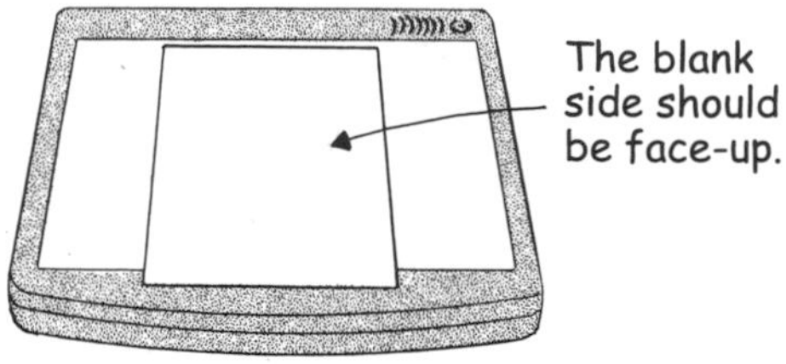
The blank side should be face-up.

5. Secure your manuscript paper in position over the other sheet with removable tape.

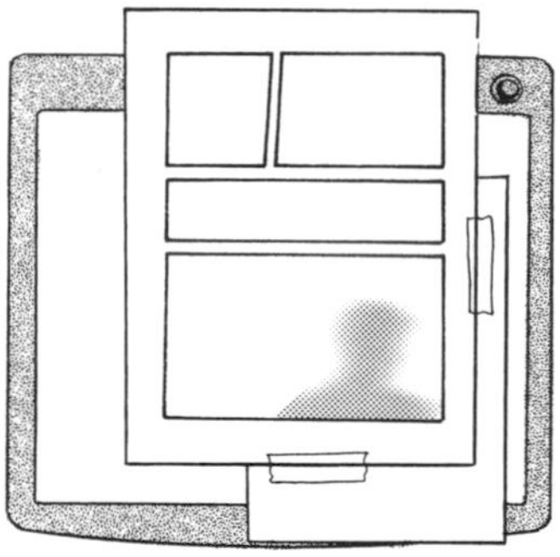

6. Now trace over the details of your drawing.

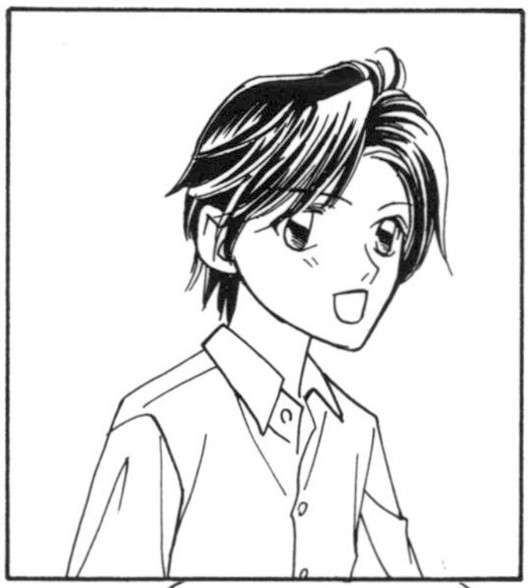

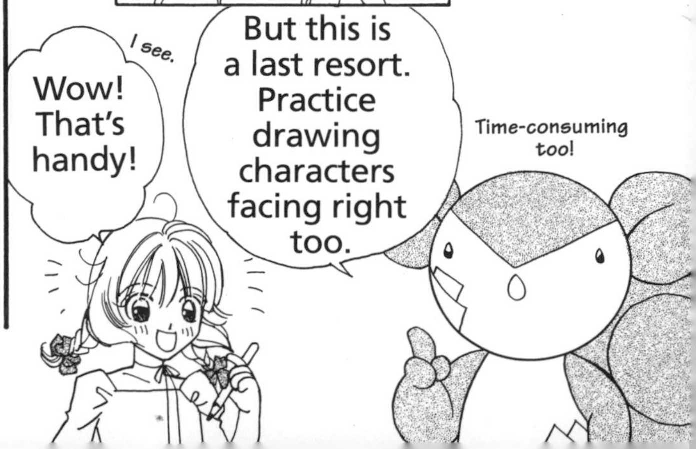
Wow! That's handy!
I see.
But this is a last resort. Practice drawing characters facing right too.
Time-consuming too!

EYES

Eyes best show a character's individuality.

Beginners can try copying the styles of their favorite manga artists and then develop their own individuality.

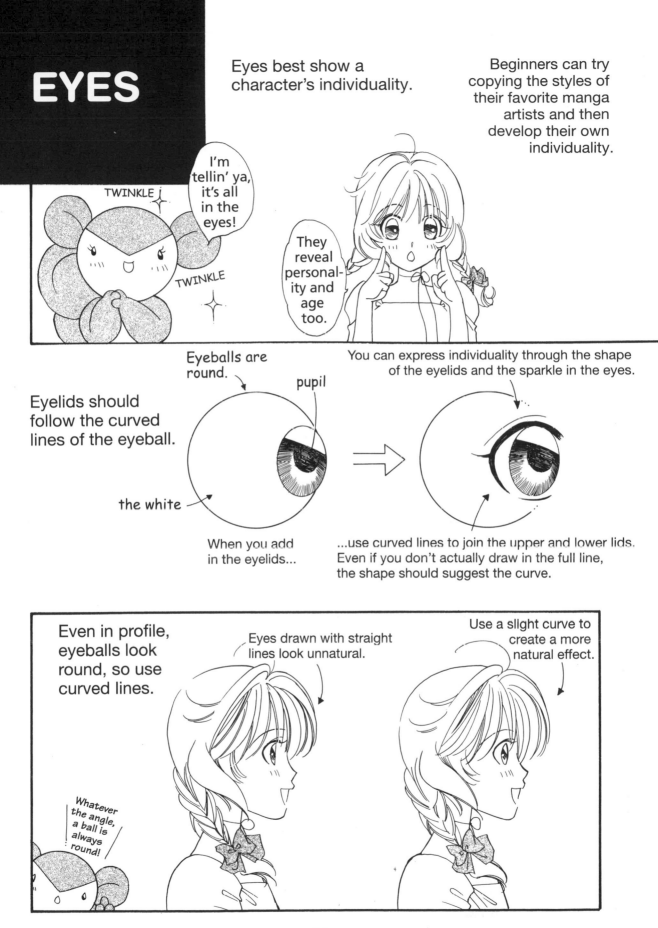

TWINKLE

I'm tellin' ya, it's all in the eyes!

TWINKLE

They reveal personality and age too.

Eyelids should follow the curved lines of the eyeball.

Eyeballs are round.

pupil

the white

When you add in the eyelids...

You can express individuality through the shape of the eyelids and the sparkle in the eyes.

...use curved lines to join the upper and lower lids. Even if you don't actually draw in the full line, the shape should suggest the curve.

Even in profile, eyeballs look round, so use curved lines.

Eyes drawn with straight lines look unnatural.

Use a slight curve to create a more natural effect.

Whatever the angle, a ball is always round!

When facing forward, the eyes are symmetrical.

When looking to one side, the eye furthest away looks smaller...

...and a bit narrower.

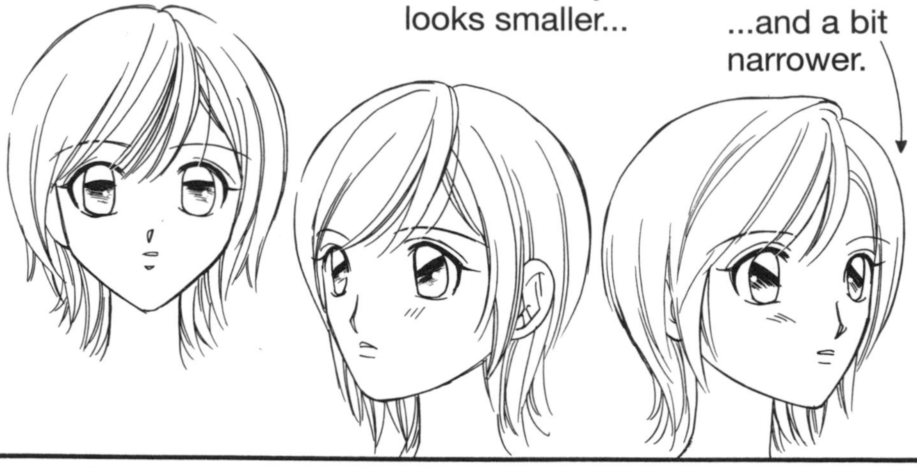

Eyes in profile appear narrower than eyes facing forward.

EYES FACING FORWARD

EYES IN PROFILE

The eye on the far side of the face is no longer visible.

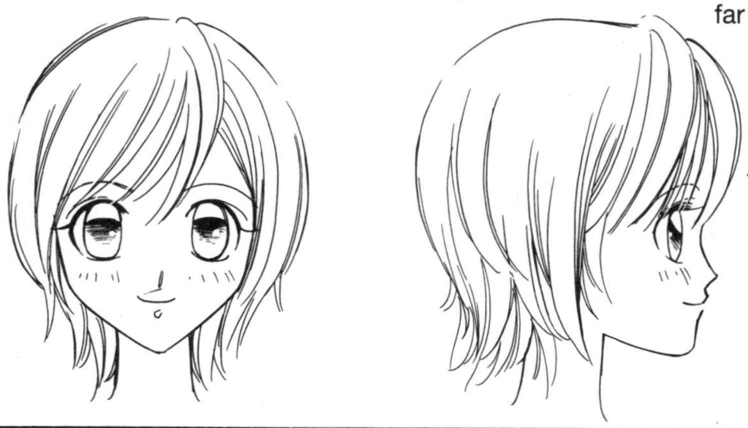

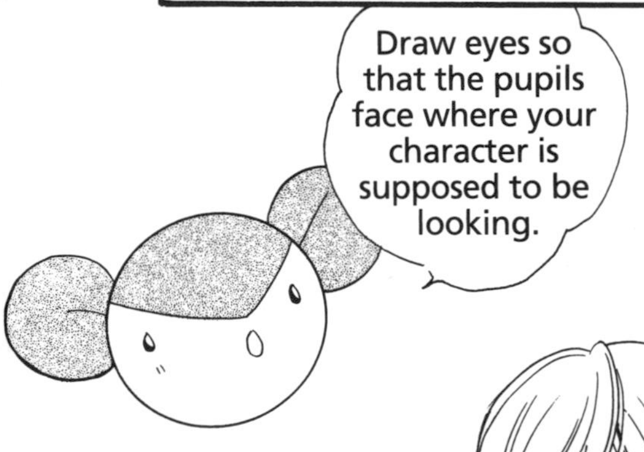
Draw eyes so that the pupils face where your character is supposed to be looking.

When looking up, the pupils should be further away from the lower eyelid.

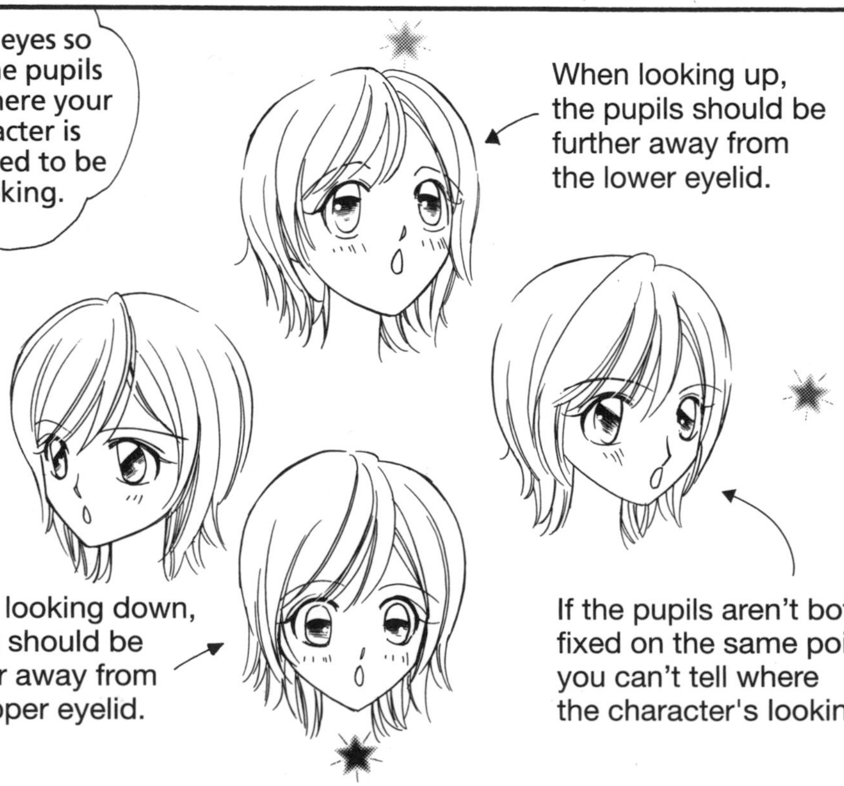

When looking down, pupils should be further away from the upper eyelid.

If the pupils aren't both fixed on the same point, you can't tell where the character's looking.

BOYS' EYES

GIRLS' EYES

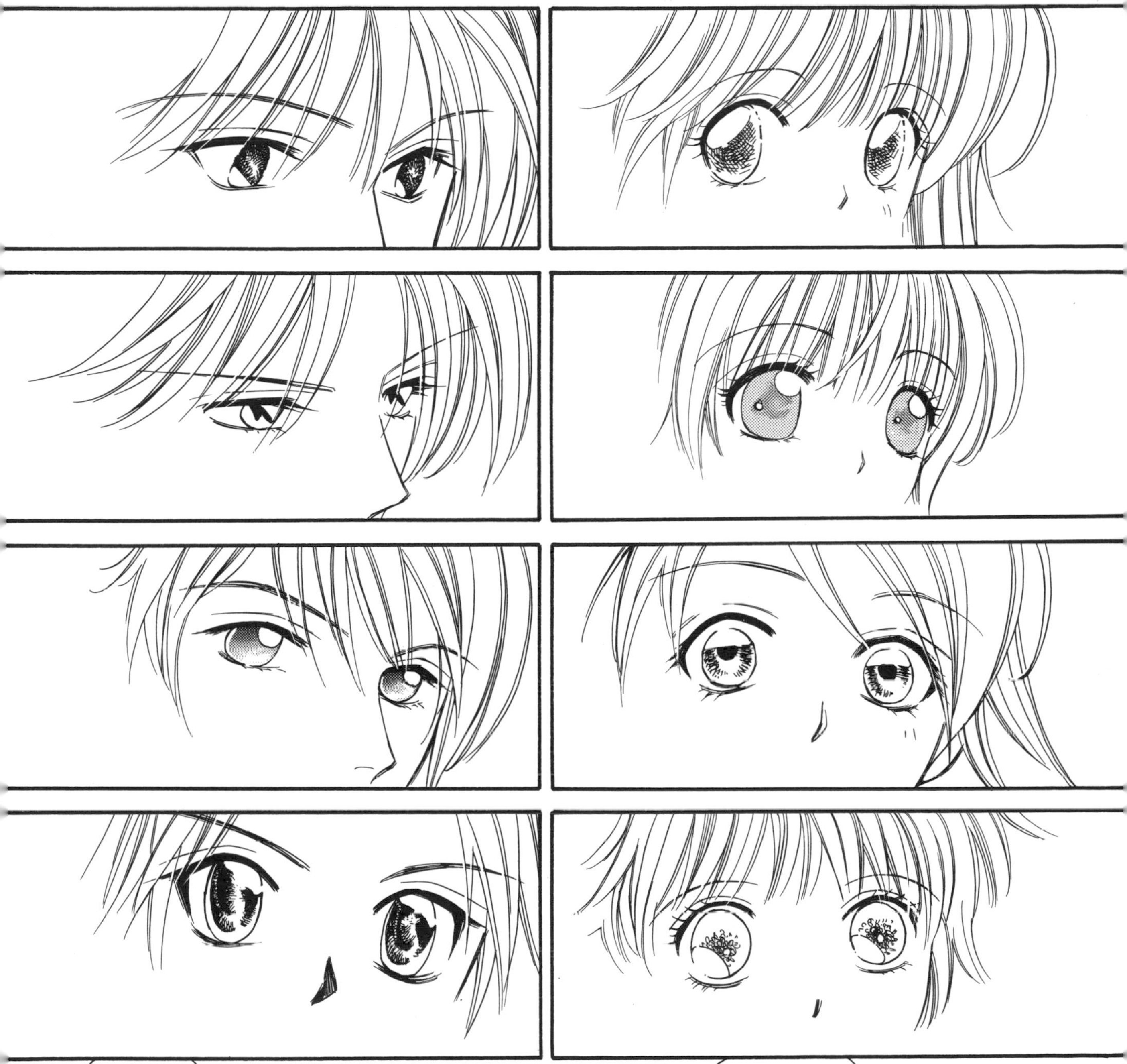

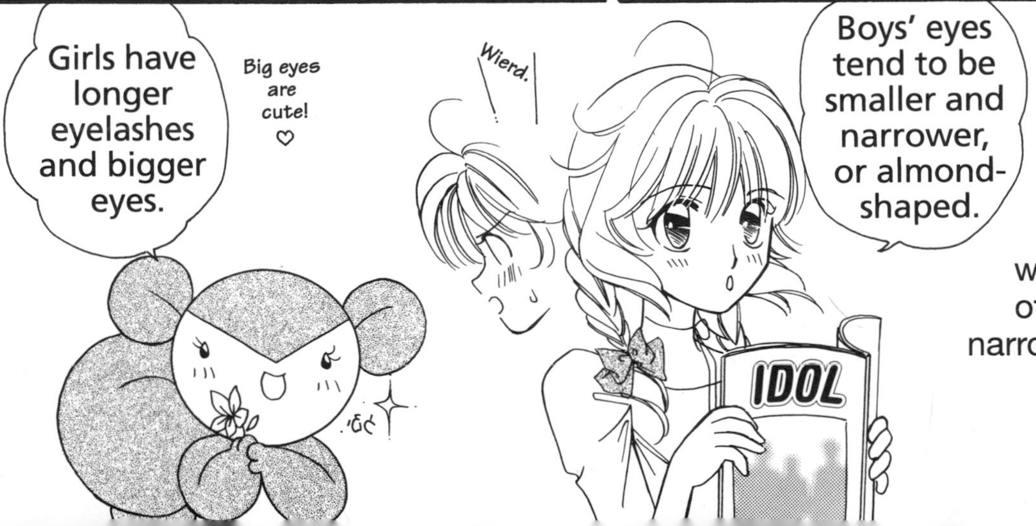
Girls have longer eyelashes and bigger eyes.
Big eyes are cute! ♡
Wierd.
Boys' eyes tend to be smaller and narrower, or almond-shaped.
IDOL

Children tend to have large, black pupils, while adult eyes often tend to be narrower or smaller.

HAIR

Straight, shiny black hair, shimmering golden hair... Try drawing all kinds!

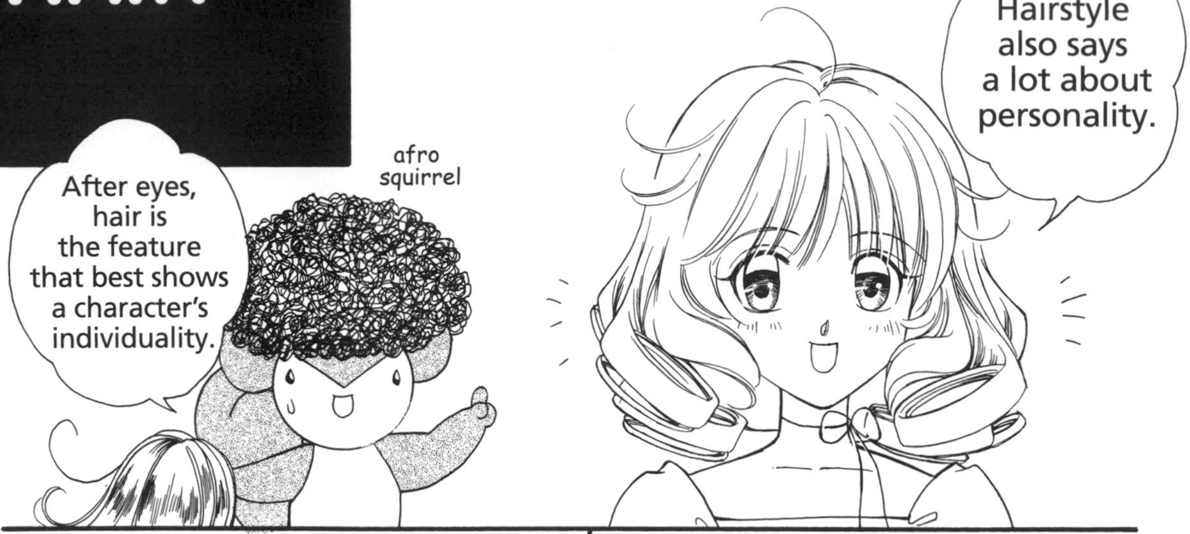
After eyes, hair is the feature that best shows a character's individuality.
afro squirrel
Hairstyle also says a lot about personality.

HIGHLIGHTS IN BLACK HAIR

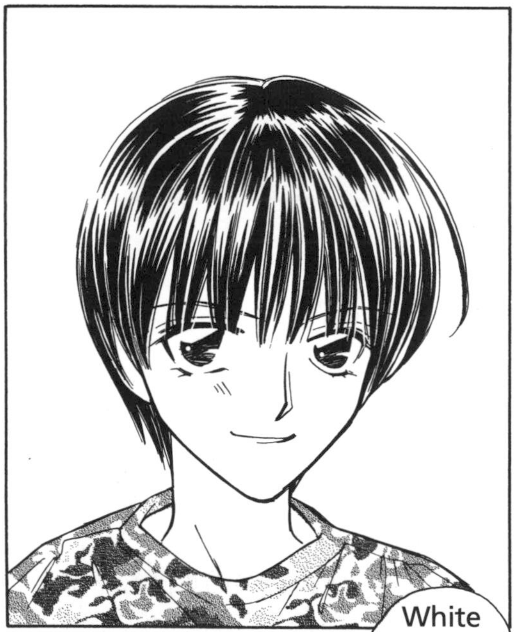

Leave some white to indicate texture and shine in black hair.

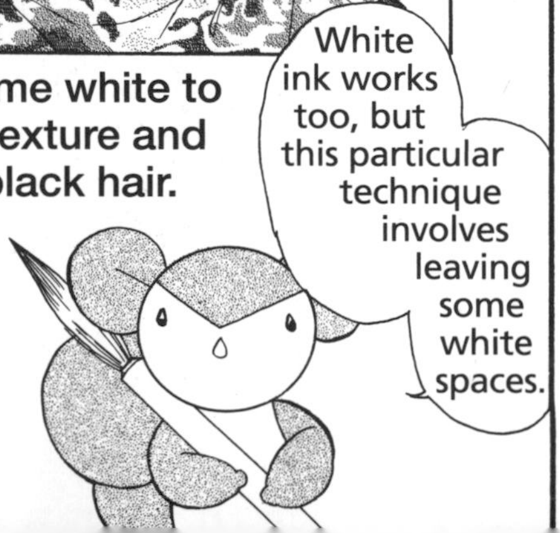
White ink works too, but this particular technique involves leaving some white spaces.

Ink in areas which do not catch the light.

1. Don't ink in areas which catch the light.

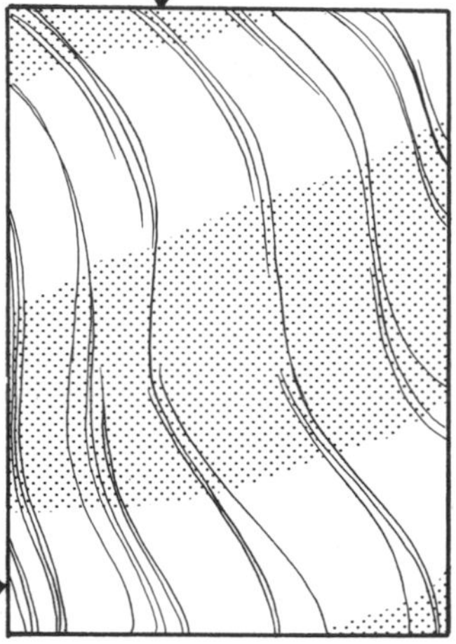

These areas should be left white.

2. Always follow the shape of the hair.

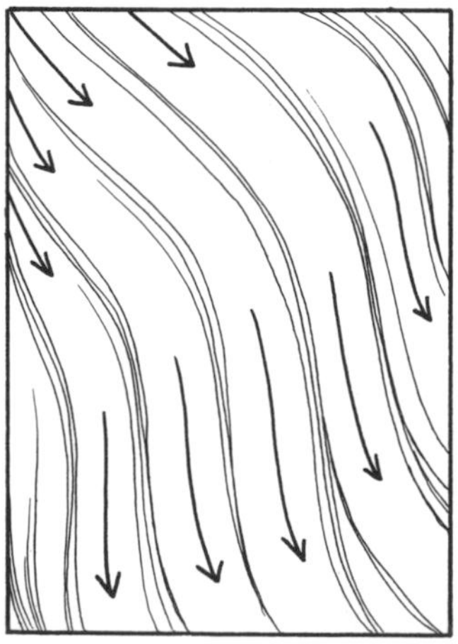

Stick to flowing curves—no straight lines!

HOW TO DO HIGH-LIGHTS

We suggest using a pale blue pencil to sketch in the highlights. This way, you won't have to erase afterwards.

But you can use an eraser over ink, like this.

Clearly mark beforehand the areas you wish to highlight. Marking the areas you wish to ink in with diagonal lines can be helpful.

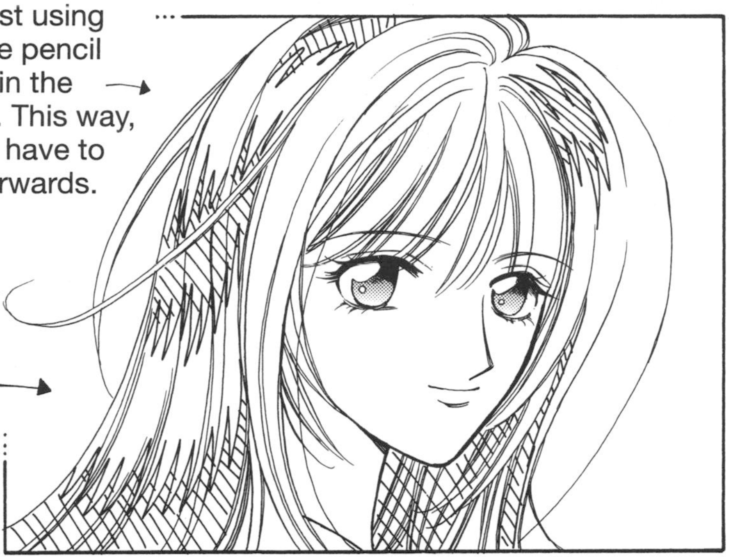

Sharp points are most effective.

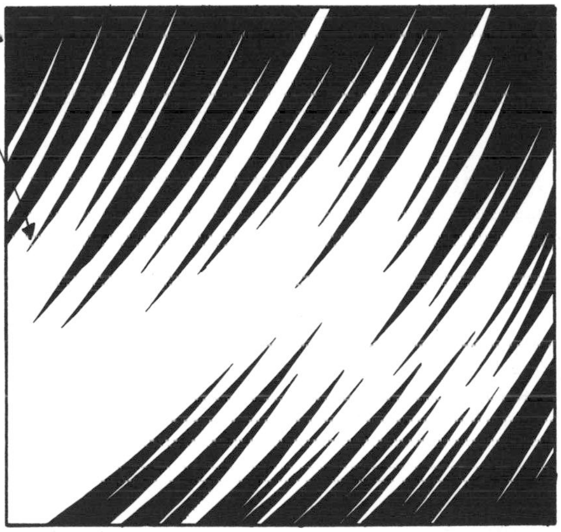

The knack is to brush lightly back and forth, like this.

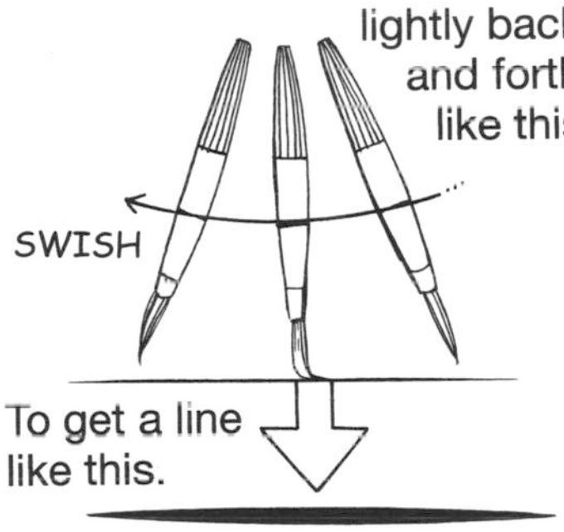
SWISH

To get a line like this.

Make clusters of lines, like this.

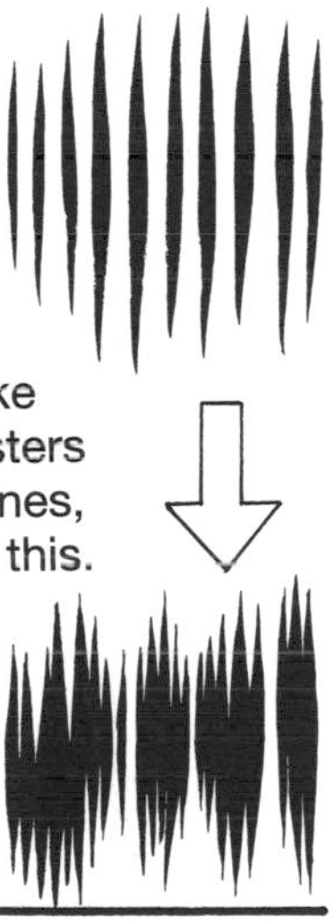

There are several styles of highlights.

Normal

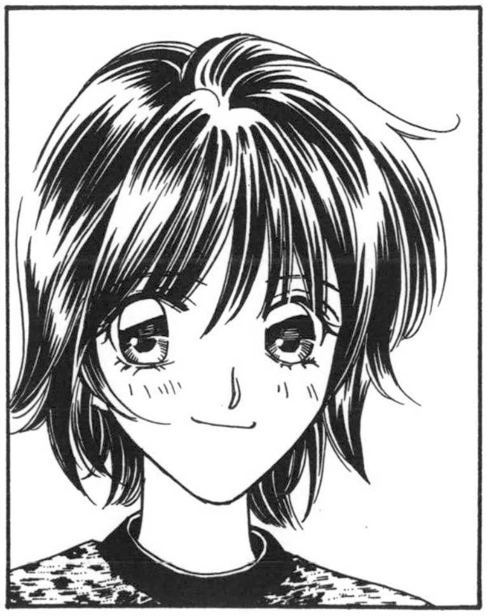

Streaky

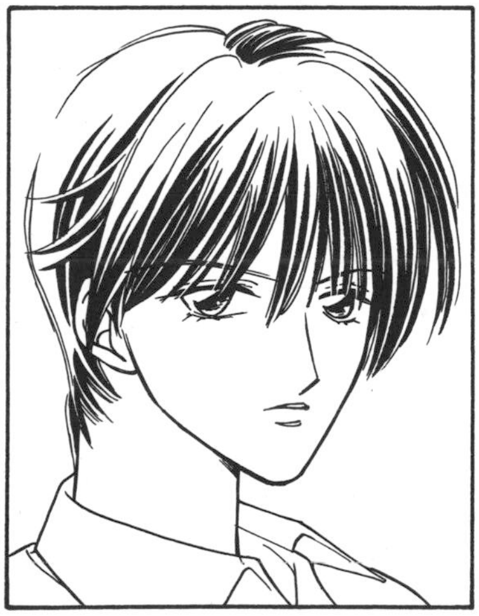

Animation style

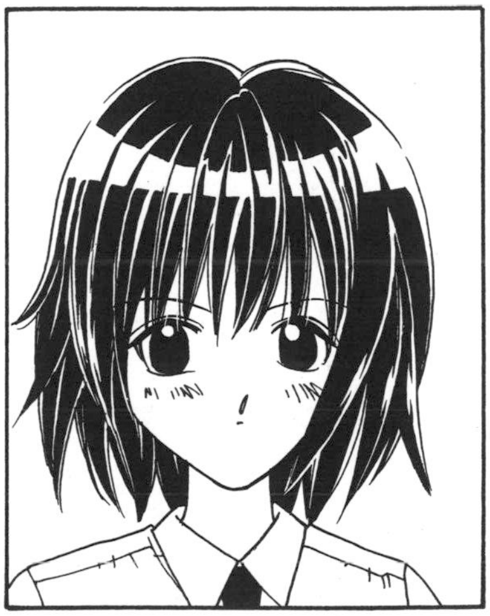

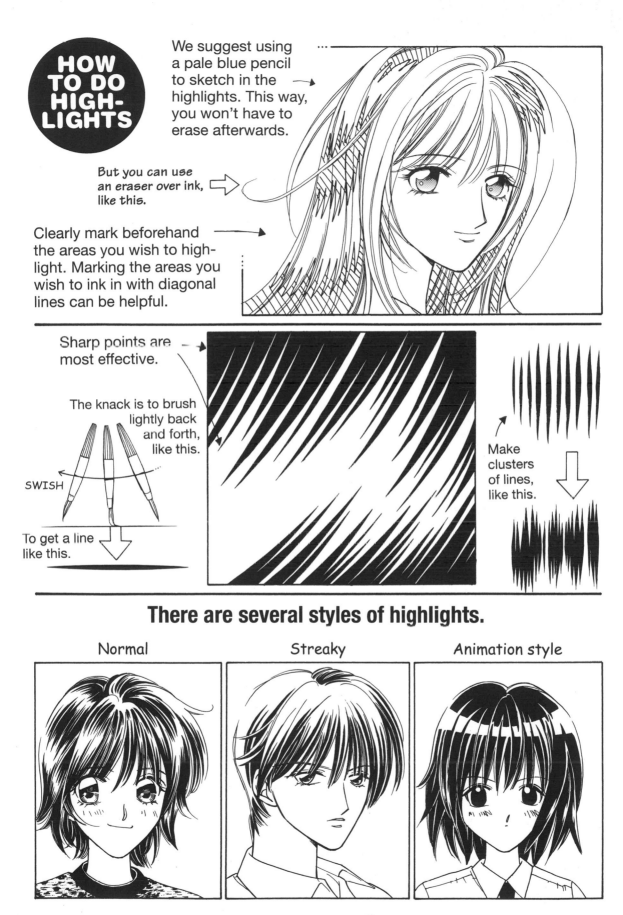

IMPORTANT!

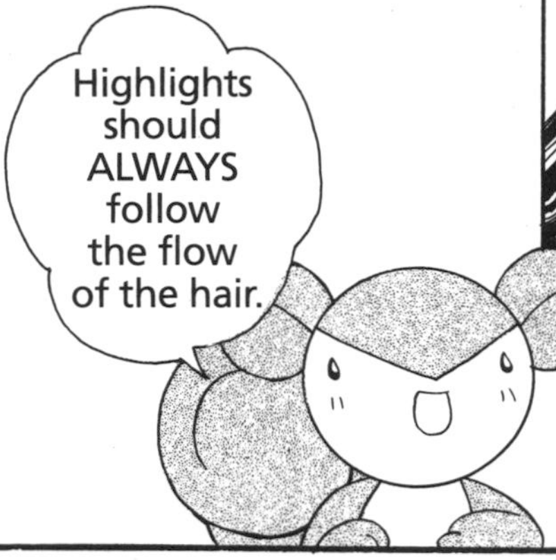
Highlights should ALWAYS follow the flow of the hair.

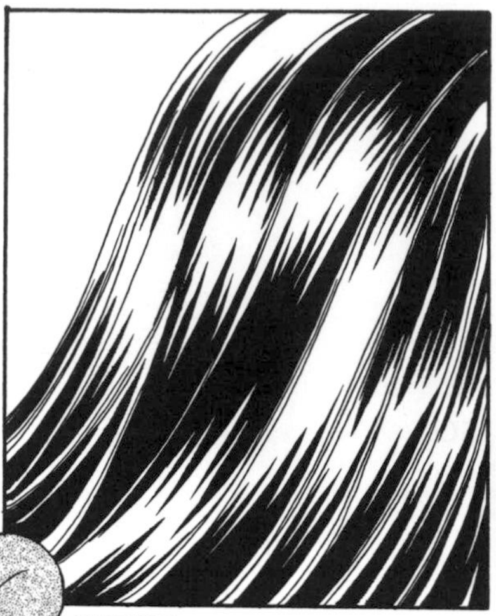

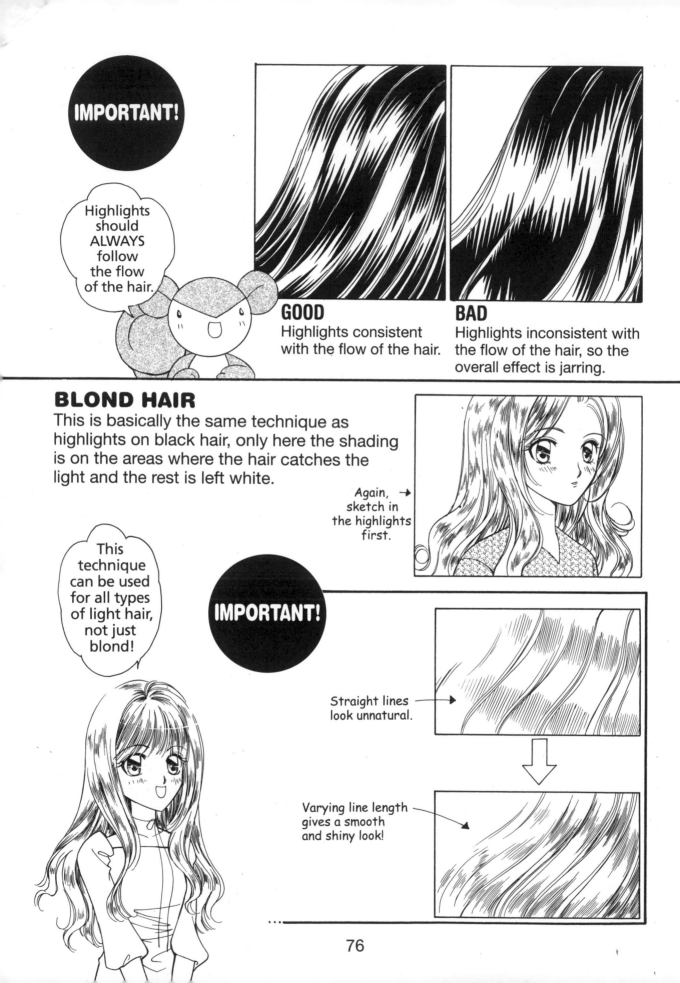

GOOD
Highlights consistent with the flow of the hair.

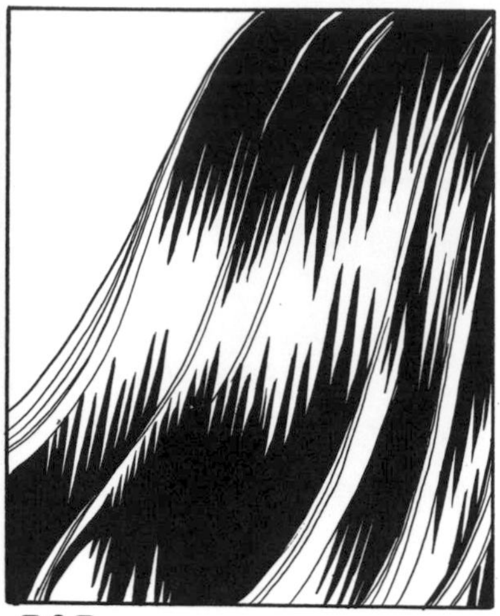

BAD
Highlights inconsistent with the flow of the hair, so the overall effect is jarring.

BLOND HAIR

This is basically the same technique as highlights on black hair, only here the shading is on the areas where the hair catches the light and the rest is left white.

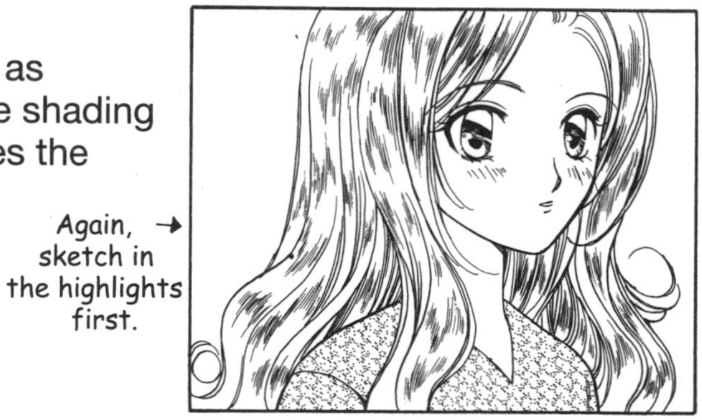
Again, sketch in the highlights first.

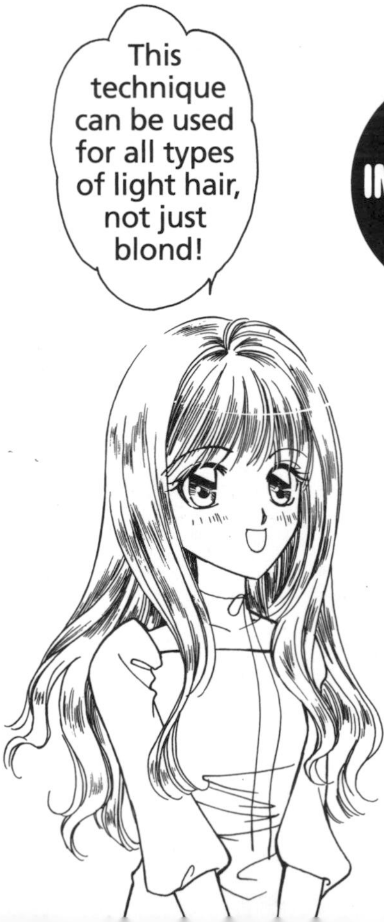
This technique can be used for all types of light hair, not just blond!

IMPORTANT!

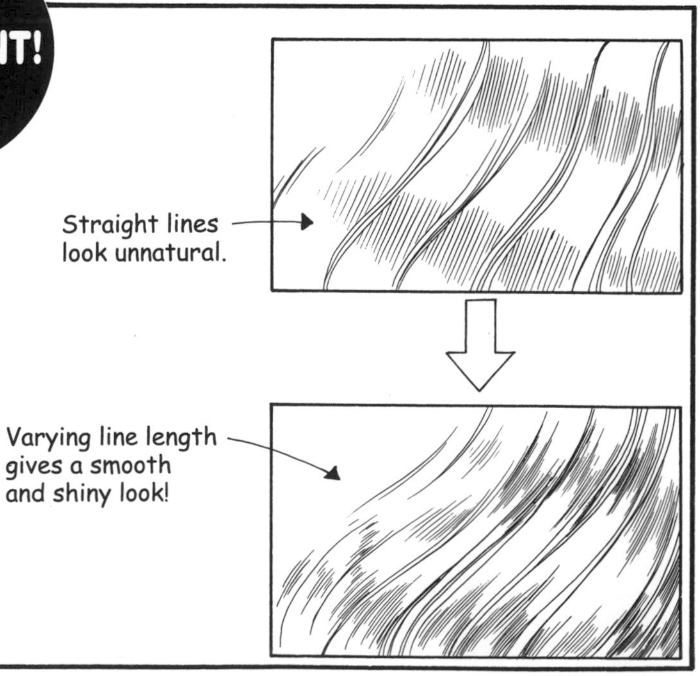
Straight lines look unnatural.
Varying line length gives a smooth and shiny look!

Screen tone comes in handy if you're drawing several characters, or for special effects.

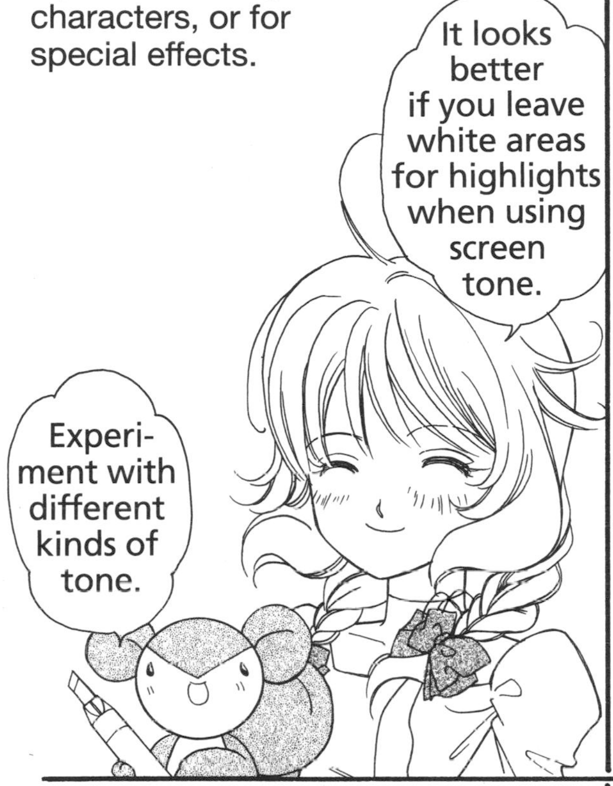
It looks better if you leave white areas for highlights when using screen tone.
Experi-ment with different kinds of tone.

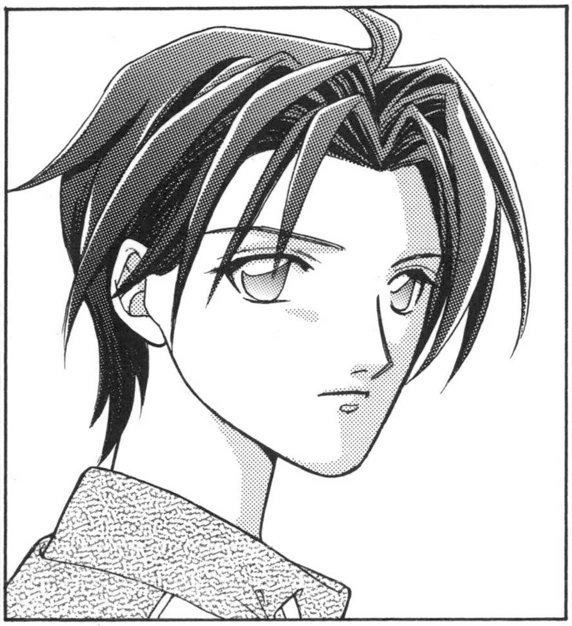

GRADATION TONE ON HIGHLIGHTS

You can use gradation tone on highlights too. Make sure the lighter tones are on top and the dark tones are below.

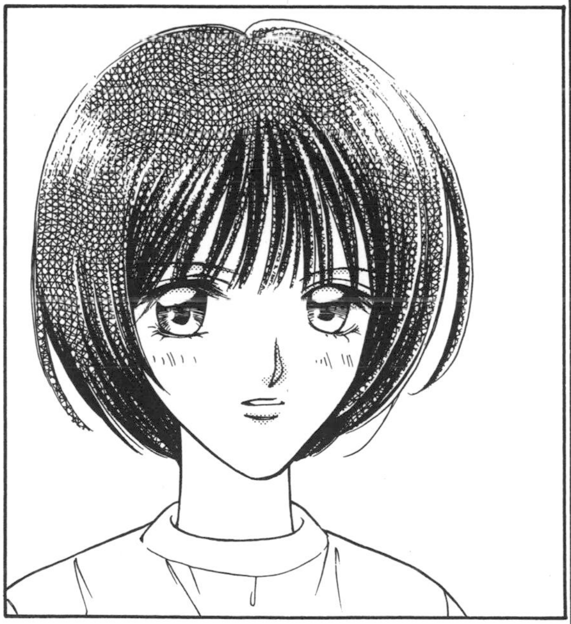

MESH PATTERNED TONE ON HIGHLIGHTS

Patterned tones are surprisingly good for hair. Here, the hair in shadow has been inked in, while a mesh patterned tone has been used on the hair catching the light.

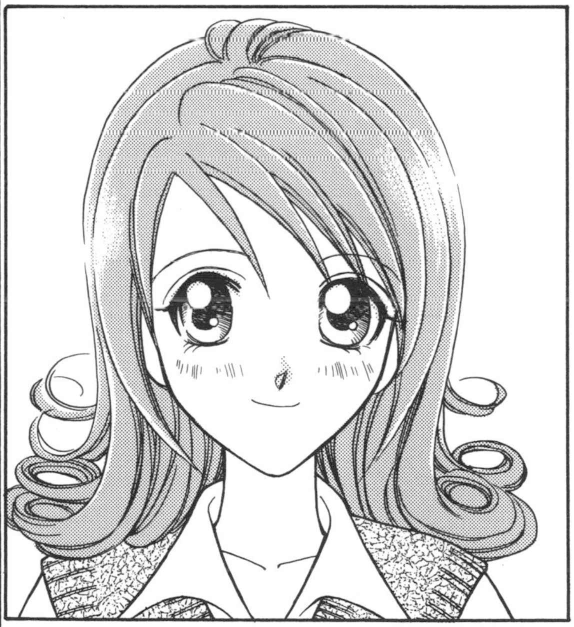

TONE AND HIGHLIGHTS

You can avoid an overly slick impression by scraping off bits of tone or adding highlights with white ink.

TIPS FROM A PRO
1

ADD SHADING!

You don't always need shading, but it does add a touch of realism and three-dimensionality. It's also effective for drawing attention to a frame.

If you want to add shading to a character, object or background, first think about which direction the light is coming from.

From the side?

Or from directly above?

It is essential to get this right, or your shading will look unnatural.

Shadow length depends on how high up the light source is.

Light from a low angle creates long shadows.

Light from a high angle creates short shadows.

From a low angle?

From a high angle?

ADD SHADING!

TIPS FROM A PRO 2

OK, so you've got the idea that the height and angle of the light determine shadow length and position. Next we'll show you how to add shading to faces.

HOW TO ADD SHADING

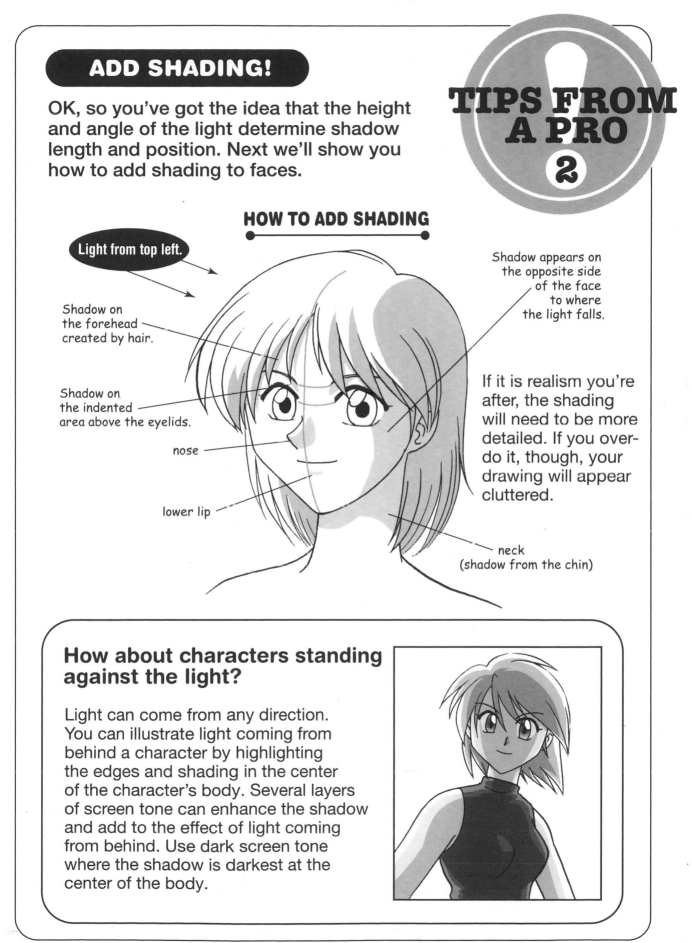

Light from top left.
Shadow on the forehead created by hair.
Shadow on the indented area above the eyelids.
nose
lower lip
Shadow appears on the opposite side of the face to where the light falls.
neck (shadow from the chin)

If it is realism you're after, the shading will need to be more detailed. If you overdo it, though, your drawing will appear cluttered.

How about characters standing against the light?

Light can come from any direction. You can illustrate light coming from behind a character by highlighting the edges and shading in the center of the character's body. Several layers of screen tone can enhance the shadow and add to the effect of light coming from behind. Use dark screen tone where the shadow is darkest at the center of the body.

TIPS FROM A PRO 3

ADD SHADING!

Light doesn't always shine with the same intensity. Use shadow length and different shades of screen tone to differentiate between night and day, and bright sunlight.

Shadows differ according to the quality of the light.

STRONG LIGHT
Use layers of dark screen tone. Make the shadows in the hair a little larger and add white high-lights around the clothing to emphasize the effect of strong light.

ORDINARY LIGHT
Outline the area to be shaded before applying the screen tone. Use 55–65 lines/inch 10% standard tone

WEAK LIGHT
Use low-density screen tone and blur the edges to get the softer feel of weak light.

Shading for effect.   Shading can radically alter a drawing.

INK

SCREEN TONE

This is used to indicate strong light such as a flash effect. Useful for adding drama or drawing attention to a frame.

The standard method of shading. Standard and gradation screen tones are the most common.

LESSON 3
SPECIAL EFFECTS

You can use special effects such as blurring
screen tone, dots, lines, mesh and flash effects
to express a character's emotions,
as well as for weather
and landscape.

SPECIAL EFFECTS

There are two ways of creating special effects: you can draw them by hand or you can use screen tone. Special effects can be used to dramatize or soften a scene.

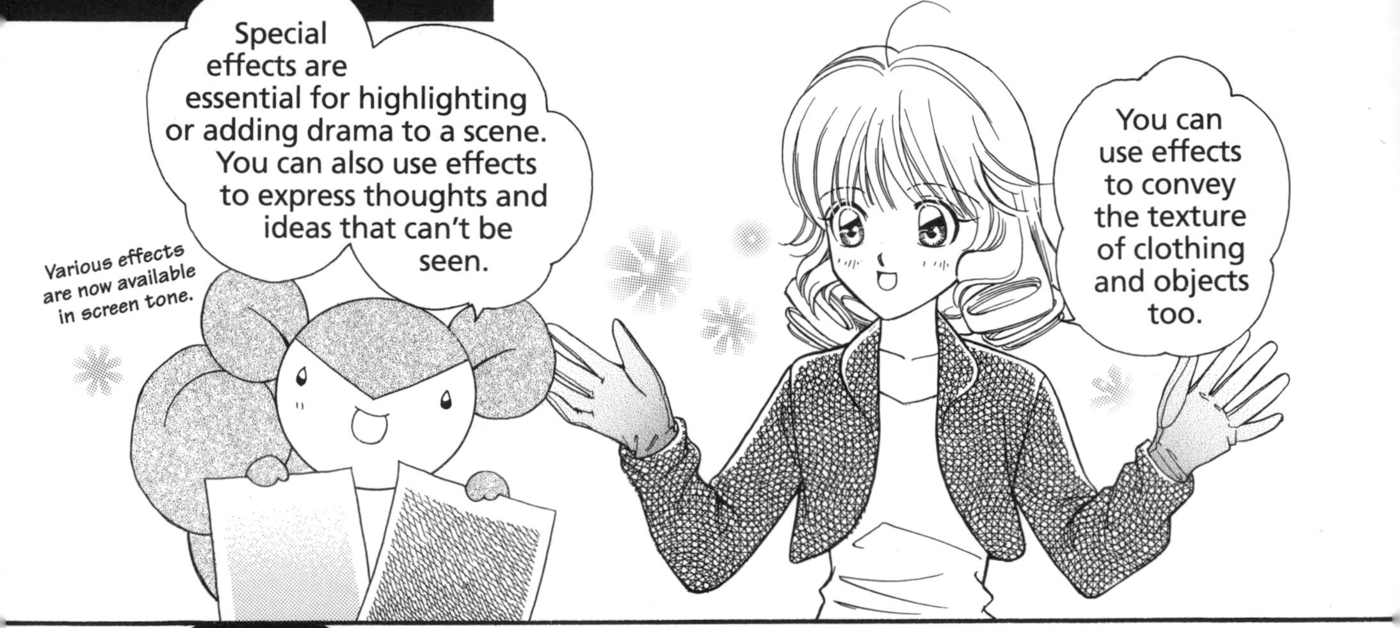

Special effects are essential for highlighting or adding drama to a scene. You can also use effects to express thoughts and ideas that can't be seen.
You can use effects to convey the texture of clothing and objects too.
Various effects are now available in screen tone.

HAND-DRAWN EFFECTS

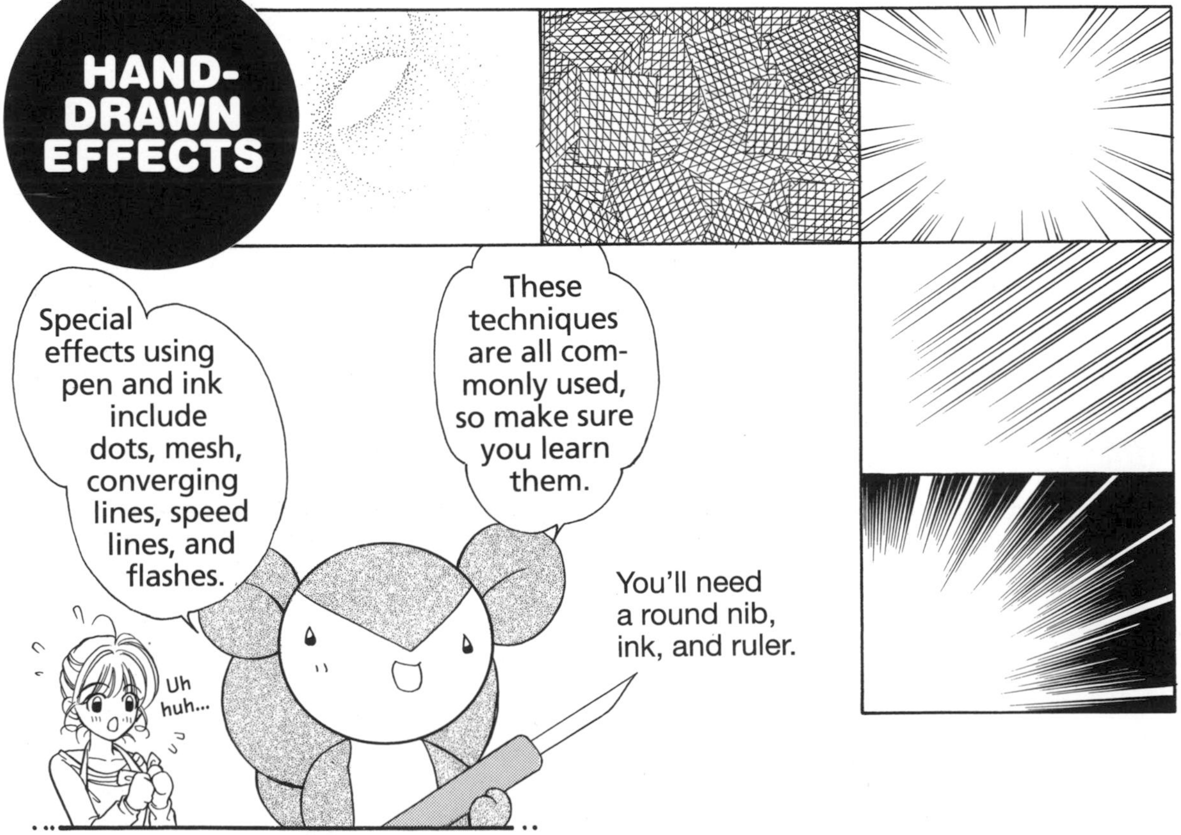

Special effects using pen and ink include dots, mesh, converging lines, speed lines, and flashes.
These techniques are all commonly used, so make sure you learn them.
You'll need a round nib, ink, and ruler.
Uh huh...

DOTS

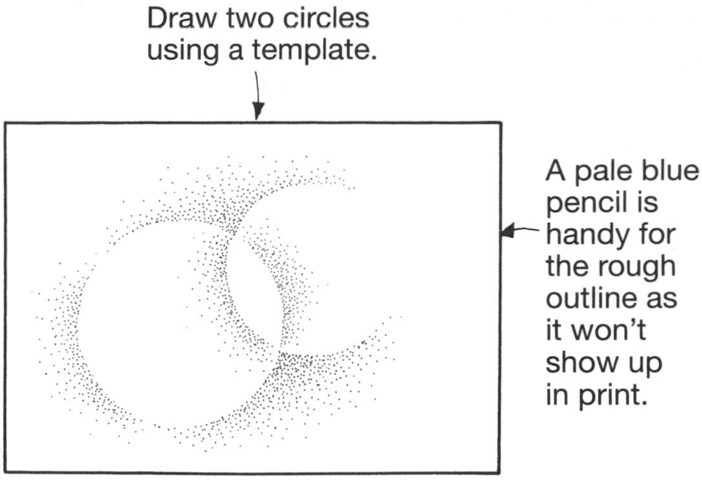
Draw two circles using a template.
A pale blue pencil is handy for the rough outline as it won't show up in print.

Try this!

This technique is often used in *shôjomanga* —the manga for young girls. It creates a light, glittery effect.

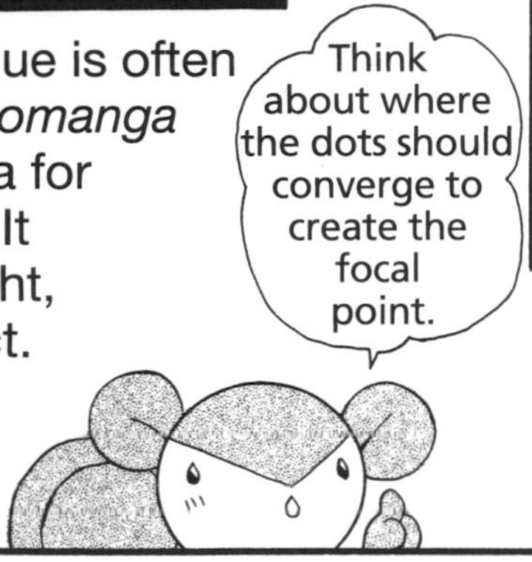
Think about where the dots should converge to create the focal point.

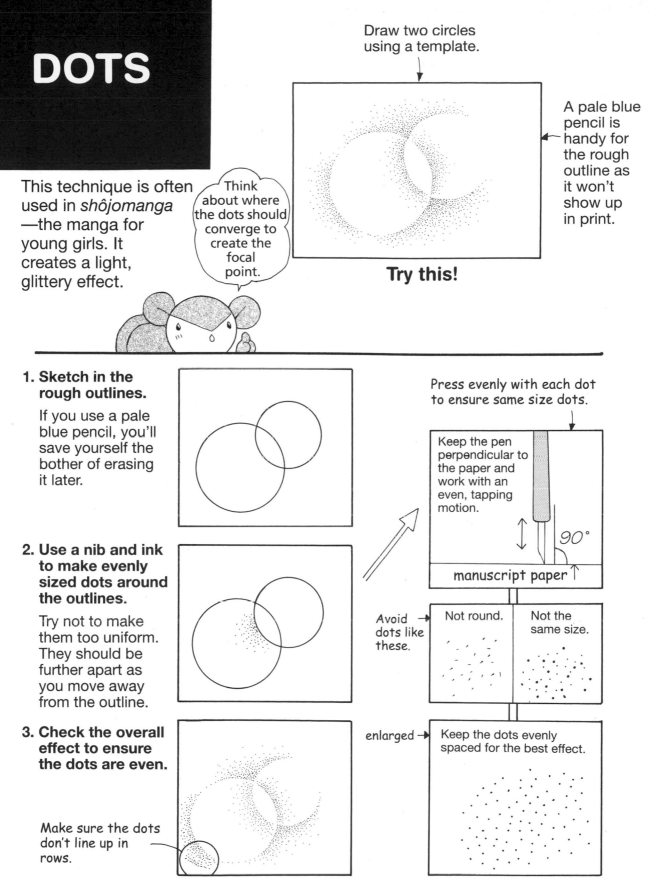

1. Sketch in the rough outlines.

If you use a pale blue pencil, you'll save yourself the bother of erasing it later.

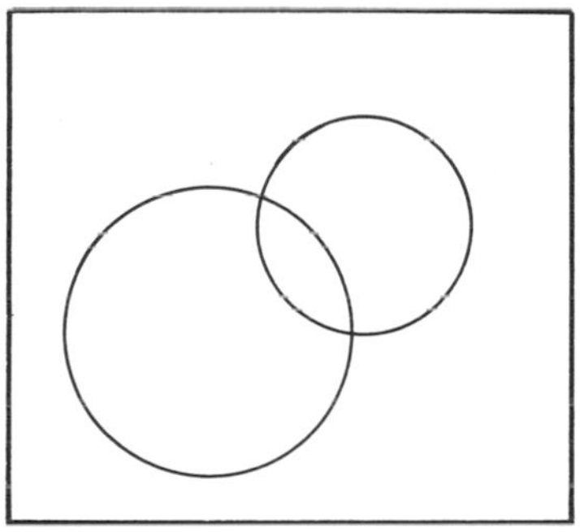

2. Use a nib and ink to make evenly sized dots around the outlines.

Try not to make them too uniform. They should be further apart as you move away from the outline.

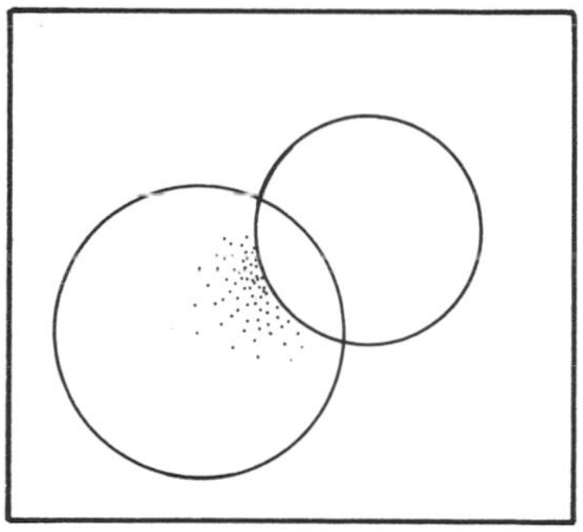

3. Check the overall effect to ensure the dots are even.

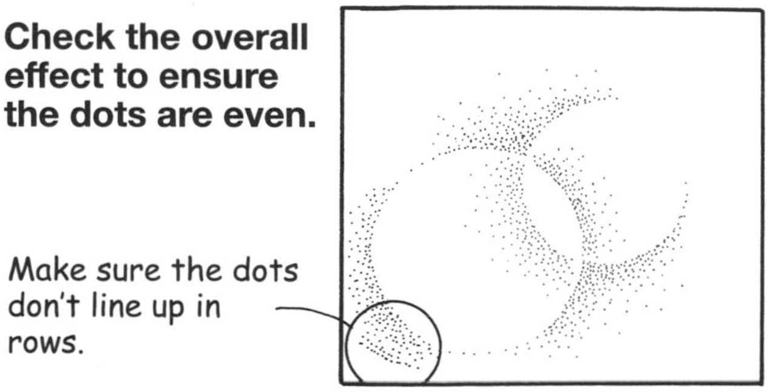
Make sure the dots don't line up in rows.

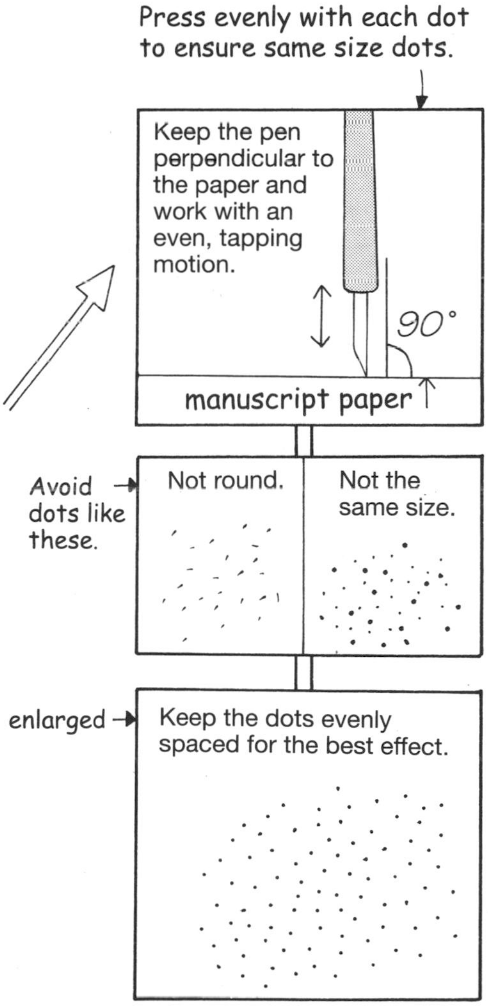
Press evenly with each dot to ensure same size dots.
Keep the pen perpendicular to the paper and work with an even, tapping motion.
90°
manuscript paper
Avoid dots like these.
Not round.
Not the same size.
enlarged
Keep the dots evenly spaced for the best effect.

Use this technique to create all sorts of patterns.

MESH

There are several kinds of mesh effects, including 2-line, 3-line, and 4-line mesh, rope mesh and gradation mesh. Here we'll show you how to do 3-line, 4-line, rope and gradation mesh effects.

Using mesh takes a bit of getting used to, but it's worth learning as you can use it in so many ways.

Mesh squirrel

Oh my!

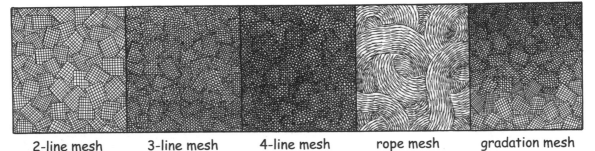

| 2-line mesh | 3-line mesh | 4-line mesh | rope mesh | gradation mesh |

HOW TO DRAW A BASIC MESH

Most artists draw freehand, but if you really can't draw straight lines, use a ruler.

The trick is to make the distance between the lines consistent.

Practice makes perfect!

The mesh effect is created with vertical, diagonal and horizontal lines.

3-line mesh and 4-line meshes are drawn like this.

3-line mesh

4-line mesh

1. Draw the rough outline of a box.

It's best to use a pale blue pencil.

Hang in there!
The beauty of this technique is that nobody can tell where you started drawing.

2. Now add more boxes, overlapping them at various angles.

Make sure all the boxes are the same shape and size throughout.

Don't make your boxes too regular or you'll spoil the effect.

3. Now fill in the boxes with your chosen mesh effect.

Use the same technique for 3-line and 4-line mesh.

FINISHED!

IMPORTANT!

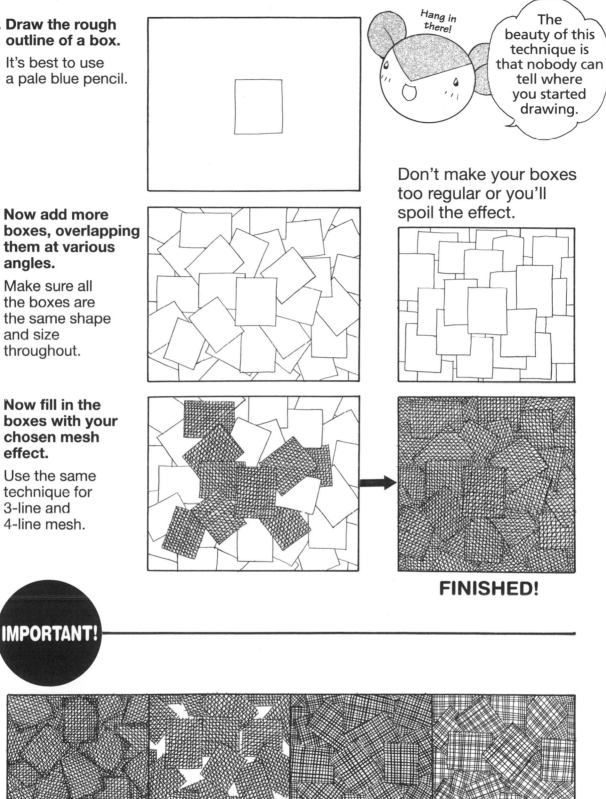

Too much overlapping creates dark patches.

Don't leave white patches.

Some lines too thick.

Lines not evenly spaced.

HOW TO DRAW GRADATION MESH

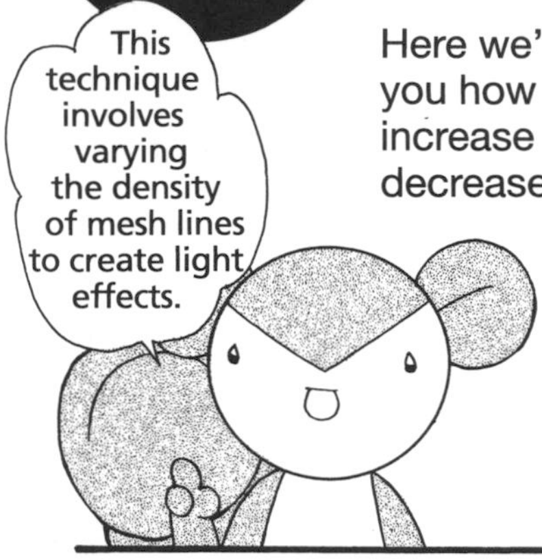
This technique involves varying the density of mesh lines to create light effects.

There are two kinds of gradation mesh.

Here we'll show you how to increase or decrease lines.

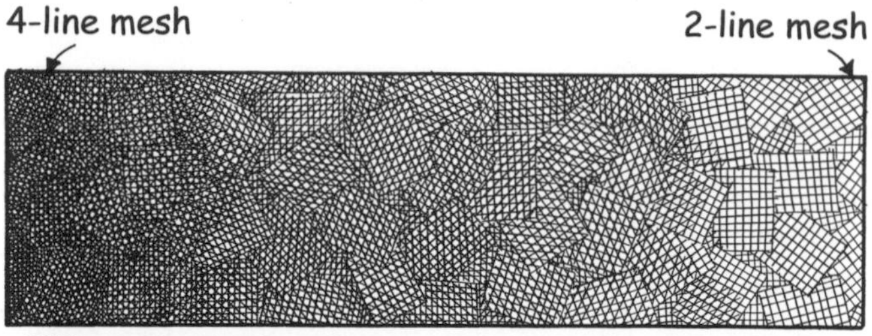
4-line mesh
2-line mesh

Different types of mesh are used, gradually decreasing from 4-line to 2-line.

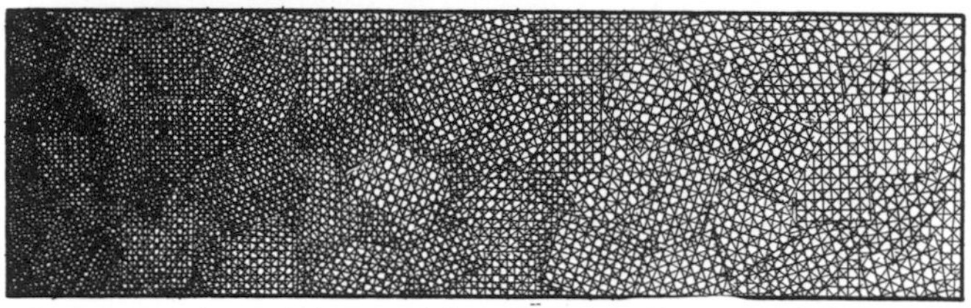

One type of mesh is used, but the density in each box is gradually decreased.

---

1. Use the same technique as before.

This time draw the first box where the mesh should be lightest.

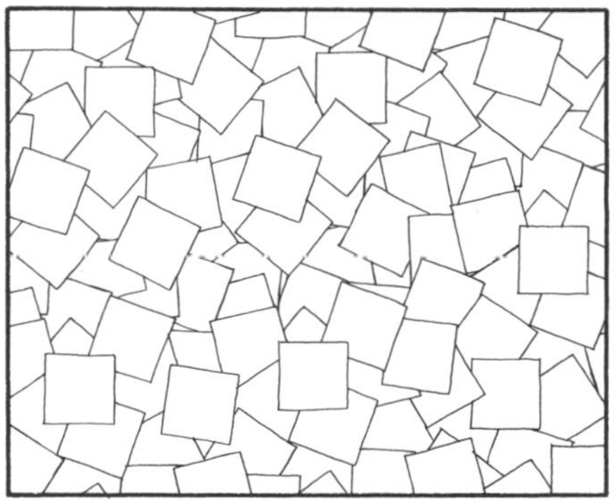

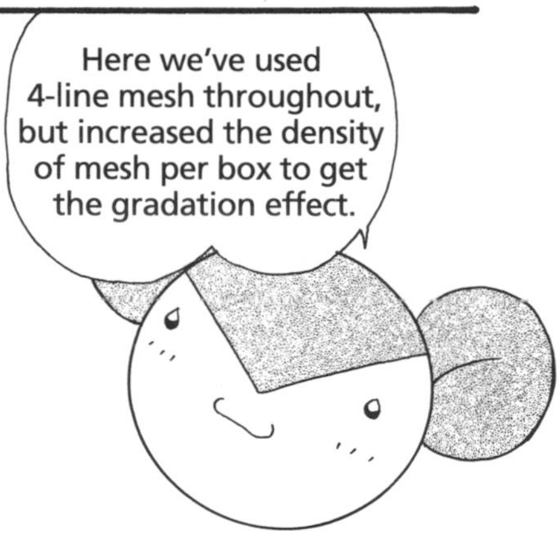
Here we've used 4-line mesh throughout, but increased the density of mesh per box to get the gradation effect.

2. Add in the mesh.

The more lines you use per box, the darker the mesh effect will be, so gradually increase the number of lines per box to make the gradation darker.

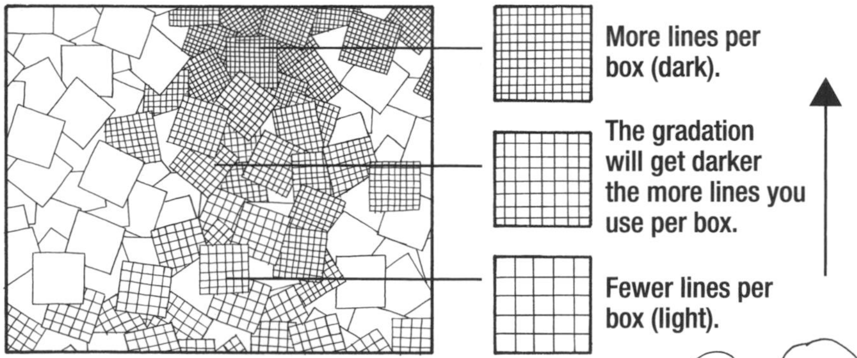
More lines per box (dark).
The gradation will get darker the more lines you use per box.
Fewer lines per box (light).

3. Check the overall effect and add finishing touches until the gradation looks smooth.

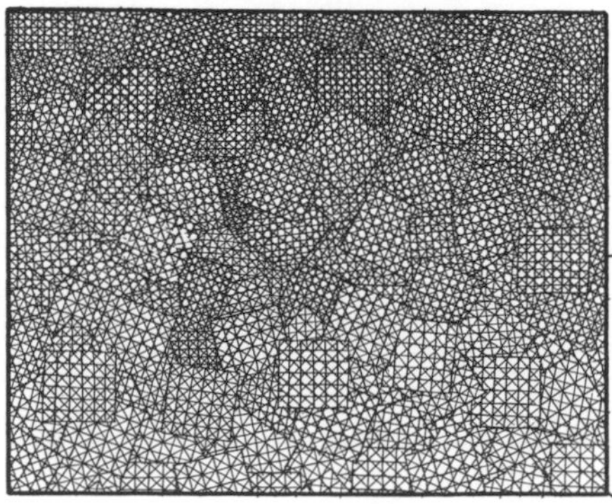

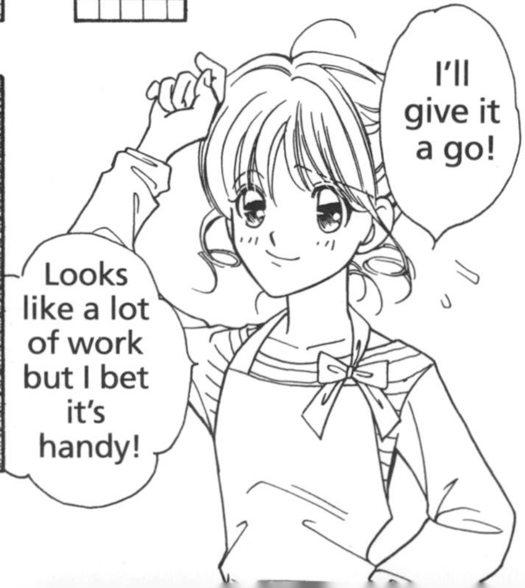
I'll give it a go!
Looks like a lot of work but I bet it's handy!

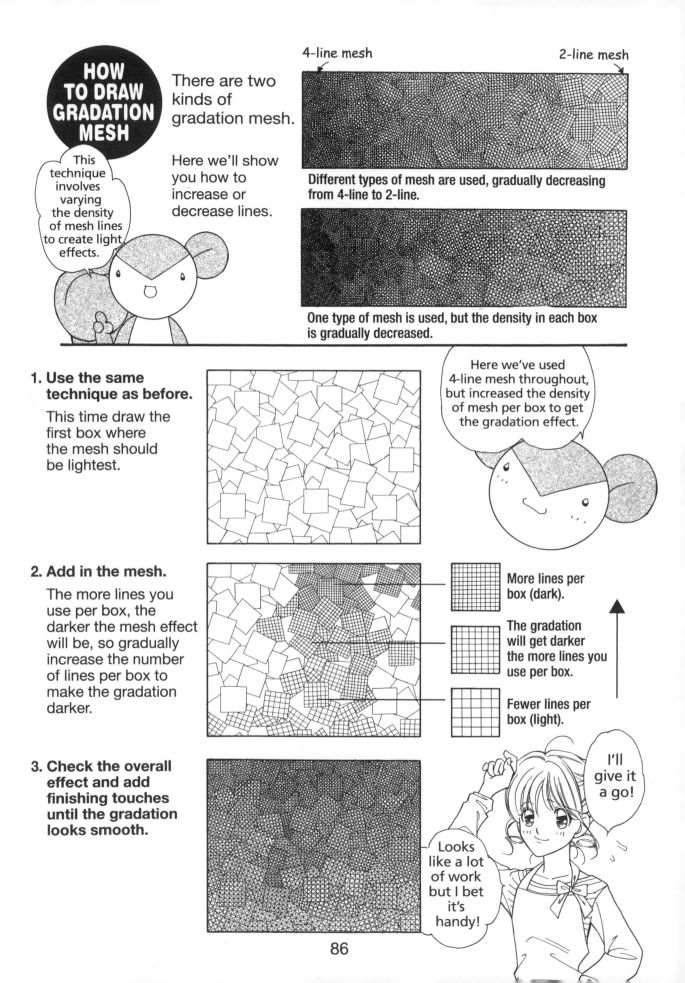

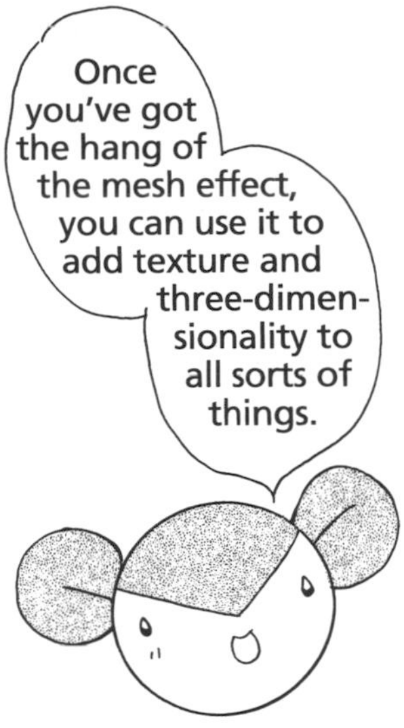
Once you've got the hang of the mesh effect, you can use it to add texture and three-dimensionality to all sorts of things.

Here we've used mesh on the walls and clothing.

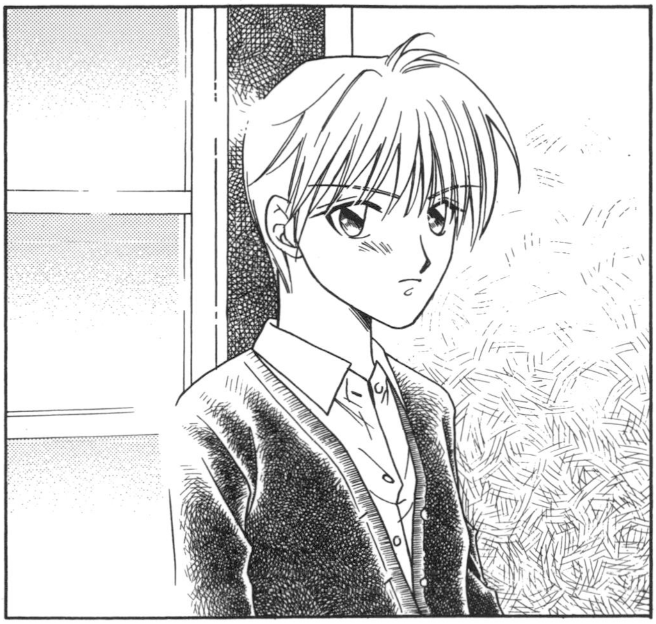

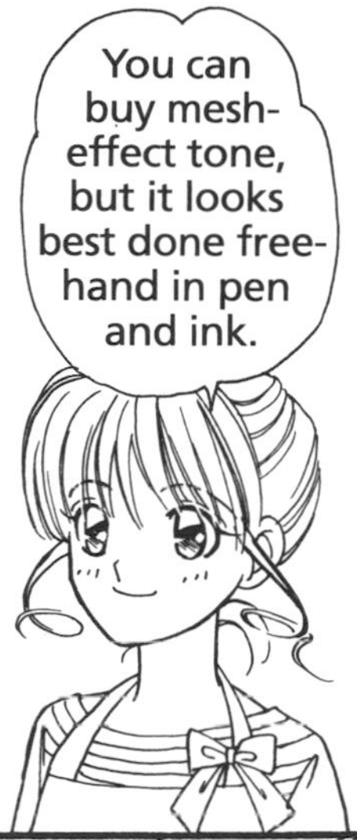
You can buy mesh-effect tone, but it looks best done free-hand in pen and ink.

CONVERGING LINES, SPEED LINES, AND FLASHES

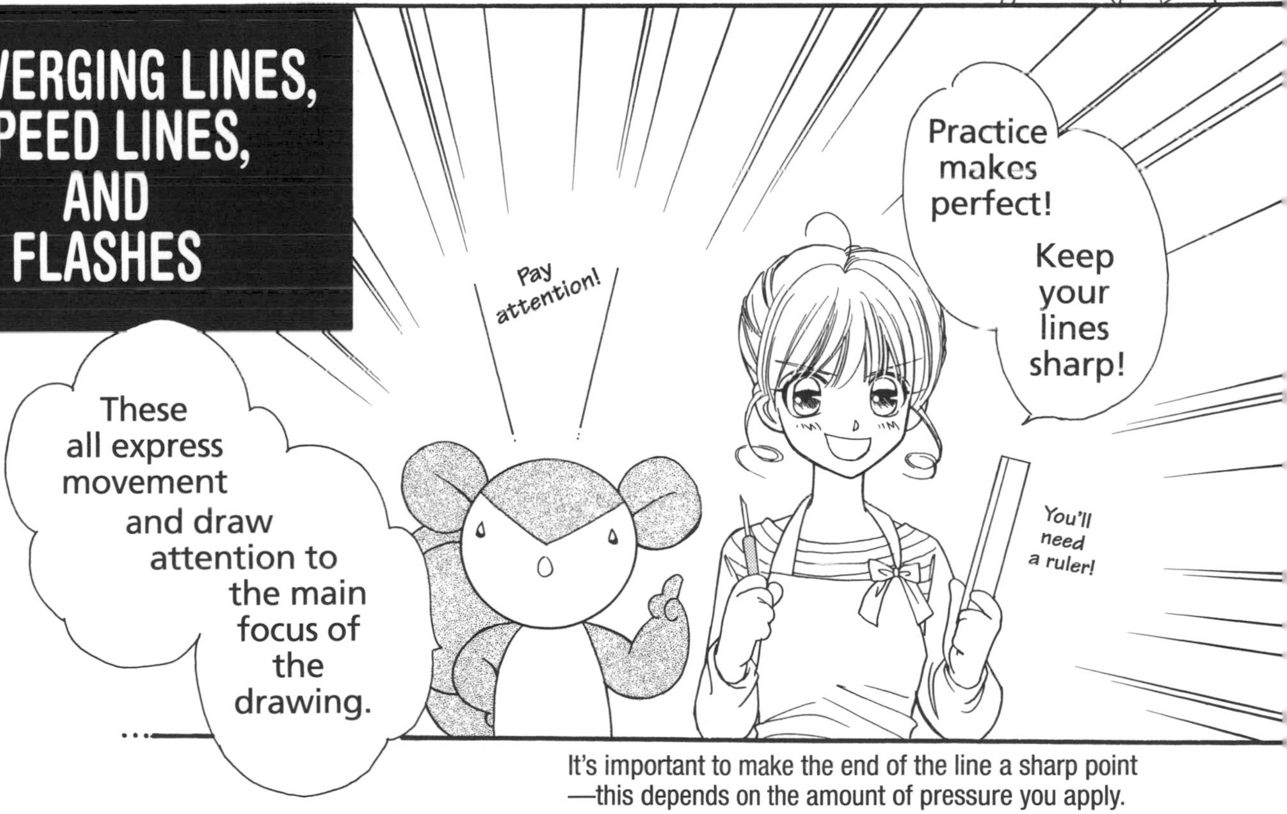
These all express movement and draw attention to the main focus of the drawing.
...
Pay attention!
Practice makes perfect!
Keep your lines sharp!
You'll need a ruler!

It's important to make the end of the line a sharp point—this depends on the amount of pressure you apply.

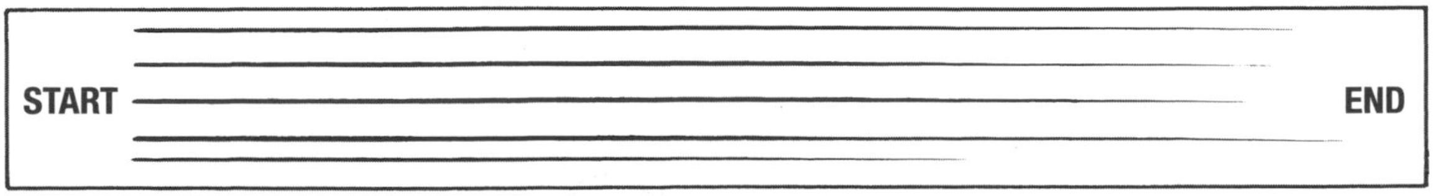
START
END

These lines have been drawn from left to right, like this arrow →

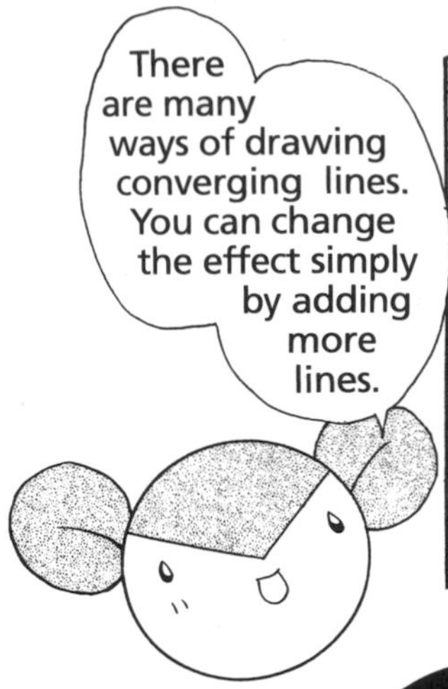
There are many ways of drawing converging lines. You can change the effect simply by adding more lines.

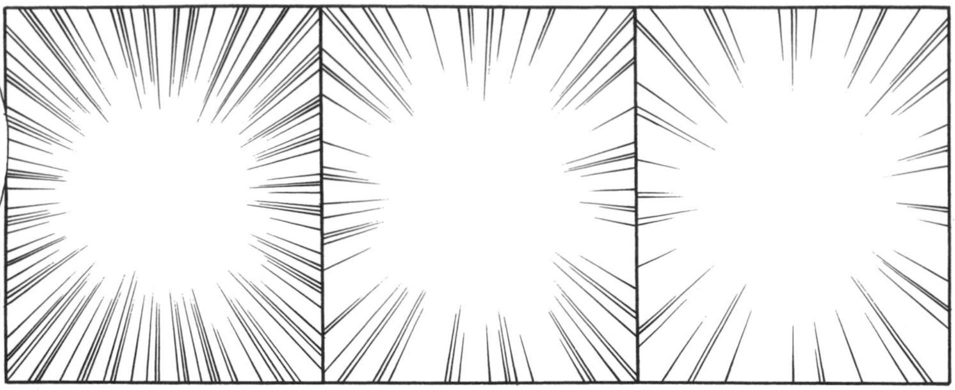

lots of lines | medium number of lines | fewer lines

HOW TO DRAW CONVERGING LINES

1. First, decide where the focus is.

Mark the point where you want the focus of the frame to be.

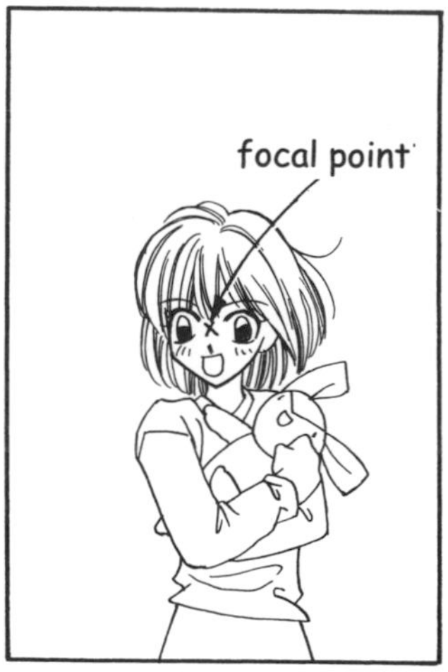
focal point

2. Roughly outline where you want the converging lines to end.

How far do you want the lines to go? Do you want them to touch the character or to create a sort of "halo" around them?

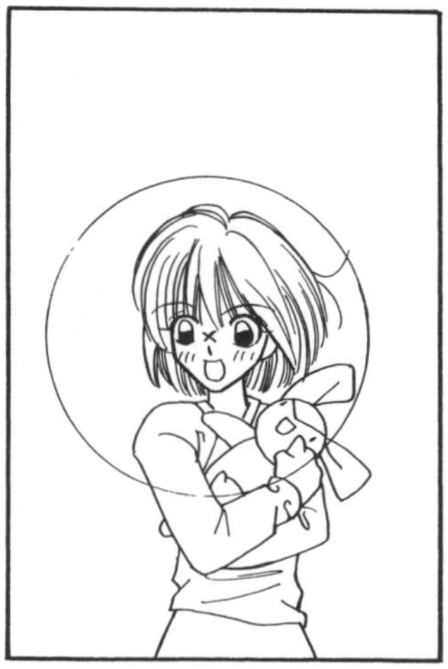

3. It's a good idea to sketch in the lines first, deciding on their position and density.

Remember a pale blue pencil is best for draft work.

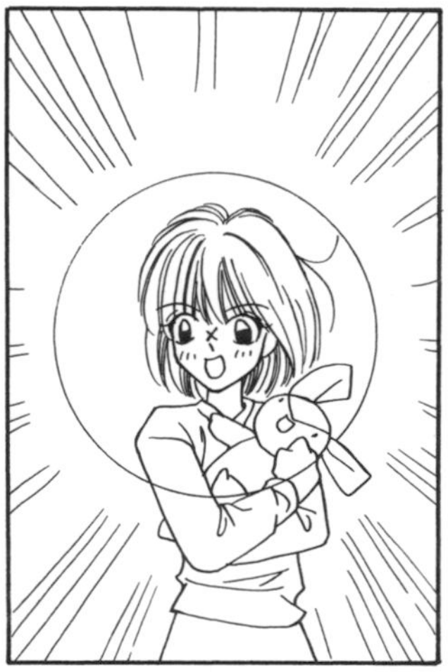

4. Use a ruler with a beveled edge and draw lines converging on the focal point.

Draw your lines from the outside in, moving counter-clockwise around the focal point.

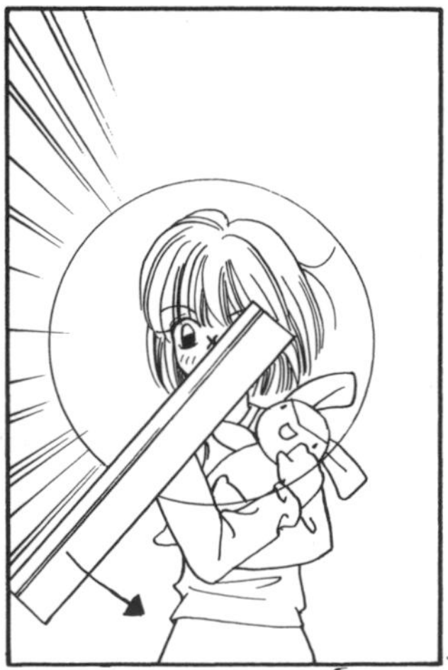

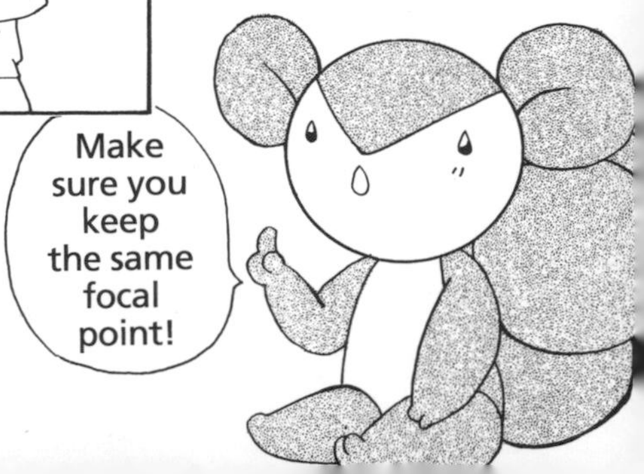
Make sure you keep the same focal point!

INEFFECTIVE LINES

These lines are → inconsistent and messy. Some parts are too thick, others too thin.

These lines ← don't converge on a single focal point. They're going all over the place.

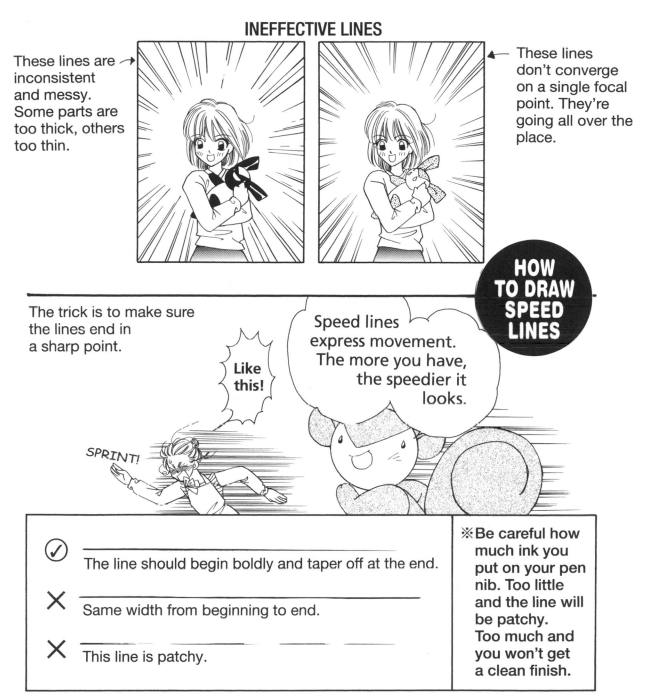

HOW TO DRAW SPEED LINES

The trick is to make sure the lines end in a sharp point.

Like this!

Speed lines express movement. The more you have, the speedier it looks.

SPRINT!

✓ _____
   The line should begin boldly and taper off at the end.

✗ _____
   Same width from beginning to end.

✗ _____
   This line is patchy.

※Be careful how much ink you put on your pen nib. Too little and the line will be patchy. Too much and you won't get a clean finish.

Fewer lines look slower.

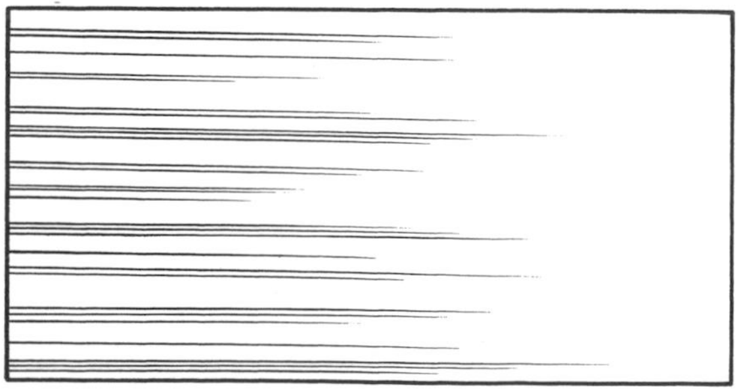

More lines look faster.

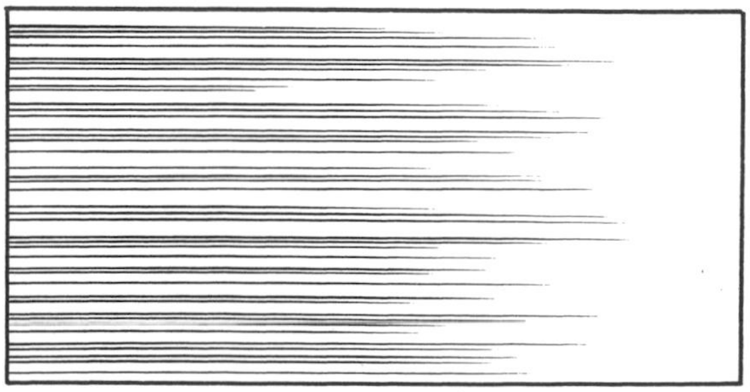

1. Sketch in the rough outline for the speed lines.

It's a good idea to use a pale blue pencil, and use a ruler to keep the lines even.

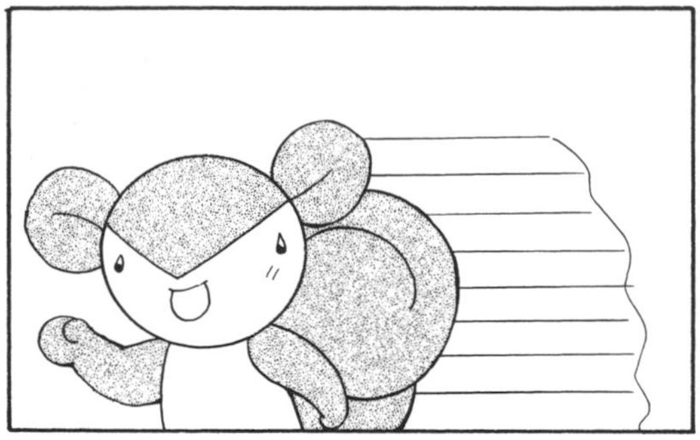

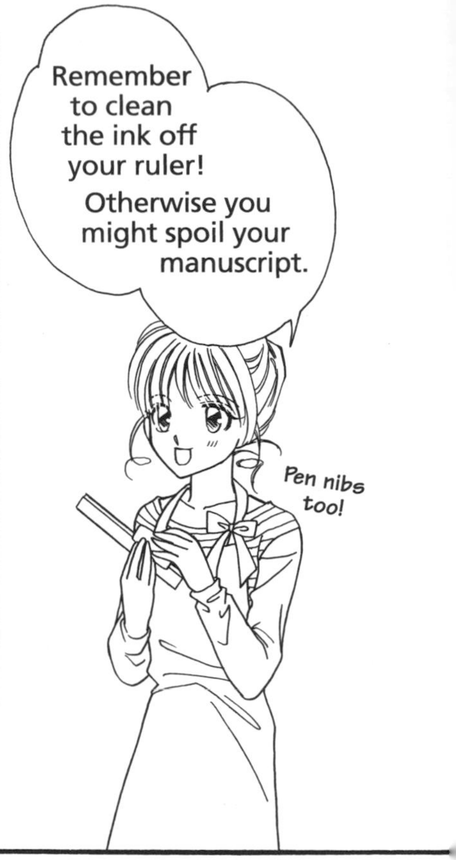
Remember to clean the ink off your ruler!
Otherwise you might spoil your manuscript.
Pen nibs too!

2. Be sure to use a ruler with a beveled edge.

Vary the lengths of the lines.

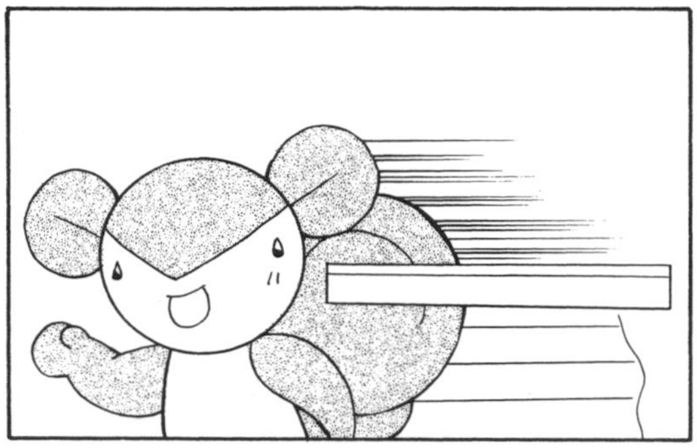

You can also try doing curved or vertical speed lines to show different kinds of movement and directions.

HOW TO DRAW FLASHES

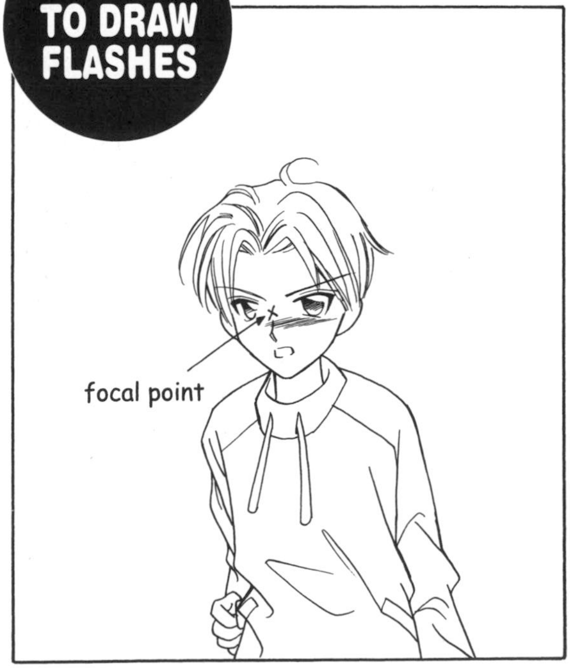
focal point

1. Mark the focal point in blue pencil.

Decide where the focus of attention should be in the frame.

This technique is perfect for that big climatic moment. It's good for both comic and serious scenes.

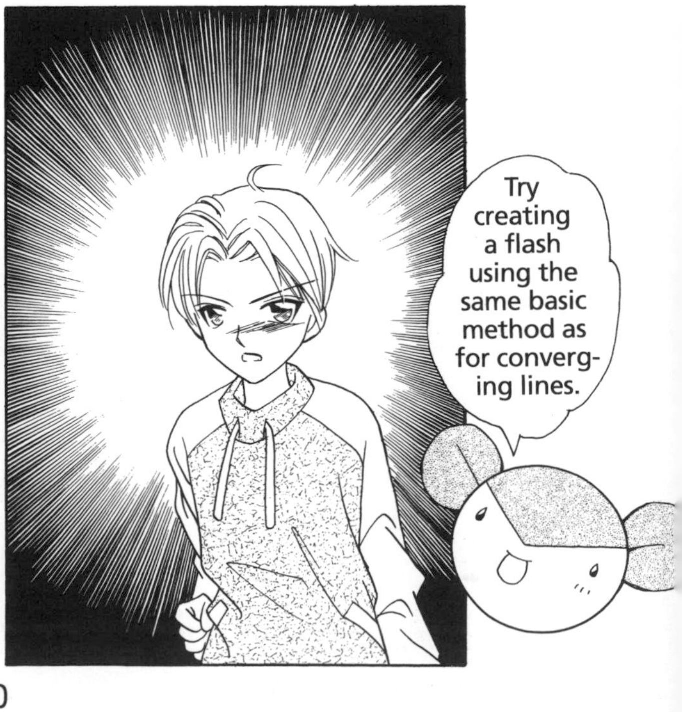
Try creating a flash using the same basic method as for converg- ing lines.

2. Sketch in the rough outline showing how far the lines should go.

This time also show where the lines should start.

Work counter-clockwise.

3. Draw in the lines keeping the ruler lined up with the focal point.

Press harder at the start of the line and taper off at the end nearest the focal point.

Draw your lines like this.

Make sure they're even.

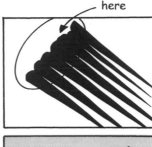

here

Make sure that the starting points of the lines are connected. This is the key to drawing effective flashes.

If you do leave any spaces, you can fill them in later with a brush pen.

4. When you've finished drawing all the lines, ink in the remaining edge of the frame with a brush pen.

Be careful not to damage the flash lines when inking in.

Don't get impatient! Pay attention to each and every line.

My mind's gone blank!

I'm going crazy!

Aah!

SCRIBBLE SCRIBBLE

HOW TO DRAW LIGHTNING FLASHES

1. Draw a few small flashes, and ink in the background.

It's best to make the flashes different sizes.

It's easier to use a small ruler.

You can get screen tone for this too.

2. Once dry, use white ink to draw in the lightning.

You can add a realistic touch by flicking some spots of white ink over the background.

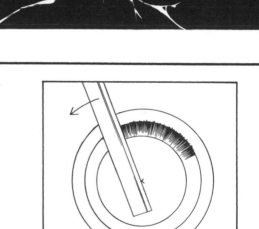

HOW TO DRAW 'SEA URCHIN' FLASHES

These can be used for all sorts of things —even speech balloons!

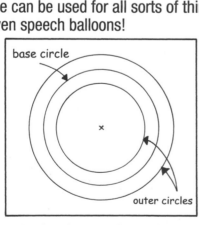

base circle

outer circles

Protect your manuscript to avoid damaging it with the compass point.

Something like this.

1. Decide on the focal point of the flash and using a compass or template first draw the base circle, indicating the starting point of the flash lines and then the outer circles to indicate where the flash lines should end.

2. Keeping the ruler lined up with the focal point, work counterclockwise around the base circle, drawing lines in the same way as standard flashes. It's easiest to go counterclockwise when drawing lines inside the base circle.

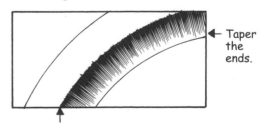

Taper the ends.

The starting points should be connected.

92

How to draw it!

Draw outline circles to indicate the length of lines.
focal point
outline circle

1. Decide on the focal point and use a compass to draw the outline circle. Keep in mind how many words you need to fit in to the speech balloon.

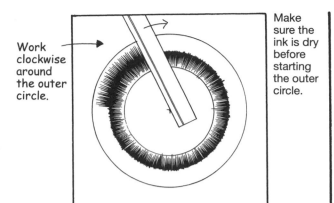

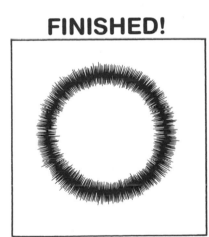

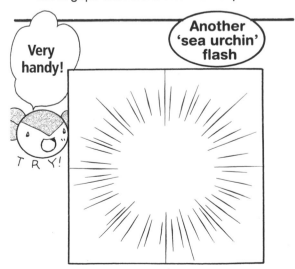

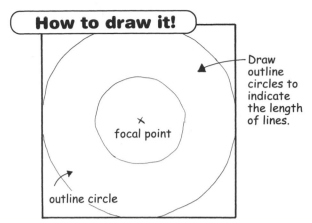

Keep your lines neat!

2. Keep the ruler lined up with the focal point and draw in the lines. As when drawing converging lines, create irregular clusters of lines of different length.

Work clockwise around the outer circle.
Make sure the ink is dry before starting the outer circle.

3. Now line up the ruler with the focal point, and draw lines outward from the base circle. Try not to leave gaps between the lines, especially at the starting points.

FINISHED!

4. Once you've finished the outer circle, check the overall effect to make sure there are no white patches left around the base circle. If necessary, ink in gaps with a fine line marker pen.

Another 'sea urchin' flash
Very handy!
TRY!

This is a really common style for speech balloons.

● Let's practice the lines!

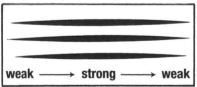

weak → strong → weak

The trick is to begin lightly, press harder midway, and end lightly so that the middle of the line is thick while both ends taper to a point.

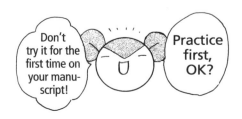

Practice first, OK?
Don't try it for the first time on your manu-script!

SCREEN TONE

These days artists often use screen tone for special effects.
All kinds of screen tone are available.
This screen tone's great!
You don't have to use just one type of tone.
You can get all kinds of effects by scraping away, cutting and layering a variety tones.

HOW TO USE SCREEN TONE—THE BASICS

1. Place the sheet of tone over the area where you want to use it. Use a snap-off blade cutter to cut around the shape, making it slightly larger than needed.

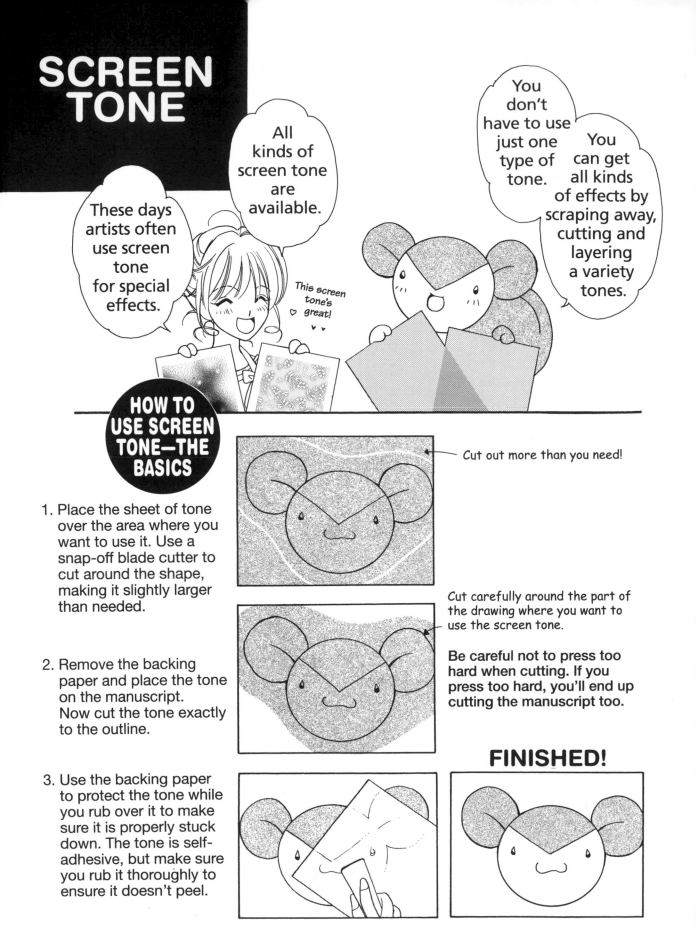

Cut out more than you need!

2. Remove the backing paper and place the tone on the manuscript. Now cut the tone exactly to the outline.

Cut carefully around the part of the drawing where you want to use the screen tone.

Be careful not to press too hard when cutting. If you press too hard, you'll end up cutting the manuscript too.

3. Use the backing paper to protect the tone while you rub over it to make sure it is properly stuck down. The tone is self-adhesive, but make sure you rub it thoroughly to ensure it doesn't peel.

FINISHED!

THE 45° RULE FOR SCREEN TONE

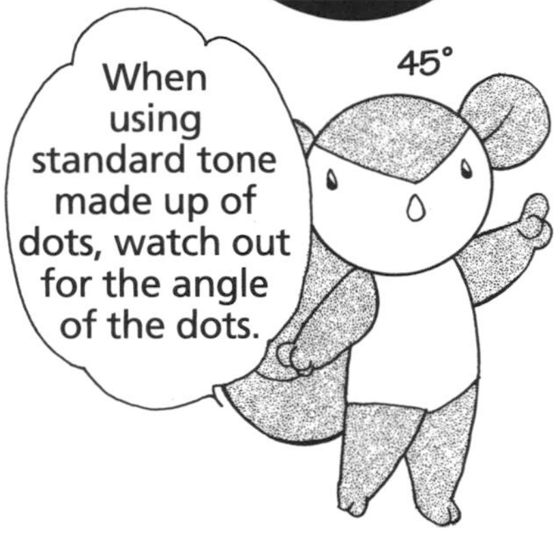
45°
When using standard tone made up of dots, watch out for the angle of the dots.

enlarged

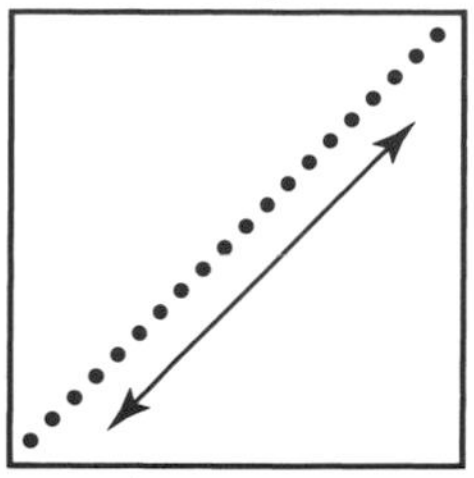

standard screen tone

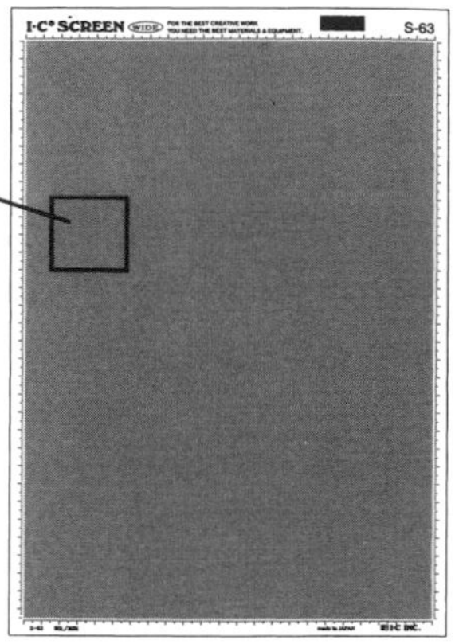
I-C® SCREEN
S-63

All standard screen tone is made up of dots lined up at 45°, as above. Remember to stick to this angle when using tone!

● **If you get the angle wrong, you'll end up with this sort of effect.**

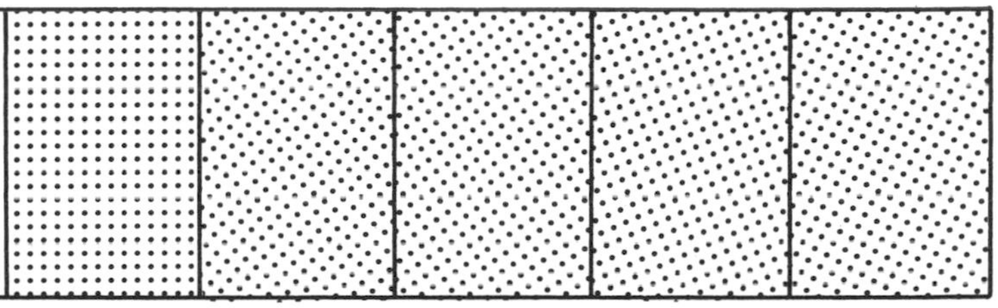

If the angle is wrong, it makes the picture look awkward.

Screen tone used at the wrong angle.

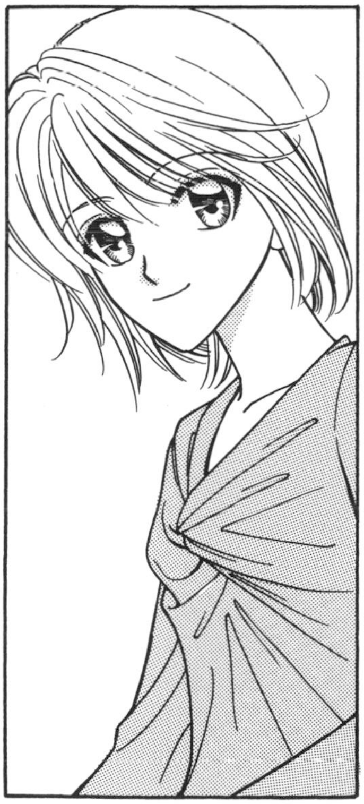

'Sand' and gradation tones are exceptions.

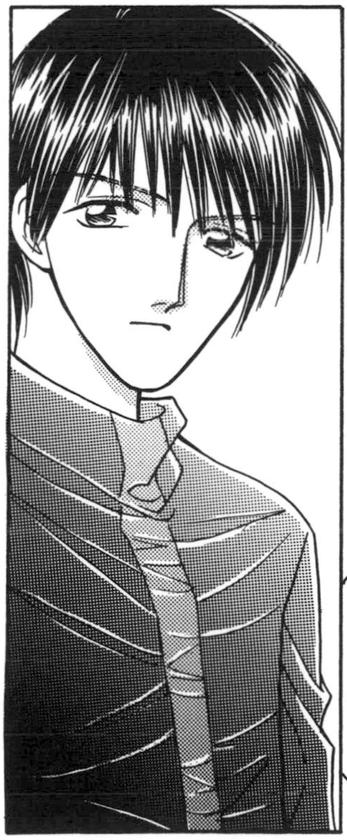

Fine dot 'sand' tone isn't printed at any particular angle, so you can use it any way you please. But make sure it is 'sand' tone—some screen tones may look like 'sand' tone but are in fact standard dot tones that need lining up.

Gradation tone is a variant of standard screen tone, but since the emphasis is on the direction and degree of light, the 45° rule doesn't apply.

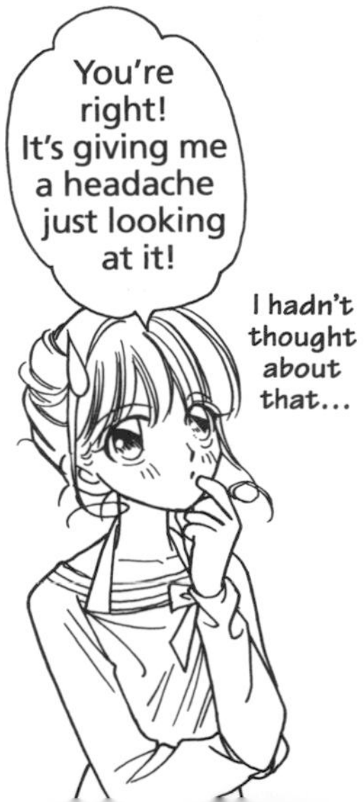
You're right! It's giving me a headache just looking at it!
I hadn't thought about that...

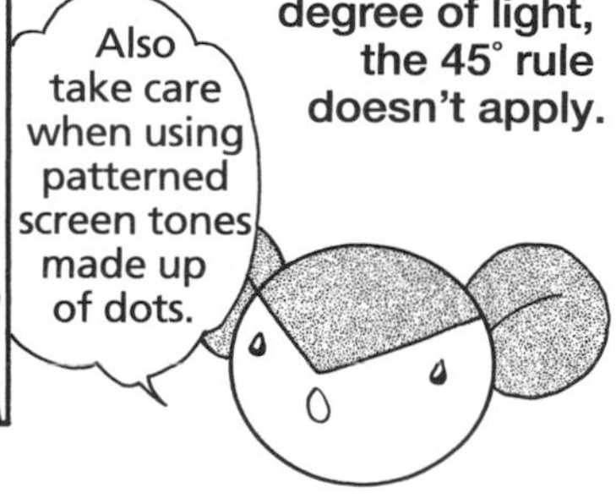
Also take care when using patterned screen tones made up of dots.

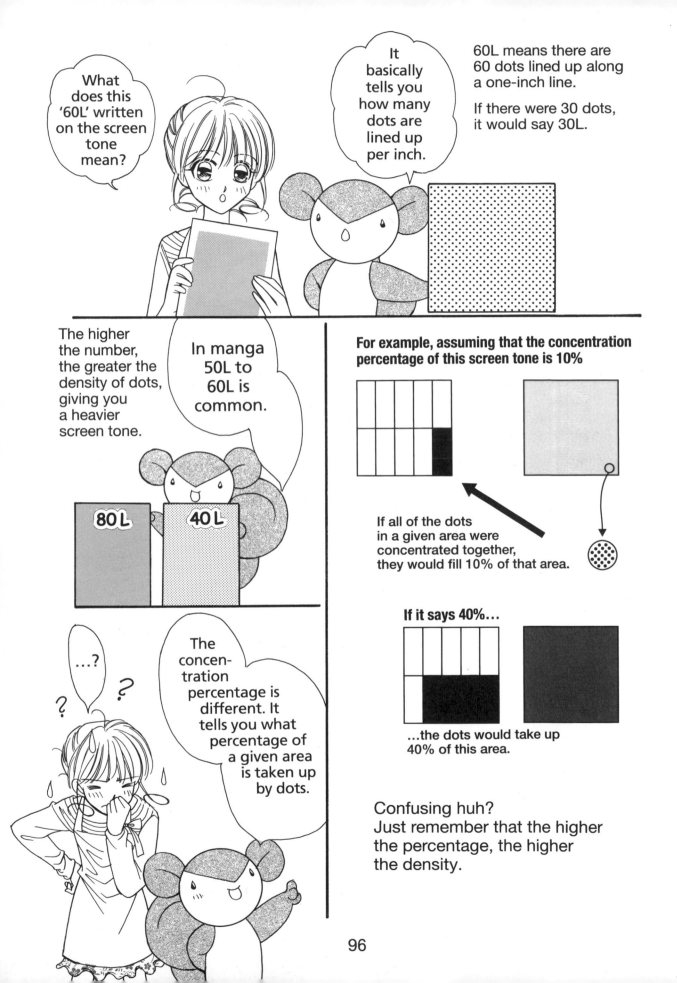

What does this '60L' written on the screen tone mean?

It basically tells you how many dots are lined up per inch.

60L means there are 60 dots lined up along a one-inch line.

If there were 30 dots, it would say 30L.

The higher the number, the greater the density of dots, giving you a heavier screen tone.

In manga 50L to 60L is common.

80 L

40 L

…?

? ? ?

The concentration percentage is different. It tells you what percentage of a given area is taken up by dots.

For example, assuming that the concentration percentage of this screen tone is 10%

If all of the dots in a given area were concentrated together, they would fill 10% of that area.

If it says 40%…

…the dots would take up 40% of this area.

Confusing huh?
Just remember that the higher the percentage, the higher the density.

96

LAYERING TONE

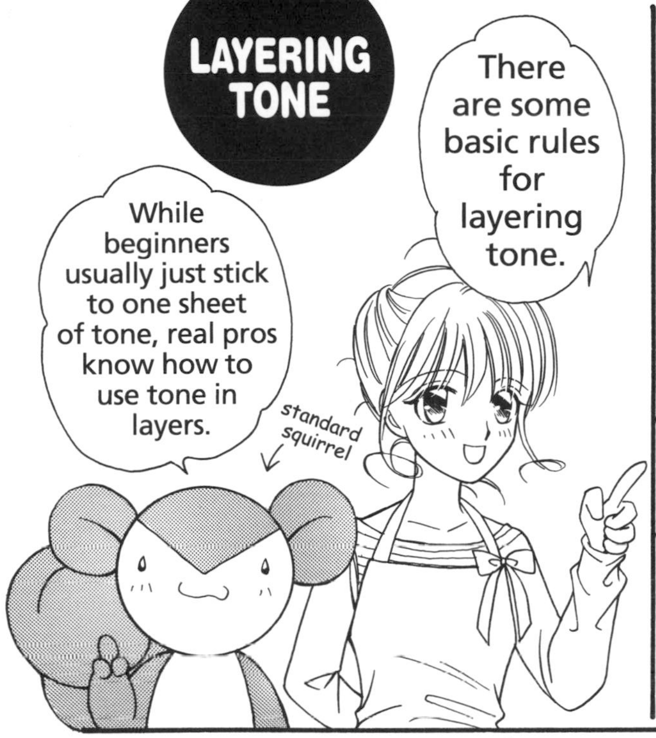
There are some basic rules for layering tone.
While beginners usually just stick to one sheet of tone, real pros know how to use tone in layers.
standard squirrel

Check to see what tone you're using, for example 60L/10%, and make sure you layer tones with the same line numbers to avoid a moiré effect.

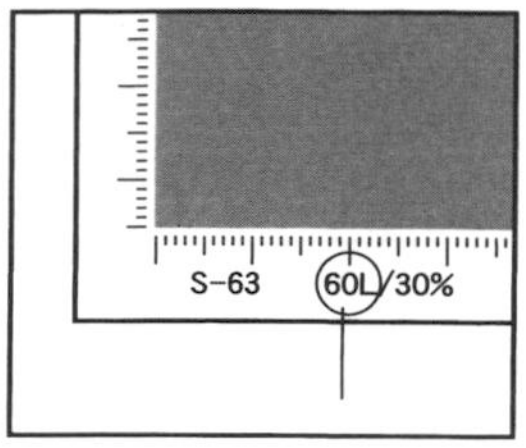
S-63
60L/30%

Only line numbers have to be the same—the concentration percentage can be different.

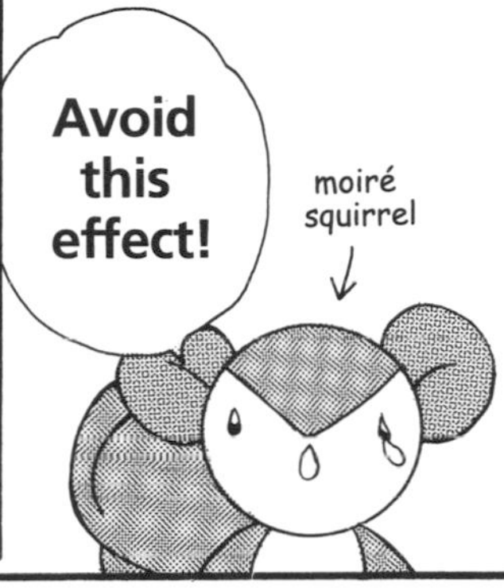
Avoid this effect!
moiré squirrel

For example, if you layer two IC products, S-61 (60L/10%) and S-63 (60L/30%) you get this effect:

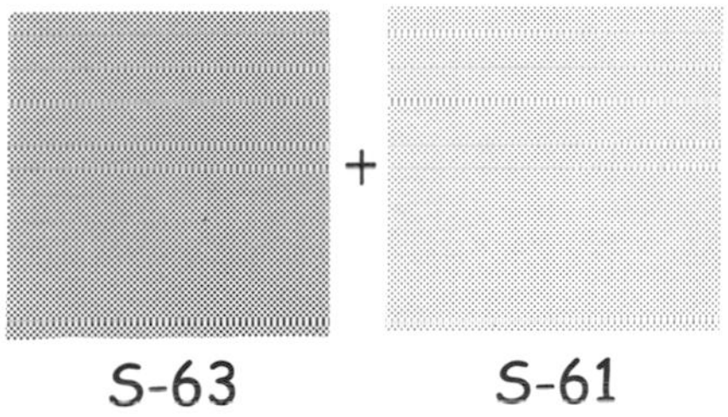
S-63
S-61

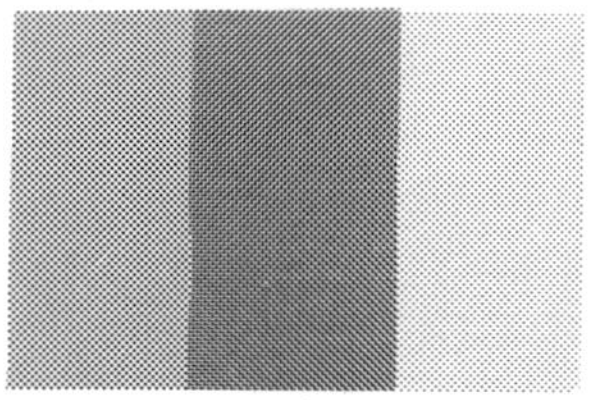

The overlap is darker.

But if you layer screen tones with different line numbers, you will get the moiré effect.
Here we have S-61 (60L/10%) layered with S-82 (85L/20%)

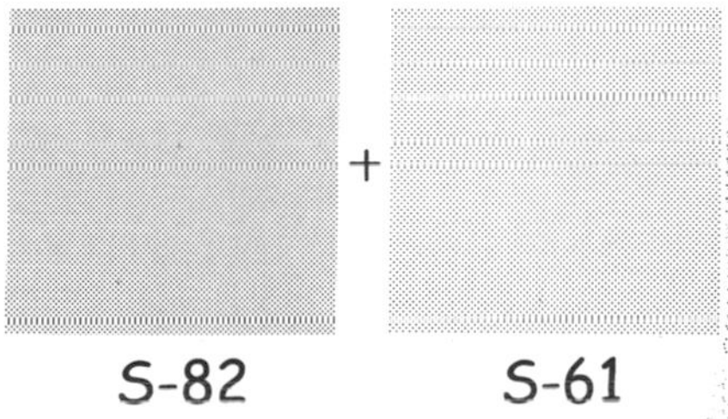
S-82
S-61

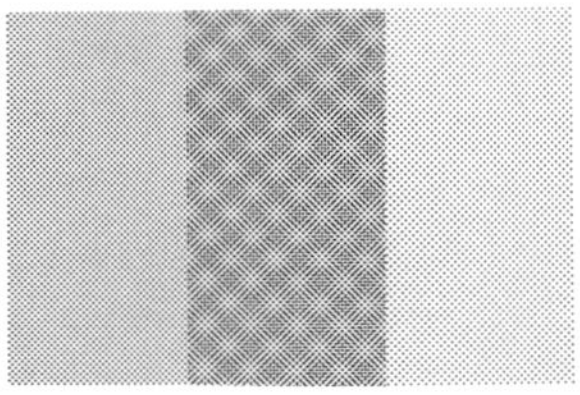

The moiré effect!
Not very cool, huh?

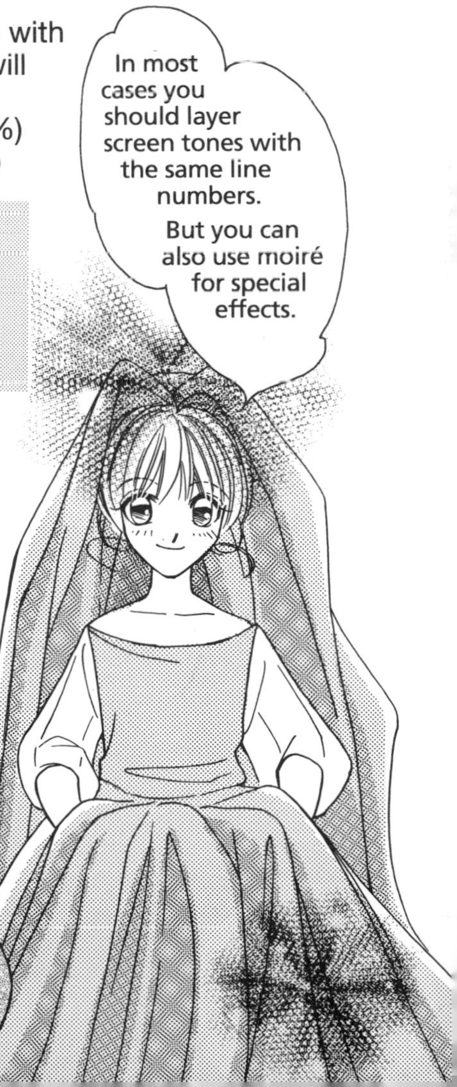
In most cases you should layer screen tones with the same line numbers.
But you can also use moiré for special effects.

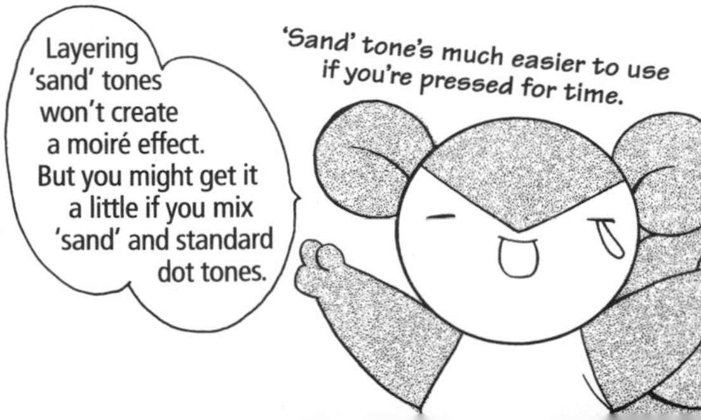
Layering 'sand' tones won't create a moiré effect. But you might get it a little if you mix 'sand' and standard dot tones.
'Sand' tone's much easier to use if you're pressed for time.

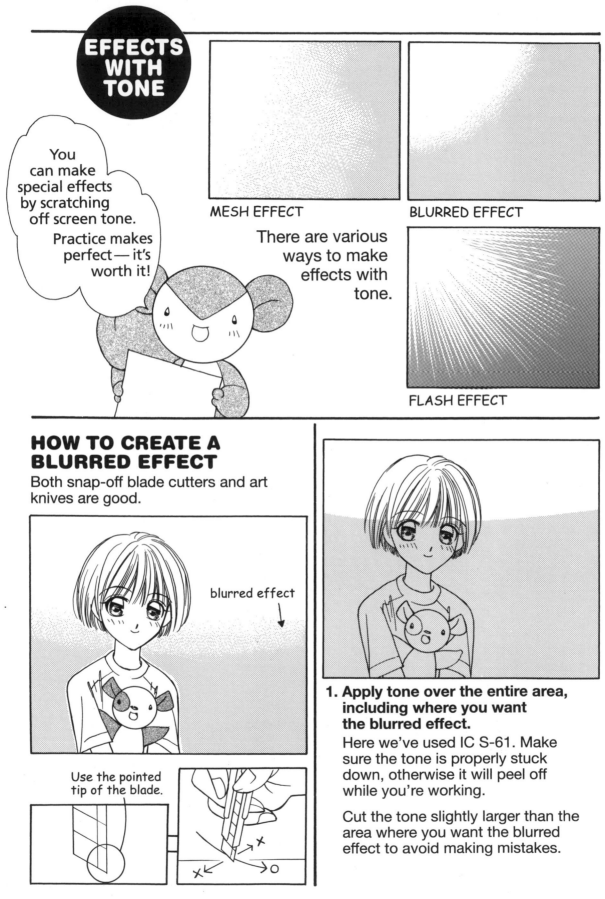

EFFECTS WITH TONE

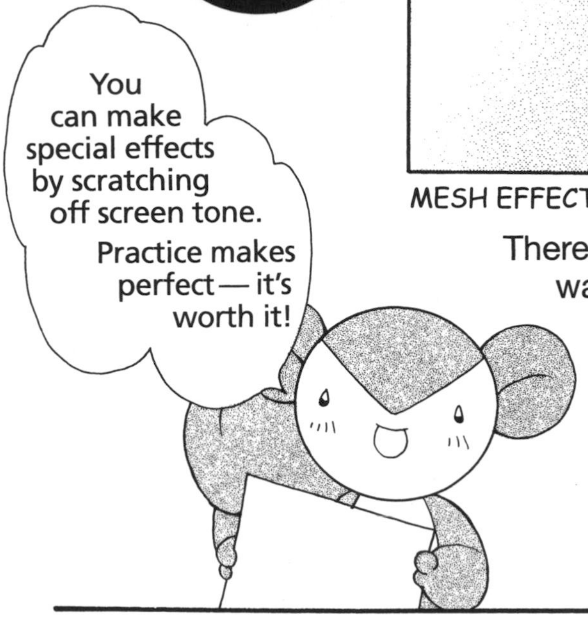
You can make special effects by scratching off screen tone.
Practice makes perfect — it's worth it!

There are various ways to make effects with tone.

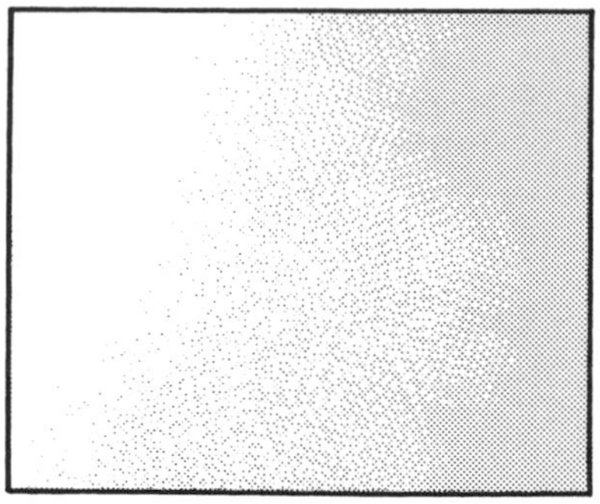

MESH EFFECT

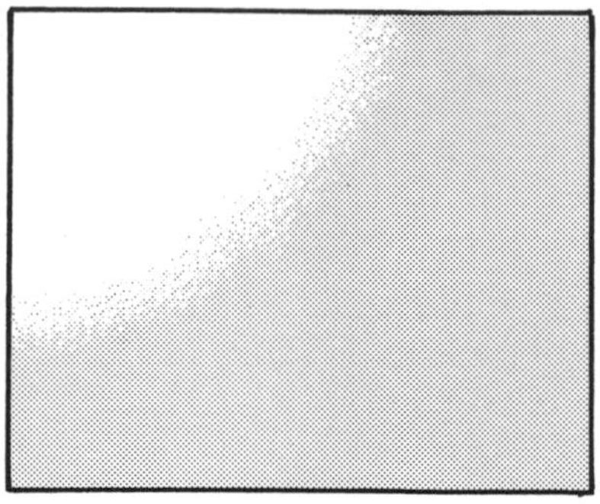

BLURRED EFFECT

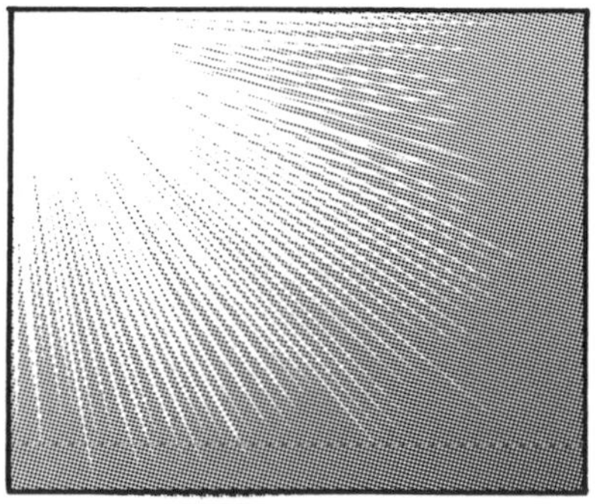

FLASH EFFECT

HOW TO CREATE A BLURRED EFFECT

Both snap-off blade cutters and art knives are good.

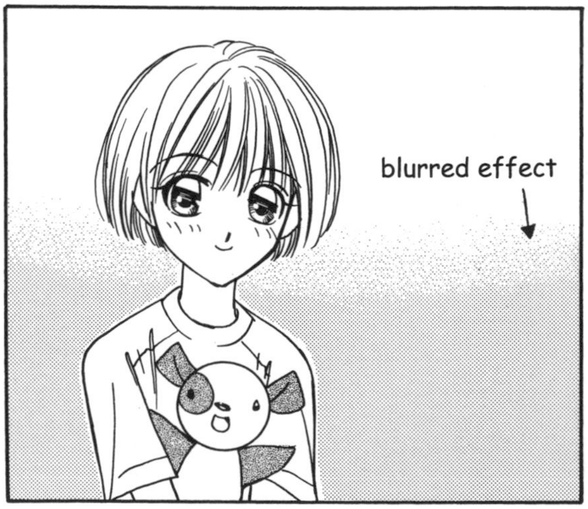
blurred effect

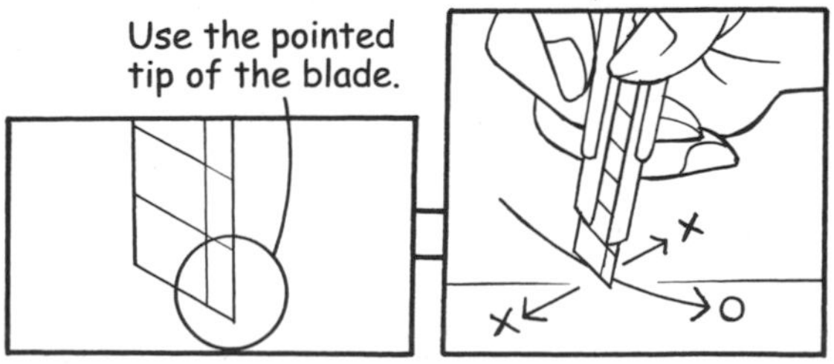
Use the pointed tip of the blade.

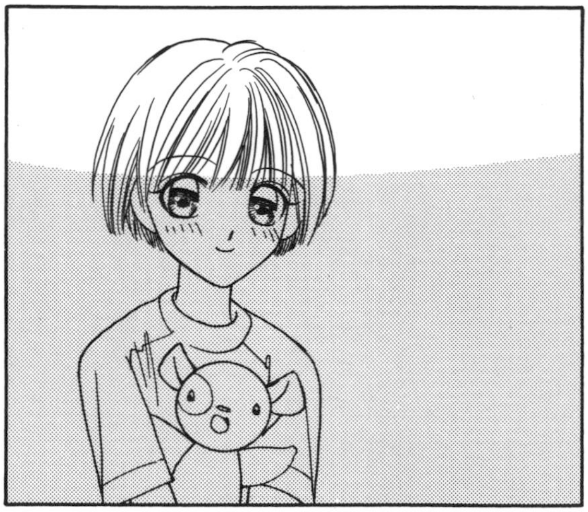

1. Apply tone over the entire area, including where you want the blurred effect.

Here we've used IC S-61. Make sure the tone is properly stuck down, otherwise it will peel off while you're working.

Cut the tone slightly larger than the area where you want the blurred effect to avoid making mistakes.

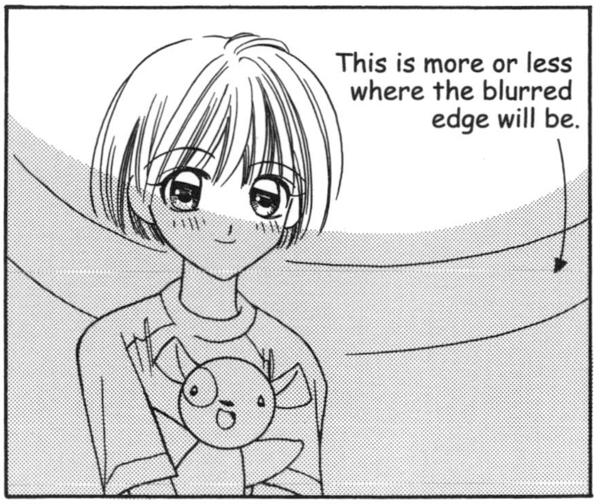
This is more or less where the blurred edge will be.

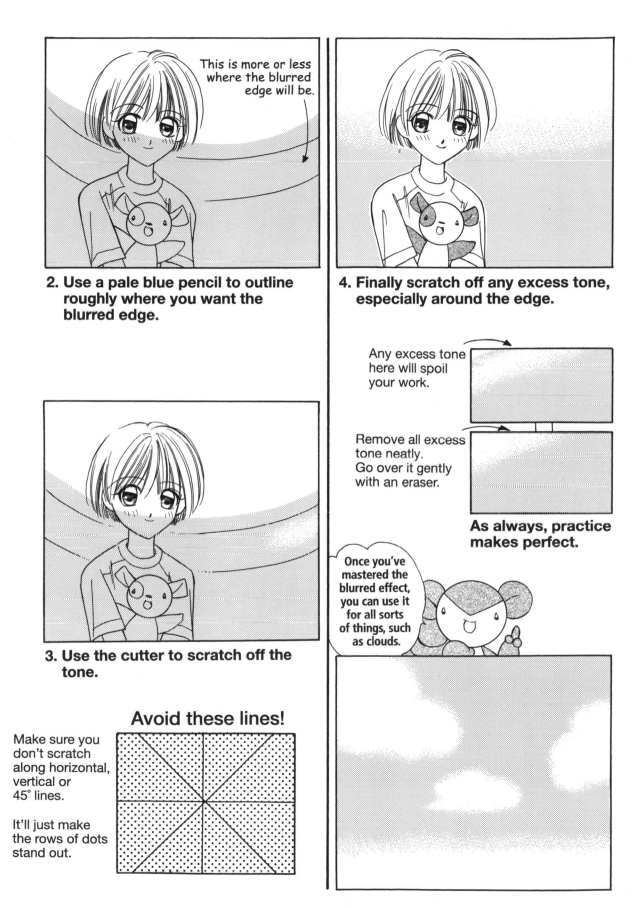

2. Use a pale blue pencil to outline roughly where you want the blurred edge.

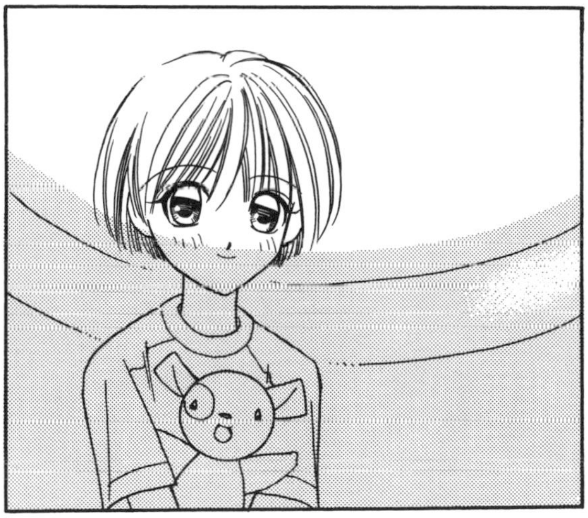

3. Use the cutter to scratch off the tone.

Avoid these lines!

Make sure you don't scratch along horizontal, vertical or 45° lines.

It'll just make the rows of dots stand out.

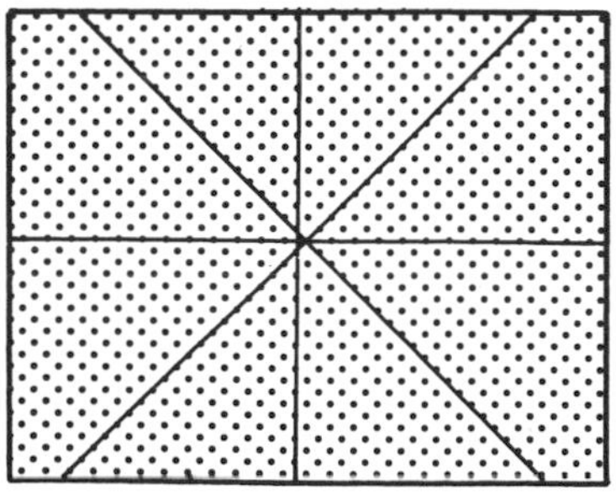

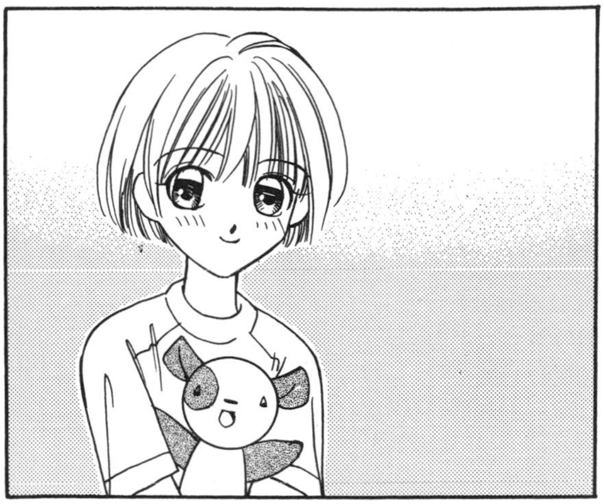

4. Finally scratch off any excess tone, especially around the edge.

Any excess tone here will spoil your work.

Remove all excess tone neatly. Go over it gently with an eraser.

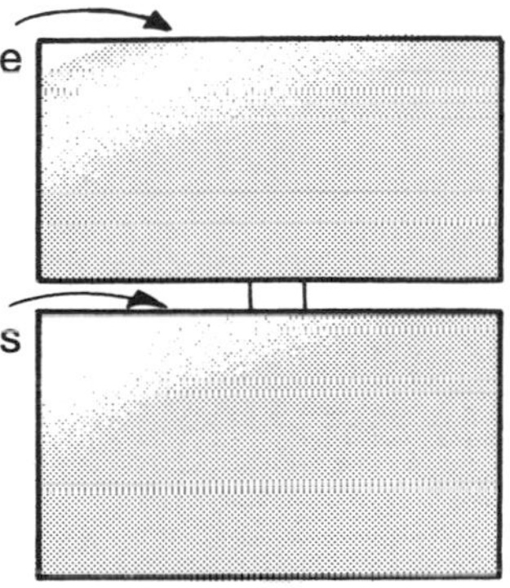

As always, practice makes perfect.

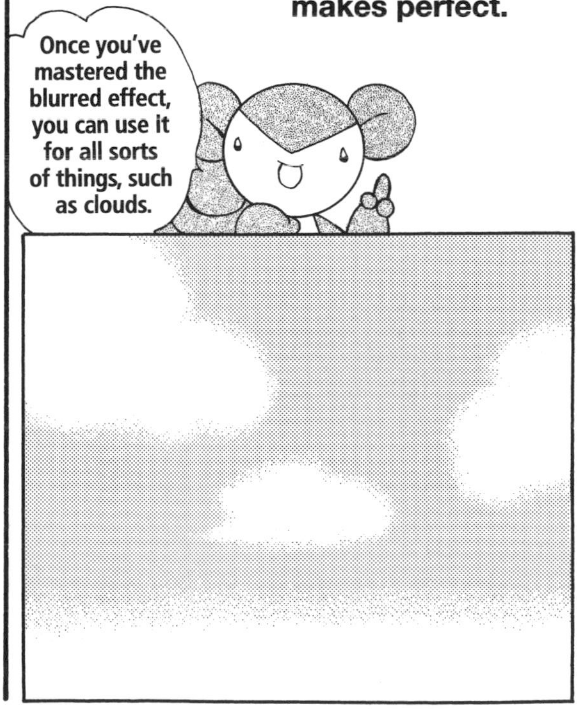
Once you've mastered the blurred effect, you can use it for all sorts of things, such as clouds.

FLASHES WITH TONE

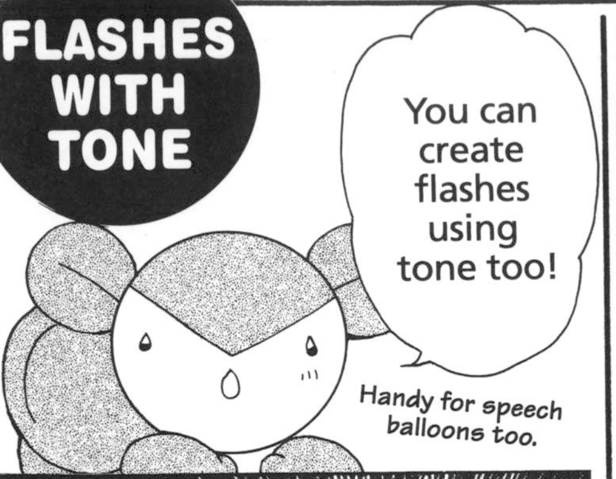
You can create flashes using tone too!
Handy for speech balloons too.

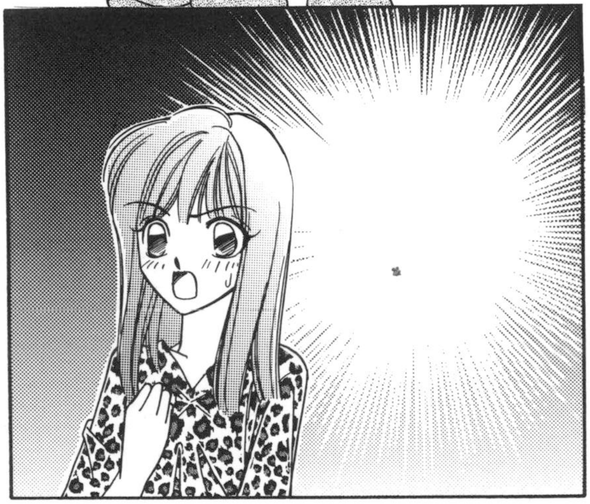

Use a snap-off cutter, with a fresh blade.

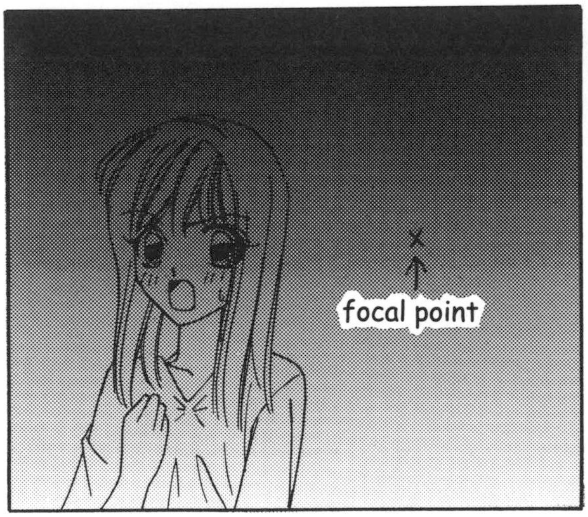
focal point

1. Mark the focal point of the flash. Apply tone.

If you're a beginner it's easier to apply tone over the whole frame. Remember to watch the angle of the dots. Also make sure the tone is thoroughly stuck down to avoid any peeling.

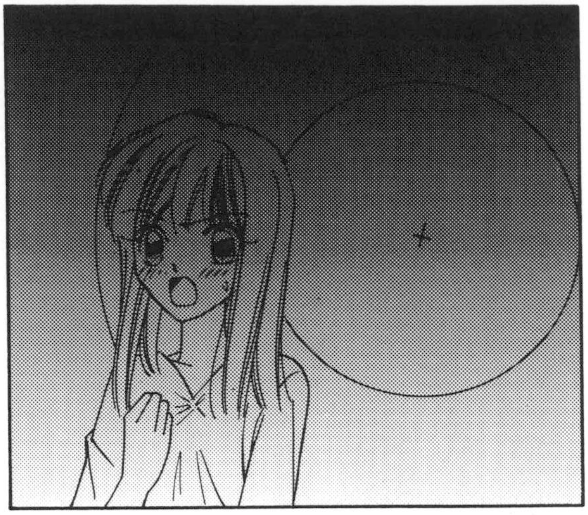

2. Using a pale blue pencil, sketch the outline of the flash on the tone.

It's easier to sketch in where you want to begin and end the flash lines. Use a compass if you like.

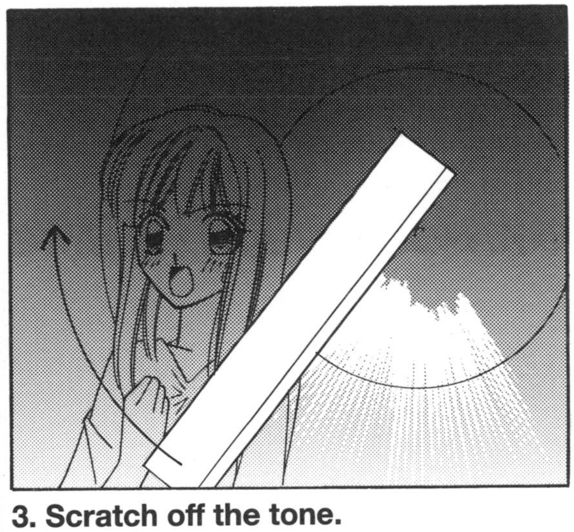

3. Scratch off the tone.

Line up the ruler with the focal point and scratch from the center outwards. Use a metal ruler with a beveled edge. The trick is to begin each cut lightly then pull away cleanly and briskly.

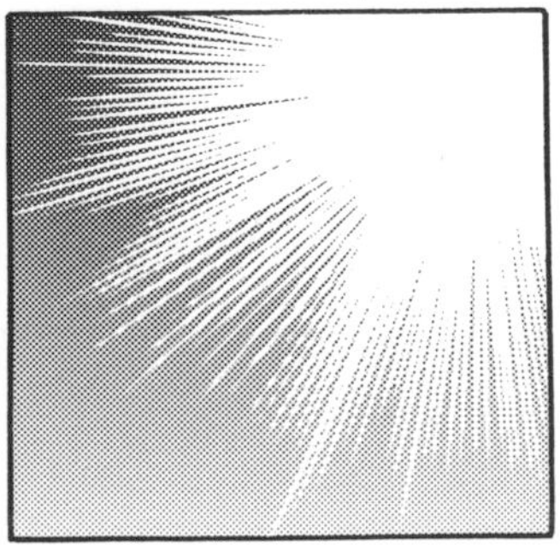

Avoid completely horizontal, vertical or 45° lines as these will make the rows of dots stand out.

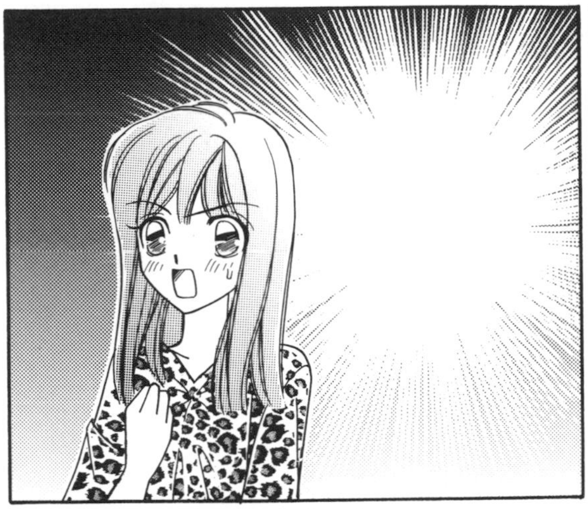

4. **When you've finished, remove any excess tone and then go over it gently with an eraser to remove any residue.**

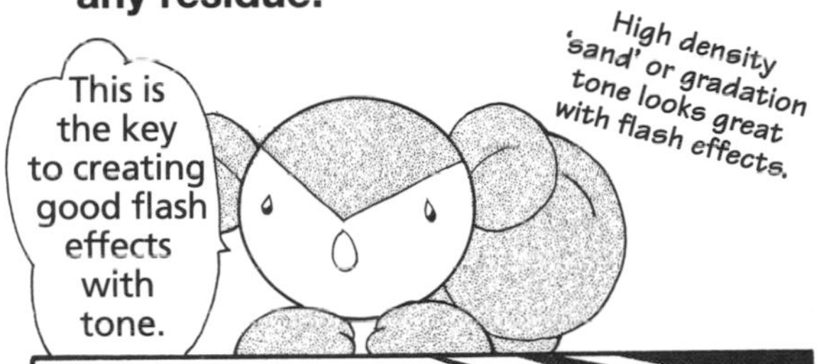
This is the key to creating good flash effects with tone.
High density 'sand' or gradation tone looks great with flash effects.

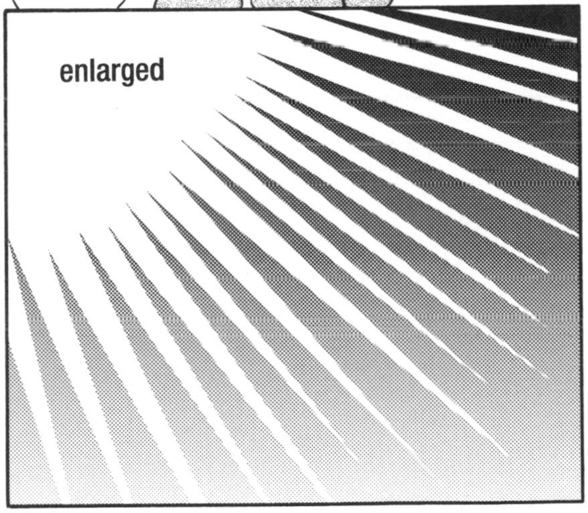
enlarged

The knack is to keep the lines sharp.

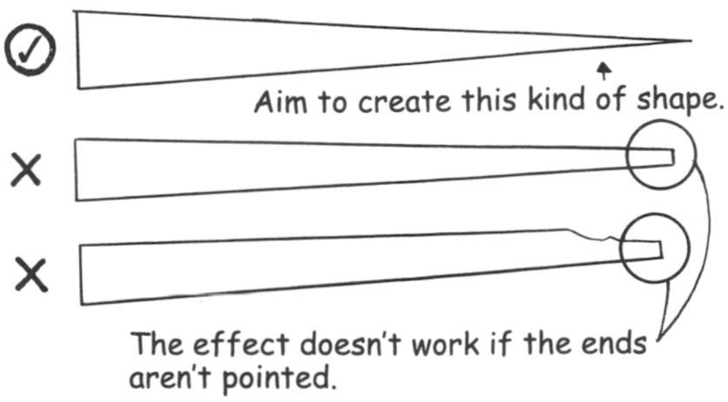
Aim to create this kind of shape.
The effect doesn't work if the ends aren't pointed.

OTHER FLASH EFFECTS WITH TONE

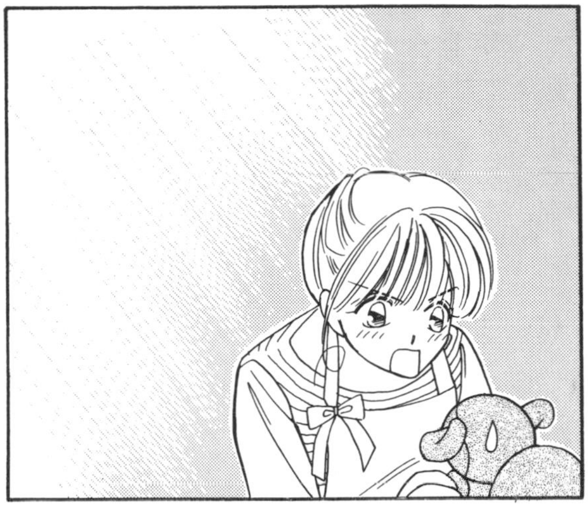

Use a metal ruler to make parallel lines. Remember to avoid horizontal, vertical or 45° lines, but make sure you keep them parallel.

A good way of removing tone debris (and you get a lot when scratching it off) is with a kneaded rubber eraser or Scotch tape. Weaken the Scotch tape by patting it on your clothes a few times.

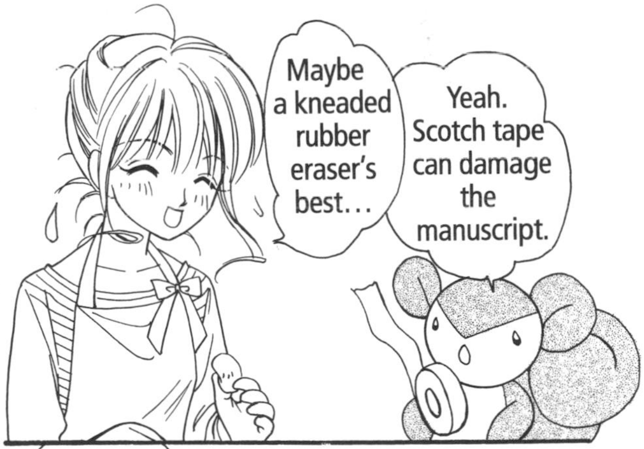
Maybe a kneaded rubber eraser's best. . .
Yeah. Scotch tape can damage the manuscript.

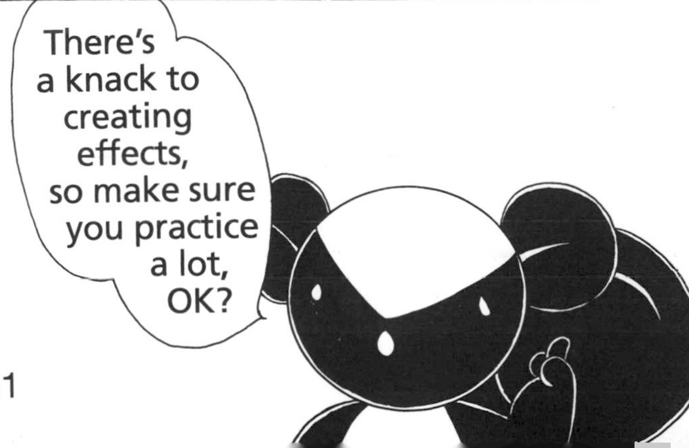
There's a knack to creating effects, so make sure you practice a lot, OK?

TIPS FROM A PRO 1

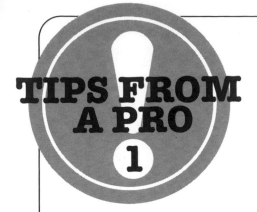

SOME MORE EFFECTS

There are some more effects which we haven't explained yet. We'll just go through them briefly here:

ROPE MESH

Sketch an outline of rope coils, keeping them curvy. Fill the coils in with a simple 2-line mesh keeping the lines equidistant. Make sure the coil width is consistent.

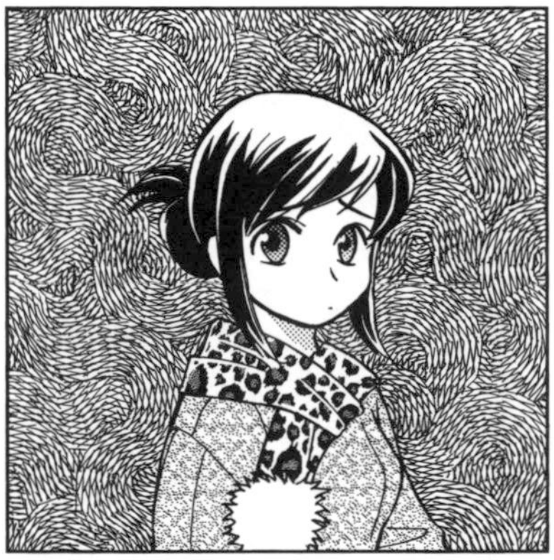

FLAMES

Often used for serious scenes, and also sometimes for comic scenes. Sketch in the outline of the flames around the character, then fill it in with a similar mesh to the rope effect above. Make the tips of the flames pointed.

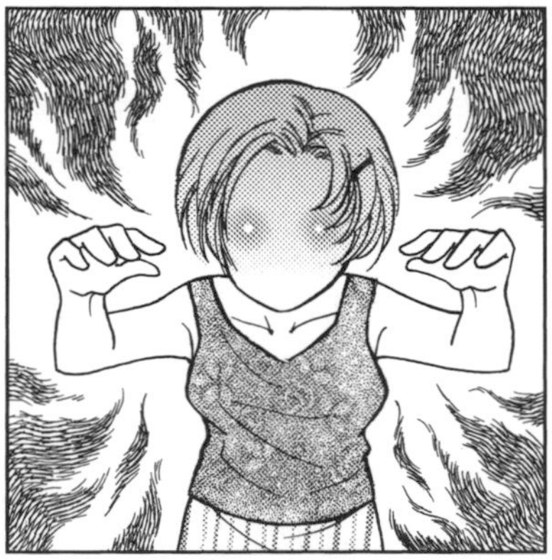

CONVERGING DOTS

This effect is a cross between dots and converging lines. It's often used to create a cheerful atmosphere. Mark the focal point, as when drawing converging lines, then sketch in some lines converging on the focal point. Now add in the marks using ink—this time use short dashes rather than dots.

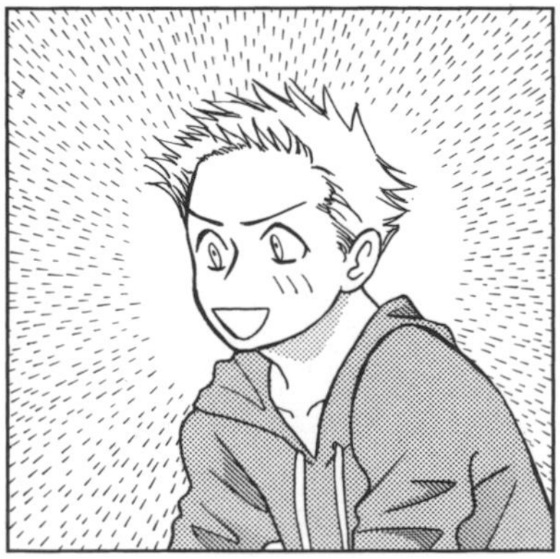

TONE FOR NIGHT OR DAY

You can vary the time of day of a scene with effective use of tone. Compare the two illustrations below and see if you can figure out which tone is used where.

DAYTIME

All tone used here is from IC

Tone numbers: S-61/S-62/S-456/S-923/S-977/S-5005/Y-1235/Y1652

TIP!

The general effect is light, so only one sheet of standard screen tone is needed for shadows on, for example, buildings, cars and trees.
This contrasts with the illustration below, where layers of standard tone on 'sand' tone have been used to create more shadow. A light standard tone has been used for the sky, scratched away to make the cloud effect. Alternatively, you can use a light sky-pattern tone.

EVENING/DUSK

Tone numbers: S-60/S-456/S-474/S-956/S-977/S-5023/Y-1237/Y1652

TIP!

Sky-pattern screen tone (S-956) has been layered here. Leaving a white area at the center of the picture gives the impression of a setting sun. You can emphasize the effect of dusk by using tone on buildings in the foreground, which don't catch much light. Use gradation tone, and layer standard and 'sand' tone to enhance the effect.

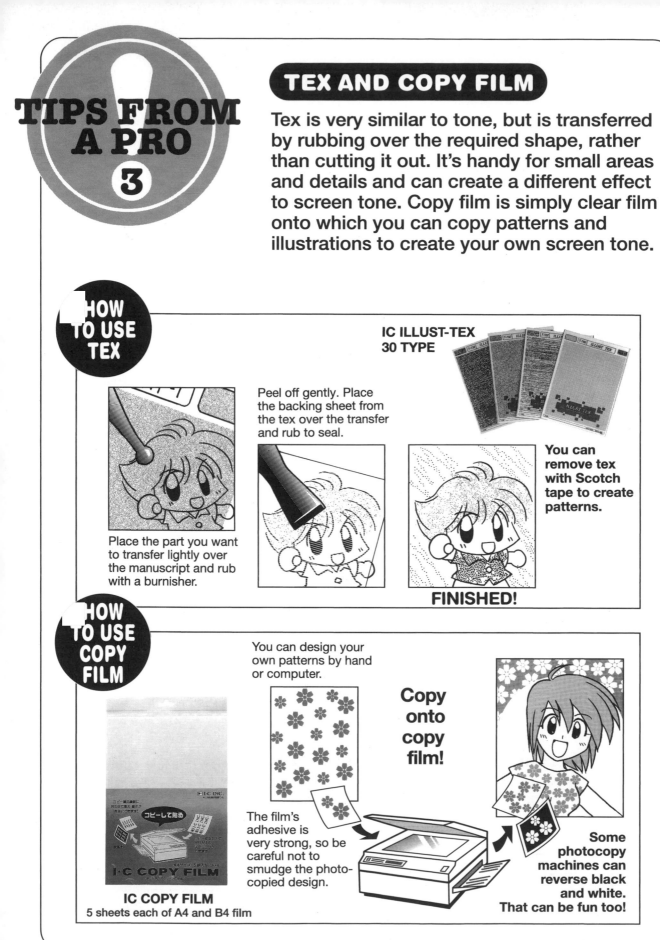

TIPS FROM A PRO 3

TEX AND COPY FILM

Tex is very similar to tone, but is transferred by rubbing over the required shape, rather than cutting it out. It's handy for small areas and details and can create a different effect to screen tone. Copy film is simply clear film onto which you can copy patterns and illustrations to create your own screen tone.

HOW TO USE TEX

IC ILLUST-TEX 30 TYPE

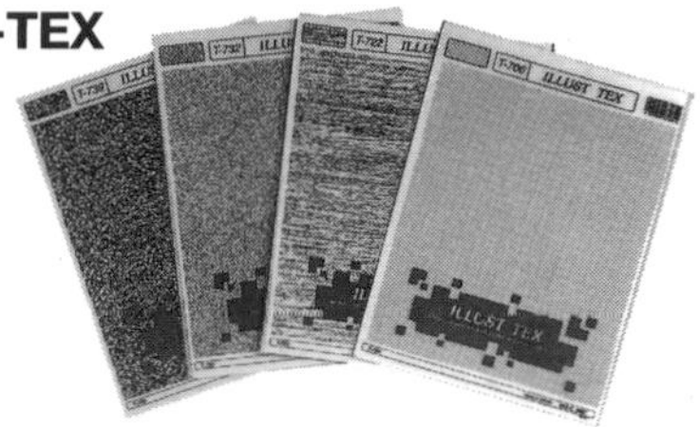

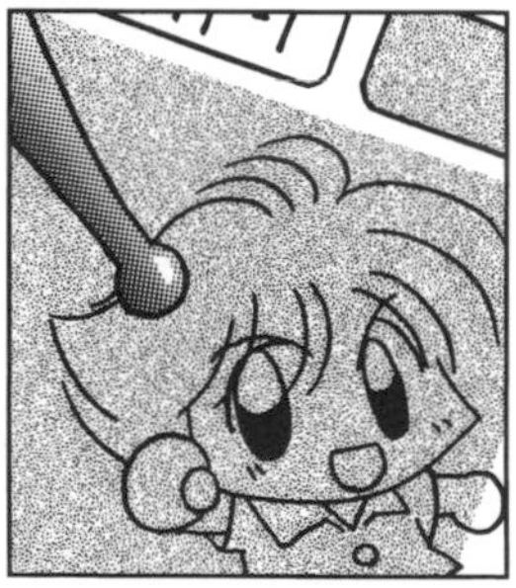

Place the part you want to transfer lightly over the manuscript and rub with a burnisher.

Peel off gently. Place the backing sheet from the tex over the transfer and rub to seal.

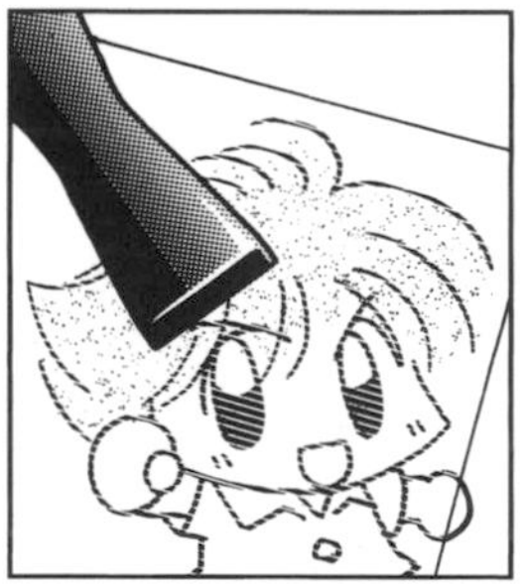

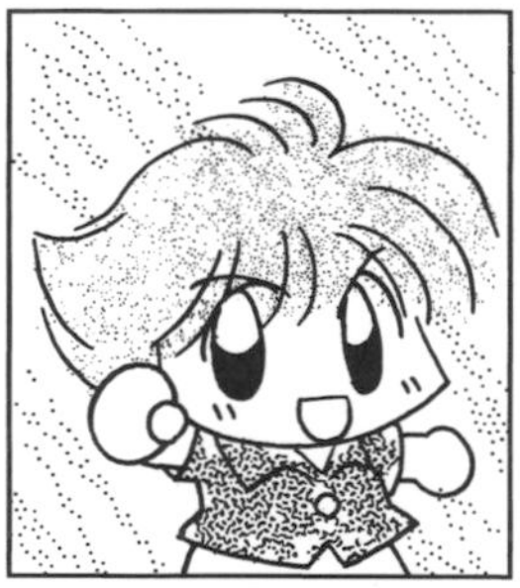

FINISHED!

You can remove tex with Scotch tape to create patterns.

HOW TO USE COPY FILM

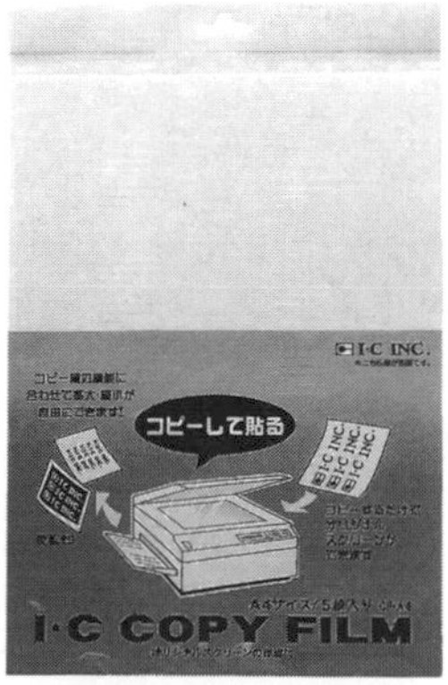
I·C INC.
コピーして貼る
I·C COPY FILM

IC COPY FILM
5 sheets each of A4 and B4 film

You can design your own patterns by hand or computer.

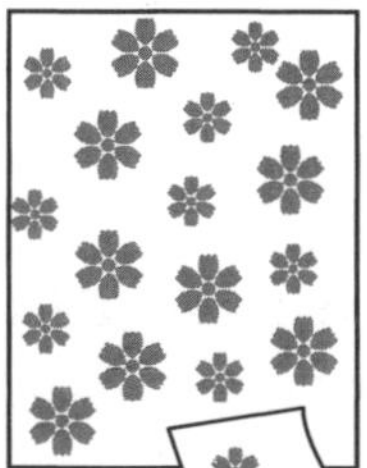

Copy onto copy film!

The film's adhesive is very strong, so be careful not to smudge the photo-copied design.

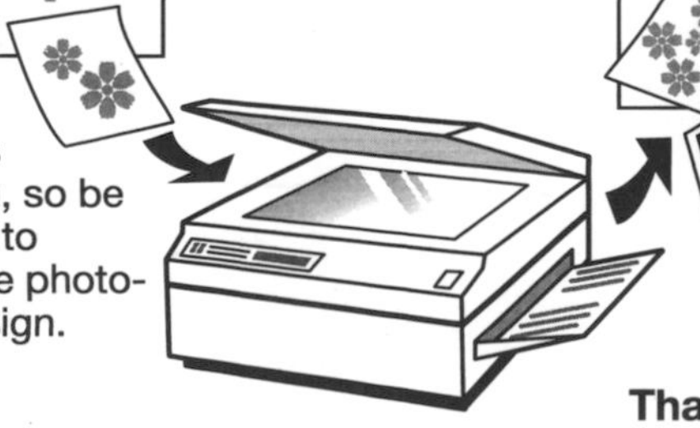

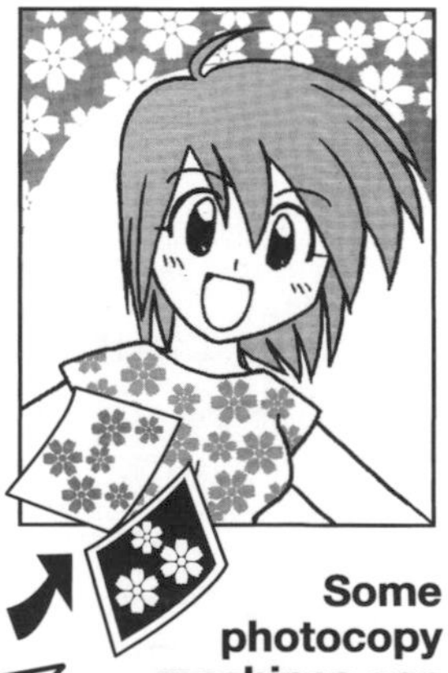

Some photocopy machines can reverse black and white. That can be fun too!

LESSON 4

BACKGROUND

**Background is an essential part of manga
—no use trying to avoid it.
Perspective, one-point perspective, vanishing point...
they all sound difficult, but are very handy once mastered.
A well-drawn background really makes a difference!**

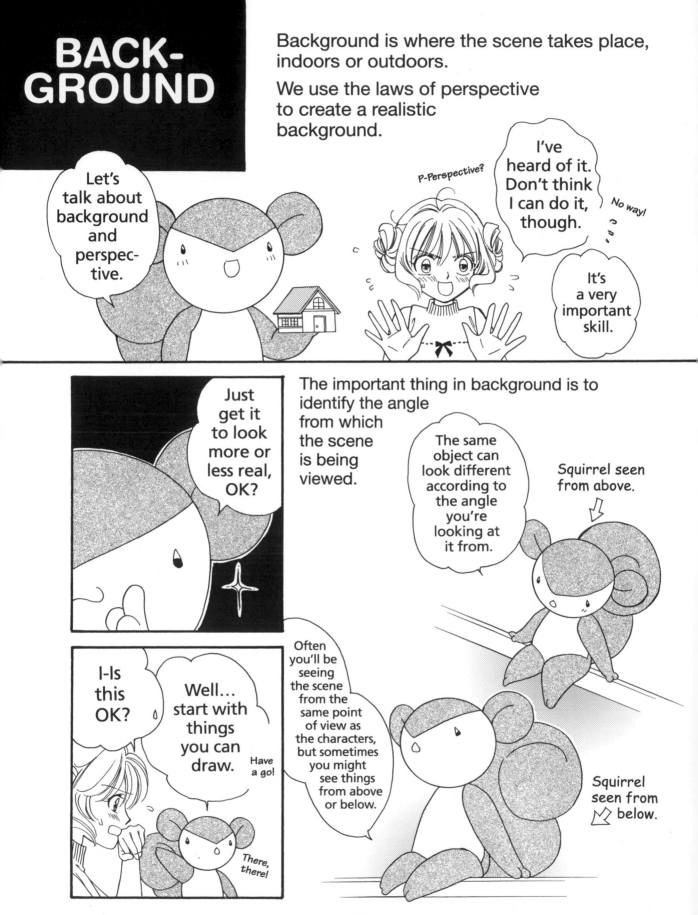

BACK-GROUND

Background is where the scene takes place, indoors or outdoors.

We use the laws of perspective to create a realistic background.

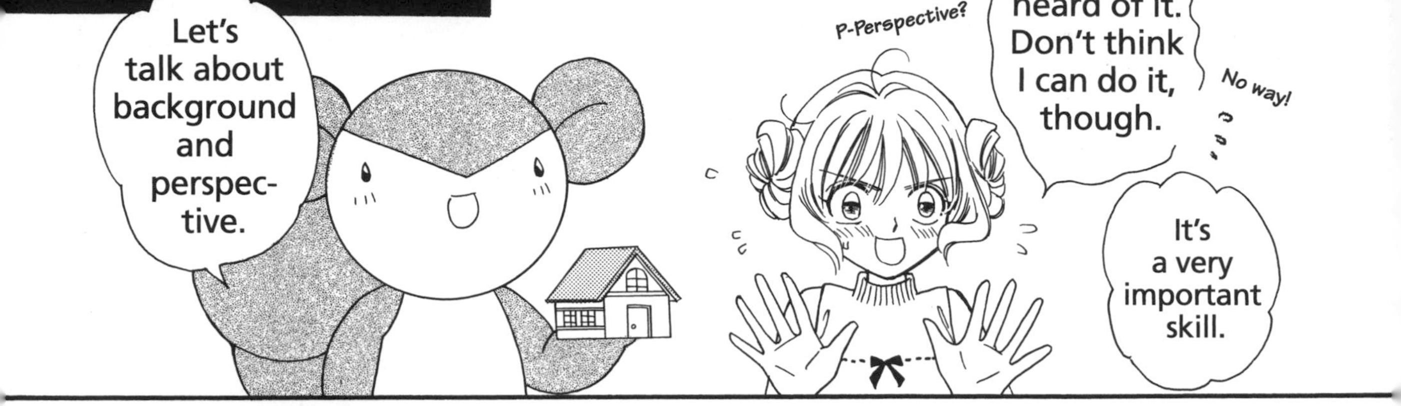
Let's talk about background and perspec-tive.
P-Perspective?
I've heard of it. Don't think I can do it, though.
No way!
It's a very important skill.

The important thing in background is to identify the angle from which the scene is being viewed.

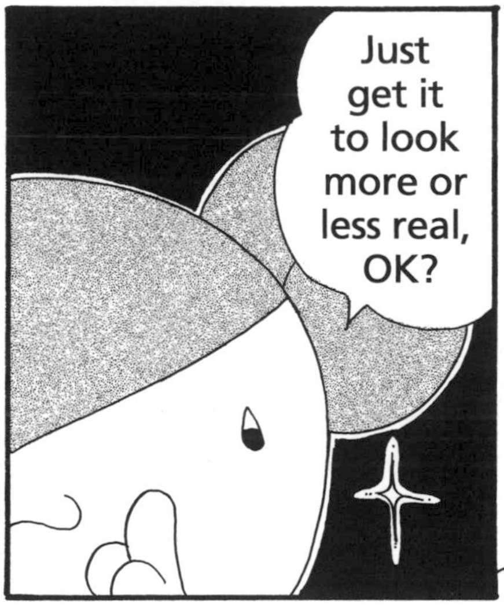
Just get it to look more or less real, OK?

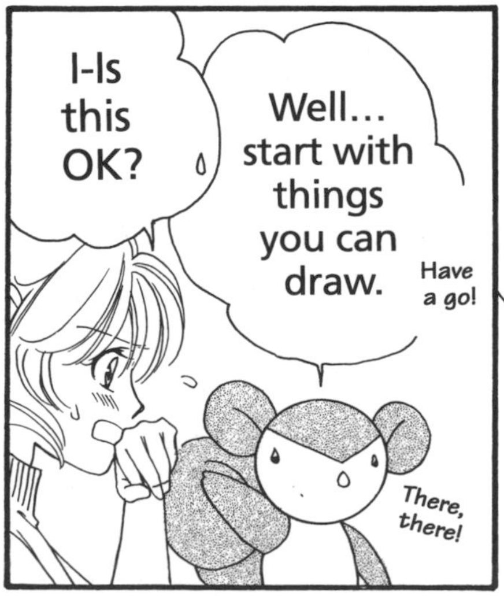
I-Is this OK?
Well… start with things you can draw.
Have a go!
There, there!

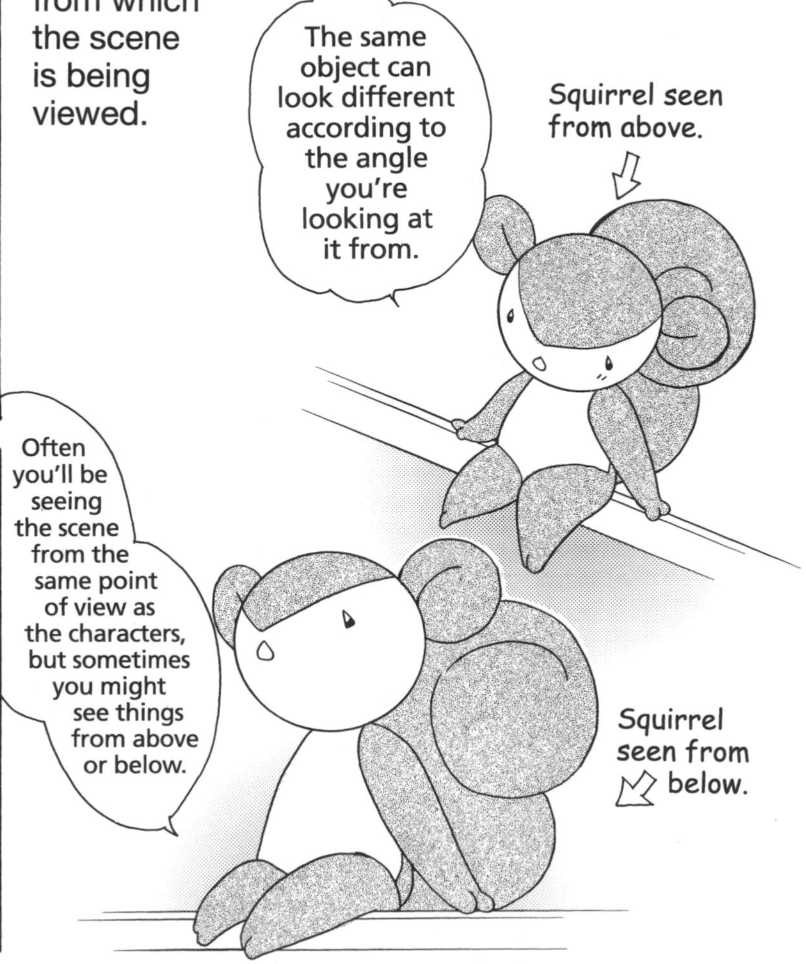
The same object can look different according to the angle you're looking at it from.
Squirrel seen from above.
Often you'll be seeing the scene from the same point of view as the characters, but sometimes you might see things from above or below.
Squirrel seen from below.

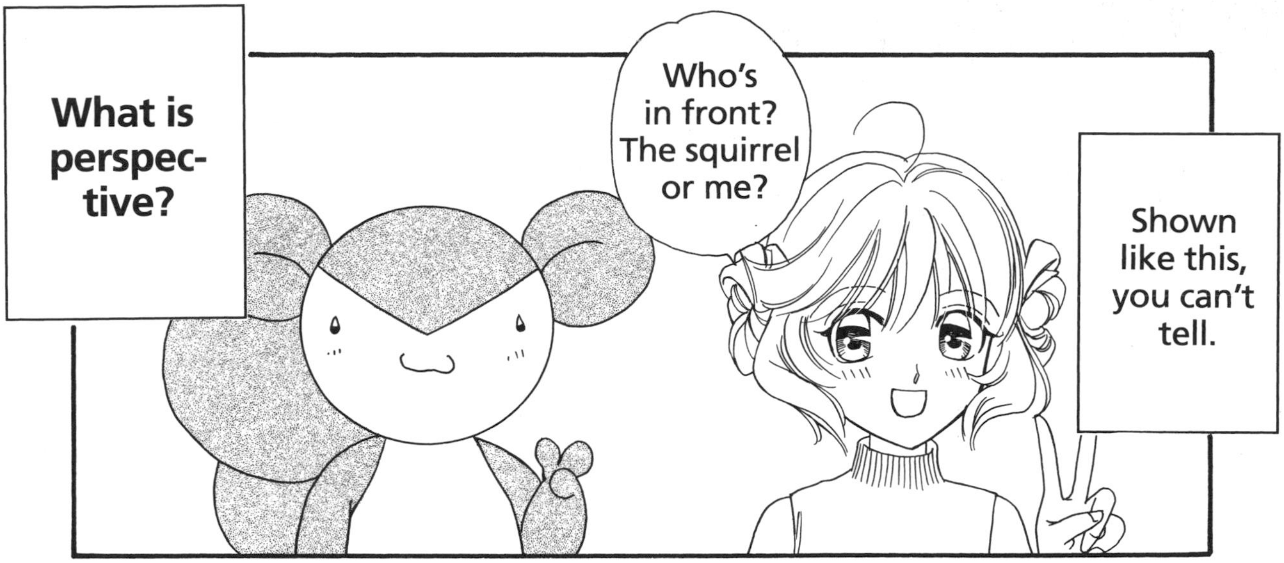
What is perspec-tive?
Who's in front? The squirrel or me?
Shown like this, you can't tell.

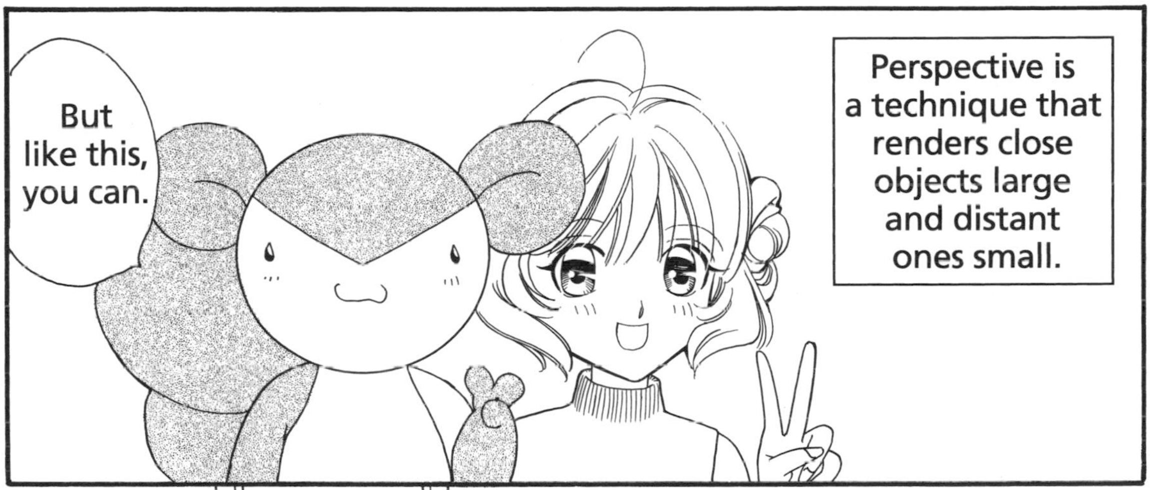
But like this, you can.
Perspective is a technique that renders close objects large and distant ones small.

If you look at this ladder held upright, the rungs are evenly spaced.

If you lay the ladder down flat, the space between the rungs appears to be closer the further into the distance. Even things the same size look bigger closeup and smaller in the distance.

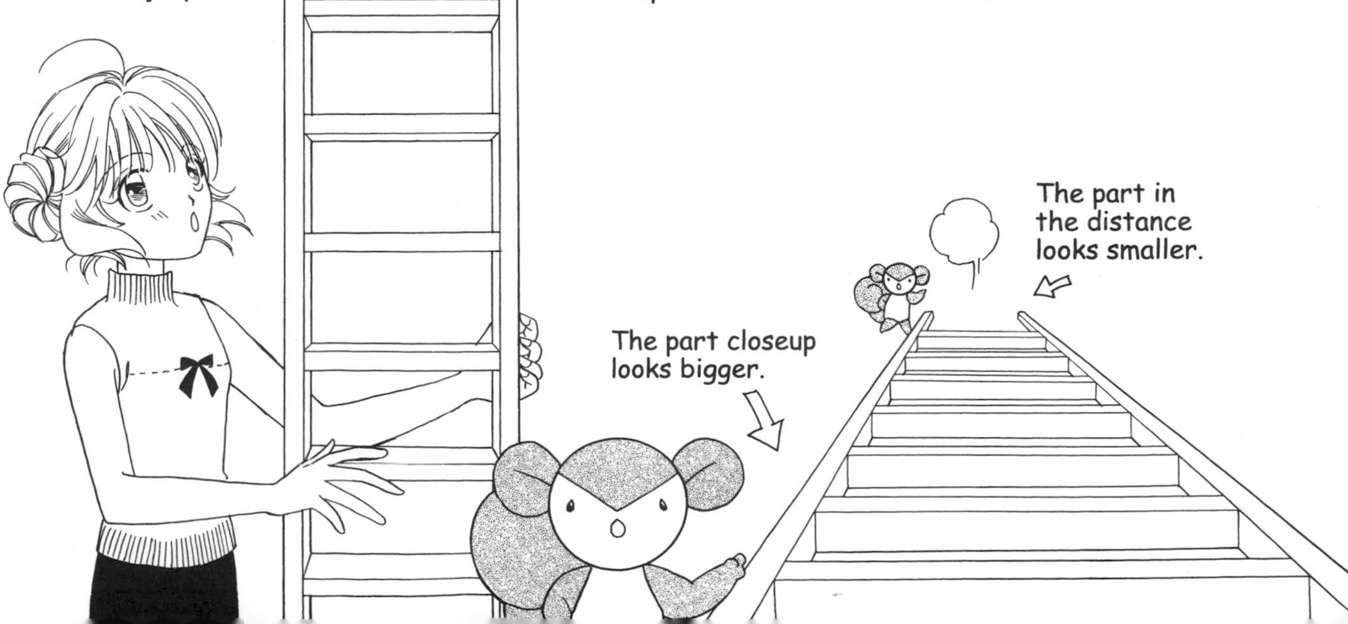
The part closeup looks bigger.
The part in the distance looks smaller.

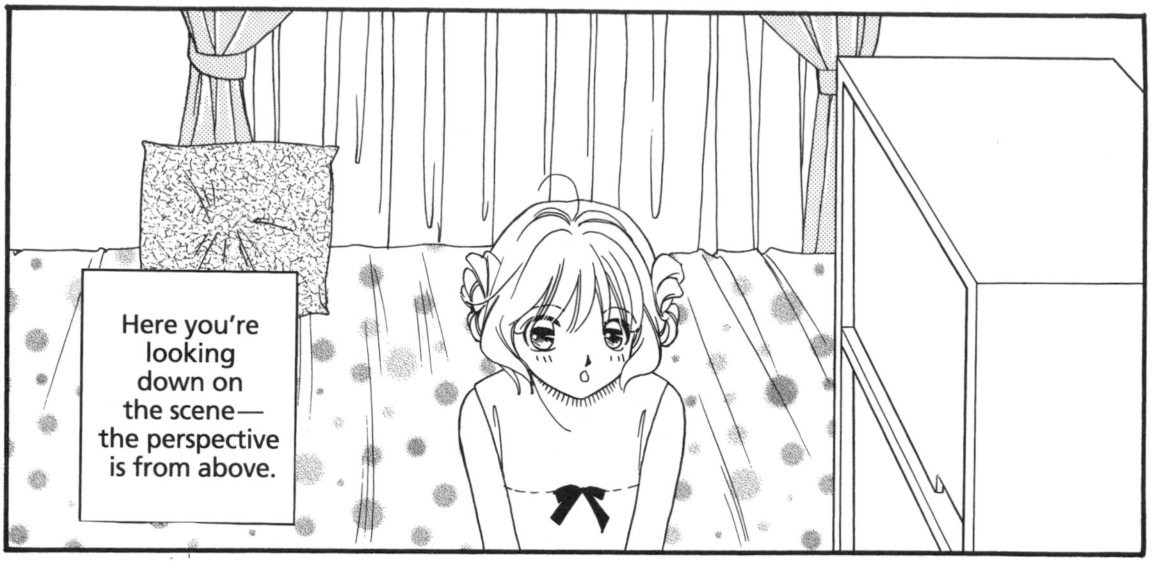
Here you're looking down on the scene—the perspective is from above.

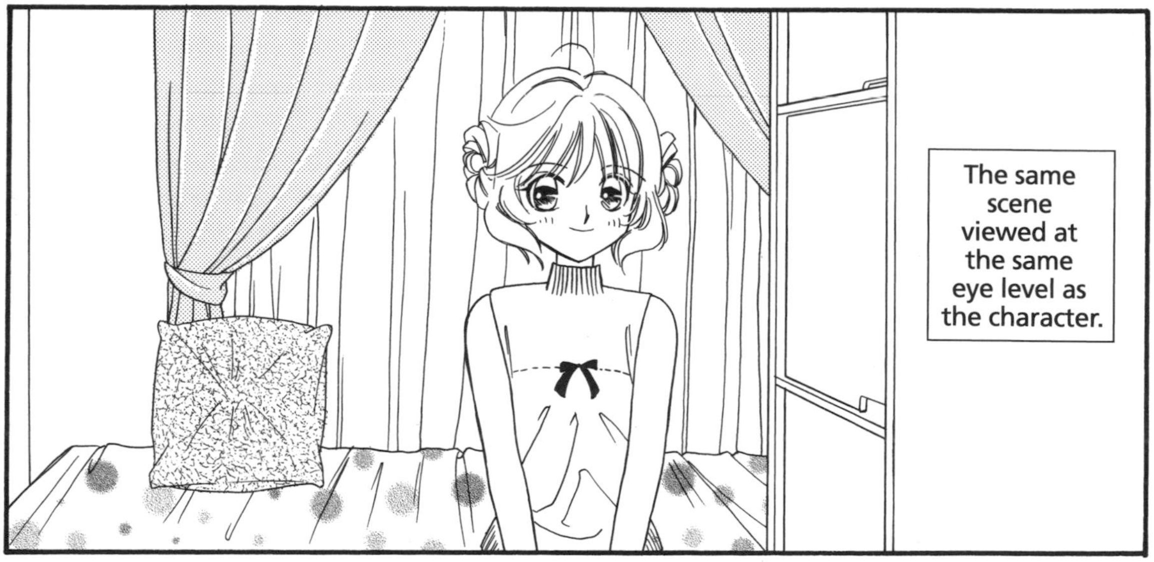
The same scene viewed at the same eye level as the character.

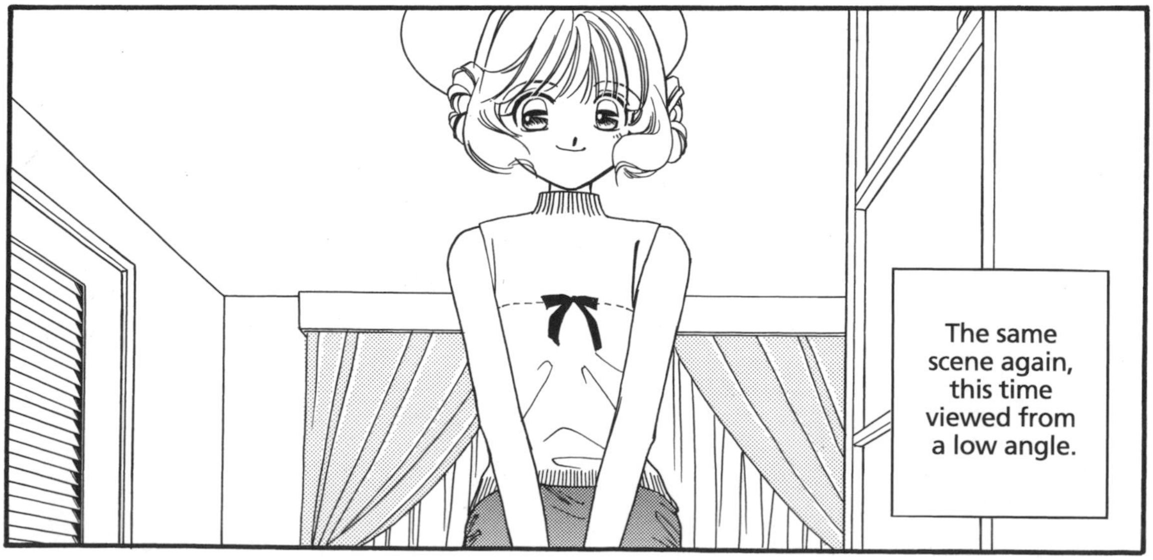
The same scene again, this time viewed from a low angle.

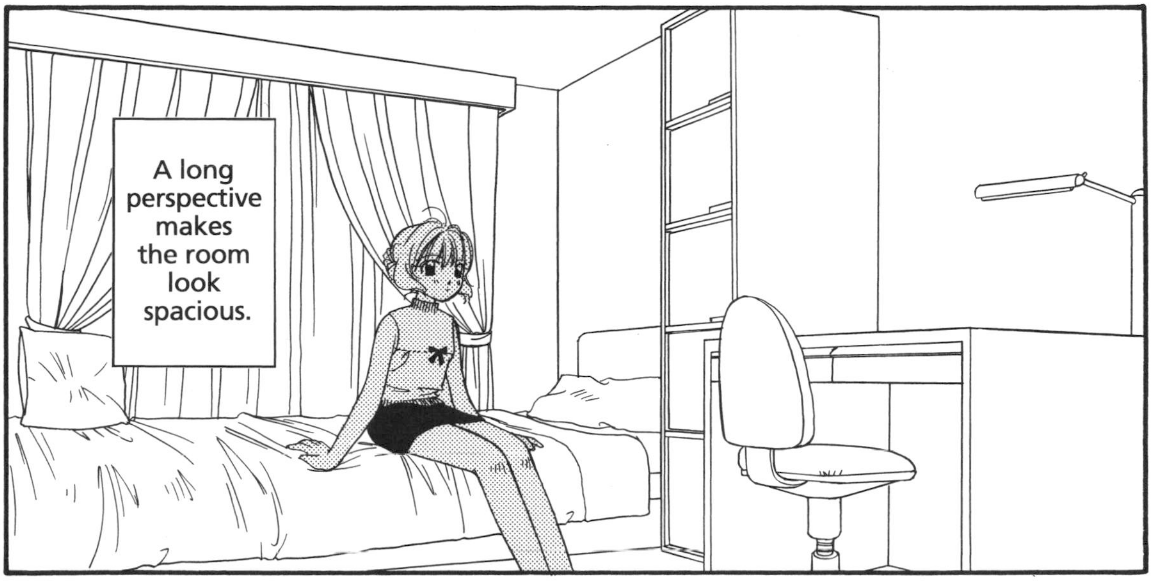
A long perspective makes the room look spacious.

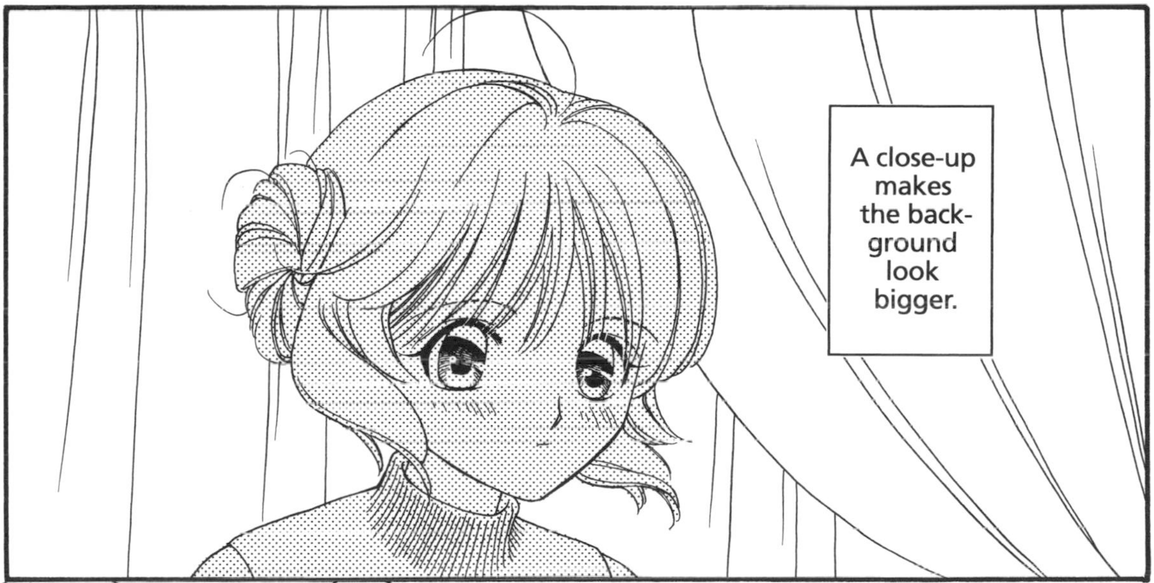
A close-up makes the back-ground look bigger.

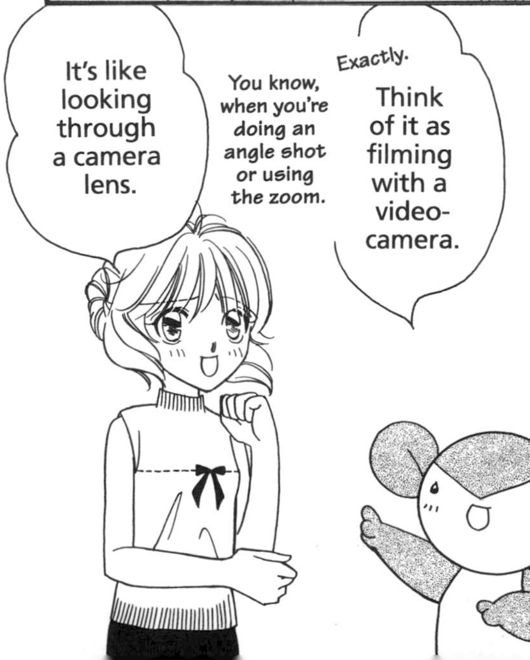
It's like looking through a camera lens.
You know, when you're doing an angle shot or using the zoom.
Exactly.
Think of it as filming with a video-camera.

In scenes where background is needed, imagine where your characters are standing and how they look. Once you've decided on that, you can make a start on drawing in perspective.

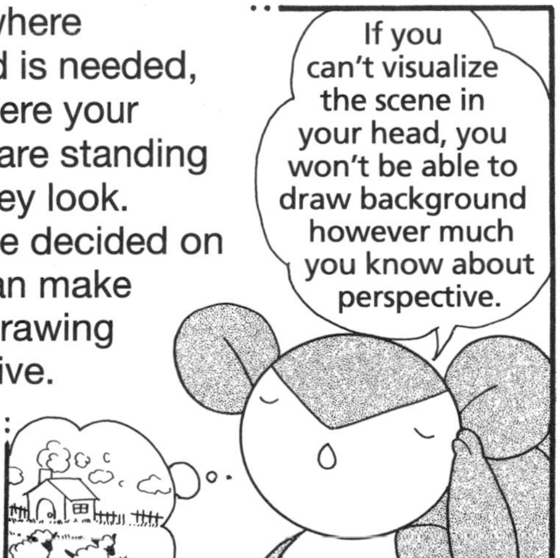
If you can't visualize the scene in your head, you won't be able to draw background however much you know about perspective.

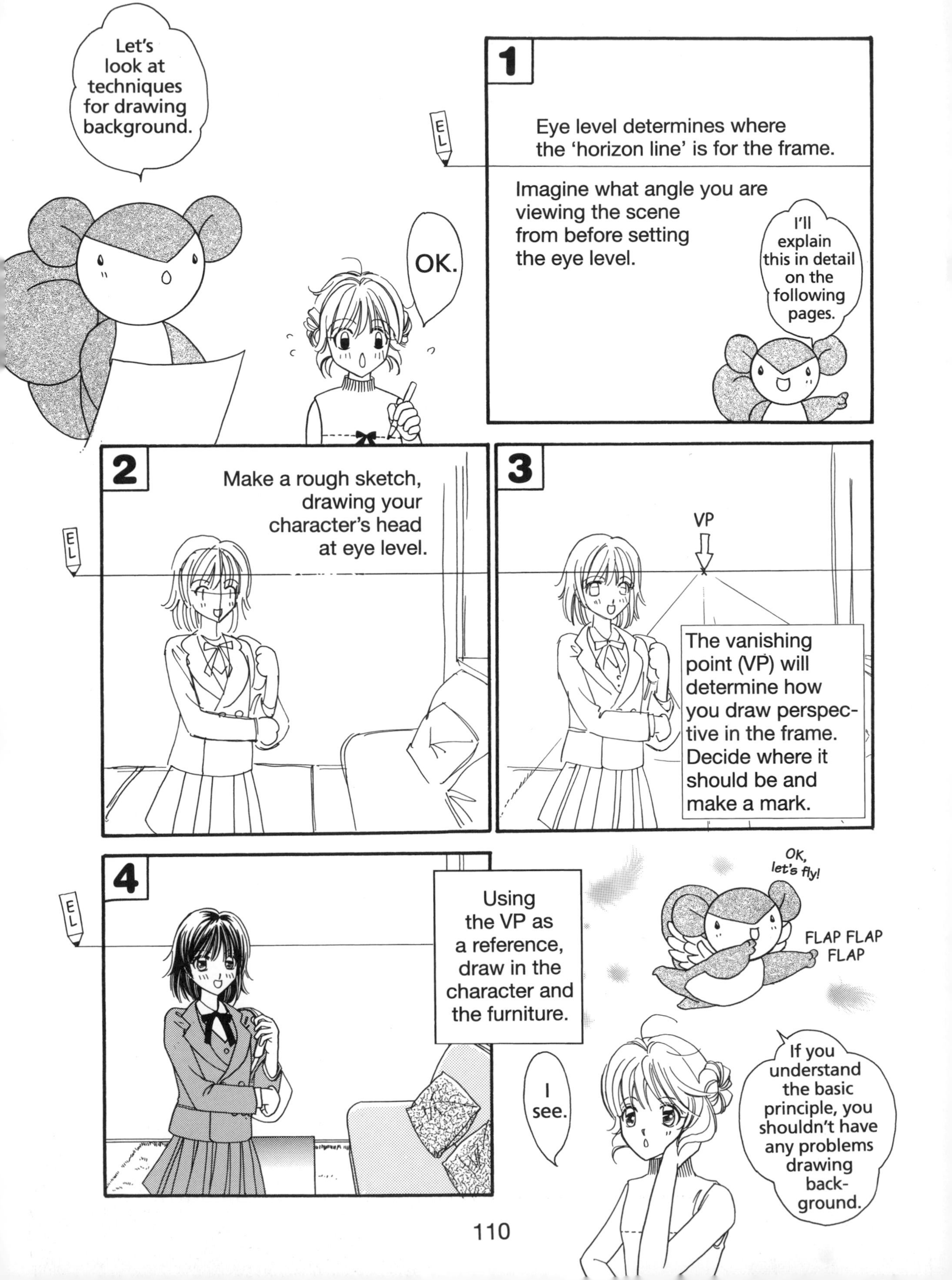

Let's look at techniques for drawing background.
OK.
EL
Eye level determines where the 'horizon line' is for the frame.
Imagine what angle you are viewing the scene from before setting the eye level.
I'll explain this in detail on the following pages.
EL
Make a rough sketch, drawing your character's head at eye level.
VP
The vanishing point (VP) will determine how you draw perspective in the frame. Decide where it should be and make a mark.
EL
Using the VP as a reference, draw in the character and the furniture.
OK, let's fly!
FLAP FLAP FLAP
I see.
If you understand the basic principle, you shouldn't have any problems drawing background.

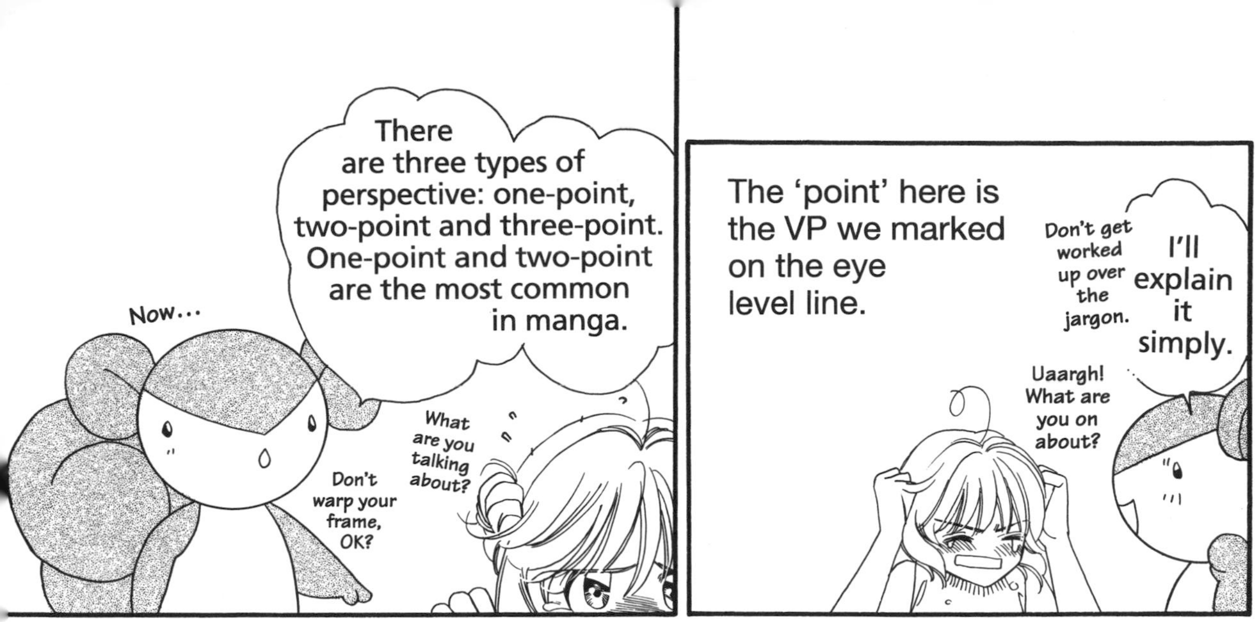
Now…
There are three types of perspective: one-point, two-point and three-point. One-point and two-point are the most common in manga.
What are you talking about?
Don't warp your frame, OK?
The 'point' here is the VP we marked on the eye level line.
Uaargh! What are you on about?
I'll explain it simply.
Don't get worked up over the jargon.

Eye level is always the same as the horizon line of the scene. It's the line that determines what angle the scene will be viewed from.

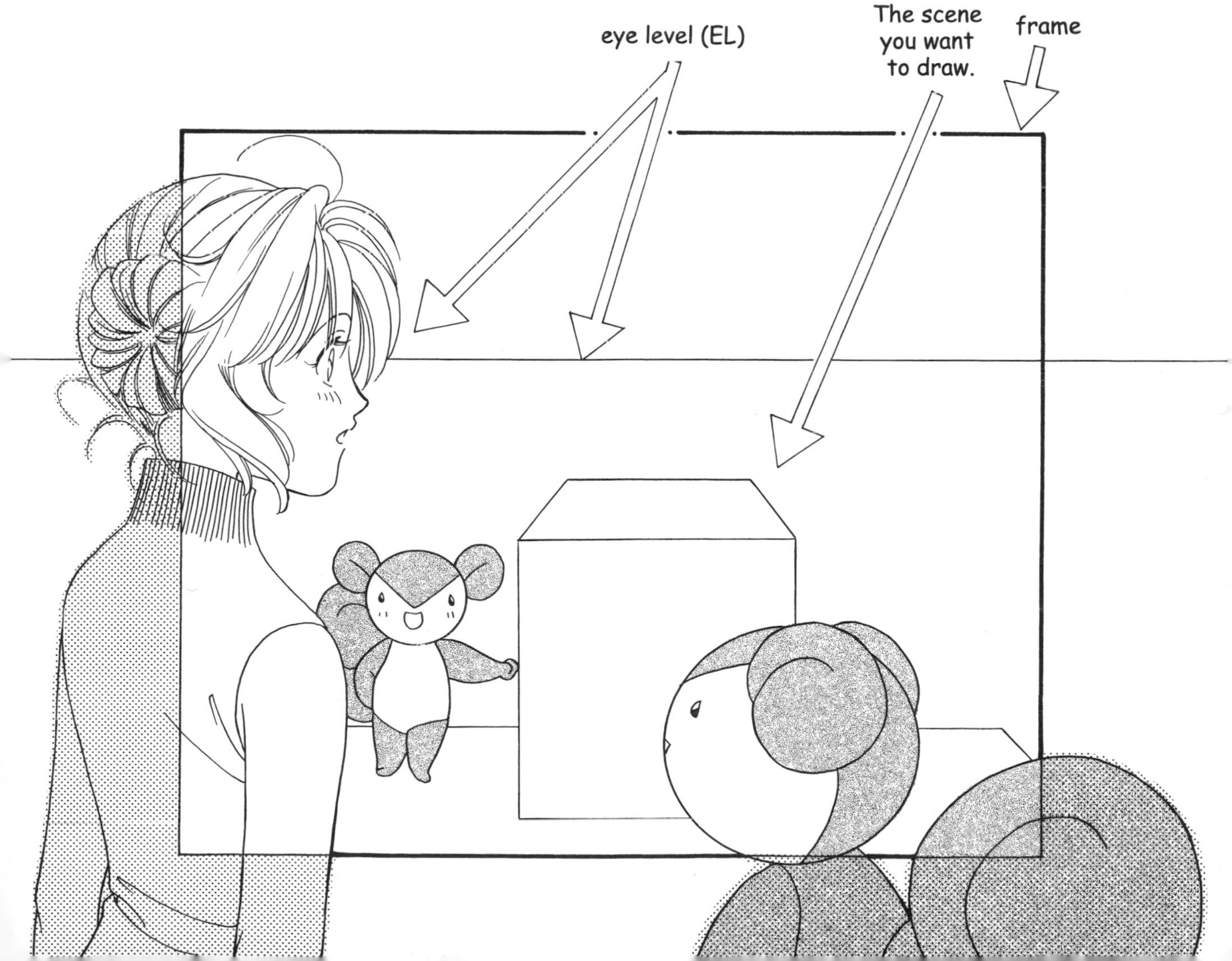
eye level (EL)
The scene you want to draw.
frame

Once you've set the eye level, you must determine the vanishing point.

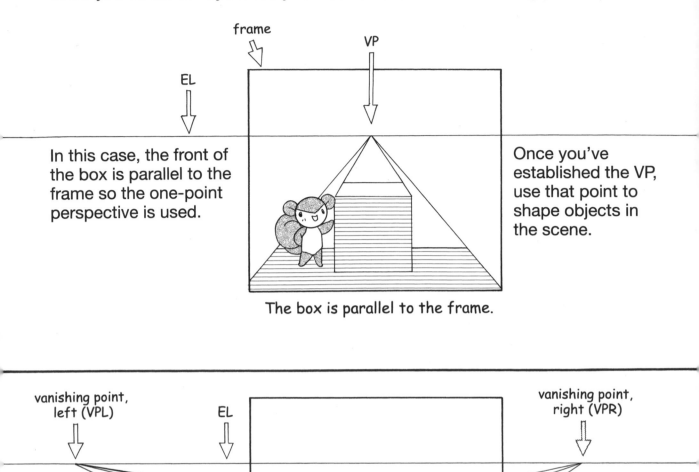

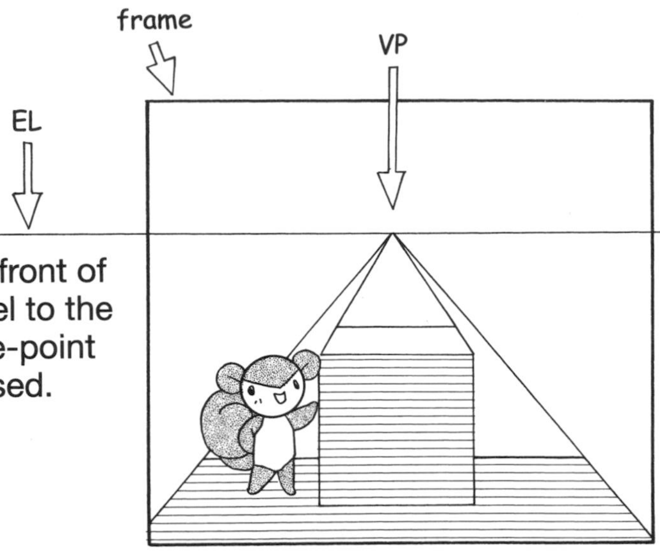
frame
VP
EL

In this case, the front of the box is parallel to the frame so the one-point perspective is used.

Once you've established the VP, use that point to shape objects in the scene.

The box is parallel to the frame.

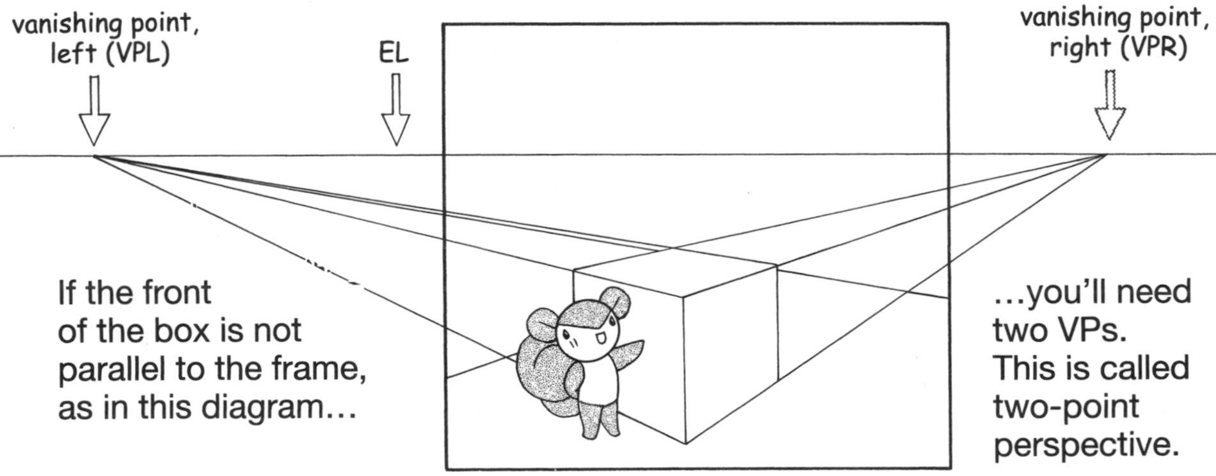
vanishing point, left (VPL)
EL
vanishing point, right (VPR)

If the front of the box is not parallel to the frame, as in this diagram…

…you'll need two VPs. This is called two-point perspective.

The box is at an angle to the frame.

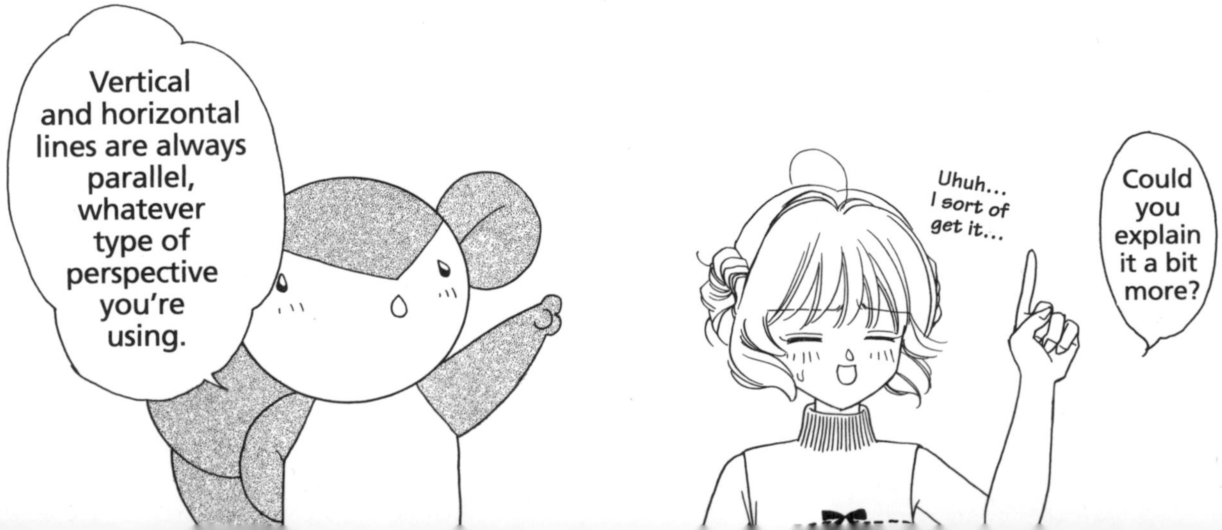
Vertical and horizontal lines are always parallel, whatever type of perspective you're using.
Uhuh… I sort of get it…
Could you explain it a bit more?

The answers are on the next page.

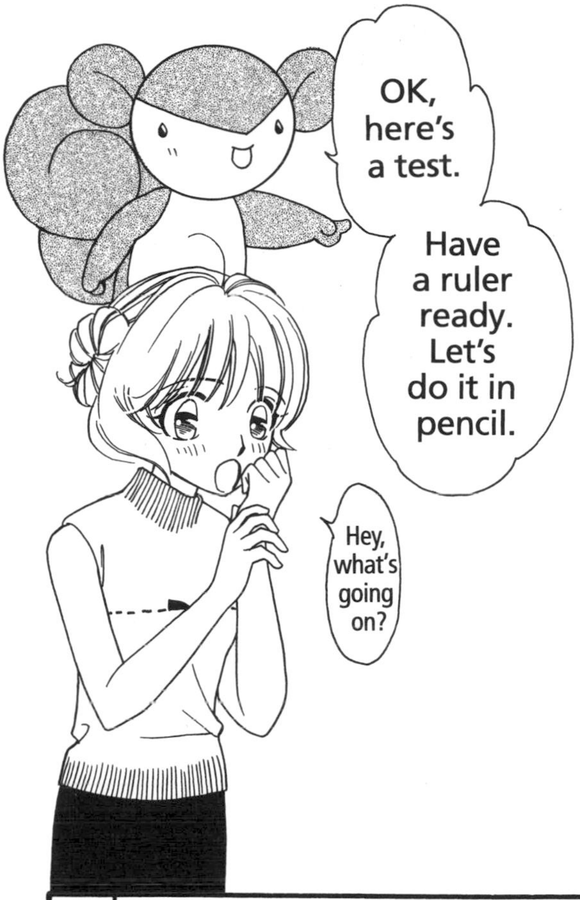
OK, here's a test.
Have a ruler ready. Let's do it in pencil.
Hey, what's going on?

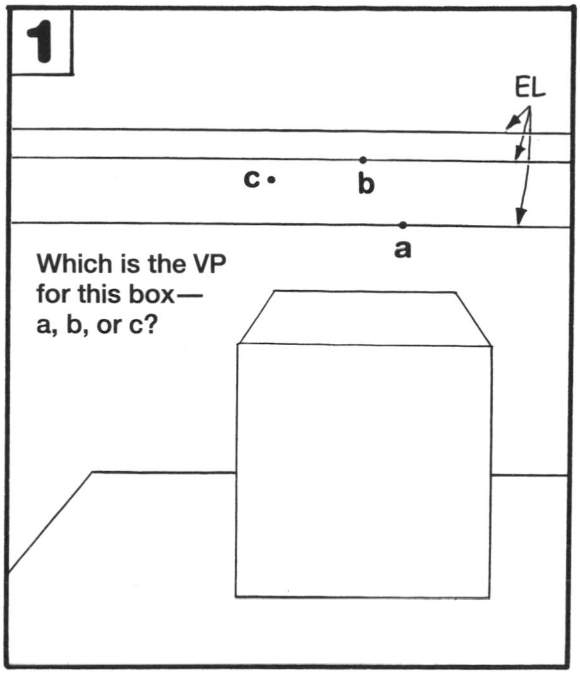
1
EL
c
b
a
Which is the VP for this box—a, b, or c?

Hint: try extending lines that aren't vertical or horizontal.

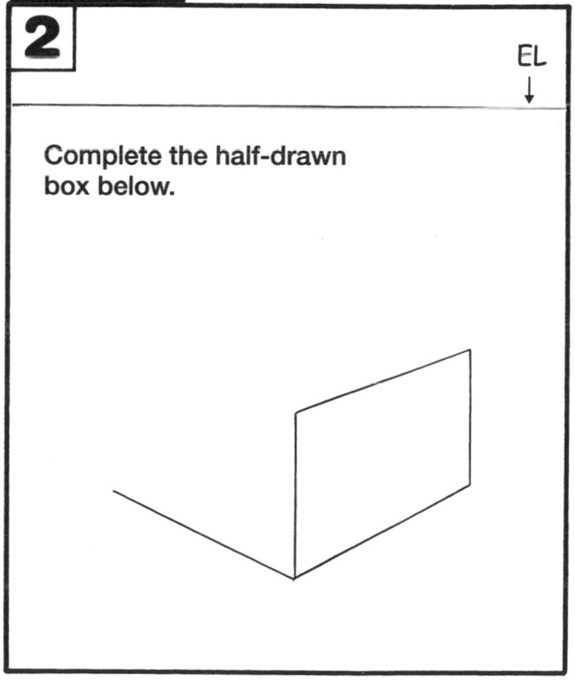
2
EL
Complete the half-drawn box below.

Hint: extend the lines at the bottom of the box to find the VP.

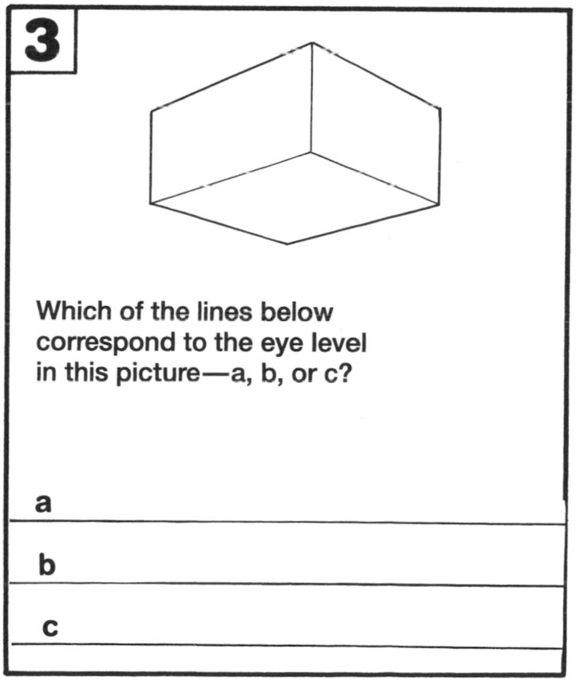
3
Which of the lines below correspond to the eye level in this picture—a, b, or c?
a
b
c

Hint: identify which line the VP is on.

Finished? Then let's have a look at the answers. If you get them all right, then you can start drawing perspective on your own.

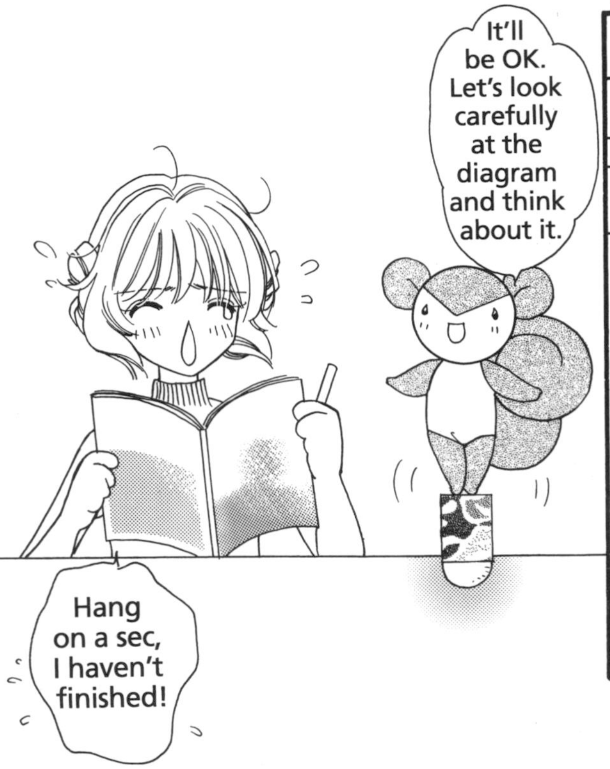
It'll be OK. Let's look carefully at the diagram and think about it.
Hang on a sec, I haven't finished!

1. The answer is b.

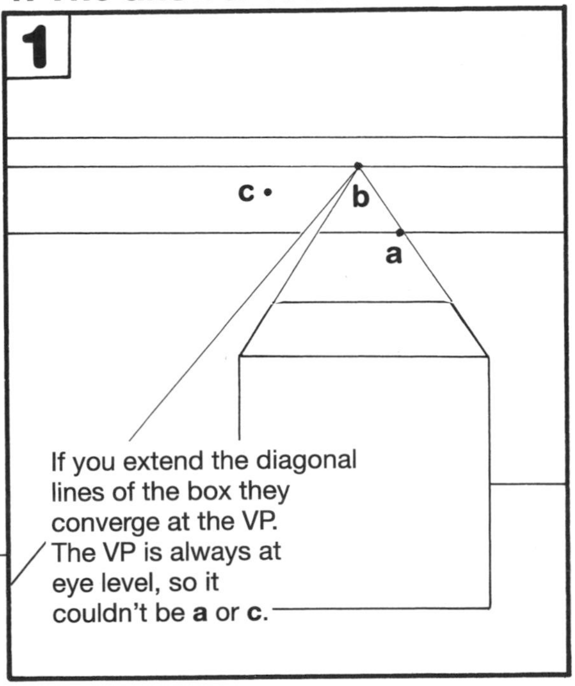
1
c
b
a
If you extend the diagonal lines of the box they converge at the VP. The VP is always at eye level, so it couldn't be **a** or **c**.

2.

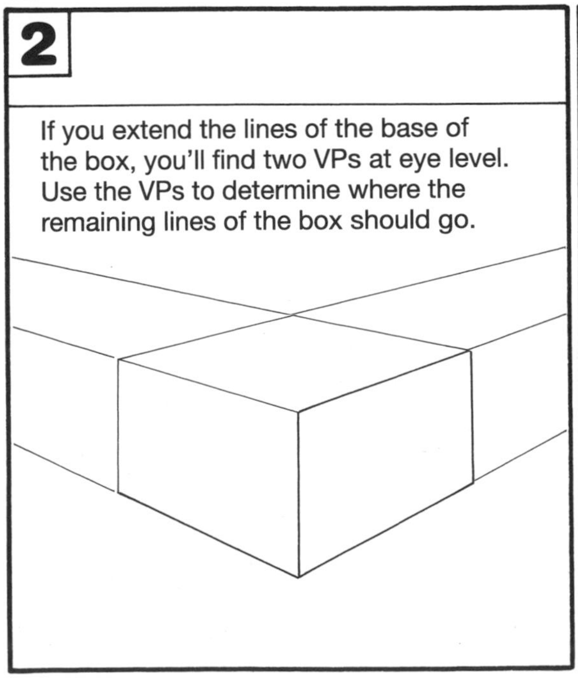
2
If you extend the lines of the base of the box, you'll find two VPs at eye level. Use the VPs to determine where the remaining lines of the box should go.

3. The answer is a.

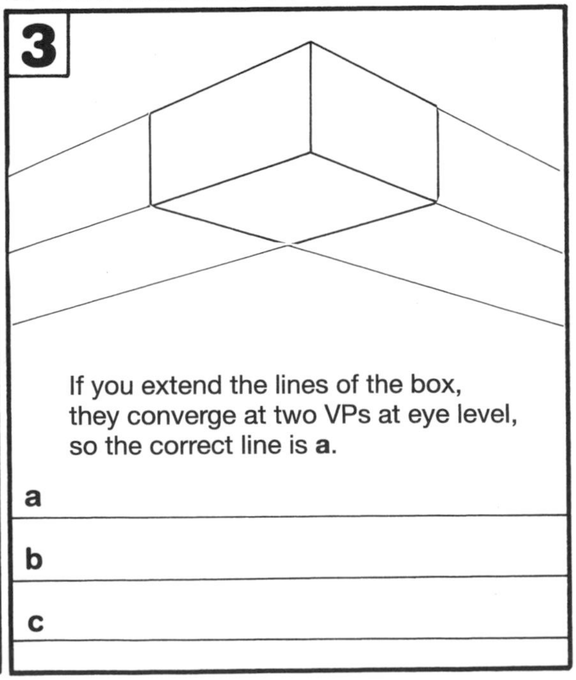
3
If you extend the lines of the box, they converge at two VPs at eye level, so the correct line is **a**.
a
b
c

ONE-POINT PERSPECTIVE

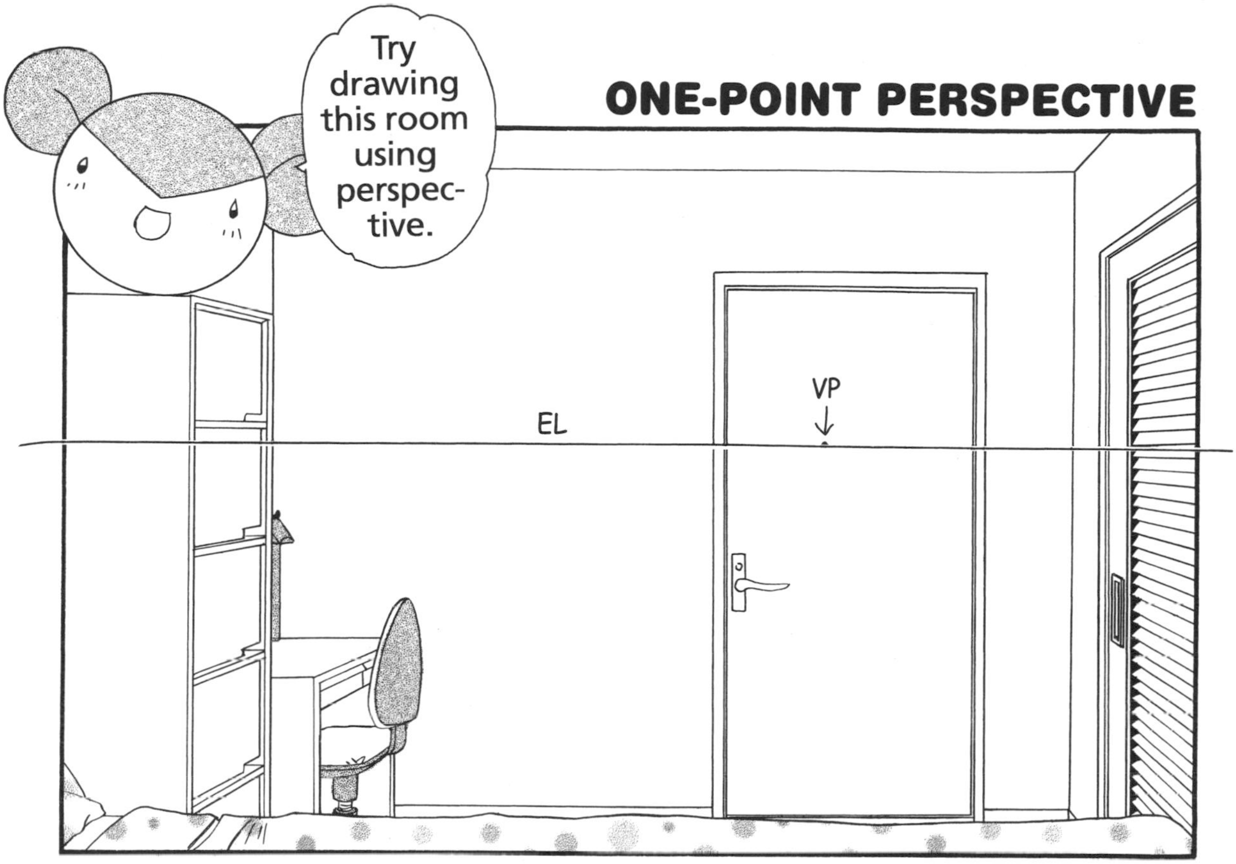

Try drawing this room using perspec-tive.
VP
EL

TWO-POINT PERSPECTIVE

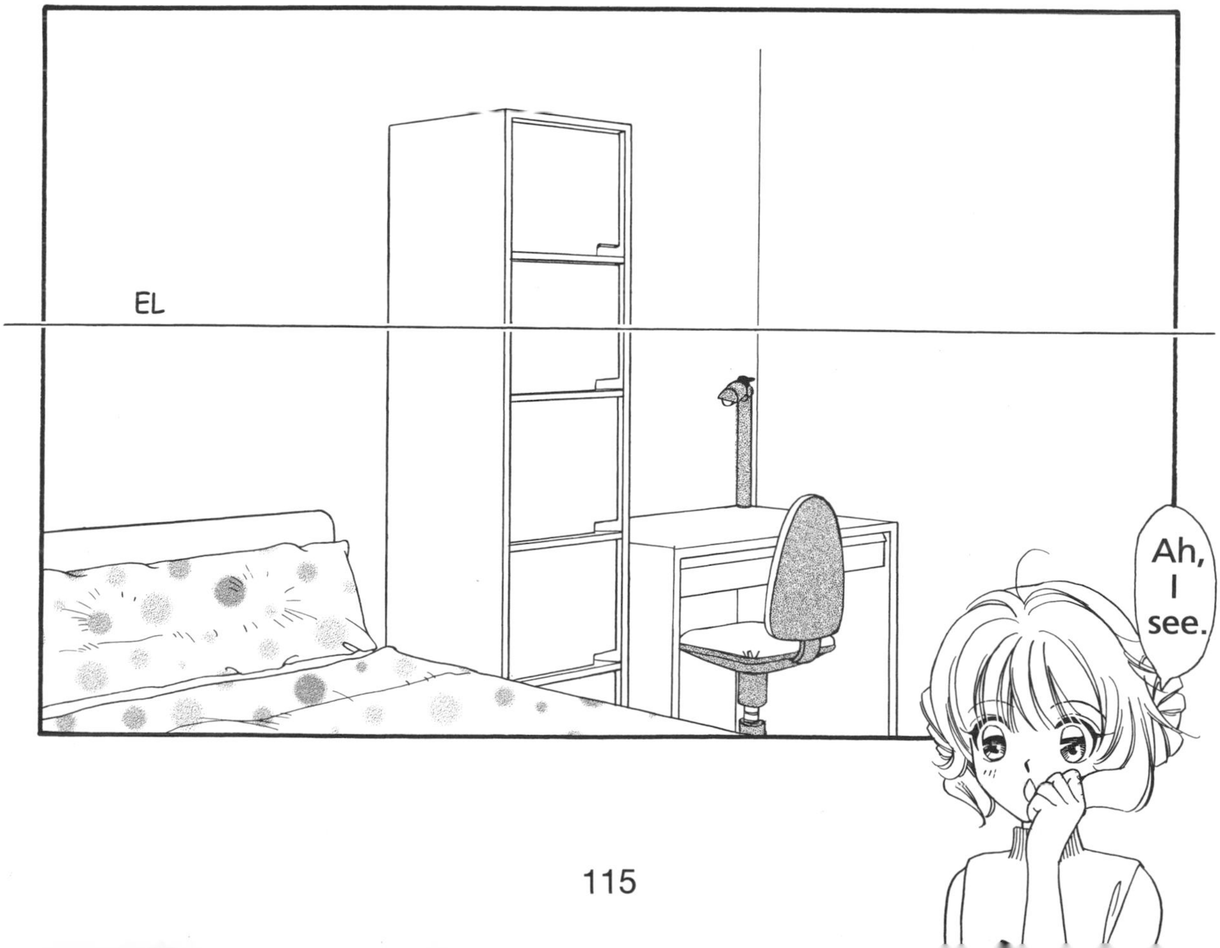

EL
Ah, I see.

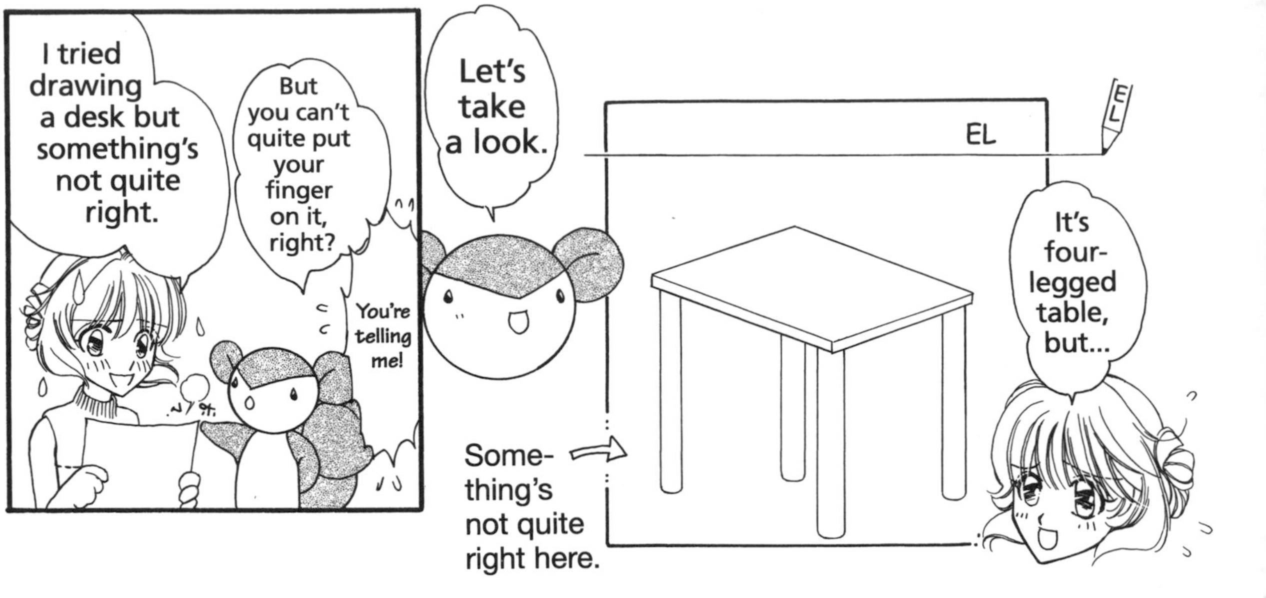
I tried drawing a desk but something's not quite right.
But you can't quite put your finger on it, right?
You're telling me!
Let's take a look.
EL
E L
It's four-legged table, but...
Some-thing's not quite right here.

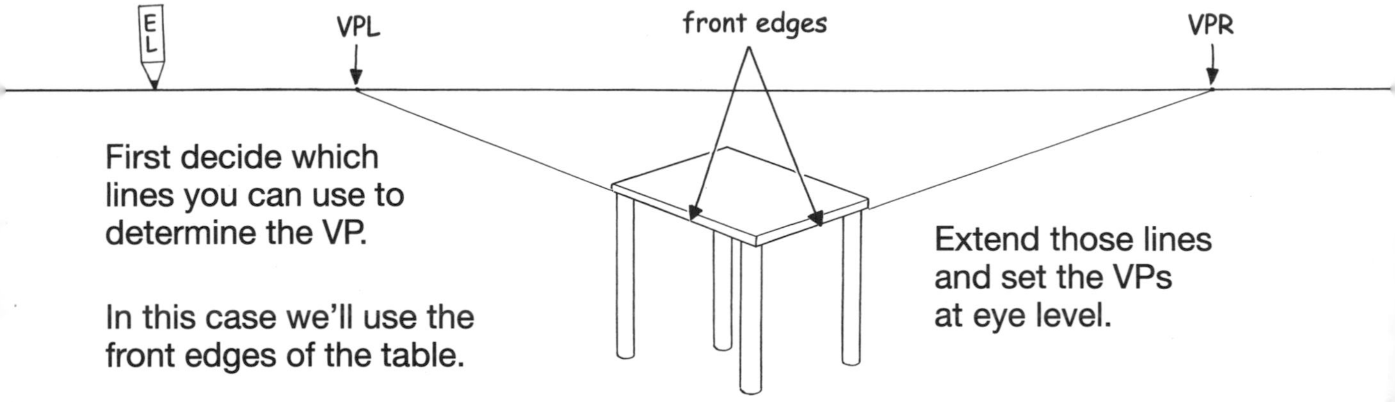
E L
VPL
front edges
VPR
First decide which lines you can use to determine the VP.
In this case we'll use the front edges of the table.
Extend those lines and set the VPs at eye level.

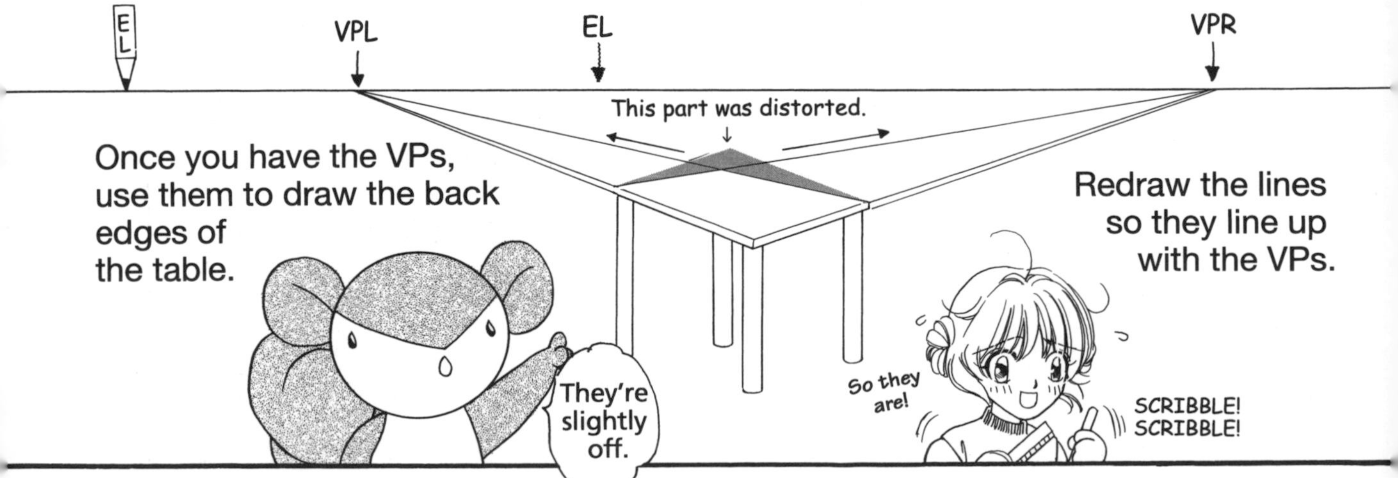
E L
VPL
EL
VPR
This part was distorted.
Once you have the VPs, use them to draw the back edges of the table.
Redraw the lines so they line up with the VPs.
They're slightly off.
So they are!
SCRIBBLE! SCRIBBLE!

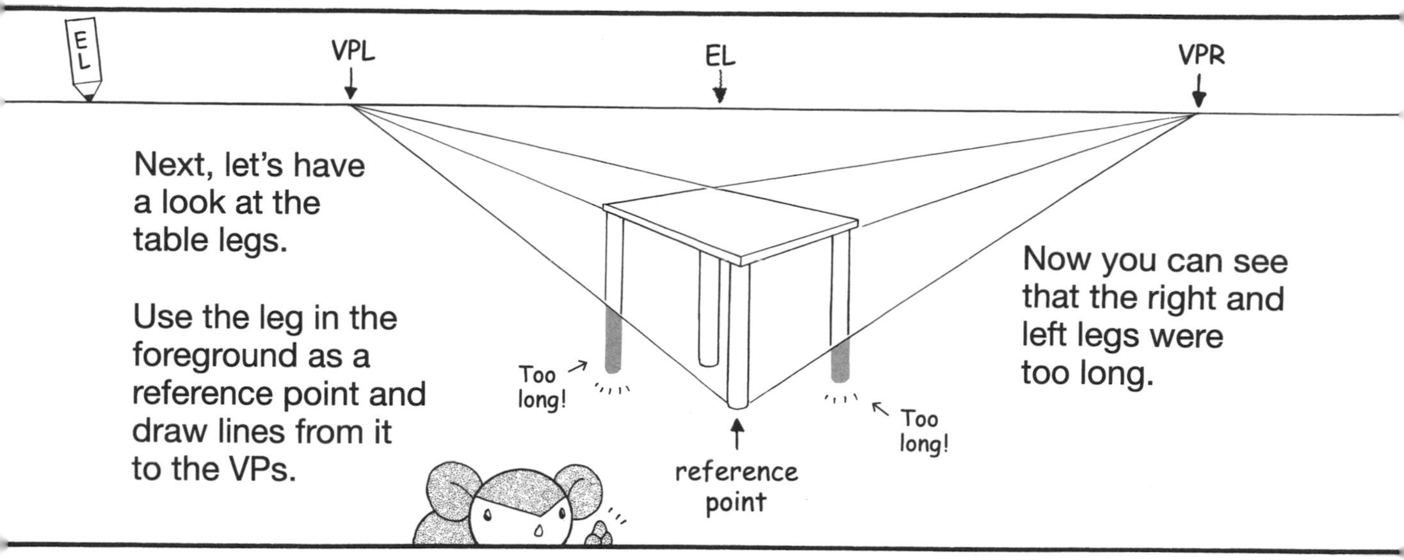
EL
VPL
EL
VPR
Next, let's have a look at the table legs.
Use the leg in the foreground as a reference point and draw lines from it to the VPs.
Too long!
reference point
Too long!
Now you can see that the right and left legs were too long.

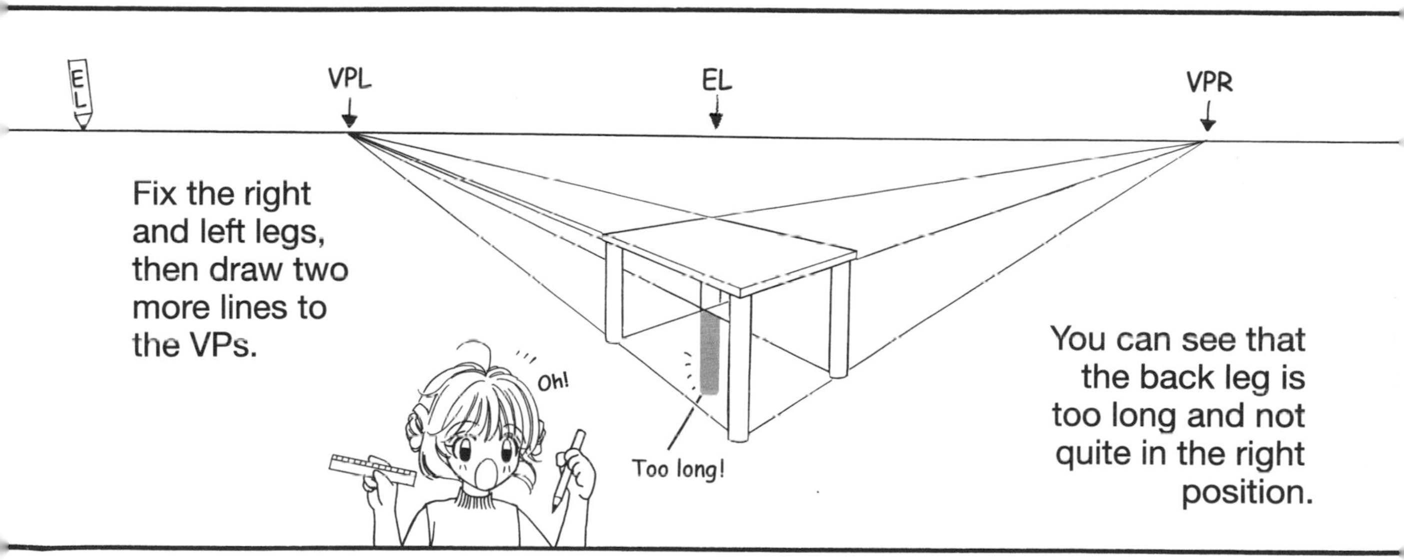
EL
VPL
EL
VPR
Fix the right and left legs, then draw two more lines to the VPs.
Oh!
Too long!
You can see that the back leg is too long and not quite in the right position.

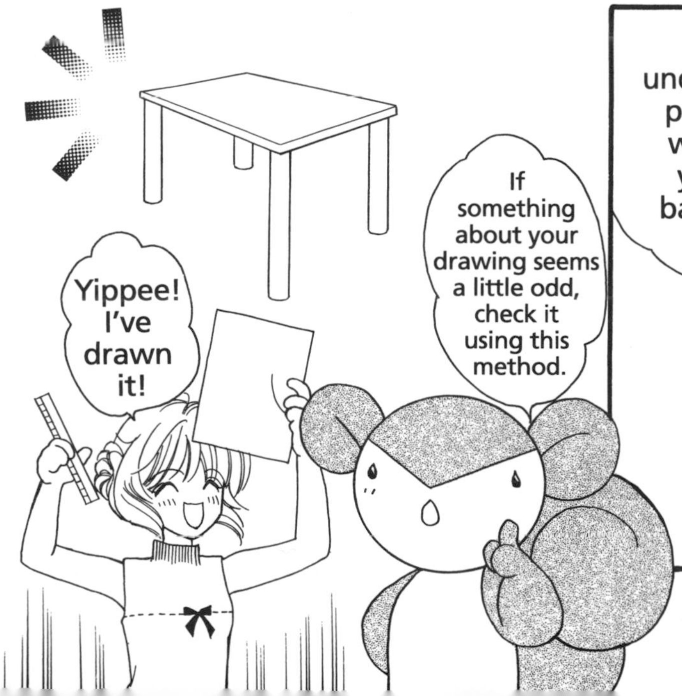
Yippee! I've drawn it!
If something about your drawing seems a little odd, check it using this method.

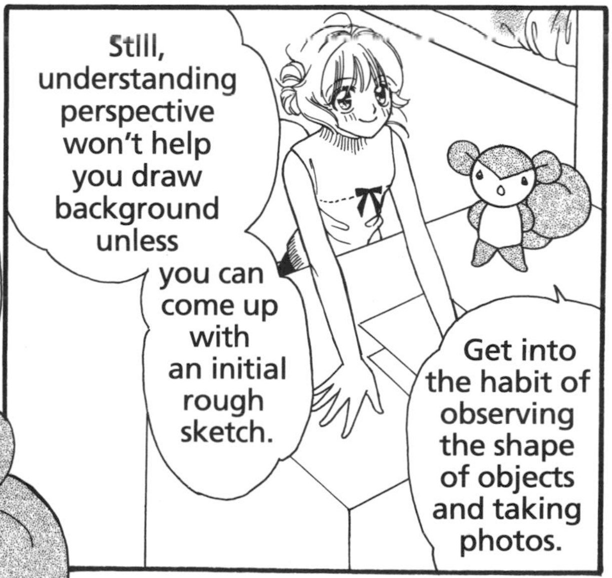
Still, understanding perspective won't help you draw background unless you can come up with an initial rough sketch.
Get into the habit of observing the shape of objects and taking photos.

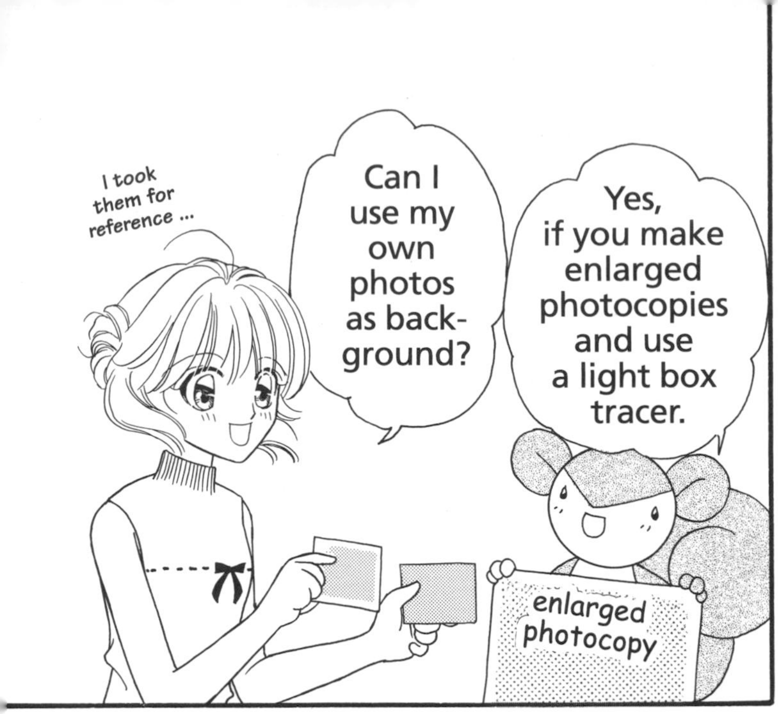
I took them for reference ...
Can I use my own photos as back-ground?
Yes, if you make enlarged photocopies and use a light box tracer.
enlarged photocopy

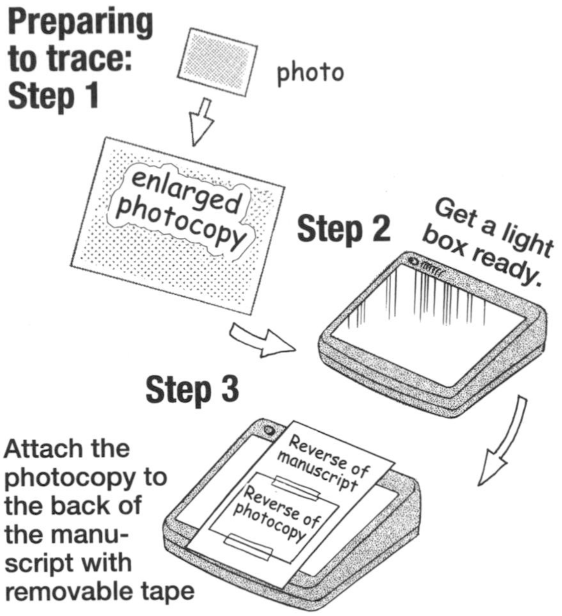
Preparing to trace: Step 1
photo
enlarged photocopy
Step 2
Get a light box ready.
Step 3
Attach the photocopy to the back of the manu-script with removable tape
Reverse of manuscript
Reverse of photocopy

Before you start tracing, look at your work on the light box to check that the size and position are right.

The eye levels in the frame and the photo must correspond.

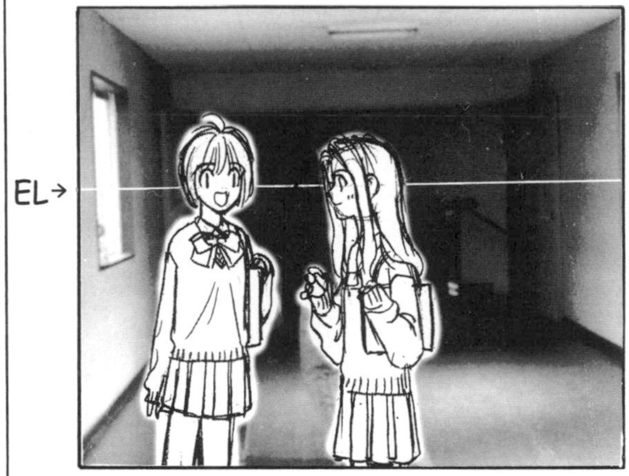
EL→

If the eye levels aren't the same, the charac-ters will look strange against the background.

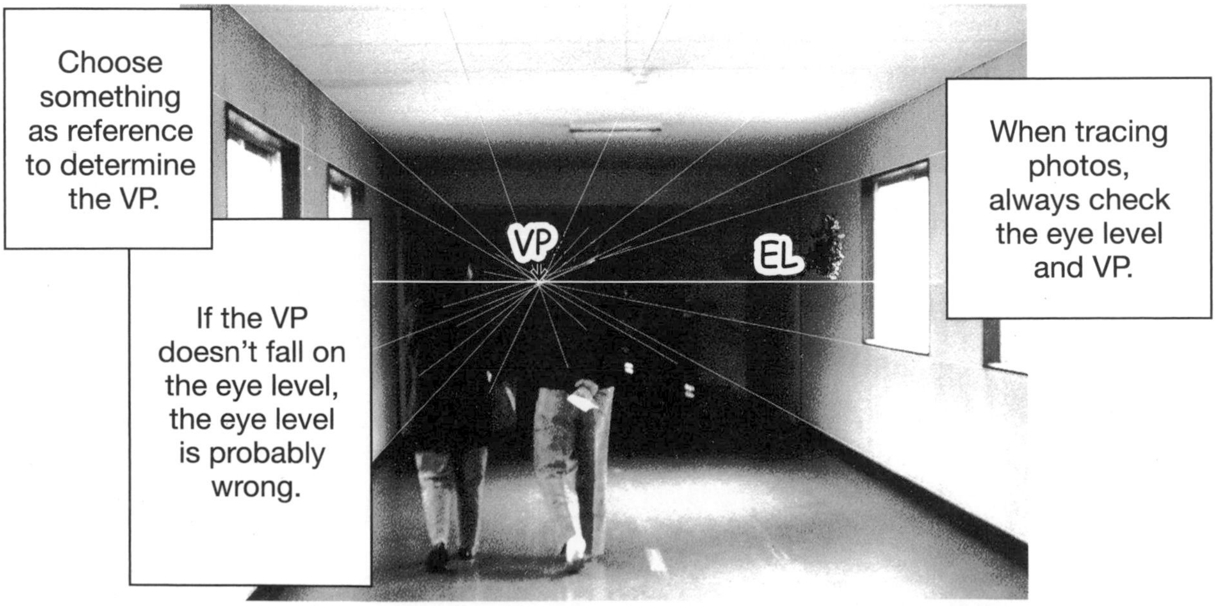
Choose something as reference to determine the VP.
If the VP doesn't fall on the eye level, the eye level is probably wrong.
VP
EL
When tracing photos, always check the eye level and VP.

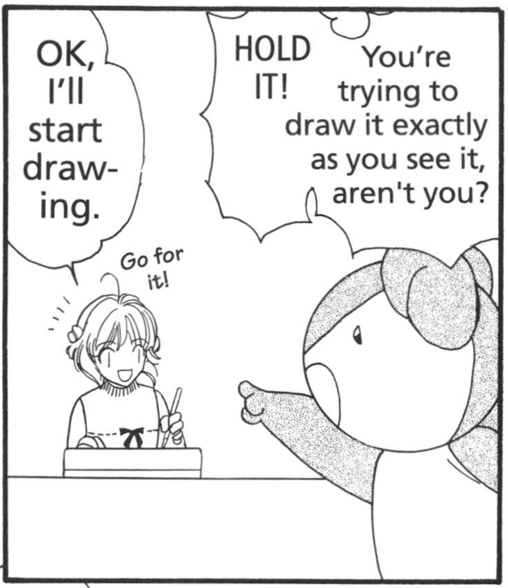
OK, I'll start draw-ing.
Go for it!
HOLD IT! You're trying to draw it exactly as you see it, aren't you?

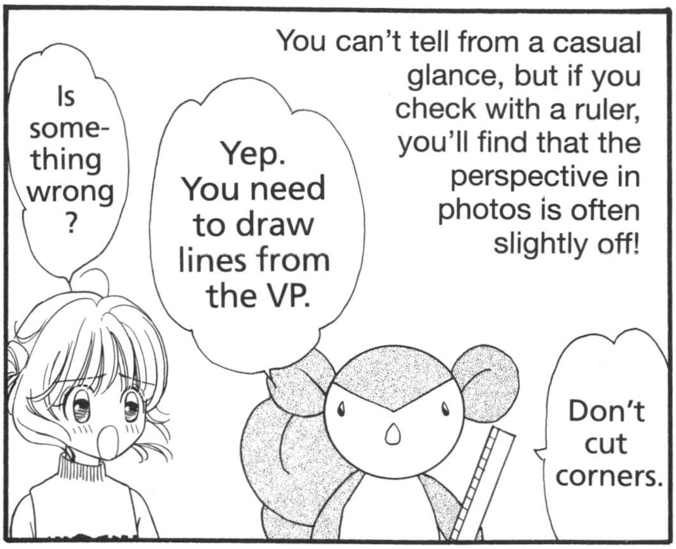
Is some-thing wrong?
Yep. You need to draw lines from the VP.
You can't tell from a casual glance, but if you check with a ruler, you'll find that the perspective in photos is often slightly off!
Don't cut corners.

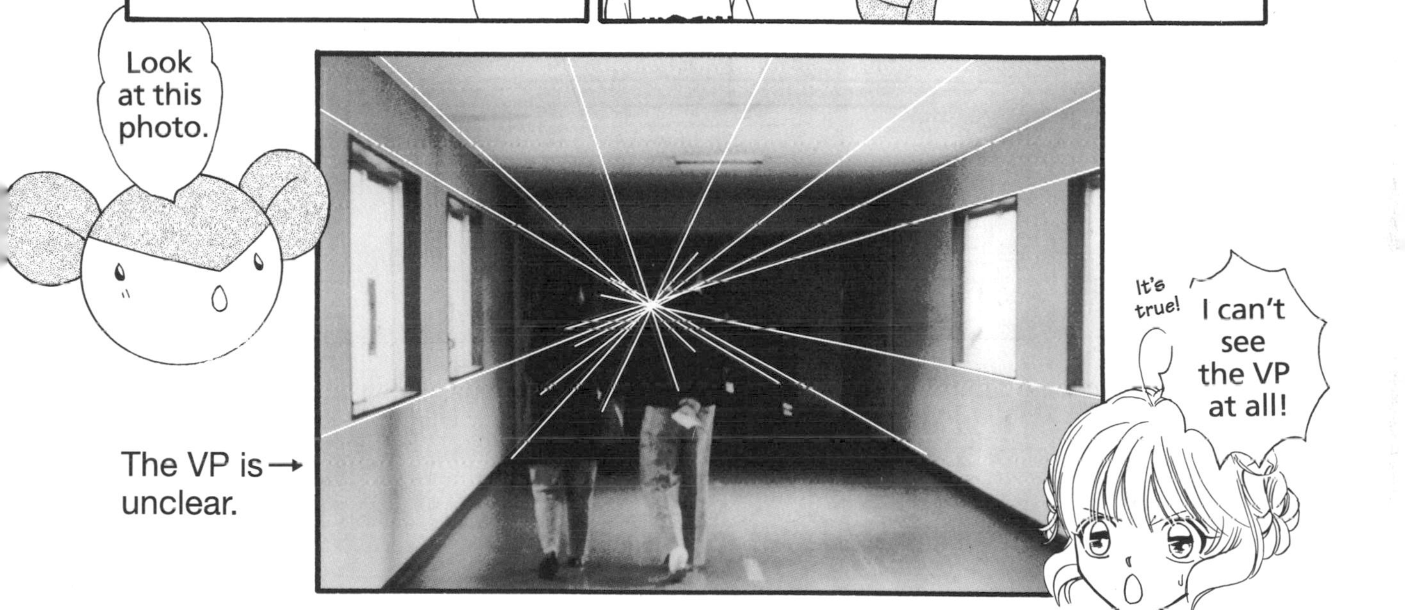
Look at this photo.
The VP is → unclear.
It's true!
I can't see the VP at all!

In this case, pick your own point on the eye level to use as a VP and draw out from there, correcting any distorted lines.

Picture traced from → the photo above, adjusted to correct the perspective.

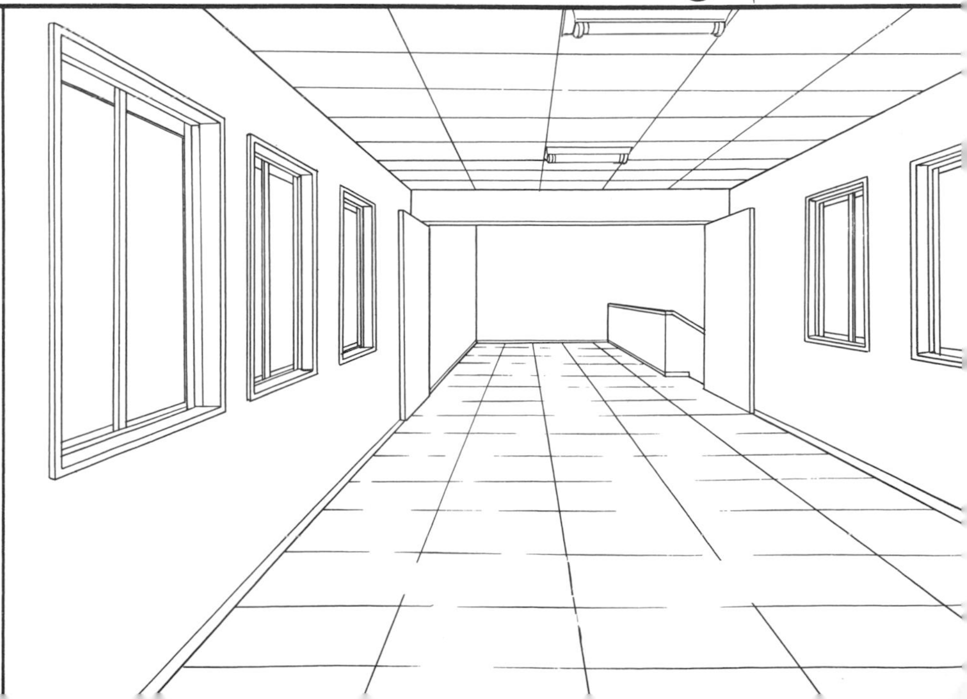

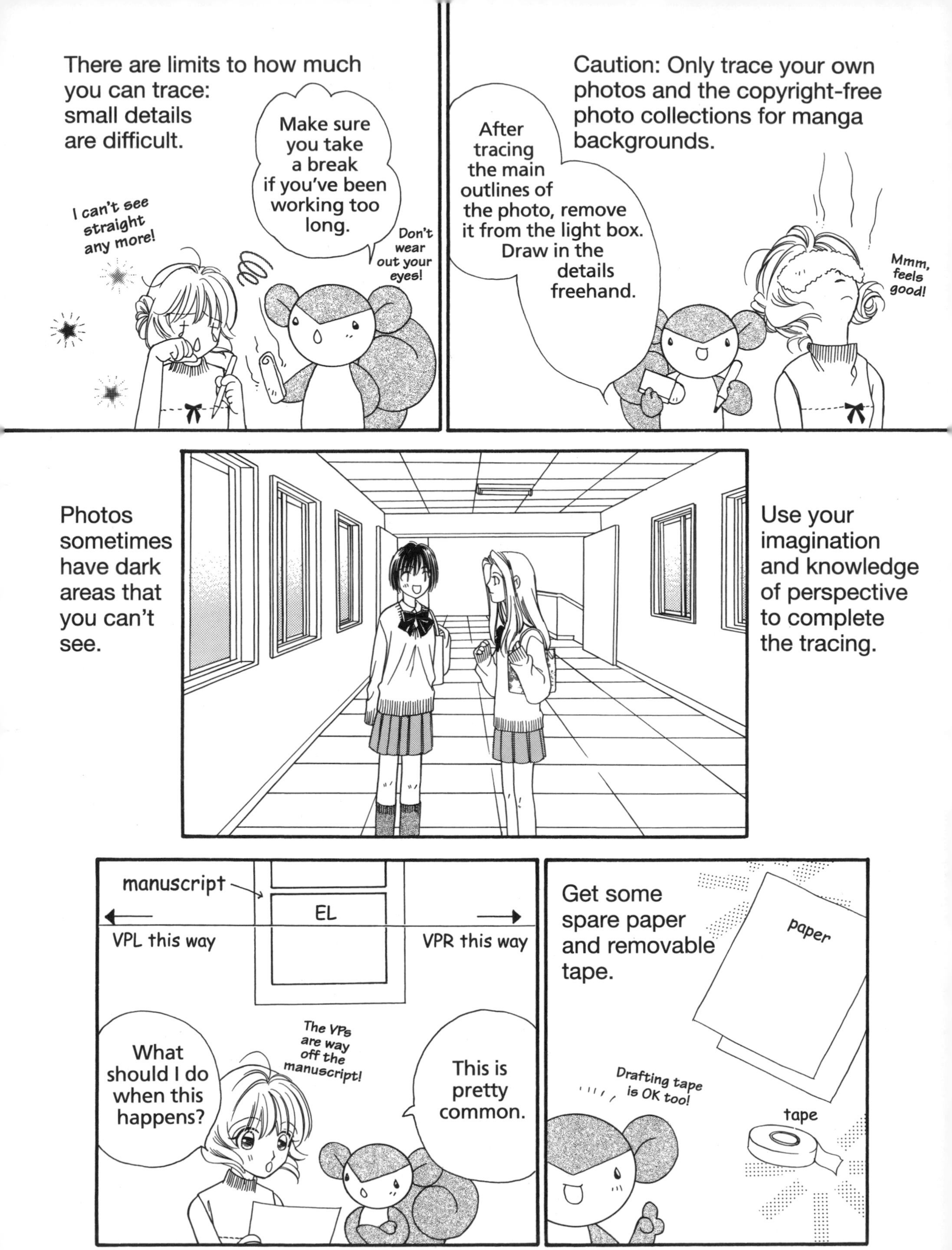
There are limits to how much you can trace: small details are difficult.
Make sure you take a break if you've been working too long.
I can't see straight any more!
Don't wear out your eyes!
Caution: Only trace your own photos and the copyright-free photo collections for manga backgrounds.
After tracing the main outlines of the photo, remove it from the light box. Draw in the details freehand.
Mmm, feels good!
Photos sometimes have dark areas that you can't see.
Use your imagination and knowledge of perspective to complete the tracing.
manuscript
EL
VPL this way
VPR this way
What should I do when this happens?
The VPs are way off the manuscript!
This is pretty common.
Get some spare paper and removable tape.
paper
Drafting tape is OK too!
tape

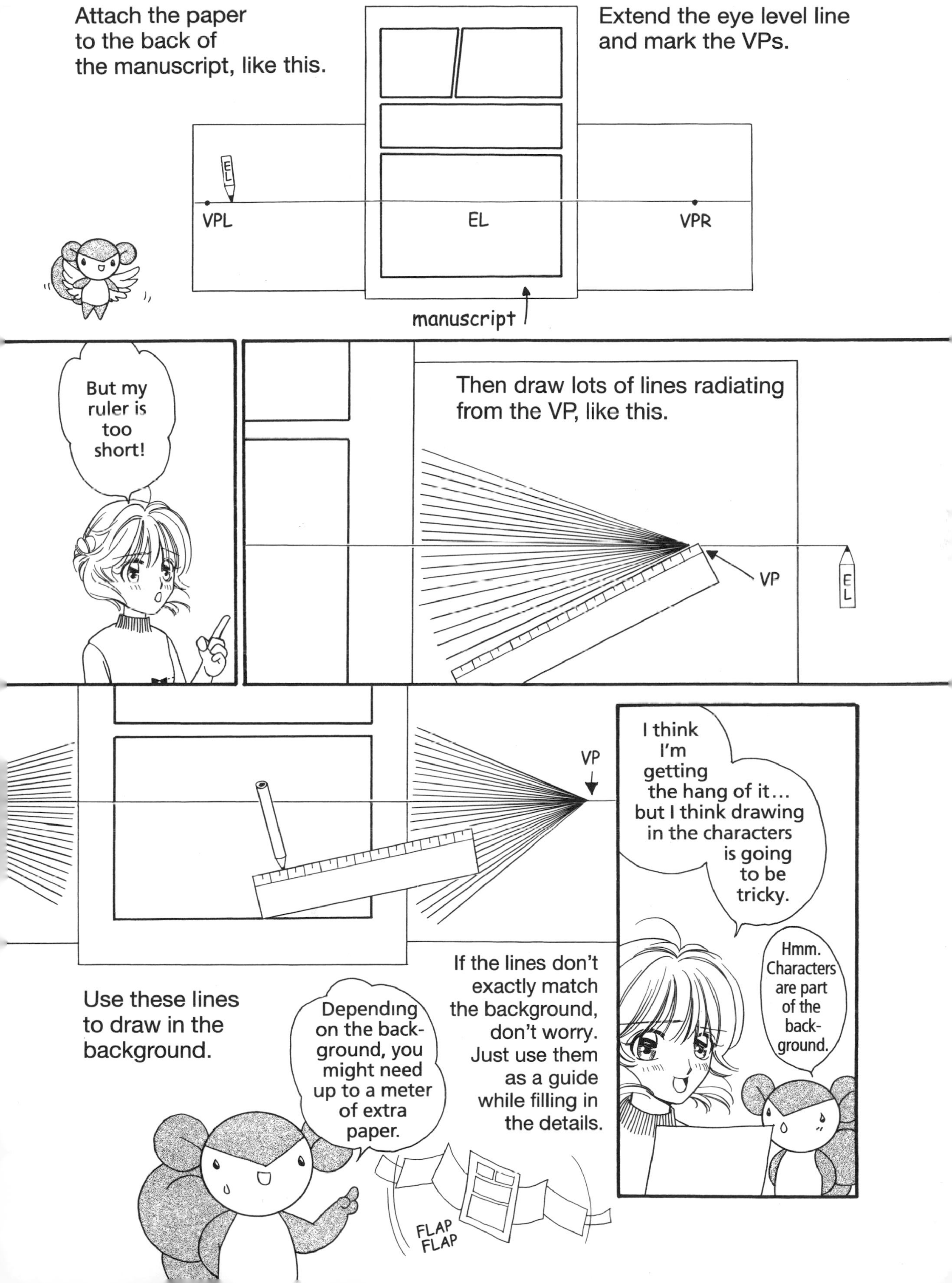
Attach the paper to the back of the manuscript, like this.
Extend the eye level line and mark the VPs.
EL
VPL
EL
VPR
manuscript
But my ruler is too short!
Then draw lots of lines radiating from the VP, like this.
VP
EL
VP
Use these lines to draw in the background.
Depending on the background, you might need up to a meter of extra paper.
FLAP FLAP
If the lines don't exactly match the background, don't worry. Just use them as a guide while filling in the details.
I think I'm getting the hang of it… but I think drawing in the characters is going to be tricky.
Hmm. Characters are part of the background.

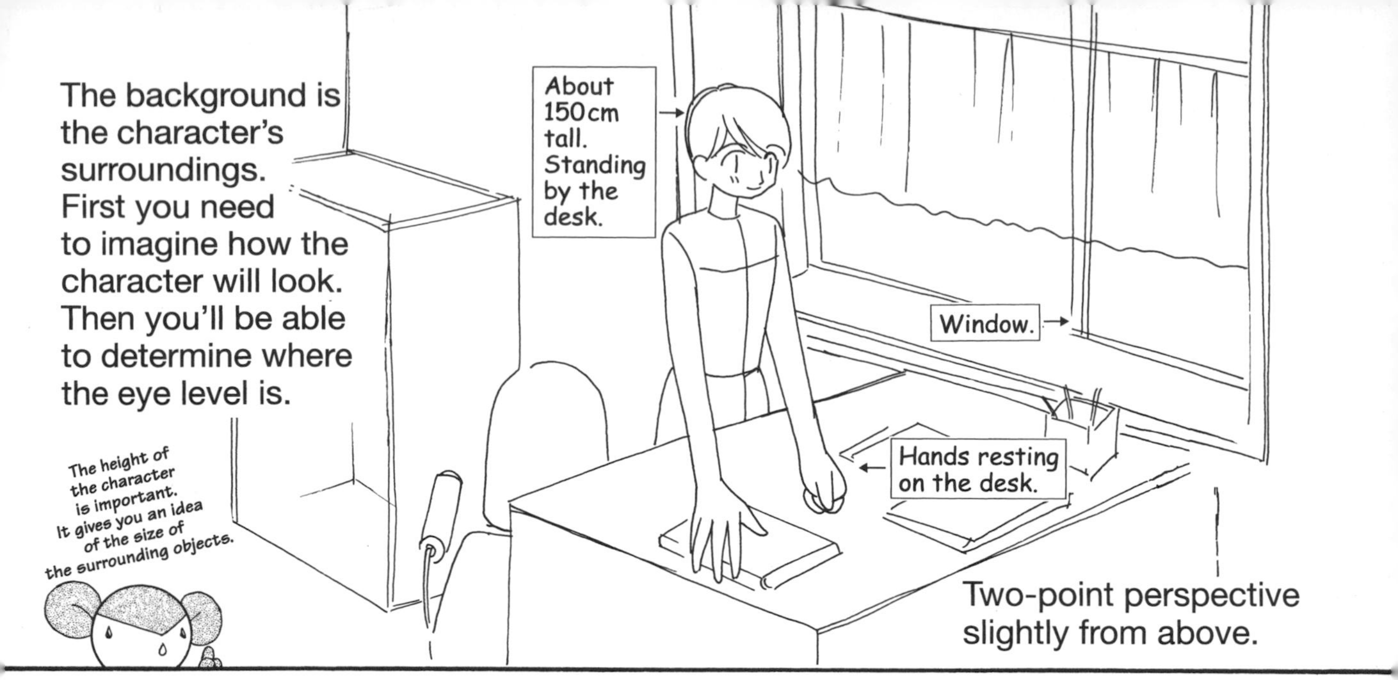
The background is the character's surroundings. First you need to imagine how the character will look. Then you'll be able to determine where the eye level is.
About 150cm tall. Standing by the desk.
Window.
Hands resting on the desk.
The height of the character is important. It gives you an idea of the size of the surrounding objects.
Two-point perspective slightly from above.

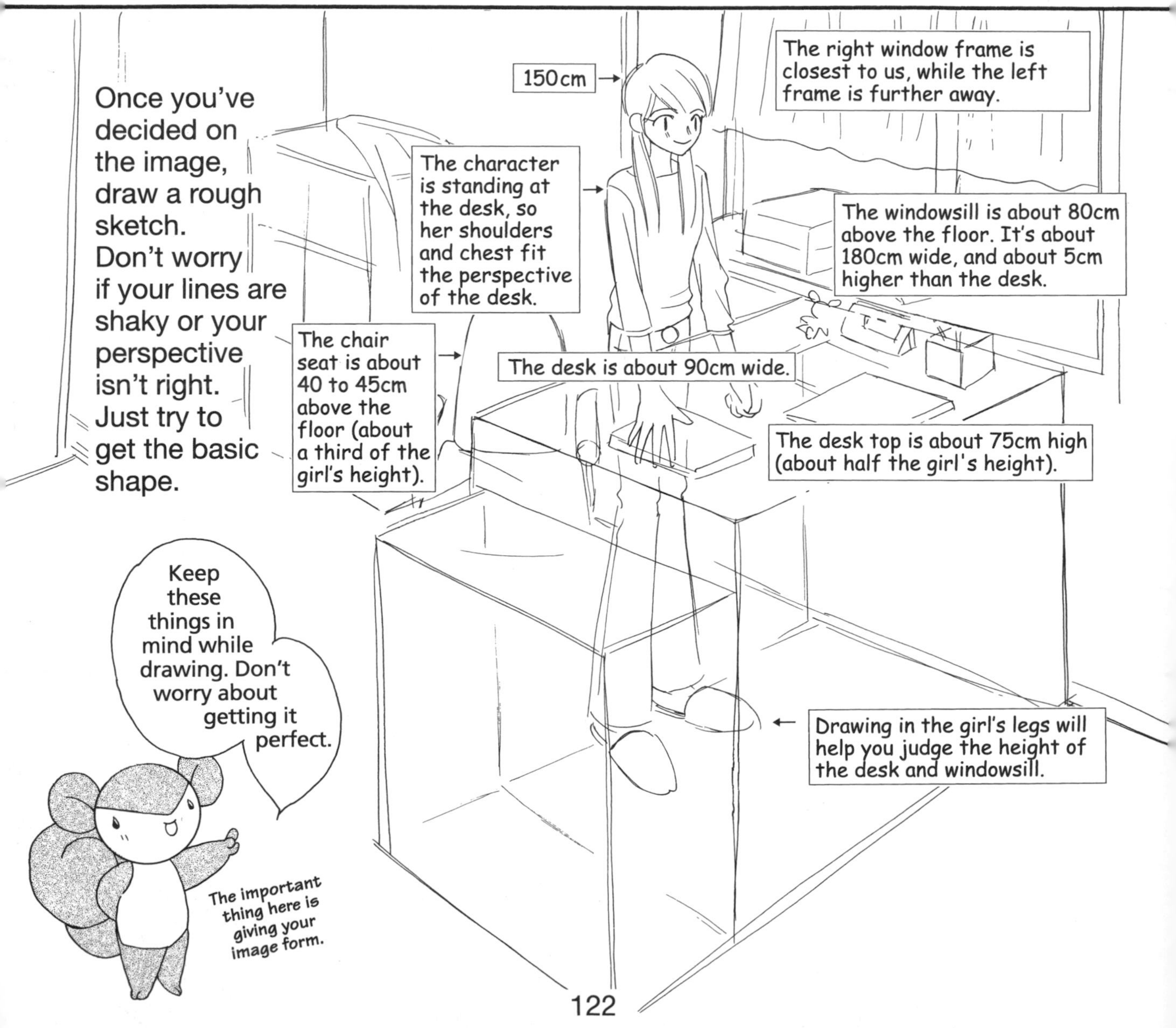
Once you've decided on the image, draw a rough sketch. Don't worry if your lines are shaky or your perspective isn't right. Just try to get the basic shape.
150cm
The right window frame is closest to us, while the left frame is further away.
The character is standing at the desk, so her shoulders and chest fit the perspective of the desk.
The windowsill is about 80cm above the floor. It's about 180cm wide, and about 5cm higher than the desk.
The chair seat is about 40 to 45cm above the floor (about a third of the girl's height).
The desk is about 90cm wide.
The desk top is about 75cm high (about half the girl's height).
Keep these things in mind while drawing. Don't worry about getting it perfect.
Drawing in the girl's legs will help you judge the height of the desk and windowsill.
The important thing here is giving your image form.

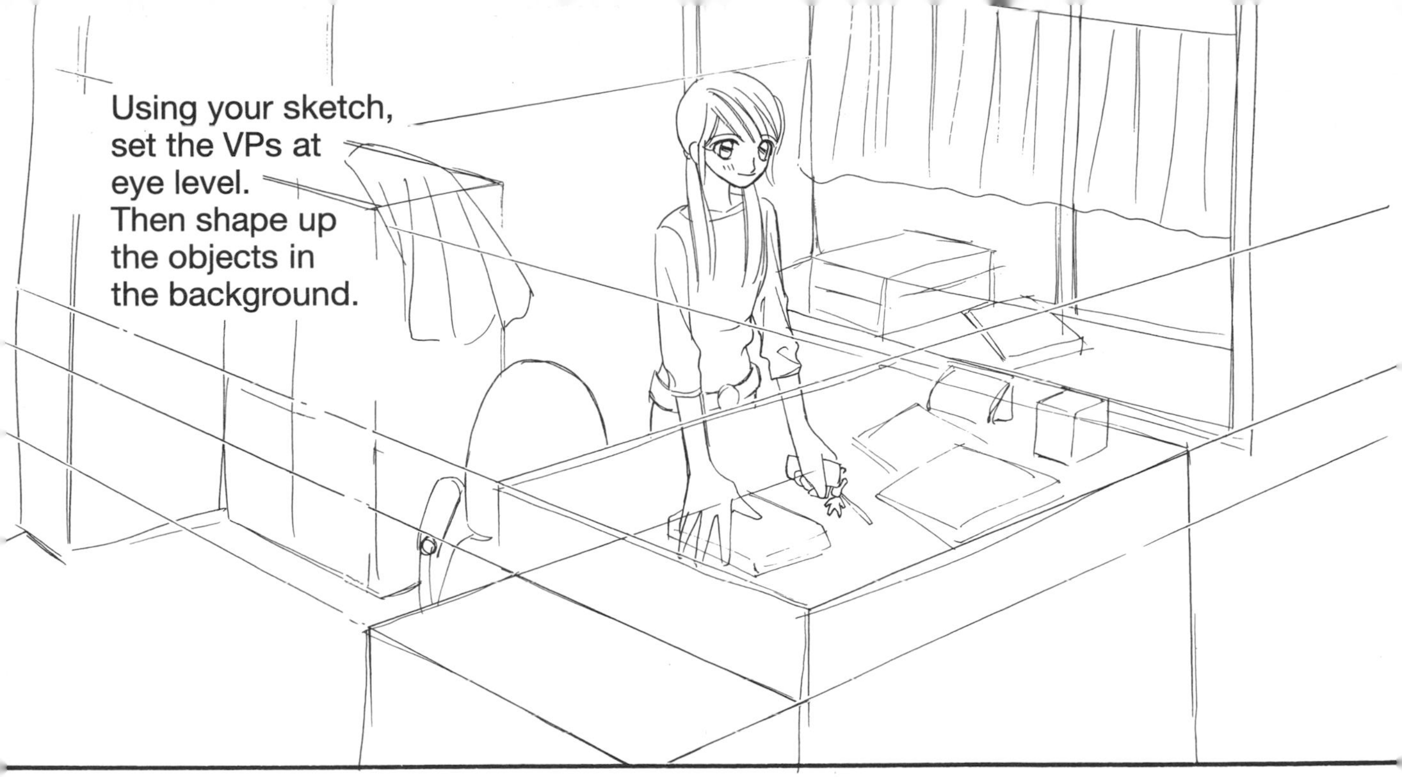
Using your sketch, set the VPs at eye level. Then shape up the objects in the background.

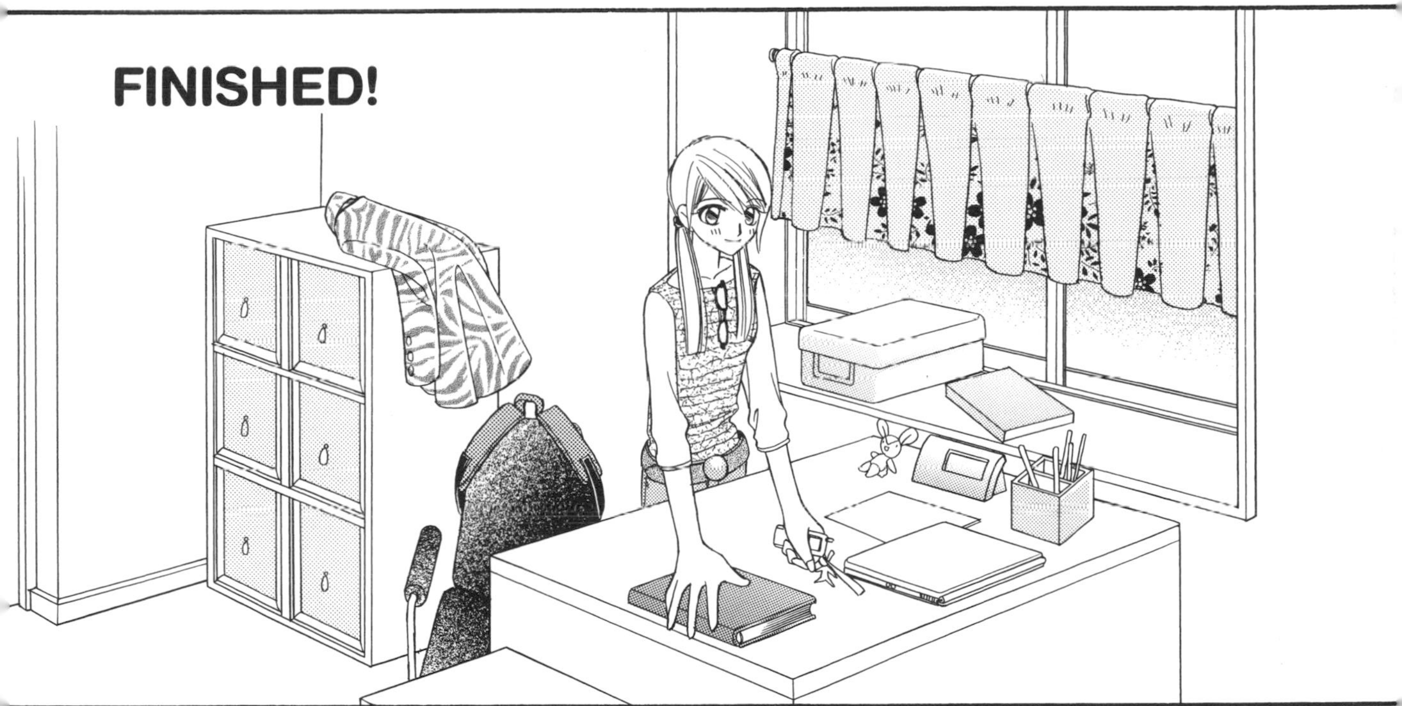
FINISHED!

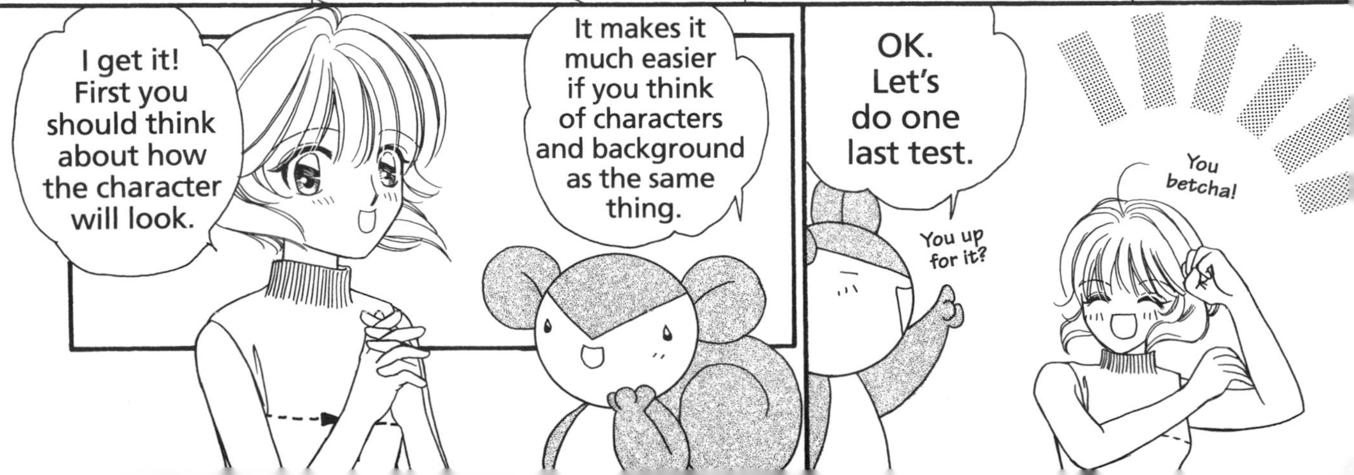
I get it! First you should think about how the character will look.
It makes it much easier if you think of characters and background as the same thing.
OK. Let's do one last test.
You up for it?
You betcha!

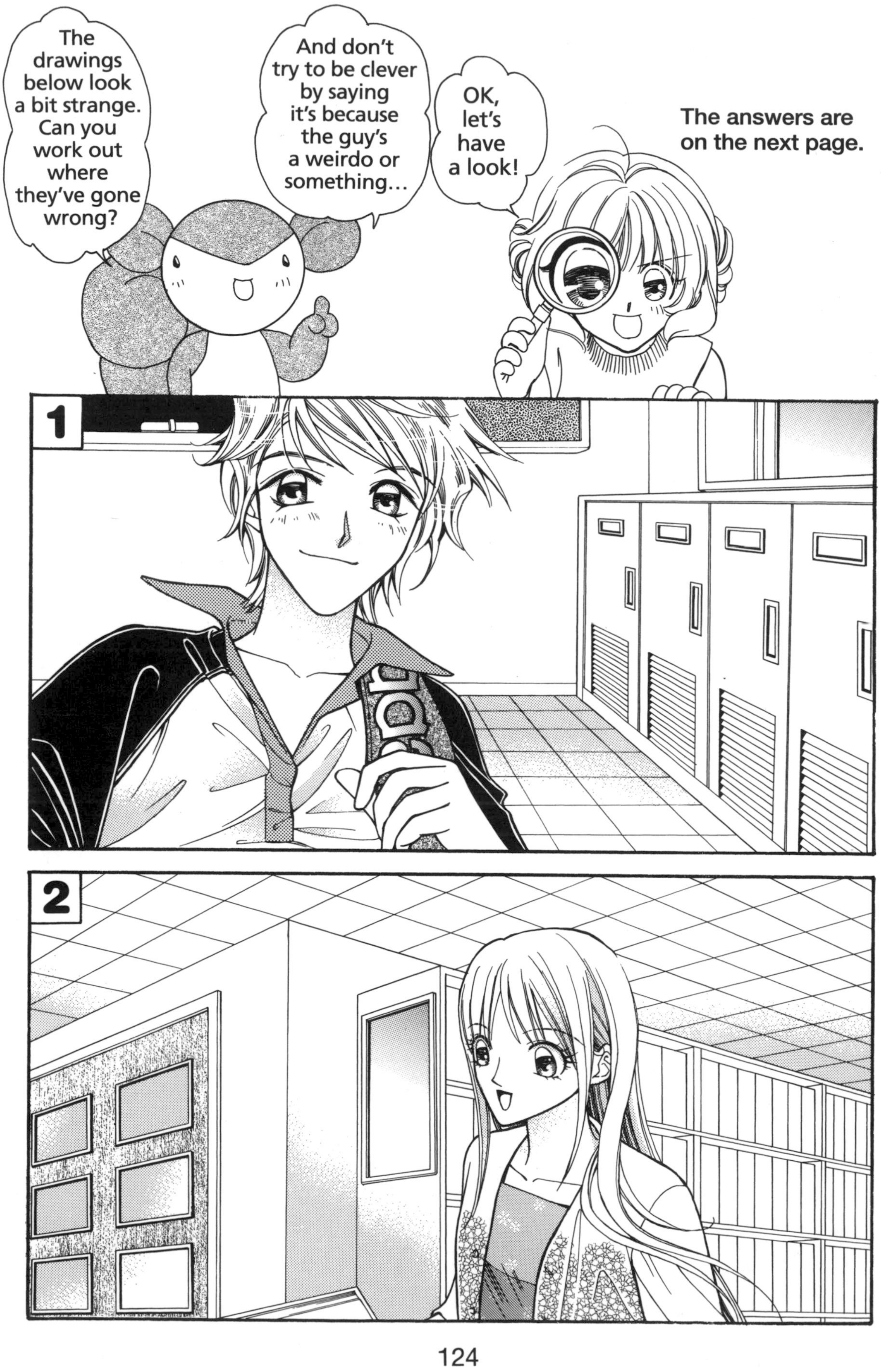
The drawings below look a bit strange. Can you work out where they've gone wrong?
And don't try to be clever by saying it's because the guy's a weirdo or something…
OK, let's have a look!
1
2

The answers are on the next page.

ANSWERS:

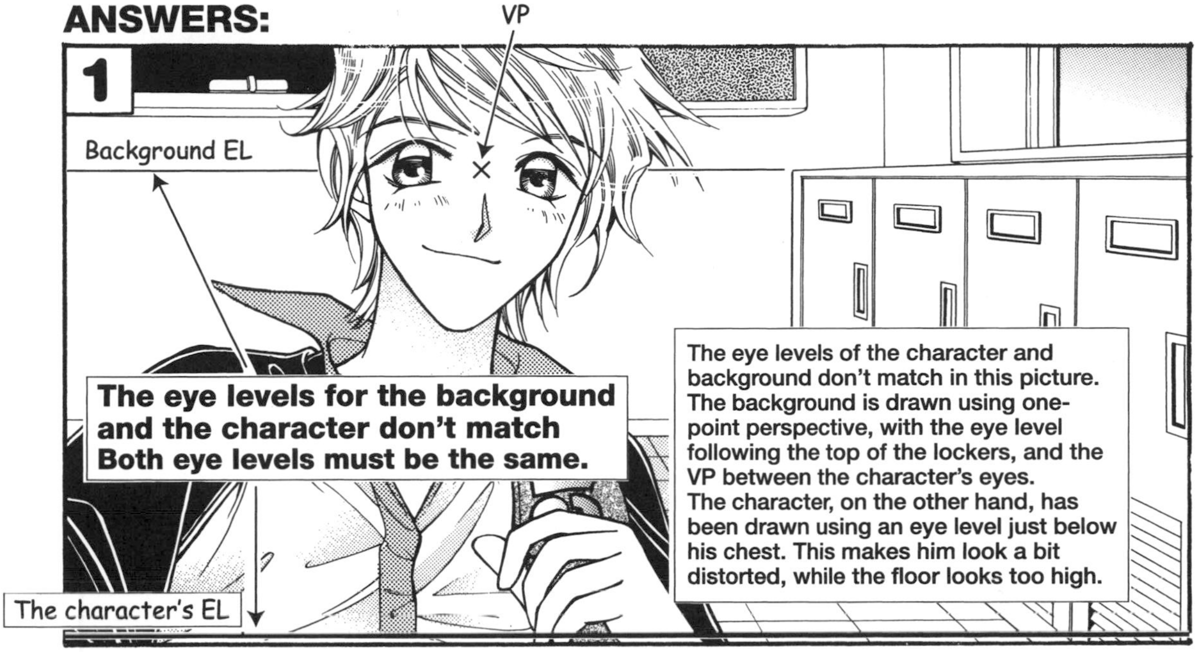
1
VP
Background EL
The eye levels for the background and the character don't match Both eye levels must be the same.
The eye levels of the character and background don't match in this picture. The background is drawn using one-point perspective, with the eye level following the top of the lockers, and the VP between the character's eyes.
The character, on the other hand, has been drawn using an eye level just below his chest. This makes him look a bit distorted, while the floor looks too high.
The character's EL

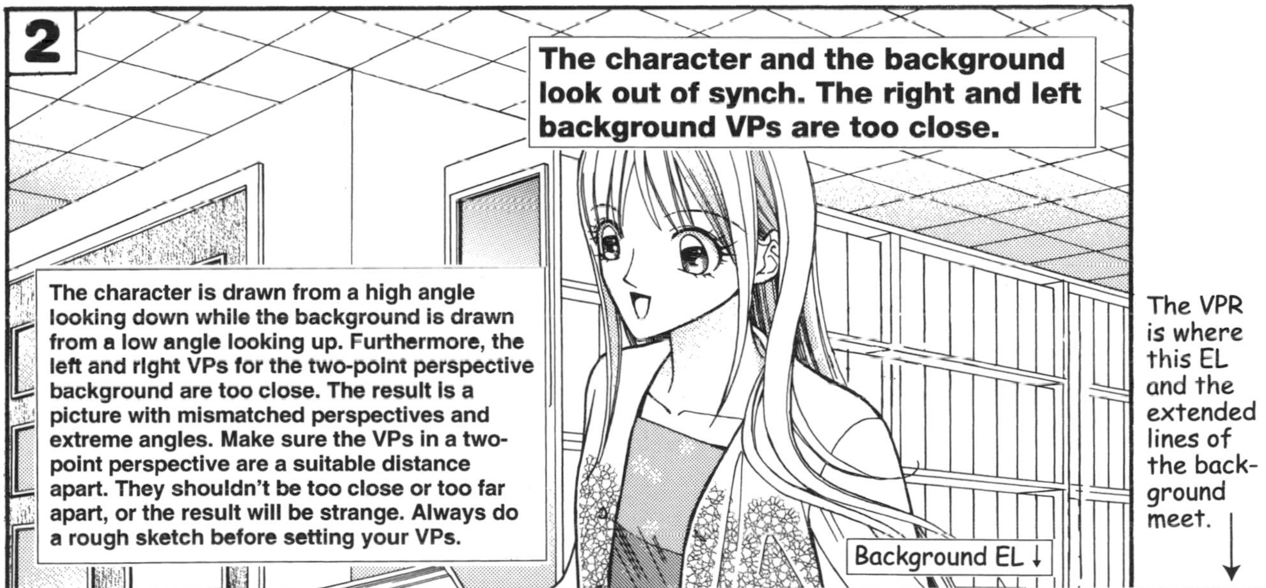
2
The character and the background look out of synch. The right and left background VPs are too close.
The character is drawn from a high angle looking down while the background is drawn from a low angle looking up. Furthermore, the left and right VPs for the two-point perspective background are too close. The result is a picture with mismatched perspectives and extreme angles. Make sure the VPs in a two-point perspective are a suitable distance apart. They shouldn't be too close or too far apart, or the result will be strange. Always do a rough sketch before setting your VPs.
Background EL
The VPR is where this EL and the extended lines of the background meet.

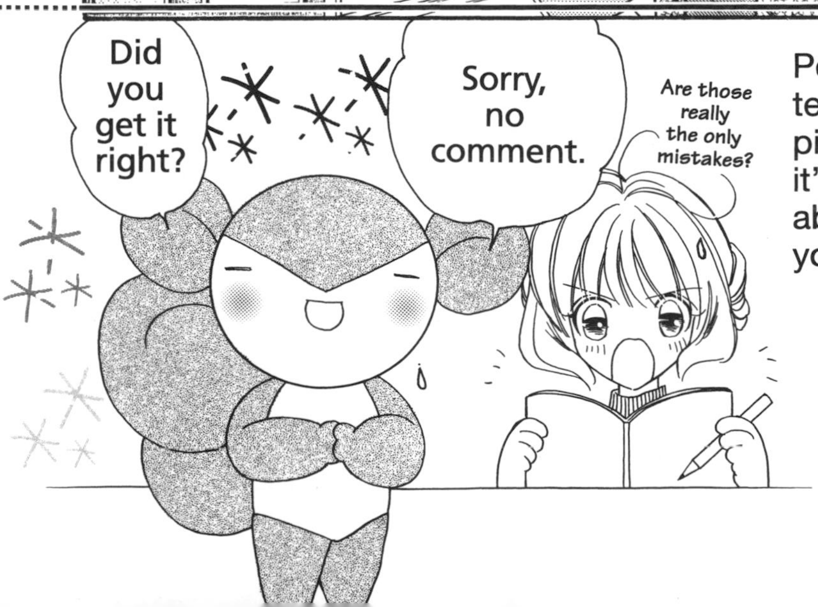
Did you get it right?
Sorry, no comment.
Are those really the only mistakes?

Perspective is an important technique, but long as your picture doesn't look strange, it's OK. Don't worry too much about detail when drawing your background.

THREE-POINT PERSPECTIVE

One- and two-point perspectives are most common in manga, but sometimes we see pictures in three-point perspective. This means there are three VPs. This method is mostly used for drawing buildings.

A picture drawn in three-point perspective

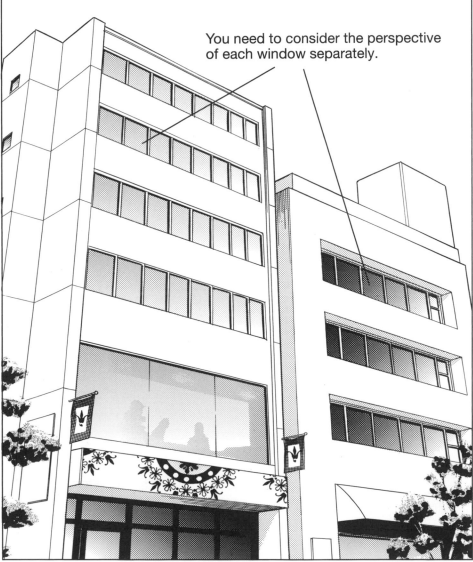

You need to consider the perspective of each window separately.

Using three-point perspective from a low angle or high angle view gives you a highly realistic, multidimensional picture. If you want to be really accurate, you would have to draw perspectives specifically for each window and floor, which would mean using many more than three VPs. Of course it's best to draw accurately, but since the characters are the most important feature in manga, there's no need to go overboard! Also more important than perfect perspective is how you arrange the frame to give maximum effect.

本書の p.20-126 は、『漫画・イラストの描き方入門』（株式会社コアデ／アイシー株式会社）を英訳したものです。

（英文版）漫画・イラストの描き方入門
Draw Your Own Manga: All the Basics

2003年9月　第1刷発行
2004年9月　第3刷発行

著　者　永友はる乃
発行者　畑野文夫
発行所　講談社インターナショナル株式会社
　　　　〒112-8652　東京都文京区音羽 1-17-14
　　　　電話　03-3944-6493（編集部）
　　　　　　　03-3944-6492（営業部・業務部）
　　　　ホームページ　www.kodansha-intl.com

印刷・製本所　大日本印刷株式会社